Teaching Nineteenth-Century Fiction

Teaching the New English
Published in association with the English Subject Centre
Director: Ben Knights

Teaching the New English is an innovative series concerned with the teaching of the English degree in universities in the UK and elsewhere. The series addresses new and developing areas of the curriculum as well as more traditional areas that are reforming in new contexts. Although the Series is grounded in intellectual and theoretical concepts of the curriculum, it is concerned with the practicalities of classroom teaching. The volumes will be invaluable for new and more experienced teachers alike.

Titles include:
Gail Ashton and Louise Sylvester (*editors*)
TEACHING CHAUCER

Charles Butler (*editor*)
TEACHING CHILDREN'S FICTION

Robert Eaglestone and Barry Langford (*editors*)
TEACHING HOLOCAUST LITERATURE AND FILM

Michael Hanrahan and Deborah L. Madsen (*editors*)
TEACHING, TECHNOLOGY, TEXTUALITY
Approaches to New Media

David Higgins and Sharon Ruston
TEACHING ROMANTICISM

Andrew Hiscock and Lisa Hopkins (*editors*)
TEACHING SHAKESPEARE AND EARLY MODERN DRAMATISTS

Nicky Marsh and Peter Middleton (*editors*)
TEACHING MODERNIST POETRY

Andrew Maunder and Jennifer Phegley (*editors*)
TEACHING NINETEENTH-CENTURY FICTION

Anna Powell and Andrew Smith (*editors*)
TEACHING THE GOTHIC

Forthcoming titles:

Gina Wisker (*editor*)
TEACHING AFRICAN-AMERICAN WOMEN'S WRITING

Teaching the New English
Series Standing Order ISBN 988–1–4039–4441–2 Hardback
ISBN 978–1–4039–4442–9 Paperback
(Outside North America only)

You can receive future titles in this series as they are published by placing a standing order. Please contact your bookseller or, in case of difficulty, write to us at the address below with your name and address, the title of the series and the ISBN quoted above.

Customer Services Department, Macmillan Distribution Ltd, Houndmills, Basingstoke, Hampshire RG21 6XS, England

---

Teaching Nineteenth-Century Fiction

Edited by

Andrew Maunder
and
Jennifer Phegley

First published 2010 by
PALGRAVE MACMILLAN

Palgrave Macmillan in the UK is an imprint of Macmillan Publishers Limited, registered in England, company number 785998, of Houndmills, Basingstoke, Hampshire RG21 6XS.

Palgrave Macmillan in the US is a division of St Martin's Press LLC,
175 Fifth Avenue, New York, NY 10010.

Palgrave Macmillan is the global academic imprint of the above companies and has companies and representatives throughout the world.

Palgrave® and Macmillan® are registered trademarks in the United States, the United Kingdom, Europe and other countries.

ISBN-13: 978–0–230–53780–4   hardback
ISBN-13: 978–0–230–53781–1   paperback

This book is printed on paper suitable for recycling and made from fully managed and sustained forest sources. Logging, pulping and manufacturing processes are expected to conform to the environmental regulations of the country of origin.

A catalogue record for this book is available from the British Library.

Library of Congress Cataloging-in-Publication Data

Teaching nineteenth-century fiction / edited by Andrew Maunder and Jennifer Phegley.
        p. cm.—(Teaching the new English series)
Summary: "This book offers practical approaches to some of the key issues and challenges involved in teaching nineteenth-century fiction at the university level, and includes annotated case studies from courses, discussions of instances of useful practice in teaching and a helpful chronology of nineteenth-century writers and texts. This new volume in the Teaching the New English series looks at how a core area of the English degree curriculum—Victorian fiction—can be taught, and issues facing lecturers and students in the field today. The book has a pedagogical slant, though chapters will also be useful for students of Victorian fiction as an overview of current debate"—Provided by publisher.
        Includes bibliographical references and index.
        ISBN 978–0–230–53780–4 (hbk.)—ISBN 978–0–230–53781–1 (pbk.)   1. English fiction—19th century—History and criticism—Study and teaching (Higher)   I. Maunder, Andrew.
II. Phegley, Jennifer.
        PR871.T43 2010
        823'.809—dc22   2009046790

10 9 8 7 6 5 4 3 2 1
19 18 17 16 15 14 13 12 11 10

Printed and bound in Great Britain by
CPI Antony Rowe, Chippenham and Eastbourne

Contents

List of Figures

Series Preface

One of many exciting achievements of the early years of the English Subject Centre was the agreement with Palgrave Macmillan to initiate the series "Teaching the New English." The intention of the then Director, Professor Philip Martin, was to create a series of short and accessible books which would take widely-taught curriculum fields (or, as in the case of learning technologies, approaches to the whole curriculum) and articulate the connections between scholarly knowledge and the demands of teaching.

Since its inception, "English" has been committed to what we know by the portmanteau phrase "learning and teaching." Yet, by and large, university teachers of English – in Britain at all events – find it hard to make their tacit pedagogic knowledge conscious, or to raise it to a level where it might be critiqued, shared, or developed. In the experience of the English Subject Centre, colleagues find it relatively easy to talk about curriculum and resources, but far harder to talk about the success or failure of seminars, how to vary forms of assessment, or to make imaginative use of Virtual Learning Environments. Too often this reticence means falling back on received assumptions about student learning, about teaching, or about forms of assessment. At the same time, colleagues are often suspicious of the insights and methods arising from generic educational research. The challenge for the English group of disciplines is therefore to articulate ways in which our own subject knowledge and ways of talking might themselves refresh debates about pedagogy. The implicit invitation of this series is to take fields of knowledge and survey them through a pedagogic lens. Research and scholarship, and teaching and learning are part of the same process, not two separate domains.

"Teachers," people used to say, "are born not made." There may, after all, be some tenuous truth in this: there may be generosities of spirit (or, alternatively, drives for didactic control) laid down in earliest childhood. But why should we assume that even "born" teachers (or novelists, or nurses, or veterinary surgeons) do not need to learn the skills of their trade? Amateurishness about teaching has far more to do with university claims to status, than with evidence about how people learn. There is a craft to shaping and promoting learning. This series of books is dedicated to the development of the craft of teaching within English Studies.

Ben Knights
Teaching the New English *Series Editor*
Director, English Subject Centre
Higher Education Academy

The English Subject Centre

Founded in 2000, the English Subject Centre (which is based at Royal Holloway, University of London) is part of the subject network of the Higher Education Academy. Its purpose is to develop learning and teaching across the English disciplines in UK Higher Education. To this end it engages in research and publication (web and print), hosts events and conferences, sponsors projects, and engages in day-to-day dialogue with its subject communities.

http://www.english.heacademy.ac.uk

Notes on the Contributors

Sofia Ahlberg earned her Ph.D. in transatlantic literature at the University of Melbourne, Australia in 2008. She teaches in the field of global fiction and publishes on transhemispheric and transatlantic issues. Her intention in and out of the classroom is to relay the larger cultural and political meanings vested in literary and generic forms as they zigzag across the Atlantic.

Janice M. Allan is Associate Head (Teaching) of the School of English, Sociology, Politics and Contemporary History at the University of Salford. She is the editor of *Bleak House: A Sourcebook* (2004) and sits on the editorial board of *Clues: A Journal of Detection*. In recent years, she has published various articles and chapters on Wilkie Collins, detective and sensation fiction, and cultural sensations of the 1860s. She is currently working on *The Sensation Novel Sourcebook* for Liverpool University Press.

Josie Billington teaches in the School of English at the University of Liverpool. Her publications on the Victorian novel include *Faithful Realism* (2002) and *Eliot's Middlemarch, Continuum Reader's Guides Series* (2008). She has also edited *Wives and Daughters*, Volume 10 of *The Complete Works of Elizabeth Gaskell* (ed. Joanne Shattock, 2006). She is currently writing a monograph study of Elizabeth Barrett Browning's creative process. She is a Fellow of the Higher Education Academy and a founder member of the British Association of Victorian Studies.

Patrick Brantlinger is James Rudy Professor of English (Emeritus) at Indiana University, where he edited *Victorian Studies* (1980–90). Among his books are *Rule of Darkness: British Literature and Imperialism, 1830–1900* (1988), *Dark Vanishings: Discourse on the Extinction of Primitive Races* (2003), and *Victorian Literature and Postcolonial Studies* (2009). With William Thesing, he co-edited Blackwell's *Companion to the Victorian Novel* (2002).

Linda K. Hughes, Addie Levy Professor of Literature at Texas Christian University, and **Michael Lund**, Professor Emeritus of English at Longwood University in Virginia, have co-authored *The Victorian Serial* (1991), *Victorian Publishing and Mrs. Gaskell's Work* (1999), and numerous articles on nineteenth-century installment publication. Dr Hughes has also written *Graham R.: Rosamund Marriott Watson, Woman of Letters* (2005) and *The Manyfacèd Glass: Tennyson's Dramatic Monologues* (1987). Dr Lund has written *America's Continuing Story: An Introduction to Serial Fiction, 1850–1900* (1993) and *Reading Thackeray* (1988).

Priti Joshi is Associate Professor of English at the University of Puget Sound. She received a Ph.D. in Literature from Rutgers University in New Jersey. Her areas of interests are: industrialism, gender, and empire; travel and colonialism; filth and disease; and the English novel, especially George Eliot, the Brontës, Dickens, and Wilkie Collins.

Teresa Mangum is Associate Professor of English at the University of Iowa. She is the author of *Married, Middlebrow, and Militant: Sarah Grand and the New Woman Novel* (1998) as well as articles on nineteenth-century human–animal relations, aging, and literature. She guest-edited a special issue of *VPR: Victorian Periodicals Review* on using magazines in the classroom (2006) and is currently preparing a special issue of *Philological Quarterly* on "Women, Writing, History" and a volume for the forthcoming *Cultural History of Women: The Age of Empire, 1800–1920* (2010).

Andrew Maunder is Subject Leader for English Literature and Creative Writing at the University of Hertfordshire. He has also worked for the Higher Education Academy English Subject Centre as part of a team involved in different teaching and learning projects relating to the teaching of English. His research interests include crime fiction, reception histories, and the short story and his work on Victorian sensationalism and the underside of nineteenth-century culture has resulted in a number of projects. These include the series *Varieties of Women's Sensation Fiction 1855–1890* (2004), *Bram Stoker* (2006) and, more recently (with Graham Law) *Wilkie Collins: A Literary Life* (2008).

Grace Moore teaches at the University of Melbourne, Australia. She is the author of many articles on Victorian and neo-Victorian literature and culture. Her book, *Dickens and Empire* (2004) was shortlisted for the 2006 New South Wales Premier's Award for Literary Scholarship. She edited *Victorian Crime, Madness and Sensation* with Andrew Maunder (2004) and she is the editor of a forthcoming book on nineteenth-century piracy (2010) as well as a guide to the Victorian novel (2010).

Richard Pearson lectures in English Literature at the National University of Ireland, Galway. He is the Director of the AHRC-funded Victorian Plays Project (victorian.worc.ac.uk), an online database of plays from *Lacy's Acting Edition*. His book publications include *W. M. Thackeray and the Mediated Text* (2000) and *The Victorians and the Ancient World* (2006).

Jennifer Phegley is Associate Professor of English at the University of Missouri-Kansas City. She is the author of *Educating the Proper Woman Reader: Victorian Family Literary Magazines and the Cultural Health of the Nation* (2004) and co-editor of *Reading Women: Literary Figures and Cultural Icons from the Victorian Age to the Present* (2005). She is writing a book on Victorian courtship and marriage and working on a collection of essays on transatlantic sensationalism.

Ruth Robbins is Head of the School of Cultural Studies at Leeds Metropolitan University. Her research interests centre on the late-Victorian period in English literature, especially the literature of Decadence, including the writings of Oscar Wilde, Arthur Symons, and Vernon Lee. Her book *Pater to Forster, 1873–1924* (2003) deals with literature written in the late nineteenth and early twentieth century. Her monograph *Subjectivity* was published in 2005. She is currently working on an anthology of nineteenth-century writing about women and the medical profession entitled *Medical Advice for Women, 1830–1914* (2009) and on a literary life of Oscar Wilde.

Talia Schaffer is an Associate Professor of English at Queens College and the Graduate Center, CUNY. Her books include *Literature and Culture at the Fin de Siècle* (2006); an edition of Lucas Malet's 1901 novel *The History of Sir Richard Calmady* (2004); *The Forgotten Female Aesthetes: Literary Culture in Late-Victorian England* (2001); and *Women and British Aestheticism* (1999), co-edited with Kathy A. Psomiades. She has published widely on late-Victorian noncanonical novels, women's writing, and material culture. Her book in progress analyses the Victorian domestic handicraft as a model for mid-Victorian realism.

Julian Wolfreys is Professor of Modern Literature and Culture with the Department of English and Drama at Loughborough University. The author of nearly twenty books and editor of more than twenty others, he is currently compiling a concordance of the works of Jacques Derrida.

Terry R. Wright is Professor of English Literature at Newcastle University. He has written several books on Thomas Hardy, including *Hardy and the Erotic* (1989), *Hardy and His Readers* (2003) and *Thomas Hardy on Screen* (editor, 2005). He has also written books on *George Eliot's Middlemarch* (1991), *D. H. Lawrence and the Bible* (2000), *The Religion of Humanity* (1986), *Theology and Literature* (1988) and *The Genesis of Fiction: Modern Novelists as Biblical Interpreters* (2007). He currently teaches a module entitled "Real to Reel: Victorian Novel to Film."

1
Introduction

Andrew Maunder and Jennifer Phegley

In 1921, in a book called *English for the English*, George Sampson, Secretary of the English Association, set down his recommendations for the teaching of literature. Sampson, a member of the committee that in the same year produced the *Report for the Teaching of English in England*, under the chairmanship of Sir Henry Newbolt, was a devotee of Matthew Arnold and shared the Victorian sage's sense that literature was a powerful force for humanizing and civilizing. Sampson thus counselled that "Personal kindness" must guide the teacher and the teacher should think more of his students' hearts than their heads. But he recognized that enthusing students about nineteenth-century literature was a problem. How to do it? They could be asked to study and imitate passages from Austen and Dickens ("models of structure and punctuation") but could they be taught to appreciate them? Sampson's advice was as follows:

> Teachers will have their own views of how to deal with long prose works, a novel by Dickens for example. Plainly, neither teacher nor class can read the whole of *David Copperfield* or *Pickwick* in a single term. It is unfair to protract the reading of any work. The class will do much by silent reading but occasionally the teacher will read scenes or passages as a treat – if his reading is not a treat he ought not to be a teacher – and occasionally members of the class will be expected to read to the others. Any book that a class finds "dry" should not be pursued to the bitter end, however sweet the teacher may think it . . . . In fact, the whole idea of compulsion is alien to the world of art. This is certain, that if you make boys read *The Fair Maid of Perth* when they would rather be reading *Ivanhoe* you will make them dislike Scott altogether. To persist with an unpopular work merely because it has been begun is to make a discipline of what should be a delight, and to disallow a rational exercise of the taste we are trying to cultivate. We must be ready to try any new adventurous experiment in education; we must be just as ready to scrap our failures. (1921, p. 89)

Ninety years on, and notwithstanding changes in class composition and required reading, many of the anxieties Sampson sought to address still remain. Indeed to log on to that part of the World Wide Web containing "The Victoria Listserv" or the "English Subject Centre" is quickly to realize that there are some questions involved in teaching nineteenth-century novelists that never seem to go away: What, for example, do we teach when we teach nineteenth-century fiction? What do we want students to read? What do we want them to get out of it? How do we encourage them to continue reading? Is there a distinction between what students read for pleasure, as recreation, and the books they study as part of their degree course? Can we teach long novels anymore? What imaginative strategies can be used to develop a more intense engagement with nineteenth-century fiction?

That these questions seem relevant and worth engaging with is doubly the case when one considers that in most higher education institutions on both sides of the Atlantic, nineteenth-century fiction remains a dominant – if not compulsory – aspect of the English literature curriculum. Although fiction is typically taught alongside poetry and drama as part of a course surveying the nineteenth century, fear of poetry means that for many students – and some teachers – novels and short stories invariably become the cornerstones of their engagement with the period. Given the focus of the present volume, it may seem slightly disingenuous to claim that this is rather apt. Yet such preferences do reflect those of our nineteenth-century ancestors themselves, those voracious readers whose desire for stories saw novel production top 900 titles per year between 1875 and 1886, reaching an incredible 1,618 by 1914 (Hammond, 2006, p. 4). "We have become a novel-reading people," announced Anthony Trollope in 1870, in his lecture "On English Prose Fiction as a Rational Amusement" (1938, p. 94)."Novels are in the hands of us all; from the Prime Minister down to the last-appointed scullery maid . . . Poetry also we read and history, biography and the social and political news of the day. But all our other reading put together, hardly amounts to what we read in novels" (p. 108). In London, Mudie's Circulating Library claimed to dispatch more than 5,000 volumes per day from its swanky headquarters in New Oxford Street (Hammond, p. 28). By the time Trollope died in 1882 from a seizure suffered whilst listening to a reading of F. Anstey's comic novel *Vice Versa* – but also worn out by so much writing and reading – a new mass of readers was emerging produced by the compulsory Education Acts introduced between 1870 and 1890. With these new readers came an accompanying expansion in the number of outlets for would-be novelists, notably a flood of new cheap magazines and papers, which gave a central place to serialized fiction and short stories. Novels, as journalist and all-round literary utility-man Frederick Greenwood observed in 1888, had become "ordinary commodities . . . [to] be sold at the drapers, & with pounds of tea" (qtd. in Waller, 2006, p. 61). "Short stories," likewise, as H. G. Wells recalled, "broke out everywhere." Moreover, there were so many magazines that, as Wells noted, even stories "of the slightest distinction" tended to find an outlet:

> Kipling was writing short stories, Barrie, Stevenson, Frank Harris; Max Beerbohm wrote at least one perfect one, "The Happy Hypocrite"; Henry James pursued his wonderful and inimitable bent; and among other names that occur to me, like a mixed handful of jewels drawn from a bag, are George Street, Morley Roberts, George Gissing, Ella D'Arcy, Murray Gilchrist, E. Nesbit, Stephen Crane, Joseph Conrad, Edwin Pugh, Jerome K. Jerome, Kenneth Graham [*sic*], Arthur Morrison, Marriot Watson, George Moore, Grant Allen, George Egerton, Henry Harland, Pett Ridge, W. W. Jacobs (who alone seems so inexhaustible). I dare say I could recall as many more names with a little effort. (1913, p. 5)

The fact that so many of these "jewels" are no longer remembered (even Wells writing in 1913 seems to have a little difficulty!) says a lot about the way literary canons are formed and constantly change, and which genres are deemed important – the novel, rather than the short story, for instance. Yet even discounting the novels and stories no longer in print or that we don't know about, it can be difficult to come to grips with the reach and variety of Victorian fiction – let alone determining how best to teach it. Henry James's famous term for nineteenth-century novels – "baggy monsters" – reflects not only their size and scope, but also their astonishing prevalence and diversity (1935, p. 84).

It is with the challenges involved in teaching a broad range of nineteenth-century fictional forms that this collection is concerned. This is a literary world that can be huge and daunting from the perspective of students, yet one that is also important and exciting. *Teaching Nineteenth-Century Fiction* includes essays by teachers from the UK, Ireland, the US, and Australia that demonstrate a variety of approaches to teaching novels and short stories while arguing for their relevance. The essays, which offer a mix of theoretical paradigms and practical applications, are the products of a revolution in literary study that has transformed how nineteenth-century fiction is deployed in the classroom.

When English literature was introduced as a subject of study at King's College London in the 1830s and when it was taught at American universities at mid-century, it was believed to be a humanizing force for moral uplift that also provided a sense of national heritage (Showalter, 2003, p. 22). Yet, that mission waned over the course of the century until it was refined and strengthened in the 1930s when, as Terry Eagleton explains it, literary studies came into its own: "in the early 1920s it was desperately unclear why English was worth studying at all; by the early 1930s it had become a question of why it was worth wasting your time on anything else. . . . English was an arena in which the most fundamental questions of human existence . . . were made the object of intense scrutiny" (qtd. in Showalter, 2003, p. 22–3). This shift in attitude toward the subject of studying literature was due in large part to F. R. Leavis, whose definition of the canon was, at least until the 1970s, the curriculum on which nineteenth-century fiction courses were often based. In *The Great Tradition* (1948), Leavis famously states that "The great English novelists are Jane Austen, George Eliot, Henry James, and Joseph Conrad" (1962, p. 9). For Leavis and the Scrutiny group, writing in the aftermath of World War II and searching for literary works that could be used to resist what they saw as the debilitating influence of modern commercial and media culture, these were peculiarly fortifying and wholesome writers whose novels embodied the possibility of a moral art, "significant in terms of that human awareness they promote; awareness of the possibilities of life" (1962, p. 10)

Leavis's attractive liberal humanist agenda made itself felt in the classroom in different ways but students' analysis was often focused on the "close reading" of a novel or story, with much attention given to plot, theme, and imagery. In the United States, this movement was embodied by "New Critics" such as John Crowe Ransom, Cleanth Brooks, Robert Penn Warren, and René Wellek, who advocated the study of "the structure of the work, not the minds of the authors or the reactions of the readers" (Leitch, 1988, p. 26). New Criticism claimed for literature a certain kind of scientific objectivity while simultaneously providing a retreat from the realm of social conflict (Showalter, 2003, p. 23). Its approach was so focused on form and language (especially symbol, imagery, and irony) that it tended to exclude even character and plot, shunning Leavis's more humanistic approach. It also, notably, neglected – if not outright rejected – nineteenth-century literature as inappropriate to its methods. Indeed, metaphysical and modern poetry were its preferred subjects and the "baggy monsters" of Victorian fiction were out of the question for the movement's formalist protocols (Leitch, 1998, p. 38).

Although it is now fashionable to disparage Leavis on the grounds that his readings are based on a narrow analysis of British fiction, his views were extremely influential in the development of the post-war study of English literature in British universities. Likewise, William Cain observes that the "attitudes, values, and emphases" of New Criticism are "[s]o deeply ingrained in English studies . . . that we do not even perceive them as the legacy of a particular movement" (qtd. in Leitch, 1988, p. 26). Methods of close reading have, of course, loosened up and now include even those "baggy monsters" of Victorian fiction. The celebrations of Leavis's "big four" as mainstays of liberal individualism, whose strengths are their social and psychological realism and their skill in creating character, have also been broken up – for good or ill – and a multiplicity of other approaches have come into play.

New interpretations have resulted from a range of twentieth-century critical developments: the resurgence of Marxist criticism as a mode of intellectual inquiry; deconstruction, taking its cue from the work of the French philosopher Jacques Derrida; and most significantly perhaps, the emergence of cultural studies, a discipline which alongside feminism, new historicism, and postcolonialism has had a very noticeable effect on the way literature is re-discovered, written about and taught. Aside from the work of Raymond Williams (*Culture and Society* [1958]; *The Long Revolution* [1961]), key statements of this shift might be said to be such works as 1982's *Re-Reading English*, edited by Peter Widdowson, or Antony Easthope's *Literary into Cultural Studies* (1991), in which the text is no longer seen as an ahistorical "self-defining object" to be treated with reverence but as something inherently linked with the power relations and ideological discourses of its time (Easthope, 1991, p. 12). For Easthope, there was nothing to distinguish literary texts from those of popular culture. Both needed to be discussed in terms of "institution, sign system, gender, identification, subject position . . . [and] the other" (p. 71). In 1982 the idea that teachers should a) consider notions of the "popular" and b) provide opportunities for texts and their students to "interact dialectically" (Widdowson, 1982, p. 21), seemed newer in certain classrooms than others. Indeed, in nineteenth-century studies the idea of cross-disciplinary work had been around for a while, perhaps because the field had been excluded from New Critical approaches. One could cite, for example, the establishment of the interdisciplinary journal *Victorian Studies* in 1956 or the publication of Richard Altick's *The English Common Reader* in 1957. Altick's book advocated the study of literature within its historical context and emphasized the role of reading audiences, both approaches that reacted against the prevailing dominance of close reading.

Since the 1980s, however, the notion of "shifting between the novel's insides and outsides" has gained impetus (Carolyn Williams, 2006, p. 304). The concept of getting students to recognize a text's "ideological work" (to use Mary Poovey's influential phrase), making them aware of its links with the historical moment of its production, has inspired a more culturally orientated criticism focused on the idea of teaching "conflict." In turn, this mixture of textual analysis and new approaches has had the effect of offering students a different picture of nineteenth-century people as "modern, self-conscious and sexually aware; as driven by consumerism and possessed of serious misgivings about domestic stability, or imperial expansion" all of which "makes them sound more like us than they did twenty years ago" (Sanders, 2007, p. 1294). Whether the characters who populate the fictional worlds of nineteenth-century Britain and her colonies are really mirrors of "ourselves" is a moot point but it is not unusual to see some authors and their texts – such as Bram Stoker's *Dracula* or Oscar Wilde's *The Picture of Dorian Gray* – sold as being "of their time," that is the 1890s, but also as works which "speak to the anxieties, desires of the twentieth [and twenty-first] century" (Davison, 1997, p. 30). It seems that changing critical trends have certainly benefited the Victorian novel, making it more popular than ever to teach.

The mention of those bogeymen Dracula and Gray brings us back to the texts offered for study on undergraduate degree programmes. The comment made in 1981 by the Oxford University Professor Christopher Ricks that "it's our job to teach and uphold the canon of English literature" may still strike a chord with some teachers but it's a job-description complicated by the fact that notions of what is canonical and what is not, have become more fluid (qtd. in Widdowson, 1982, p. 1). It was, as Raymond Williams pointed out, twentieth-century critics who tended to consign realist or popular novels to the "wide margin of the century" in favour of a more exclusive canon (1989, p. 35). But the last twenty years has seen a revolution in the definition of nineteenth-century fiction. The 1990s in particular saw growing interest in the world of so-called "genre" fiction – the novels of colonial adventure, of domestic crimes, of exotic worlds, tropical worlds, monsters, "New women," psychopathic femme fatales, vampires, savage natives, and heroic deeds of "derring-do" – all seeming to promise the syllabus a wider variety of cultural expression than existed before.

In *Doing English*, Robert Eaglestone notes: "A person who studied English and has become a teacher often teaches the texts that he or she was taught, in part because she or he was taught that these texts were the most important" (2000, p. 56). There is some truth in this but English departments are not simply safe houses for the canon of English literature. They also play a key role in reshaping it. It is still the case that teachers want to expose their classes to the best of what has been thought and felt but the days appear to have gone when courses could define the "nineteenth-century novel" by assigning *Vanity Fair* and *Middlemarch* and focusing on the universal human values Thackeray and Eliot reveal. It would also be a supremely confident teacher who would teach both novels in a single semester course. Elaine Showalter has written about the long-lasting consequences for the curriculum that have resulted from students' financing of their educations through part-time work, which leaves students with less and less time to devote to their studies. She also explores the university administration's attempts to control what courses are taught and on what timetable (2003, p. 91). This varies across institutions but in some this can be as little as two-hours of classroom time over ten weeks. Where once Thackeray's centrality to the syllabus was taken for granted and *Middlemarch* was bound to appear two-thirds of the way through a course, overworked or unmotivated students' inability to read these novels means that the texts and their authors slide off the syllabus, to be replaced by more "manageable" works – "easier" novels which are beneficiaries of the democratization/politicization of the literary canon (Mary Braddon's *Lady Audley's Secret* and H. Rider Haggard's *She* spring to mind), and which seem to provide accessible expositions of the kind of important political or formal issues presented and debated by theorists. Sitting alongside these are those texts that maintain a foothold by virtue of being comparatively short (*Hard Times, Great Expectations, Silas Marner, The*

Picture of Dorian Gray). That students are offered a different cultural experience from the previous generation is not necessarily a bad thing but it does not mean that their conceptions of nineteenth-century fiction are any less skewed than they were thirty or forty years ago.

The present collection is thus framed by changes in the student body, by changes in university administrations, and by a shift in the critical lenses used to approach nineteenth-century fiction, however these may be defined. It is, as we have noted, difficult for students to pass through a Literature programme without having to study examples of nineteenth-century fiction but it is also the case that there are many who seek it out. This may be because the names of many authors who appear on nineteenth-century syllabuses still loom large as mainstays of our cultural capital – in the US as well as in the UK. Come mid-December, it is rare, for example, not to find at least one theatre company presenting a new version of *A Christmas Carol*. These and other adaptations of classics are also regular features of the TV schedules. They attract healthy viewing figures – sometimes extraordinary ones as in the case of the BBC's 1995 serialization of *Pride and Prejudice* – and offer a carefully-tailored but nonetheless powerful, view of nineteenth-century men and women: glamorous, passionate lovers, and symbolic representatives of "Romance" and also "History" – or at least commercial filmmakers' ideas of those concepts. Some authors dominate – Austen, Dickens, Gaskell, Hardy, and – rather intriguingly – Trollope. The implication seems to be that such adaptations do not simply represent a body of entertainment but are repositories of important (British) cultural values, that they are valid for contemporary audiences. In the UK on the BBC and in the US on PBS, 2006–2007 was the TV year of *Jane Eyre* and *Bleak House*; 2007–2008 featured *Cranford* and three Jane Austen adaptations, culminating with *Mansfield Park* starring former "Dr Who" assistant Billie Piper as an unlikely Fanny Price. In 2008 "Masterpiece Theater," the PBS series that brings many BBC productions of Victorian novels to American audiences, capitalized on the success of the previous year's serialization of *Bleak House* by making Gillian Anderson (star of the 1990s hit series "The X-Files" who received an emmy-nomination for her performance as Lady Dedlock) the new spokesperson for the series (now divided into "Masterpiece Classic," "Masterpiece Contemporary," and "Masterpiece Mystery!"). Anderson replaced Alistair Cooke and brought a younger, hipper persona to the previously stodgy face of nineteenth-century adaptations. With the launch of the new "Masterpiece Classic" series, Victorian novels appear to be front and centre for American viewers who, in 2009, enjoyed productions of *Tess of the D'Urbervilles*, *Wuthering Heights*, *Oliver Twist*, *Little Dorrit*, and *The Old Curiosity Shop*. The new season was hosted by Laura Linney, another fresh and beautiful award-winning actress who was recently honoured for her role as Abigail Adams in the HBO mini-series "John Adams." Interestingly, the use of Linney as the face of Masterpiece Classics ties British literature to American history in a subtle way, making the celebration of nineteenth-century British fiction a part of American cultural heritage. So, in thinking about the preconceptions students bring to nineteenth-century fiction and the way in which they consume it – or manipulated versions of it – we might also note that teaching nineteenth-century fiction seems to be a matter of alerting students to different ways in which literary texts can be reworked but also bringing them face to face with – and even attempting to sell to them – the original – sometimes more ideologically disagreeable – but no less interesting – words on the page.

* * *

As a result of these ever-shifting critical and cultural perspectives about how we define and teach literary texts, a new field devoted to the study of teaching literature has developed. While the teaching of composition has always produced engaged discussions of the intersections between theory and practice, literature faculty have been slower to participate in such conversations. George Levine points out that "One doesn't have to look too far to notice how many university English departments are divided into two nations: the part that teaches writing and is therefore also likely to be concerned with the teaching of teachers, and the part that 'does' literature" (2001, p. 8). The academic journal *Pedagogy*, which published Levine's essay in its inaugural issue, set out to "create a new way of talking about teaching by fusing theoretical approaches and practical realities" (Holberg and Taylor, 2001, p. 1). In the years following the launch of *Pedagogy*, there have been other signs that the "two nations" Levine denounces are beginning to productively merge.

Books in the Modern Language Association's "Approaches to Teaching" series, usually focused on particular literary texts, were among the first to collect essays that discuss actual classroom practices in order to encourage new approaches to teaching key works such as George Eliot's *Middlemarch* (1990) and Charles Dickens's *Bleak House* (2009). While many of these early collections include brief, practically-oriented descriptions of classroom practice that neglect theoretical paradigms, these volumes were a crucial first step toward valuing pedagogical scholarship and remain an important model. The proliferation of guides on Victorian literature that are now flooding the market further highlight the increasing attention paid not only to canonical authors and texts, but also to entire fields and genres of study. *The Cambridge Companion to the Victorian Novel* (2000) as well as *The Cambridge Companion to Gothic Fiction* (2002) and *The Cambridge Companion to Crime Fiction* (2003) were quickly followed by Blackwell's "companion" series, which includes *A Companion to the Victorian Novel* (2002), and Continuum's latest books *Victorian Literature and Culture* (2007) and *The Victorian Literature Handbook* (2008). Such guides are intended to introduce students to important issues related to their field of study and to make teaching the literature of those fields easier by providing trustworthy contextual and background information. Responding to the turn back towards historical and cultural approaches to literary study, these guidebooks aim to recontextualize nineteenth-century fiction. However, they do not complete the process of pedagogical engagement because they do not usually directly address classroom practices.

Even more promising are the increasing number of books that attempt to wed pedagogical approaches in the classroom to movements in the field of literary studies, such as Elaine Showalter's *Teaching Literature* (2003) and Tanya Agathocleous and Ann C. Dean's *Teaching Literature: A Companion* (2003), which explore teaching practices across the whole spectrum of the literature, with some attention to nineteenth-century British fiction. In his foreword to the latter book, Levine proclaims that "the best indication that this book will have done its work effectively would be the publication fairly soon of similar books, concerned with the problems of teaching literature, not by the Modern Language Association" but by major university presses since "the profession (and the institutions that publish its work) has not taken teaching as the sort of 'contribution to knowledge' that makes for a major entry on the 'CV'" (vii). It is hoped that *Teaching Nineteenth-Century Fiction* is yet another sign that the state of the profession Levine describes is beginning to change and that we are providing a new example of "the way in which we can, at last, begin to restructure the system of paradoxes and self-contradictions that have made the teaching of literature such an oddly anomalous activity – the work we faculty get paid to do, but the work that remains, in the structures of university compensations, most ignored institutionally" (p. xii).

Teaching Nineteenth-Century Fiction attempts to address a more focused topic than other collections of its kind. The essays examine what is taught in nineteenth-century fiction courses in the light of the constantly changing canon; indicate how key critical approaches can be taught effectively through nineteenth-century fiction; and discuss the relationship between the literary text and the literary, cultural, and historical contexts surrounding it, and its importance for students. Together, these essays offer a partial chronology of nineteenth-century fiction writers and texts together with an exploration of issues relating to text selection and course design. Also included at the end of chapters are sample syllabuses, the inclusion of which is intended to give a (very) brief snapshot of how nineteenth-century literature courses are currently being organized in different institutions across the globe.

The chapters which follow thus focus on a number of recurrent issues that regularly crop up in relation to the teaching of nineteenth-century fiction, though teachers working in other periods may also recognize some of them. In Chapter 2, Janice Allen discusses the changing shape of the canon – from Walter Scott and Jane Austen, publishing in the 1800s, through Newgate fiction and the emergence of realism and sensationalism, to the "New Woman" fictions and imperial romances of the fin de siècle. Given these changes it is clearly useful for English Studies students to have a sense of how their discipline has altered, how notions of aesthetic value regularly shift and the roles that the "canon function" plays "in the production, circulation, classification and consumption of literary texts" (p. 23).

It is not simply the texts which change. Feminism, colonialism, deconstruction, psychoanalysis and the deeply held interest in the relation between literature and other forms of discourse underlie a whole host of readings and re-readings of nineteenth-century fiction over the last twenty years. Inevitably there has arisen a sense on the part of teachers that students need to know about these developments. Julian Wolfreys provides his perspective on the use of theoretical approaches to nineteenth-century fiction in Chapter 3, analysing the impact of theory on students. Wolfreys explores the difficulties in talking about "theory *and* the novel" at the same time as highlighting some of the benefits to student – and teacher – of re-thinking what it is to read with theory and what might take place in teaching a nineteenth-century course in which "theory" is supposed to figure. Wolfreys argues that "it is not a question of learning a theory so that "practically" they can "apply" something "useful" to a novel, as though the novel were soft jelly being poured into a mould" but rather "the close and patient reading of "theory" can serve to illuminate ideas already at work in the novel, which in the drive for narrative content the student might otherwise overlook" (p. 37).

The acknowledgment of the novel's place within the history of nineteenth-century ideas has been one of the most positive developments in recent criticism, even if it has meant that critics have perhaps spent too much time trying to link its proponents to Darwinism, Comtism and a whole variety of other "isms" that make the study of the novel a heavily academic pursuit. More accessible for students perhaps are concepts relating to empire, imperialism, and the deeply held interest in the relations between literature and forms of colonial and postcolonial discourse. These underlie Patrick Brantlinger's essay which forms Chapter 4. Brantlinger explores some of the ways in which British imperialism serves as a backdrop to several of the nineteenth-century novels commonly taught in literature courses, before suggesting some of the ways students might be encouraged to deal with this topic.

The idea of reading nineteenth-century fiction in an interdisciplinary context is one of the themes taken up by Teresa Mangum in Chapter 5. Mangum discusses two approaches to teaching Bram Stoker's *Dracula* that ask students to become engaged interdisciplinary scholars. The first outlines a moot court project that involves students in "the overlapping practices of literature and law," while the second asks them to consider the "survival, reinterpretation, and critique of nineteenth-century literature and culture in the world of the graphic novel" (p. 64).

The questions of context and text selection are part of the discussion taken up by Talia Schaffer in Chapter 6. Taking up the issue of canon formation discussed by Janice Allen, this chapter focuses on the challenge of including women writers on a crowded syllabus. It begins with canonical figures – Jane Austen, the Brontës, Elizabeth Gaskell – with whom most teachers – and some students – have had experience – but those are also authors who bring considerable baggage with them. In a recent article, "Reader, I Triumphed: Complicating the Appeal of *Jane Eyre*" Simon Dentith has written of the (understandable) "popular simplification" of nineteenth-century novels by women on the part of twenty-first-century readers and the tendency to read them "as narratives of heroic women 'beating the odds.'" As Dentith points out, recasting Jane Eyre as a "triumphant liberal narrative" is not implausible and is clearly what makes it appealing to many contemporary readers (2005, p. 19). In a discussion of what she terms "over-identification," Schaffer takes up this issue and suggests possible solutions. She then moves on to focus on less-well known writers and the benefits of making their inclusion part of one's pedagogy.

In Chapter 7, Jennifer Phegley suggests via a case study how a specialist module focusing on a particular sub-genre might be organized. The chapter takes as its central example a relatively new addition to nineteenth-century fiction courses: the sensation novel. Phegley surveys the place of sensation fiction in the current curriculum by examining on-line course syllabuses and publishers' lists of sensation novels in print. She then explains how she developed and revised a course focused on sensation novels. She advocates for the importance of a sustained focus on the genre as a way of mapping out the criteria critics (past and present) have used to justify the divisions between high and low culture and the formation of the literary canon.

Another popular sub-genre, the ghost story, is the basis for Chapter 8. Ruth Robbins explores the short story as a quintessentially nineteenth-century form arising out of a particular set of publishing and market contexts. Robbins argues that in terms of undergraduate teaching, the nineteenth-century ghost story has some marked advantages, especially in entry-level modules. Because the primary texts are, by their nature, very brief, students are able to develop their reading skills, critical vocabulary, and comprehension of the conventions of narrative fiction across a wide range of materials and do so in ways that are often not possible where the primary materials are longer. Robbins outlines particular assignments that are conducive to the study of short fiction and provides an analysis of how Henry James's *The Turn of the Screw* can provide a model for the study of narrative (un)reliability that is directly tied to the culture's often troubled relationship to concepts of desire.

In Chapter 9, Richard Pearson explores the benefits of introducing students to the visual/literary interface with which nineteenth-century readers were so familiar. In recent years the subject of nineteenth-century novelists and their illustrators has attracted a substantial amount of scholarly attention from literary critics, art historians, and those working in the field of publishing history. Scholars have explored a diverse range of themes, including the relationship between illustration and text, the study of illustration-as-narrative, or as-marketing ploy, and the ideological role played by illustration within, for example, discourses of gender, class and national identity. As with Chapters 5 and 13, part of Pearson's focus is on how teachers practise interdisciplinary approaches to the nineteenth-century novel – approaches which allow connections and contrasts, invite consideration of ideological messages, and allow students to approach nineteenth-century fiction through a range of forms (book illustrations and covers, narrative paintings, prints). Using *Great Expectations* as a case study, this chapter examines how the use of illustrations or paintings expands or complicates students' understanding of the texts they read, of narrative, and of nineteenth-century culture more generally.

Readers who have encountered nineteenth-century novels in their original publishing format (which, in many cases involved not only illustrations but part-issue as well, either separately or in a magazine), will know that this conjures up a very different prospect from the one which confronts us in modern editions. It is with this way of encountering fiction that Linda Hughes and Michael Lund are concerned in Chapter 10. They examine historical, theoretical, and pragmatic reasons to introduce students to fiction in the context of magazine culture, ranging from enhanced understanding of fiction's form and relation to the literary marketplace to students' increased engagement with novels read in parts over the course of a term or semester. The discussion of pedagogical strategies includes, among others, individual or multiple novels read serially in introductory and advanced courses and undergraduate and graduate research in periodicals to probe nineteenth-century fiction's intertextual relations.

Earlier in this chapter we suggested that, to the extent that they engage readers of a given culture at a certain moment with the nineteenth-century novel, film and television adaptations are as influential as all those other examples of canon building and literary criticism in which different generations take part in acts of "revision." The term "revision" is here used in the sense that John Wiltshire uses it in his *Recreating Jane Austen*, i.e. as the act of looking back, "of seeing with fresh eyes, of entering an old text from a new critical direction" at a particular moment (2001, p. 38). In Chapter 11, Terry Wright focuses on a number of recent film and television adaptations (mainly from the 1990s and 2000s), attempting to analyse conventions which they share with novels and other narrative techniques for which "translation" is necessary from one set of codes (those of the novel) to another (those open to film and television). Among the examples considered are recent versions of *Wuthering Heights*. Questions explored are the role of the narrator (for which an alternative needs to be found in film), the nature of characterization (very different in written narrative than on screen), and the issue of ideology (how it is possible to portray an author's world-view in film or television adaptations). Studying film and television adaptations of nineteenth-century fiction, the chapter argues, can alert students to conventions they have internalized but have often not consciously analysed and articulated.

This is also a theme taken up by Grace Moore in Chapter 12. She explores ways in which contemporary fictional re-imaginings of the nineteenth century can play a role in broadening students' sense of nineteenth-century fiction, its recurrent motifs and ideologies. Perhaps the most famous and groundbreaking examples of this kind of fiction are Jean Rhys's *Wide Sargasso Sea* (1966), John Fowles's *The French Lieutenant's Woman* (1969) and A. S. Byattt's *Possession* (1990), although Michael Sadleir's 1943 take on the shadier elements of Victorian society in *Fanny By Gaslight* (greeted with shock and outrage at the time of publication) is a reminder that this particular sub-genre has a longer history. Whilst these and other popular examples – Peter Carey's *Jack Maggs* (1997), Sarah Waters' *Fingersmith* (2003) and Michael Faber's *The Crimson Petal and the White* (2003) – determinedly shrug off the bedclothes of inherited tradition, it is also possible to see this kind of post-modern representation in terms of "writing back" (to use a term popular in postcolonial criticism), but also as determinedly historical and respectful, with a definite awareness of contemporary fiction's indebtedness to the past and present.

The idea of writing backwards and forwards – and sideways – also features in Sofia Ahlberg's essay "Transatlanticism," which forms Chapter 13. Until relatively recently, nineteenth-century fiction has been taught from a nationalist perspective with tutors and students working within a nationally framed literary history. The division of literary studies into "British" and "American" often goes unquestioned. In some instances there might be some discussions about the representation of American subjects in works by British authors – Antony Trollope or Wilkie Collins perhaps – or vice versa. But as Ahlberg points out it is also worth thinking about some of the other links to be made between British and American writers and writing in the nineteenth century and some of the acts of reciprocity and exchange that occur over and beneath the Atlantic ocean and which, given the supposedly "special" relationship existing between the two countries, are worth pursuing. Looking at real and imaginary encounters between America and Britain from both sides of the Atlantic encourages students to consider the art of fiction in the nineteenth century as not exclusively a national art. Transatlantic literary studies, it is suggested, encourages students of nineteenth-century English fiction to view writers from this period in terms of what Edward Said calls their "worldliness" (1993, p. 13). As Alhlberg puts it: "A precursor to globalism, the hemispheric context of the nineteenth-century text provides fascinating pointers on how to read literature in the wider context of religion, race, capitalism, and colonialism – then and now. A transatlantic reading encourages students to bring their own experience as global citizens into the classroom" (pp. 198–9).

The final two essays in this volume return to the issue of how students might be further encouraged to think about fiction via the cultural conditions within which texts were produced and consumed. In Chapter 14, Josie Billington considers the challenges not just of contextuality but what Peter Barry in *English in Practice* (2003) has usefully described as "total textuality" i.e. "the different kinds of textuality which can be seen as 'in play' (to varying extents) in works of literature" (2003, p. 48). Barry suggests that these will include:

> *Textuality* (also known as "the words on the page")
> *Intertextuality* (roughly the words on related pages)
> *Contextuality* (the social, cultural, and historical context of the work)
> *Multitextuality* (the textual variants of the work itself)
> *Peritextuality* (also known as literary criticism – the works alongside the text)

Taking her cue from Barry, Billington's essay starts from the premise that the big and necessary challenge to students in this era of interdisciplinary research is thinking about fiction in relation to other nineteenth-century discourses. Students will generally be familiar with the use of secondary criticism and programmes will usually provide library instruction in the use of relevant online research bibliographies. However, Billington argues that one of things which helps develop students as scholars – particularly in the transition from undergraduate to postgraduate work – is the literary training they undergo in the use of manuscript and primary sources to help generate research projects. Billington suggests something of the originality and richness which can derive from working creatively with primary sources and/or using them for ancillary conceptual, contextual, or framing support, whilst drawing attention to some of the practical, intellectual, and developmental-learning issues surrounding the issue of textuality which are integral to growing into postgraduate study.

One of these issues is of course the World Wide Web. In the final essay, Priti Joshi asks whether the internet can enhance students' understanding of nineteenth-century fiction, whether it can add to the complexity and nuance of their engagements? As Helen Rogers notes in a recent round table discussion hosted by the *Journal of Victorian Culture*, "the new technologies offer much more than resource enhancement and advanced search tools" but she observes, too, how teaching with technology raises concerns about sustainability, out-datedness, and plagiarism (2008, pp. 56–7). As Joshi argues in the present volume, using the internet involves taking on board two seemingly contradictory lessons: that scepticism about using technology in teaching is healthy and necessary *and* that technology can be thoughtfully used to advance learning. By way of example, Joshi explores the use of online maps alongside Dickens's *Oliver Twist* to discuss some potential possibilities of the use of web material before posing some larger questions: should we use technology at all? Should we simply use those aspects of technology that allow us to post materials for common use? If we deploy technology in the classroom, how might we frame its introduction? What sorts of assignments scaffold or enhance the primary material rather than detract from it? How might we manage its demands on our time?

As the essays in this volume reveal, approaches to teaching nineteenth-century fiction remain more diverse than ever. A number of very different versions of what constitutes a nineteenth-century literature course exist and co-exist. The essays included suggest once again that such different constructions of nineteenth-century fiction are the result of productions of cultural politics, of positions being constantly formed and held, challenged and subverted but also of nineteenth-century fiction's own diversity and complexity. This same complexity means, of course, that the directions in which future developments might go are numerous. For example, if teachers of the 2000s are not now as obviously concerned with the "best" of what has been written as they might have been ninety years ago they are more alert to texts' involvement in the creation of social discourse and to the anxieties that fiction may manipulate or conceal. They are slowly beginning to be conscious too of the cultural and economic milieu in which fiction was produced and consumed and are anxious to convey this to their students. The recognition that nineteenth-century fiction covers a vast canvas, that nineteenth-century readers enjoyed lots of different kinds of stories and that students are interested in exploring similarly widely is one point on which there is general agreement.

Works cited

Barry, Peter, *English in Practice: In Pursuit of English Studies* (London: Arnold, 2003).

Davison, Margaret (ed.), *Bram Stoker's Dracula: Sucking Through the Century, 1897–1997* (Toronto: University of Toronto Press, 1997).

Dentith, Simon, "Reader, I Triumphed: Complicating the Appeal of *Jane Eyre,*" *English Subject Centre Newsletter 9* (November 2005), pp. 19–25.

Eaglestone, Robert, *Doing English: A Guide for Literature Students* (London: Routledge, 2000).

Easthope, Antony, *Literary into Cultural Studies* (London: Routledge, 1991), 12.

Hammond, Mary, *Reading, Publishing and the Formation of Literary Taste* (Aldershot: Ashgate, 2006).

Holberg, Jennifer L. and Marcy Taylor, "Editor's Introduction." *Pedagogy: Critical Approaches to Teaching Literature, Language, Composition, and Culture,* 1.1 (2001), pp. 1–5.

Hutchinson, Linda, "Beginning to Theorize Postmodernism," *Textual Practice,* 1:1 (1987), pp. 10–31.

James, Henry, *The Art of the Novel: Critical Prefaces* (London: Charles Scribner's, 1935).

Leavis, F. R., *The Great Tradition* (Harmondsworth: Penguin, 1962).

Leitch, Vincent B., *American Literary Criticism from the Thirties to the Eighties* (New York: Columbia University Press, 1988).

Levine, George, "The Two Nations." *Pedagogy: Critical Approaches to Teaching Literature, Language, Composition, and Culture*, 1.1 (2001), pp. 7–19.

——, "Foreword." Tanya Agathocleous and Ann C. Dean (eds.), *Teaching Literature: A Companion* (Palgrave Macmillan, 2003), pp. vii–xii.

Macdonald, Peter D., *British Literary Culture and Publishing Practice 1880–1914* (Cambridge: Cambridge University Press, 1997).

Poovey, Mary, *Uneven Developments: The Ideological Work of Gender in Mid-Victorian England* (Chicago: University of Chicago Press, 1988).

Rogers, Helen, "Searching Questions: Digital Research and Victorian Culture," *Journal of Victorian Culture*, 13.1 (Spring 2008), pp. 56–7.

Sampson, George, *English for the English. A Chapter on National Education* (Cambridge: Cambridge University Press, 1921).

Sanders, Valerie, "Where Next in Victorian Literary Studies? – Historicism, Collaboration and Digital Editing," *Literature Compass*, 4 (2007), pp. 1292–302.

Showalter, Elaine, *Teaching Literature* (Oxford: Blackwell Publishing, 2003).

Trollope, Anthony, *Four Lectures*. Ed. Morris L. Parrish (London: Constable & Co., 1938).

Waller, Philip, *Writers, Readers and Reputations: Literary Life in Britain 1870–1918* (Oxford: Oxford University Press, 2006).

Wells, H. G., *The Country of the Blind* (London: Thomas Nelson and Sons, 1913).

Widdowson, Peter (ed.), *Re-reading English* (London: Methuen, 1982).

Williams, Carolyn, "Genre Matters: Response," *Victorian Studies*, 48:2 (2006), pp. 295–304.

Williams, Raymond, "When was Modernism?," in *The Politics of Modernism*, ed. Tony Pinkney (London: Verso, 1989), pp. 31–5.

Wiltshire, John, *Recreating Jane Austen* (Cambridge: Cambridge University Press, 2001).

2

The Canon: Mapping Writers and Their Works

Janice M. Allan

> Every week beholds a new irruption of emigrants into the
> sunny land of fiction, sadly disturbing the old balance of
> power, and introducing a fearful confusion of names and
> habits. Within a few years, all the proprieties of the domain
> have been violated by the intrusion of hordes of ruffians,
> pickpockets, and vagabonds. Sir Charles Grandison finds
> himself face to face with Jack Sheppard, and no scorn spar-
> kling in the eyes of Di Vernon can abash the impudence of
> Mr. Richard Turpin. The swagger of vulgar villainy, the lisp of
> genteel imbecility, and the free and easy manner of Wapping,
> are now quite the rage in the Elysian fields of romance.
>
> (Whipple, 1848, p. 354)

The title of this chapter names two incommensurate bodies: nineteenth-
century fiction and the canon. The first is unwieldy, almost monstrous, in
its proportions; an estimated 60,000 novels were published between 1855
and 1890 alone (Maunder, 2005, p. 20). Such figures, moreover, do not take
into account the explosion of serialized fiction within the growing number
of popular periodicals launched during the same period. Within such publications, as Margaret Oliphant suggests, "There are stories to begin with,
stories to end with, and stories in the middle" (1858, p. 204). Such was the
growth in the production of popular fiction that a critic writing for *Tait's
Edinburgh Magazine* could declare, without irony, that the "'age of iron,' the
'age of steam,' and all the various epithets by which that period of time
in which we live is distinguished at every progressive step, seem about to
retire before the newer one of the 'age of cheap literature'" (Anon., 1852,
p. 118). Resisting, for the moment, the urge to qualify and question, we may
simply state that the canon is, in contrast, a much more select and circum-
scribed body consisting of a mere handful of works. Out of the thousands
of published nineteenth-century authors, Francis O'Gorman's recent – fairly
standard – list of the "acknowledged great names of Victorian fiction"

includes only nine: Charlotte and Emily Brontë, Charles Dickens, George Eliot, Elizabeth Gaskell, Thomas Hardy, Henry James, William Makepeace Thackeray, and Anthony Trollope (2002, p. 2). Although this group of writers collectively published well over a hundred novels, this represents little more than a drop in a vast sea of fiction produced during the period.

Over the past few decades, the canon – as both a body of works and a certain Kantian conception of aesthetic value – has undergone a series of profound challenges, both theoretical and material, that has robbed it of much of its former authority. The pioneering work of such feminist critics as Ellen Moers (*Literary Women*, 1976) and Elaine Showalter (*A Literature of Their Own*, 1977) initiated an ongoing process of literary recuperation and canon revision that has dramatically changed our perception of nineteenth-century writing. Others, such as the post-colonial critics Chinua Achebe ("An Image of Africa: Racism in Conrad's *Heart of Darkness*," 1977) and Gayatri Spivak ("Three Women's Texts and a Critique of Imperialism," 1985), reminded us that the question of *how* to read is just as important as *what* to read (see Chapter 3 for a discussion of how trends in literary theory have altered the terrain of the literature classroom). In more recent years, the shift towards a more thoroughly historicized understanding of cultural production and consumption has radically undermined the universalist notion of "intrinsic value" upon which the concept of the canon is based. Indeed, there is now a widespread recognition that, "All value is radically contingent, being neither a fixed attribute, an inherent quality, or an objective property of things but, rather, an effect of multiple, continuously changing, and continuously interacting variables" (Hernstein Smith, 1988, p. 30). Today, most scholars are happy to acknowledge that the "canon" (its problematic status now signalled by scare quotes) reveals more about the time and circumstances of its construction than the works it reifies.

The impact of such changes has not been limited to our scholarly research, it has also had a profound impact on both how and what we teach. The fact that Elizabeth Gaskell, for too long relegated to the margins as a "minor" writer, is now a curriculum staple is only a particularly obvious example of this. It is no longer surprising to find a popular novel by Mary Elizabeth Braddon or Wilkie Collins on undergraduate curricula, nor is the appearance of working-class writers and forms uncommon. Yet as Anne Marie Beller has recently argued, "in spite of an unprecedented rise within Victorian Studies, of research into 'popular' genres and writers, the traditional canon continues to dominate the nineteenth-century syllabus at undergraduate level" (2007, npn).[1] Certainly more work is required in order to answer the thorny question of how we, as teachers, might design and deliver a curriculum that moves beyond, without simply abandoning, "the established greats" in order to equip our students with a better sense of that vast body, both amorphous and heterogenic, that is nineteenth-century fiction. Without purporting to offer a definitive answer to this question, this chapter investigates how we might begin to bring the two disproportionate bodies named in the title into a more equitable relationship. Rather than advocating the incorporation of any particular non-canonical text, or texts, it explores a range of pedagogic and pragmatic issues relating to integrationist curriculum design.[2] At the same time, I should acknowledge from the outset that the underlying assumption that drives my argument forward is that we must reassess not only *what* our students read but *how* they read. In the words of Antony Easthope, this will "entail not just a change in the object of study (additional texts) but a transformation in the *method* of study" (2003, p. 5).

A final (related) introductory word about cartography. A typical attempt to chart the vast terrain of nineteenth-century fiction might begin with Walter Scott and Jane Austen, publishing in the 1800s, through Newgate fiction (Edward Bulwer-Lytton or William Harrison Ainsworth) and on to the publishing phenomenon that was Charles Dickens. The next stop would inevitably be the Gothic-inflected realm of the Brontës. From there, it might trace the emergence and development of social problem fiction (Elizabeth Gaskell) and domestic realism (Anthony Trollope or George Eliot), before moving on to the sensation novel (Wilkie Collins, Mary Braddon or Ellen [Mrs Henry] Wood), the latter providing a well travelled route to New Woman's writing (Sarah Grand or George Egerton) and then fin de siècle decadence (Oscar Wilde). While this map covers a good deal of ground (certainly a module's worth), it also leaves wide expanses wholly unexplored. One might, of course, address such gaps through an additional or alternative map, but what we must recognize is that such efforts will not address the fundamental problem that all maps – and, according to my analogy, all canons – "organize information according to systems of priority and thus, in effect, operate as arguments, presenting only partial views, which construct rather than describe an object of knowledge" (Gilbert, 2004, p. 16). Thus this chapter, as indicated by its title, is interested in mapping rather than maps: the process of canonization rather than any particular canon. Focusing on the verb as opposed to the noun, it argues that it is not a map or even a variety of maps – necessarily partial, distorted and distorting – that we need to offer our students but, rather, a heightened degree of reflexivity about the process of mapping (canonization) itself. For as Pamela K. Gilbert argues, maps "have generally been accorded a disproportionate truth value by their readers, and often even by their makers, who should know better" (ibid.). It is precisely this "truth value" that we must enable our students to question.

From the canon to the curriculum

In *Cultural Capital: The Problems of Literary Canon Formation*, John Guillory suggests that "works not included on a given syllabus appear to have no status at all" (1993, p. 30). Frank Kermode states the case even more succinctly: "every reading list is a canon of sorts" (cited in Widdowson, 1999, p. 24).

Without denying the pivotal role of the education system in the production and distribution of cultural capital, I would suggest that such assertions give little credit to the present generation of students, many of whom, while demonstrating a limited knowledge of specific literary texts, are increasingly savvy about cultural production, the production of culture, and the relativity of "value." That said, it is only by destabilizing and demythologizing the relationship between the curriculum and the canon that we can move our students from a passive acceptance of maps as an object to an active engagement with the process of mapping as a subject. Consider, for example, the following statement from a recent volume of pedagogical essays, *Teaching British Women Writers: 1750–1900*: "When one can eliminate a dependency on the literature by males and teach a work for its own merits, without using a comparison/ contrast method to argue legitimacy, then clearly the work in question has a place in the canon" (Simmons, 2005, p. 94). Such an approach may well *open* the curriculum/canon (there appears to be a seamless transition between the two) but it is based upon the same exclusionary and hierarchical principles it is designed to redress. By employing the ever-elusive criteria of "merit," as well as maintaining a boundary between "legitimate" and "illegitimate" texts, it leaves the *idea* of the canon untouched. What we must recognize is that while the number of academics who maintain that a text needs to be canonical in order to form part of the curriculum is dwindling, there is still a tendency to assume that curricular inclusion represents the first step towards canonization. *Pace* Guillory and Kermode, integration into the curriculum should not be viewed as the same thing as integration into the canon. Indeed, only when we fully sever this tie between curriculum and canon will we be able to move our students beyond a questioning of individual canons (which canon, whose canon?) to an interrogation of the idea of the canon itself.

As a first step towards decoupling the curriculum from the canon, it may be productive to distinguish between *aesthetic* value and what Thomas O'Beebee, in his pragmatic study of genre, calls *"use*-value" (1994, p. 17, italics added). In other words, our decisions about what to teach should be based, not on an outmoded idea of a text's intrinsic "merit" but, rather, on the potential uses to which a text was and can be put, both in its original context and within today's lecture theatres and seminar rooms. Of course, not the least important of such uses would be a text's ability to shed light upon contemporary and current constructions of aesthetic value, as well as the social and political imperatives by which they were, in part, determined. Other use-values would be determined by the learning outcomes of the individual module, or overall programme, but would likely include a consideration of the following: Does the text reveal something about the mode and mechanics of literary production and consumption? Will it allow students to identify and explore the contradictions inherent within contemporary ideologies? Is a particular theme or issue writ large within the text, providing students with an accessible introduction to a topic? and so on.

Unfortunately, the substitution of use-value for merit does not eliminate evaluative judgements from curricular design – decisions about which texts are most useful are as contingent and subjective as traditional constructions of aesthetic value. Nor should we mask this from our students.[3] On the other hand, because the potential uses to which a text was and can be put do not correlate, in any simple way, to its aesthetic merits, adopting O'Beebee's concept of use-value creates a more neutral terrain which neither excludes nor privileges either canonical or non-canonical texts. There is, in short, no *pre-determined* reason why an "acknowledged great" text like *Middlemarch* (1871–2) should, in the context of one particular module or programme, have a greater use-value than a popular work by Arthur Conan Doyle. Within another context, however, *Bleak House* (1852–3) might prove more useful than *The Woman in White* (1859–60) or any other sensation novel.

From what? To how?

It is, at this point, worth pausing to reflect on the teaching practices required by an integrationist curriculum. Introducing a range of non-canonical fiction will, no doubt, enhance our students' appreciation of the breadth and diversity of nineteenth-century literary production. But our pedagogical practices may still bear the imprint of traditional understandings of aesthetic value, obscuring the positive impact of curricular change. Consider, for example, what it suggests to our students if a canonical writer or text is given more class time than a non-canonical writer. Or again, if library resources are unequally distributed, resulting in an abundance of material devoted to Charles Dickens or George Eliot and a corresponding paucity of resources on working-class writing or detective fiction. Of course there *are* more resources available on canonical writers and texts (at least of the traditional monograph variety), but the increasing body of scholarly material devoted to popular genres and writers, including that which is now available electronically, via subject-specific databases, goes a considerable way to redressing this imbalance. What we must ensure is that such materials are represented in our course bibliographies and reading lists. It may well be that such equitable treatment of non-canonical works is nothing more than basic good practice, but it is crucial to achieving a truly integrationist approach to the teaching of nineteenth-century fiction; an approach where non-canonical works are not regarded as anomalous nor positioned in terms of alterity.

It is, perhaps, only appropriate that the model that best captures the curricular approach advocated above is the nineteenth-century magazine: the medium through which so much fiction of the period was disseminated. As Laurel Brake reminds us:

> the magazine format, bringing together as it does a range of authors, topics and kinds of article into a single but serialised text, offers to

twentieth-century readers a cheek by jowl structure which alerts us to the nuances of difference – categories of gender, genre, class, ideology, discourse – which allegedly more seamless texts are claimed to repress. (1997, p. 54)

It is this "cheek by jowl" structure, coupled with a refusal to elide "the nuances of difference," that renders the magazine format such an enticing pedagogical model for the integrated teaching of canonical and non-canonical fiction. Like a well-designed syllabus, it allows, in the words of Edwin P. Whipple cited at the beginning of this chapter, a diversity of texts to come "face to face" with each other and enter into dialogue. But where this nineteenth-century critic could detect only "a fearful confusion of names and habits," today's academics see a productive site of both consonance and contestation. Within this site each text is allowed to impact on the others – readings continually generating re-readings – in both rehearsed and sometimes unexpected ways. Indeed, a text's potential for cross-fertilization may be considered one of its most important use-values. Revisiting *Jane Eyre* after *Lady Audley's Secret*, for example, opens the text to new readings relating, not only to contemporary constructions of the relationship between gender and madness, but also to a range of issues relating to the professionalization of the woman writer, class (innate or performative?), marriage and narrative structure, and the politics of perspective.

This is not the only way in which the magazine format functions as a useful model for reading. Implicit within the idea of the canon is a preference for an ahistorical methodology that concentrates on the literary, rather than extra-literary, aspects of a text. In contrast, O'Beebee's more pragmatic notion of use-value requires a commitment to contextualization in order to realize more fully the various *uses* to which nineteenth-century fiction was and could be put. Although this issue is treated by Linda Hughes and Michael Lund in Chapter 10 of the present collectin, it is, at this point, worth reminding ourselves that contextualization is implicit within the very form of the magazine where "each piece is instantly and always contextualized, embedded in a matrix of other pieces which make up the issue in which it appears, and extends to the issues before and after" (ibid., p. 54). Thus the magazine format usefully foregrounds how "imaginative literature was demonstrably integrated into [a] cacophony of discourses" (ibid., p. 63). Within this "cacophony," moreover, there are no rigid boundaries between text and context. Thus the magazine model of reading encourages a more genuinely interdisciplinary approach to nineteenth-century writing.

The canon function

In advocating a clear distinction between the curriculum and the canon I am in no way predicting, *à la* Roland Barthes, the canon's demise. However much they may evolve and multiply, canons will always be with us.

Exercising a profound effect on our reading and reception of literary texts via our horizon of expectation, we ignore them only at our peril. And thus, while the canon should not determine the curriculum (nor should the curriculum be viewed as a canon), we must never simply occlude distinctions between "high" and "low" or "legitimate" and "illegitimate." For as Tricia Looten asserts, attention to such constructions "can open up new understandings of specific conflicts over literary and cultural value" (1996, p. 13). Thus, the canon, as a subject, demands a place within our curricula. In order to ensure that the emphasis remains squarely on mapping as a process, rather than maps as an object, I would suggest, even more specifically, that what we must equip our students with is an understanding of what might be called the canon function: the crucial roles that it plays in the production, circulation, classification and consumption of literary texts. The reference to Foucault is deliberate for, like the author function, the term canon function recognizes both its necessity (in that it continues to operate and to exercise certain effects) and its status, not as transcendent and autonomous, but rather, as a historically-determined discursive construct.

While few would question the imperative that our students appreciate the various functions of canonicity, it is less clear how this might be accomplished. In an era when more and more students are combining study with paid employment and/or caring responsibilities, we must think carefully about simply expanding the curriculum in order to allow for a consideration of the canon function. What text or texts, moreover, would in this respect prove most useful? In response I would argue that the inclusion of even one well-chosen example of nineteenth-century literary criticism can, without constituting an undue burden on the syllabus, provide lasting insight into the operations and functions of canonicity. Moreover, what our students garner from an encounter with the judgements of critics such as Margaret Oliphant, Geraldine Jewsbury, John Morley, or E. S. Dallas, can have a significant impact on how they read the rest of the curriculum.[4] At the same time, by asking our students to interrogate a piece of criticism, rather than accept its assertions and assumptions without question, we will also enable them to develop important critical thinking and research skills. With such a high potential use-value, it is difficult to understand why contemporary reviews and criticism have not assumed a more prominent place within mainstream nineteenth-century curricula. Certainly we can no longer use the excuse that our students do not have access to such sources for there is a wealth of material available on the internet.[5] Furthermore, the relative brevity of the literary review, combined with the ease with which they may be accessed (via electronic links on our virtual learning environments), make contemporary literary criticism a popular choice with students who grumble about the number of weighty texts they are required both to read and to buy.

As an illustration of how novel criticism can illuminate what I am calling the canon function, I would like to conclude with a discussion of how

Margaret Oliphant's 1867 *Blackwood's Edinburgh Review* article, "Novels," might be put to use within the classroom. With a plethora of materials to choose from, it may be helpful to identify the criteria that informed my choice but which might also be employed in defence of an alternative selection. In the first place, Oliphant's review includes examples of what are identified as both "high" and "low" literature. This, in itself, is not unusual but her determination to "make as distinct a separation as the printer's skill can indicate between the lower and the higher ground" (p. 275), aids the students in their first attempts to distinguish the qualities attributed to each category. Secondly, Oliphant's concentration on sensation fiction (including works by Mary Braddon, Edmund Yates, and Rhoda Broughton) makes this a particularly fertile source for an exploration of the operations of canonicity. For while every genre from the Newgate novel to high realism has its own story to tell about the canon function, few are as revealing as the sensation novel.[6] In Chapter 7, Jennifer Phegley explores how sensation fiction, as a genre, enhances the students' understanding of nineteenth-century culture. Here, I would argue that the use value of the criticism generated by this fiction is equally high. Because of its cross-class appeal and blurring of working- and middle-class literary properties, the critical response to sensation fiction was characterized by a strong sense of what Pamela Gilbert calls "critical surveillance, a need to categorize, to name and contain" (1997, p. 36). As a result, the signs and tokens of the canon function (naming, containing, categorizing) are writ large for the student. Even less attentive readers are struck by the multiple references to diseased bodies, disordered appetites, and spiralling mania. Furthermore, the slipperiness with which the term "sensation" is employed, here and elsewhere, is evidence of a generic instability that allows the term to function as a more generalized signifier of cultural anxiety. Thus the concept of sensation sheds light on more than the literary texts so labelled. As Winifred Hughes suggests, "What a culture considers 'sensational,' what gives it the creeps, can tell us a good deal about it" (2005, pp. 276–7). The final and wholly pragmatic reason behind my choice is that a full text electronic version of Oliphant's review is available via The Internet Archive (see note 5).

Moving on to the question of how this review article might best be put to use in an exploration of the canon function, it may be helpful to quote a portion of the opening paragraph.

> English novels have for a long time – from the days of Sir Walter Scott at least – held a very high reputation in the world, not so much perhaps for what critics would call the highest development of art, as for a certain sanity, wholesomeness, and cleanness unknown to other literature of the same class. This peculiarity has had its effect, no doubt, upon those very qualities of the national mind which produced it. . . . The novel,

which is the favourite reading of the young – which is one of the chief amusements of all secluded and most suffering people – which is precious to women and unoccupied persons – has been kept by this understanding, to a great degree pure from all noxious topics. That corruption which has so fatally injured the French school of fiction has, it has been our boast, scrupulously kept away from ours. It was something to boast of. We might not produce the same startling effects; we might not reach the same perfection in art, which a craftsman utterly freed of all restraints, and treating vice and virtue with equal impartiality, may aspire to; but we had this supreme advantage, that we were free to all classes and feared by none. (p. 257)

As the ability to read criticism critically is an acquired skill – and one which is underdeveloped in many of our undergraduates – we need to equip the reader with a set of specific directives to apply to Oliphant's text. Clear guidance will also ensure that the students' attention is focused firmly on a range of issues relating to the operations of canonicity. The following are a useful point of departure for the consideration of any contemporary piece of criticism:

1. Who is the author and what level of authority do they represent themselves as possessing? Where does this authority come from?
2. What criteria are employed by the critic in determining the merit of a literary text and/or distinguishing between "high" and "low"?
3. How many of these criteria can be defined and/or objectively measured?
4. How many of these criteria relate to literary (formal or aesthetic) qualities?
5. How many of the critic's judgements relate to extra-literary issues (such as contemporary constructions of gender, class and/or race)?
6. What are the assumptions (literary, cultural, political and so on) behind the author's statements?
7. Which discursive fields are employed in the argument and what might the choice of fields reveal about the culture of the period?
8. What are the "blind spots" and contradictions inherent within the argument?
9. What uses does the critic assign to literature?

The exploration of such issues, even within a limited context, such as the extract cited above, can prove surprisingly illuminating for students. Without the space to enter into a detailed analysis of the canon function within Oliphant's argument, I will comment on only the most salient features of its opening. Most important is Oliphant's frank and repeated admission that the "high reputation" of English novels (which here include those of Scottish Walter Scott) has little to do with their "literary merit" (p. 260).

This immediately denaturalizes the students' assumptions about literary valuation, planting seeds of scepticism about the very idea of canonicity. These seeds are then nurtured by Oliphant's focus on the texts' point of consumption – the vulnerable female reader – to the almost total exclusion of a consideration of their formal features. Finally, the location of value outside the text (in its ability to uphold and reflect a certain construction of national identity) foregrounds the contingency and historicity of judgement, as does Oliphant's stark and sustained opposition between robust English health and foreign disease.

The exercise described above is just one of many ways that we can enhance the critical skills needed to interrogate the idea of the canon and problematize notions of aesthetic value. However we decide to impart this skill set, impart it we must. Until it assumes a prominent place within our learning aims and outcomes, the benefits of teaching a novel by John Frederick Smith, G. P. R. James, or any of the other best selling authors of the period, will be unnecessarily limited. Only when our students are equipped with an understanding of what I have called the canon function can they become active explorers of the uncharted terrain of nineteenth-century fiction. Then, and only then, will the possibilities of an integrationist curriculum be realized through an integrationist reading practice.

Appendix: sample syllabus: Victorian literature

Aims and Objectives: This module introduces a range of Victorian texts – novels, poetry and non-fiction – in the context of the social and cultural history of the period. It encourages an appreciation of the diversity of intellectual and political activity in the period and invites a reassessment of received ideas about the Victorians. Students should note that a good acquaintance with secondary reading related to the period and its literature is important.

Delivery: This is a Level Two core module and is delivered via two weekly lectures and a weekly tutorial. Lectures are theme-based and will refer to a number of different primary texts from the primary reading list below.

Assessment: One short close reading assignment of 1000 words (15%); one tutorial essay of 1500 words (25%); one final two hour exam (60%).

Week 1

- Introduction to the Victorian Period
- Writing the City: representations and strategies: Hector Gavin's *Sanitary Ramblings* and Frederick Engels' *The Condition of the Working Class in England* ("The Great Towns")

Week 2

- Constructions of Class and Class Struggle: *Bleak House* and *Aurora Leigh*
- Reading Victorian Poetry (How to undertake a close reading of poetry)

Week 3

- *Mary Barton* and Social Problem Fiction
- Reading Victorian Prose (How to undertake a close reading of prose)

Week 4

- Literary Production and the Construction of Value
- The Right to Write and the Will to Read: Reading Women/Women Writers

Week 5

- Working-Class Voices: Philip Connell's "A Winter Night in Manchester"
- Detecting "Connexions": *Bleak House*

Week 6

- *Jane Eyre*: Deploying Otherness
- Constructing the Fallen Woman: Reading Esther(s)

Week 7

- The Poetry of Christina Rossetti: "Goblin Market"
- Poetic Form and the Dramatic Monologue: Robert Browning's "My Last Duchess"

Week 8

- The Rise of Science: from Lyell to Darwin
- Science v. Faith: Tennyson's *In Memoriam*

Week 9

- Sensation Fiction: *Lady Audley's Secret*
- Reading the Pastoral in Nineteenth-Century Writing

Week 10

- Celebration or Lament?: *The Woodlanders*
- Moving Towards the fin-de-siècle

Week 11

- Urban Identities: Sherlock Holmes's "The Man with the Twisted Lip"
- *Dracula* in Context

Week 12

- Reading *Dracula*
- Revision Lecture

Notes

1. Beller's insightful analysis of these issues has inevitably influenced my own thinking and I am grateful to her for a productive exchange of views while working on this chapter.
2. I use the term integrationist to designate a curriculum that cuts across traditional boundaries between high and popular literature, bringing texts into unexpected but meaningful association in order to allow students to perceive new relationships between them. This chapter does not address separatist approaches to the teaching of non-canonical fiction. While there may be certain benefits to such an approach where, for example, popular fiction is the subject of its own module, I believe that it does not lend itself to a questioning of the idea of canonicity as well as an integrationist mainstream curriculum. For a detailed discussion of such issues, please see Chapter 7 below.
3. Catherine Burroughs, for example, believes in offering her students a "'backstage' tour" of her courses, using an explicit analysis of the syllabus as a springboard to the larger critical issues within the field (2005, p. 140).
4. From the early 1850s, Margaret Oliphant was a regular reviewer for *Blackwood's Edinburgh Magazine* while Geraldine Jewsbury contributed a scarcely credible 1700 reviews to the *Athenaeum* between 1848 and 1871. Editor of the *Fortnightly Review* (1867–1882) and the *Pall Mall Gazette* (1880–83), John Morley was also a prolific and influential literary critic. E. S. Dallas was the literary editor of *The Times* throughout the 1850s and first half of the 1860s, as well as a regular contributor to the *Saturday Review* and the *Pall Mall Gazette*.
5. Most academics working within the field of nineteenth-century studies are well acquainted with the digitised resources available via The Online Books Page (http:// onlinebooks.library.upenn.edu/) including, for example, *Blackwood's Edinburgh Magazine* (vols. 53–94) and *Littell's Living Age* (vols. 1–227), but the treasures to be found on the Internet Archive (www.archive.org/) are less familiar. A small sample of the serials available within this online digital library includes: *Macmillan's Magazine* (82 complete volumes from the period of 1859 to 1905); *Cornhill Magazine* (67 complete volumes from the period stretching between 1860 and 1922); a complete run of *Household Words* (1850–1859) and the first 20 volumes of *All the Year Round*, covering the full span of Dickens's tenure as editor (1859–1870).
6. For a particularly insightful analysis of this issue see R. Nemesvari, "'Judged by a Purely Literary Standard': Sensation Fiction, Horizons of Expectation, and the Generic Construction of Victorian Realism," in K. Harrison and R. Fantina (eds.) *Victorian Sensations: Essays on a Scandalous Genre* (Columbus: The Ohio State University Press, 2006), pp. 15–28.

Works cited

Anon, "Literature," *Tait's Edinburgh Magazine*, 19 (February 1852), pp. 118–29.

Arnold, Matthew (1869), *Culture and Anarchy*. Ed. J. Dover Wilson (Cambridge: Cambridge University Press, 1971).

Beller, Anne-Marie, "Teaching Victorian Popular Fiction and the Problems of Literary Value," paper delivered at Victorian Literature: The Canon and Beyond Conference (University of Chester, 2006).

Brake, Laurel, "Writing, cultural production, and the periodical press," in J. B. Bullen (ed.) *Writing and Victorianism* (London and New York: Longman Press, 1997), pp. 54–72.

Burroughs, Catherine, "Teaching Women Playwrights from the British Romantic Period (1790–1840)," in J. Moskal and S. R. Wooden (eds.) *Teaching British Women Writers 1750–1900* (New York: Peter Lang, 2005), pp. 140–59.

Easthope, Anthony (2003) "But What is Cultural Studies," in S. Bassnett (ed.) *Studying British Cultures: An Introduction* (London and New York: Routledge, 2003), pp. 3–19.

Gilbert, Pamela. K., *Disease, Desire and the Body in Victorian Women's Popular Novels* (Cambridge: Cambridge University Press, 1997).

——. *Mapping the Victorian Social Body* (New York: State University of New York Press, 2004).

Guillory, John, *Cultural Capital: The Problem of Literary Canon Formation* (Chicago and London: The University of Chicago Press, 1993).

Hernstein Smith, Barbara, *Contingencies of Value: Alternative Perspectives for Critical Theory* (Cambridge, MA: Harvard University Press, 1988).

Hughes, Winifred, "The Sensation Novel," in P. Brantlinger and W. B. Thesing (eds.) *A Companion to the Victorian Novel* (Malden, MA and Oxford: Blackwell Publishing, 2005), pp. 260–78.

Lootens, Tricia, *Lost Saints: Silence, Gender, and Victorian Literary Canonization* (Charlottesville, VA: University of Virginia Press, 1996).

Maunder, Andrew, "Mapping the Victorian Sensation Novel: Some Recent and Future Trends," *Literature Compass* (2005), pp. 1–32.

Nemesvari, Richard, "'Judged by a Purely Literary Standard': Sensation Fiction, Horizons of Expectation, and the Generic Construction of Victorian Realism," in K. Harrison and R. Fantina (eds.) *Victorian Sensations: Essays on a Scandalous Genre* (Columbus: The Ohio State University Press, 2006), pp. 15–28.

O'Beebee, Thomas, *The Ideology of Genre: A Comparative Study of Generic Instability* (University Park, PA: The Pennsylvania State University Press, 1994).

O'Gorman, Francis, *The Victorian Novel* (Oxford: Blackwell Publishing, 2002).

Oliphant, Margaret,"The Byways of Literature – Reading for the Million," *Blackwood's Edinburgh Magazine*, 84 (1858), pp. 200–16.

——."Novels," *Blackwood's Edinburgh Magazine*, 102 (1867), pp. 257–80.

Simmons Jr., James. R, "Pedagogy and Oppositions: Teaching Non-Canonical British Women Writers at the Technical University," in J. Moskal and S. R. Wooden (eds.) *Teaching British Women Writers 1750–1900* (New York: Peter Lang, 2005), pp. 91–100.

Whipple, Edwin. P , "Novels of the Season," *The North American Review*, 67 (1848), pp. 354–69.

Widdowson, Peter, *Literature* (London and New York: Routledge, 1999).

3
"Theory" and the Novel

Julian Wolfreys

I

"Theory and the novel": this title makes me not a little uneasy; for one thing it sounds like an analogical substitution for "death and the maiden." In my scenario, the novel becomes the innocent victim of some predatory and ultimately fatal force, a force which it is the fate of the novel in all its virgin purity to suffer. This is not entirely fanciful, as you would realize had you heard, as I did, "Start the Week" (Radio 4; 31 March 2008). Novelist Maggie Gee spoke of what she saw as the problem facing students of English in terms of the amount of language which was "dead" and "abstract" they were expected to read. Misha Glennie, author of *McMafia* – a book on organized crime – observed that students were forced to read theory before reading "actual" works of literature. Maggie Gee responded that with the introduction of theoretical materials "something hideous began . . . this mad language of . . . " Whilst she was searching for the word "poststructuralism," Andrew Marr gleefully interjected "structuralism," which sounded as if it had an exclamation mark after it, if not being spelt in capital letters. Having found her word eventually, Gee then remarked that theory was the Emperor's new clothes, described it as mad once more, and confidently proclaimed "it will disappear," at which point Marr uttered the phrase "completely bonkers." It was as if a David Lodge novel had suddenly broken free of its parallel universe and stepped into mine.

Whilst teachers, or indeed actual students, might find such an exchange bizarre and/or irritating, it does point to a set of assumptions which often underlie attempts to talk about this subject. Not least of these is the sense that there is this thing called "theory" and that "it" can be taught as a set of theorems and procedures, as a series or system of propositions or principles vis-à-vis its presumed object or subject. And, moreover that this is to be pursued quite separately and often prior to, the "proper" business of reading and interpreting the novel. Once teacher and students have understood and come to terms with "theory," with so-called "literary theory,"[1] then they can put it behind them, and get on with the business at hand, informed as they now are by a set of theorems, little metaphorical spanners and wrenches, which, taken out of the institutional tool box, can be applied to literary analysis of a given text, such as "the novel."

Can we talk about "theory *and* the novel" then? I find the idea problematic. Some would say, that's just me being "theoretical." After all, we all know that there is "theory" and then there is "the novel." Well, yes, and no. Institutions, universities, colleges, other places of higher education, teach modules on "theory" whilst also teaching modules on "the novel": "introduction to the novel," "the novel in the nineteenth century," and so on. "Theory" appears in similar ways on course handbooks and web pages. This is far from uncommon, and the practice in departments of literature is to make material the "theoretical" assumption behind the very idea of "theory." Institutionally, "theory" is placed, located and given an identity, as (a) preliminary, coming before the study of literature-proper (as if there were such a thing) and (b) therefore contextual. "Theory," institutionally speaking, is preparatory material rather than as something in its own right. However, in such an approach "theory" is ill-served – and so too, as a consequence, is the student of literature.[2] This is especially so if that which is gathered in the name of "theory" is treated as merely contextual and only preliminary, seen as solely for the purposes of mechanical and repetitive application, and then applied as mere support to the proper work of reading literature, which should be historical and aesthetic. What follows is a discussion of how this might be avoided and the benefits to student – and teacher – of re-thinking what it is to read with theory.

II

First, another anecdote: in a departmental meeting, the subject of a forthcoming visiting speaker was raised, and a colleague inquired as to the title of the visiting speaker's talk. Another colleague replied that the talk concerned the Brontë sisters, and gave the precise title. The title contained words like "phenomenological," "methodological," and "deconstructive." This raised a slight laugh from the colleague who had enquired, with some additional smirks and knowing, complicit looks from others. At the risk of interpreting this moment, I would imagine the mirth came from what was seen as a combination of what for some would be jargon or theoretical buzz-words (even now, 30–40 years after "theory" was first imported into departments of literature), and the sense on the part of those who were amused that such an approach to the Brontës was inappropriate, anachronistic even. Anachronism is here read as the untimely "application" of particular modes of thought and inquiry to texts to which – the argument would go – are inappropriate to such forms of analysis because *Jane Eyre, Wuthering Heights,* et al. were written historically prior to the development of those modes of philosophically inflected consideration. Put another way, a phenomenological or "deconstructive" approach to the Brontës is wrong because the types of discourse identified as "theoretical" belong to a period, or periods, after the Brontës wrote. Such a way of reading could not take account of the contexts of production (social, cultural, political) and so removed itself from a "properly" historical account.

This kind of argument seems to me to be flawed on several accounts. First, it has to be asked, can one ever recover the histories that make up a text? Is it ever possible to reconstruct the totality of history out of which a text appears, and which that text then mediates through its own encoded signs of its historicity? The answer is no; not only is a totality impossible, there is also no direct access to another period, the forms of its thought, its cultural practices, and so on. However dogged my research, however much I may believe my approach to be empirical, I can only ever read from within the complex matrix of cultural forces that make up and inform – inscribe – my own subject-position. This is not to say that I cannot recover the traces of a history, but that I must always recognize that my interpretation is not neutral, however naively I may assure myself I read.

The point here is that there is not one history but multiple histories for which one must account. Different texts – even those published in the same year or written by the same author – speak of, and to, their histories in differing ways. No one historical approach can account for this, and making comparative judgements between texts, extracting "evidence" selectively from them in order to promote a single historically-based argument, generated from a monolithic overview of a moment in the past, seems to me to be both politically and ethically suspect, not to mention an act of violence.

Second point: whatever objections there may or may not have been to the departmental research paper when it was presented, this always has more to do with how cogently and coherently the speaker or writer presents the reading of *Wuthering Heights* – or whichever novel is being read. Thus, before we can even come onto the matter of "theory" it has to be stated that no "theoretical" reading is, necessarily, inappropriate as such. One of the things we need to tell students is that there are only good readings and bad readings; or, to refine this somewhat, there are readings of texts that are more sensitively handled and less sensitively handled. It must necessarily also be the case that every reading must always begin not from a fixed intellectual position imposed on the text. Instead, every reading begins only as a response to the singularity of said text, starting from a recognition that one is not imposing a reading but instead articulating, finding, a reading dictated by that text. It might be worth noting that the text the reader responds to relies on the assumption, as Derek Attridge puts it, that this text exists as "a set of coded signals," which become a novel in "a specific reading," and "within which [process] the reader too comes into being" (2004, p. 87).

If this can involve a recognition that particular types of representation are comprehensible via the reader's apprehension of philosophical or political discursive models, the act of critical reading might – and only might – generate what Attridge calls a creative reading of the text. What I have called the critical reading is what Attridge terms a "literary reading" (2004, pp. 86–7). The "literary reading" is that process by which, being "embedded in the culture of which literature . . . [and a particular literary form such as a novel] is a part, one . . . deploy[s] one's familiarity with the conventionalized routines of the literary institution." This, Attridge argues, involves the reader in a "great deal of patient labour [which] is unavoidable if a responsible reading is to be achieved." However, this is only the beginning. The creative reading, being "both passive and active," involves one in the effort of doing justice to the singularity of the text (as Attridge has it), whilst also letting that singularity, the otherness of the text in all its "strangeness" or anomalous difference "happen" to one, thereby experiencing the text in its otherness (2004, p. 85).

Without wishing to raise a laugh from readers of this chapter similar to those in my own department who laughed at the title of the research paper to be given, and so to escape any accusations of using "theoretical (so-called) jargon (so-called)," the alterity, the singularity, the strangeness experienced in the event of reading might well be the sign or trace of the historical – although this is not something that one can guarantee before one's encounter with the text. However scholarly a particular theoretical approach may be, it must also – in its responsibility to the text – be prepared for the unexpected and address this as it is, as it arrives. The textual anomaly – the odd image, trope, scene, that which opens a gap in logic and comprehension, or that about which a text remains silent – this is what remains to be read, and to which we teachers and our students must learn to attend.

III

The resistance to certain manifestations of "theory" and the privileging of "theoretical" readings favouring the historical and the material can perhaps be traced to the reading history of the nineteenth-century novel in universities, and the justifications made for it. For a number of years in literary study the novel was seen as a poor relation to poetry or drama. However, since 1948, with the publication of F. R. Leavis's *The Great Tradition*, and subsequent works by Wayne Booth and Dorothy Van Ghent, the attempts to articulate, if not a "theory," then a poetics *of* the novel has demanded that we take our commentaries on its origins and manifestations somewhat more seriously. Yet for many critics the justification for reading or studying the novel has often been on some historical ground or other. To invert an argument put forward by David Carroll, because literature, and the novel especially, is representational, it is taken as producing scenes, people, speeches, and events which offer the reader something extra beyond the immediate event or experience being described on the page, i.e.:

> a particular and recognizable historical, social or psychological reality or, in a more abstract manner, a figure of an ideal, mythical, metaphysical "reality". . . . The "outside" is assumed to exist before its representation and thus to be the origin of representational literature, to be present in itself before it is represented in literature – which means that this "outside" is defined by other means than "strictly literary" ones and assumed to exist in itself before it is "figured" and recognized for what it is in literature. (1980, p. 201)

The Marxist or quasi-Marxist dismissal of theoretical models of reading other than those explicitly materialist or historicist, allied to the assumption that what is on the page is a representation or even a "reflection" of the world and that it is our job, as critics to read the world, has to do with a wish to justify one's own reading act by turning to the "outside" of the text. This is easier said than done for, as the good reader will already know, there is no outside-the-text. History, society, culture: all are terms – mere concepts. Nonetheless there has been a certain inevitability about this type of reading especially amongst leftist, pseudo- or quasi-leftist critics. Its origins seem to lie in György Lukács' *Theory of the Novel* (1916), in which the nineteenth-century novel is held up as "the epic of the contemporary world" in which characters are seen as individuals but also as representatives of particular historical or social forces of the period. Thus when Lukács wrote that the novel was the epic for disintegrated civilizations and disenchanted worlds, his postlapsarian inflection led him to remark that the novel "thinks in terms of totality" (1971, p. 56). Nothing is less the case in fact; novels in the nineteenth century are vast, densely woven irregular matrices of heterogeneous materials. It is only a certain type of critic who, incapable or unwilling to think in anything other than terms of totality, sees totality everywhere, and sets out, Quixote-like, to try and prove it. In fact, like "theory," the novel resists being neatly packaged. Both are manifestations which come about by the chance of historical and material forces. In this respect, literary language itself is "theoretical," to the extent that, comprised of differing and heterogeneous discourses, it weaves a mediated network. It invites us to attend to language as language, the purpose of which is, in engaging with the historical moment, to generate not merely a representation but a rhetorical reading of material conditions, translated into the literary, and therefore available as ideological critique of the materiality of history. The role of "Theory" in the classroom then is to make the "rhetorical" reading of the nineteenth-century author's own rhetorical reading available. This is because, in treating language as language, it asks the student to take seriously the power with which language is invested.

IV

A final anecdote, this time from my own teaching practice and set in a class on literary theory, an "introduction" placed somewhat idiosyncratically in the senior or fourth year of a North American institution, and placed there also as one of two quasi-compulsory courses (*quasi-* because you had to take one or the other; there was a limited choice through a kind of institutional get-out clause, making sure that students could avoid encountering "pure" theory if they so chose, or thought they chose). One day, in being asked a question, I found myself having to step back every time I tried to frame an answer, to open onto broader, and more complex frames. The question, a two-parter, had to do, perhaps ironically, with the reason for theory at all, the student having asked something along the lines of this: if theory is important, why is it only introduced to us in our final year? And, given that we are all English Majors, who apparently know how to read very well (having got high scores in high school, and gained access to a highly selective university with an international research reputation), why do we need to be taught other ways of reading? This question arose at the beginning of the seminar, that moment when one or two people are still coming in, others are switching off mobile phones, a few are finishing a conversation, and so on; or, if not at the beginning then in that curious margin slightly before the beginning but after the point where the seminar has begun, which was positioned rhetorically by the student asking the question, in this way: "before we got going with this week's reading, I'd like ask a quick question." The question may have been quick, in that rhetorical formula involving an apologia, which students use regularly, but the answer was anything but, taking over the seminar and lasting 43 minutes. This left 5–6 minutes in which to discuss "this week's reading." But what is one to do?

Readers of this volume will recognize the difficulties here. On the one hand, the teacher has a responsibility to this student, which exceeds any seminar plan or institutional regulation about how class time should be spent. On the other hand, to respond to an individual student in this manner means that the teacher is not doing what is required according to certain rules, conventions, and so forth, and is neglecting or giving short shrift to every other. Before any calculation one encounters a "crisis" and one is forced to decide in response to the undecidable; or, as Jacques Derrida remarks, "I am responsible to any one (that is to say to the other) only by failing in my responsibilities to all the others . . . Whether I want to or not, I will never be able to justify the fact that I prefer or sacrifice any one (any other) to the other . . . What binds me to singularities, to this one or that one . . . remains finally unjustifiable." Or as he puts it rather more directly: "How would you justify the fact that you sacrifice all the cats in the world to the cat that you feed at home every day for years, whereas other cats die of hunger at every instant?" (2008, p. 71). Teaching is not the same as feeding cats, but the principle governing what is ultimately unjustifiable is a matter of degree, rather than kind. Thus there is always the unexpected which can erupt in the true choices one makes.

Of course, I can imagine someone observing, "well Wolfreys could have just told the student to come and see him in office hours and they would discuss the point." The point here is that there is in teaching – as well as in reading – always the possibility of an excess that erupts from within, that which throws a spanner in the works, where the works rely for their smooth operation on a production-line assembly mode of knowledge acquisition, as one fits or equips the student. However, to go back almost to where I began: theory and practice are inseparable. If this particular section of this essay is "Derridean" in its ethics – and I would like to believe it is, but not for the reasons I imagine haunt the objection I've invented, above – this has to do not with a theory and a practice of teaching, or even a theory and a practice of teaching theory, a theory and practice of teaching theory in relation to the nineteenth-century novel, etc., and so on, and so forth. Rather, this section emerges itself as a response to the editors' (natural) request that I say something about actual teaching.[3]

V

What, then, might take place in teaching a nineteenth-century course in which "theory" is supposed to figure? First, ask questions of yourself – and students – about those very practices of thought where you don't think, where habitually you take something as "read," or that you assume that something "goes without saying." If something goes as read, and without saying, its mute inscription is all the more pervasive. Ask why do certain forms of language – the language of "theory" – make you uncomfortable, and avoid the immediate fall back into the obvious answers. Also consider the fact that in other disciplines one is expected to master certain discourses or language praxes – mathematics or physics for example. Yet, with "English literature" or "literatures in English" we are doing professionally what we do anyway (the phrase "reading for pleasure" springs to mind). There is behind whatever implicit assumptions are at work here, the idea that there is something "natural," "inevitable," "self-evident" in what we do and how we do it, when we're doing reading or when we're doing what passes for reading but which is, already, a programme by which we are written as liberal humanist western Europeans or North Americans, the parameters and protocols of which we all share, more or less. Even – or perhaps especially – political criticism shares the same, or similar, often humanist values, and justifies its own departure from the "normative" or "conventional" mode of reading out of political necessity, the demands of demystification and so on.

So, one aspect of "theory" is to question fundamentally what it is we think we're doing when we read. Having to learn a new language with difficult concepts behind it, can appear unnecessary at best, pernicious at worst. Students of nineteenth-century novels can gain much from "theory" however (as can students of any literary form or period), for the following reason: it is not a question of learning a theory so that "practically" they can "apply" something "useful" to a novel, as though the novel were soft jelly being poured into a mould, or as if "theory" were a template, into which the novel could be made to "fit" once "theory" had rubbed off its rough edges. Rather, the close and patient reading of "theory" can serve to illuminate ideas already at work in the novel, which in the drive for narrative content the student might otherwise overlook. Equally, the novel can be shown as a medium for the exploration of philosophical ideas in particular cultural and historical moments, which ideas are given shape and form, or given face – what in classical rhetoric would be called prosopopoeia – through characters, the worlds they inhabit, and the interactions between those characters in those sites, at specific historical moments, and in relation to the local materiality of the singular world they exist in and serve to define through their experiences.

Secondly, there is the potential for students to gain a great deal from the engagement with "theory," not least the ability to reason in complex ways that challenge habits of thought and assumptions about their world and the world depicted through novels. In being hybrid and heterogeneous, "theory" exposes the student to a complex of different disciplinary modes of thinking. These include historical and ideological discourses, discourses of contemporary science, practices in linguistics and an understanding of otherwise silent and unconscious modes of thought as revealed through psychoanalysis. Additionally there is the encounter with the discourses of philosophy, often those developing out of ontology and phenomenology, as well as aesthetics, which place at centre-stage questions concerning the meaning of being and the ways in which the human subject perceives and so interprets the world. Were one to advocate "theory" in its own right (again supposing such a thing existed, and one could speak, both of an "it" and an "in its own right"), such concerns should be more than enough, if not to justify "theory" then at least to explain what is important, urgent even. However, what can also be said here, through analogy, is that the nineteenth-century novel in its many guises and through the various modes of realist presentation that are assumed in the novels Dickens, Trollope, Gissing, Thackeray, the Brontës, Gaskell, Oliphant, and so on, is, though different, also oddly similar to the web that goes by the name "theory." The same and yet not the same, it too asks questions of history, ideology, politics, language, questions of value, both economic and aesthetic, what laws define a society, what gives meaning to human life, how one interprets the world, and so forth.

Conveying these ideas in a classroom situation is, of course, tricky. One possible practice is that small passages, no more than a couple of paragraphs, be given over to close reading, in seminars, and in written exercises. If possible, find a passage in a given thinker (Lacan or Kristeva, perhaps, or indeed, any critic or "theorist" you might employ) and compare it with a passage from a novel in which the subject is, if not similar, then, at least, in some way discernibly related through its different modes of representation and the play in which these modes engage. Where, for example, Kristeva speaks of abjection in relation to coroporeality, *jouissance* and violence (1982, p. 10), consider as a contrast the passage in Gaskell's *Cranford* where the story of a cat being forced to take an emetic is shared amongst a group of genteel ladies (1998, pp. 125–6).[4] And this passage, in turn, might be turned towards a discussion of analogy, catachresis, modes of signification and, in short, pussy vomit as a model for *pure* literary production, for what Derrida calls a "non-exchangeable productivity in terms of sensible objects or signs of sensible objects (money for example)" (1998, p. 271). Conveying that the function of artistic and literary activity "is essentially *parodic*" (Eagleton, 1978, p. 51) Gaskell's narrative of fabulous regurgitation, a metaphorical regurgitation of the narrative and the displacement of vomit into narrative iterability coming back and up over and over again, admits of "neither . . . use-value nor . . . exchange value" (Derrida, 1998, p. 271).

   Another way to approach the two passages is not to find simply overlaps or analogous resemblance but to read both passages rhetorically or "poetically," considering tropes, metaphors, other figures of speech, and how they operate in the extracts in question. One might take, again to give an example, a passage from Lacan's well-known essay on returning to Freud, "The Agency of the Letter in the Unconscious or Reason since Freud" (1977, pp. 146–78). In the second section of this essay, "The Letter in the Unconscious" Lacan offers a "definition" of "the topography of the unconscious" in relation to the signifier and, by extension chains of signification expressed in writing, as this "topography" is to be expressed as an "algorithm" (p. 163). Why, we might pause to ask, is this figure of "topography" appropriate? Is it appropriate, and what is Lacan doing in "representing the unconscious through the figure of a map and then substituting that trope with another, this time one from the symbolic logic of mathematics? What is the relation between topography and writing, mapping and other forms of inscription? What does thinking the unconscious as a map, or thinking a literary text as a map for that matter, change in our perception of literary form, the supposed linearity of narrative, structures of literary representation and so forth? Already the Lacanian excerpt throws up all kinds of questions that we can ask of literary texts. It enables a different thinking, a thinking of difference in relation to our habitual practices of reading the literary. But to take this further, one should observe how Lacan's text is a series of interplays between linear text and algorithmic diagrammes, thus (pp. 163–4):

It is a matter, therefore, of defining the topography of this unconscious. I say that it is the very topography defined by the algorithm:

S

-

s

From this point, Lacan develops a series of increasingly complex algorithms, qualifying their presentation as symbols through discussion of metaphor, metonymy and metonymic structure (1977, p. 164). Against this one might read, or seek to unravel the symbolic and metonymic logic at work in an extract from Thomas Hardy's *Far from the Madding Crowd*. In this, Gabriel Oak and Jan Coggan, in pursuit of Bathsheba Everdene, stop to decode differ- ent forms of horse's hoof-prints (2000, pp. 184–6). There is more than mere similarity here between the Lacanian and the Hardyan world of symbol and signification, though this is undeniably significant and worth exploration. Both texts, more significantly, are available to us as explorations and plays with the limits of competing epistemologies and modes of representational logic. In *Far from the Madding Crowd*, in its first volume edition at least rather than the Wessex edition, Hardy introduces diagrams of the prints. Coggan stops before some tracks, of which the narrator records that "the footprints forming this recent impression were full of information as to pace: being dif- ficult to describe in words, they are given in the following diagram" (p. 184). On the page before the reader appear two parallel, hand-drawn lines within which are shapes resembling horse's hooves at different distances. Hardy reproduces such prints several more times (pp. 185–6), each set developing, like Lacan's algorithms, yet remaining resolutely at the limits of legibility. In these pages Coggan deciphers the tracks, both for Oak, whose knowledge is scanty and of the most general kind at best, but also, importantly, for the reader. Not only is the pace translated, so too is the fact that the horse being tracked is recently shod, and that it is lamed eventually. Such is what we are given to read in the "mystic charactery" of the hoof-prints (p. 186). Whether it is the late Victorian novelist remarking on the difficulty in expressing verbally the significance of the signs, or the Freudian-structuralist analyst elaborating on the function of the subject in the work of signification, each passage offers important insight into that which is, for want of a better word, "theoretical" at the heart of narrative discourse, and with that, the epistemological historicity of a given text, which remains as encrypted as it may be said to give up its meanings. More than this, they offer an anal- ogy between the structure of the unconscious and the structure of a novel, which itself not only speaks of but engages in a performativity through the very different examples – for both texts do the very things about which they speak, in, as it were, so many signs of their times.

In any situation, the teacher should always ask questions that are dictated by the text. By this I mean, the question should be formulated as a response to the text, whether "theoretical" or fictive, as if the text were asking the question. For example:

Why does Dickens in *Dombey and Son* allegorize train travel as some mani- festation of Death? Why is that manifestation itself quasi-anthropomorphic or prosopopoeic?

In chapter forty-seven of *Bleak House*, consider the powerful passage where Joe, the road sweeper is found to be dead. What takes place in that strange and disquieting instance of parabasis, where Dickens addresses the nation, and Queen Victoria herself? Is this realism? What is going on in such a gesture?

Take the passage from chapter fifty-six of *Middlemarch*, where George Eliot introduces Timothy Cooper, a labourer. Why is he allowed to step forward, to speak for himself? What is the function of voice as witness?

Why is there endless reference to optics and vision, visibility and visuality in *The Pickwick Papers* when, ostensibly, such references in all their frequency have little to do either with narrative or representation of a given scene? (Asking the student to notice a network of figures, which often persist for no immediately apparent reason, can produce very important "theoretical" discussions, which reveal much about a novel beyond what it has to tell us on its surface.)

The idea here is that the question should focus on that which in representation or narrative goes unremarked. Much time in seminars is taken up with talking about character motivation or psychology as if the character were not a construct of language. This is then extended to the reading of narrative trajectory. Yet if there is a fundamental question one might ask, this would be to invite students to consider *why* something anomalous appears in a novel. An alternative would be to call such a reading to a halt and focus on *how* a passage produces effects in a reader.

From these questions, it should be clear that "theory" is not something one "applies." "It" is a series of modes of thought and critical engagement from multiple and diverse intellectual locations, which cannot all be made to fit together in the neat package labelled "literary theory." Instead, the classroom should be a place in which students practice conceptual thinking so that they can be enabled to formulate appropriate questions for themselves. Given that the novel works through the medium of a narrator or "narrator-effect" (for there is no narrator there, only what Colin MacCabe calls a metalanguage, a language commenting on the language and behaviours of invented characters), it is, I believe, important to introduce the student to notions of ontology, the meaning of being, and how ontological definitions are formed, and, equally, it is important to introduce the student to matters of perspective *as* perception. Even in the most seemingly omniscient "voice," the interpretation of places, scenes, and peoples is based on a subjective translation of the material world. As a reader one is thus always subject to a phenomenological filter – even if the writer might believe he or she is simply presenting the world as it is. This in turn can lead to the student being introduced to the subject of how language as a structural system operates. Why does a particular word or group of words produce an effect or meaning, which other synonymous and non-synonymous substitutions do not? Additionally, attention paid to the role of seemingly purposeless meshes of metaphors and tropes, and linguistic or rhetorical devices can also direct the student to the historicity of the text. Thus, the student need not be introduced to "theory" as such but to that which "theory" is grounded in: the investigation of conceptual frames and structures and the historicity of their production.

Finally, there is the question of "how" in this assessment-driven age, does the teacher give the students the chance to best show that they've got the hang of this thing called "theory"? The main driver should be that students should be encouraged to invent their own responses. They need to respond as faithfully and as ethically as possible to the text. It is, therefore, inadvisable to dictate essay questions which direct the student to searching out "cookie-cutter" answers and other formulaic reactions. This chapter thus ends with four suggestions:

Detailed acts of close reading, supported with careful research, can work effectively.

Placing a "theoretical" passage, not as a question, but in some relation to a passage from a novel of the nineteenth century, and asking the student to explore that relation, to invent it (invention being used here in the sense of finding what is already there rather than creating something supposedly new), can produce surprising results.

Discourage so-called "secondary" materials. Everyone has marked an essay where the student has included twenty or more sources, which has all the resemblance of an omelet's ingredients before they're cooked: nothing adds up to much and it's not particularly digestible. Another way to put this is to say that undergraduates become anxious about the number of sources and mistake the activity of research in its practical gathering mode for the process of intellectual reflection (or "theorization") productive of an argument or insight. Ten articles or books on Elizabeth Gaskell might make the student familiar with a number of authoritative statements on Elizabeth Gaskell, but will not necessarily produce for the student an insight into that author.

A statement from a thinker conventionally perceived as a "theorist" might, inasmuch as, in not being directly about the author in question, enable the student to think about a more general problematic and so come to interpret a novel in the light of a more oblique questioning. Apprehending Smike, and Nicholas Nickleby's relation to him is not just a matter of understanding the abuses of the ragged schools that Dickens was keen to expose; it is irreducible to that. Beginning to think Smike beyond that merely historical context is a beginning of an ethical engagement that, I would argue, is closer to what pulses in Dickens's writing than mere historical fact.

Appendix: sample syllabus: Victorian literature

Centuries are the children of one mighty family, but there is no family-likeness between them. We ourselves are standing on the threshold of a new era, and we are already hastening to make as wide a space, mark as vast a difference as possible, between our own age and its predecessor. (Letitia Elizabeth Landon, *On the Ancient and Modern Influence of Poetry* (1832))

Fundamentally, form is unlikeness . . . every difference is form. (George Eliot, "Notes on Form in Art" (1868))

So much we can see; darkly, as through the foliage of some wavering thicket . . . (Thomas Carlyle, *Sartor Resartus* (1833–34))

Aims and Objectives: The purpose of this module is to introduce you to the broad sweep of Victorian Literature, its concerns, its interests, and its reflections of the culture from which it comes and which generates it. The nineteenth century is a period in which the cultural perception of one's historicity is transformed. It is, as one critic has put it, marked by the "trauma" of becoming historical.

What does this mean, though? What is the Victorians' sense of history, of the past, cultural memory, and their own historicity, their place or groundedness in time? How does this consciousness – which is, inevitably, a self-consciouness – come to be mediated in imaginative literature? At the same time, however, what is the relationship between a sense of being "in history," of being a material being, a sense of the past, and one's own "modernity" or "unlikeness" between oneself and one's predecessors? These are the questions which it is the aim of this module to address. At the same time, and in order to throw those questions into relief, we will be reading short theoretical essays which challenge epistemological assumptions behind both the Victorian texts in question and those which you put to work in reading a nineteenth-century text.

Schedule:

Week 1

- Introduction: the Victorians and Us

Week 2

- "Poetry, National Identity, and Historical Consciousness": Karlin, ed., *The Penguin Anthology of Victorian Verse*: Selections
- Theoretical Text: Jacques Derrida, "Che cos'è la poesia?"

Week 3

- "An Amazonian Society": Gaskell, *Cranford*
- Theoretical Text: Julia Kristeva, extracts from *Powers of Horror*

Week 4

- "Melodrama, History, & the Self": Dickens, *Dombey & Son*
- Theoretical Text: Jacques Rancière, extracts from *The Names of History*

Week 5

- Dickens, *Dombey & Son*
- Theoretical Text: Jacques Rancière, extracts from *The Names of History*

Week 6

- "A Use in Measured Language": Tennyson, *In Memoriam A.H.H.*
- Theoretical Text: Jacques Derrida, extracts from "How to Avoid Speaking: Denials"

Week 7

- Browning, Selections from Karlin ed., *Penguin Anthology*
- Theoretical Text: Paul de Man, "Phenomenality and Materiality in Kant"

Week 8

- "The Sensational": Collins, *The Woman in White*
- Theoretical Text: Freud, "The 'Uncanny'"

Week 9

- Collins, *The Woman in White*
- Theoretical Text: Freud, "The 'Uncanny'"

Week 10

- Lewis Carroll, *Alice's Adventures in Wonderland*
- Theoretical Text: Gilles Deleuze, extracts from *The Logic of Sense*

Week 11

- "Architects of Modernity": Hardy, *A Laodicean*
- Theoretical Text: Martin Heidegger, "Building Dwelling Thinking"

Notes

1. I say "so-called" for two reasons: first, the name "theory" assumes, however implicitly, an undifferentiated body of knowledge with an equally homogeneous ontology. That body of knowledge is not defined by what comprises it, but by the fact that, from the outside it can be called "theory," as opposed to other forms of writing, which supposedly are not "theoretical" in any way. Such a supposition is nonsense. The nineteenth-century novel, often concerned with economics, engages with this "theory." Second, "theory" is so-called, because, as I elaborate, the assumption in academic departments is that theory is entirely separable from other more obviously literary forms. From this point forward, the phrase "so-called" is implied wherever theory in the singular is referred to, and theory is placed in quotation marks in order to invite the reader to hold off from an unthinking and uncritical acceptance of the term, and more specifically its use in academic contexts.
2. I should immediately qualify the foregoing remark by saying that what I am about to narrate is not intended to expose anyone's resistance to, or lack of comprehension concerning, "theory." Rather, it is to identify a central concern in this essay, which has to do with how much or how little "theory," is accommodated on its own terms, or the extent to which "it" has become habituated or habitual; or, to push the point further, the question is one concerning the fact that multiple and different modes of thinking, having been reduced to and so neutralized by this catch-all identity "theory," has been positioned institutionally and found, if not a home, then a lodging place with greater or lesser shows of hospitality.
3. Because of the limits of length imposed by the publisher, a lengthy commentary on the ethics of teaching, framed in a performative discourse, has been cut from the essay. If you wish to receive a copy of this discussion, please email me at J.Wolfreys@lboro.ac.uk. I will be happy to send you either the discussion or a version of the essay with the discussion in its originally intended place.
4. For a comprehensive discussion of the scene in Gaskell, see Chapter Two, "Our Society: *Cranford*," from my *Dickens to Hardy 1837–1884* (2007, pp. 51–80).

Works cited

Attridge, Derek, *The Singularity of Literature* (London: Routledge, 2004).

Barbaras, Renaud, *Desire and Distance: Introduction to a Phenomenology of Perception*. Trans. Paul B. Milan (Stanford: Stanford University Press, 2006).

Carroll, David, "Representation or the End(s) of History: Dialectics and Fiction," *Yale French Studies*, 59 (1980), pp. 201–29.

——. "Economimesis." *The Derrida Reader: Writing Performances*. Ed. Julian Wolfreys. (Edinburgh: Edinburgh University Press, 1998), pp. 264–93.

Derrida, Jacques, *The Gift of Death, Second Edition, and Literature in Secret*. Trans. David Wills (Chicago: University of Chicago Press, 2008).

——. *Sketches By Boz and Other Early Papers 1833–39*. Ed. Michael Slater (London: J. M. Dent, 1994).

——. *Selected Journalism 1850–1870*. Ed. and Int. David Pascoe (London: Penguin, 1997).

Dickens, Charles, *Bleak House*. Ed. and Int. Nicola Bradbury. Preface Terry Eagleton (London: Penguin, 2003).

Eagleton, Terry, *Criticism and Ideology: A Study in Marxist Literary Theory* (London: Verso, 1978).

Gaskell, Elizabeth, *Cranford*. Ed. Elizabeth Porges Watson. Int. and notes Charlotte Mitchell (Oxford: Oxford University Press, 1998).

Hardy, Thomas, *Far from the Madding Crowd*. Ed and Int. Rosemarie Morgan, with Shannon Russell (London: Penguin, 2000).

Hegel, G. W. F., *Phenomenology of Spirit*. Trans. A. V. Miller. Foreword J. N. Findlay (Oxford: Oxford University Press, 1977).

Kristeva, Julia, *Powers of Horror: An Essay on Abjection*. Trans. Leon S. Roudiez (New York: Columbia University Press, 1982).

Lacan, Jacques, "The Agency of the Letter in the Unconscious or Reason since Freud," *Écrits: A Selection*. Ed. and trans. Alan Bass (New York: W. W. Norton & Co., 1977), pp. 146–78.

Lukács, György, *The Theory Of The Novel: A Historico-Philosophical Essay on the Forms of Great Epic Literature* (London: MIT Press, 1971).

McLaughlin, Kevin, "Losing One's Place: Displacement and Domesticity in Dickens's *Bleak House*," *MLN*, 108:5 (December 1993), pp. 875–90.

Merleau-Ponty, Maurice, *The Prose of the World*. Ed. Claude Lefort. Trans. John O'Neil (Evanston: Northwestern University Press, 1973).

Mighall, Robert, *A Geography of Victorian Gothic Fiction: Mapping History's Nightmares*. (Oxford: Oxford University Press, 1999).

Miles, Robert, *Gothic Writing 1750–1820: A Genealogy* (London: Routledge, 1993).

Natanson, Maurice, "Phenomenology, Anonymity, and Alienation," *New Literary History*, 10:3 (Spring, 1979), pp. 533–46.

Wolfreys, Julian, *Dickens to Hardy 1837–1884: The Novel, the Past, and Cultural Memory in the Nineteenth Century* (Basingstoke: Palgrave Macmillan, 2007).

4
Empire

Patrick Brantlinger

Before the advent of postcolonial literary criticism, which is usually dated from Edward Said's *Orientalism* (1978), most studies of nineteenth-century British fiction had little to say about the colonies or the Empire.[1] That was largely because, from Jane Austen through George Gissing, most novelists focused on domestic settings and characters. Austen wrote during and shortly after the Napoleonic Wars, which ended with the Battle of Waterloo in 1815. Nevertheless, though soldiers and sailors appear in her novels, they are ordinarily minor characters, and while some of them have served, like Colonel Brandon in *Sense and Sensibility* (1811), in India or elsewhere, none of the scenes in her novels takes place abroad. So, too, in *New Grub Street* (1891) and *The Odd Women* (1893), Gissing has very little to say about places and events beyond Britain, and that is true as well of Thomas Hardy's Wessex novels and of most of Elizabeth Gaskell's and George Eliot's fiction.

In *Culture and Imperialism* (1993), however, Said argues that the Empire is never entirely absent even in Jane Austen's novels. His main example is *Mansfield Park* (1814), in which Sir Thomas Bertram leaves for Antigua to look after the management of his plantation there. Said writes:

> According to Austen we are to conclude that no matter how isolated and insulated the English place (e.g., Mansfield Park), it requires overseas sustenance. Sir Thomas's property in the Caribbean would have had to be a sugar plantation maintained by slave labor (not abolished until the 1830s): these are not dead historical facts but, as Austen certainly knew, evident historical realities. (1993, p. 89).

Though Austen barely hints at slavery, Fanny Price is curious about it; by 1814, when *Mansfield Park* was published, Austen was certainly well-aware of the antislavery crusade. And the British Empire is key in Gissing's *The Whirlpool* (1897), whose protagonist Harvey Rolfe advocates a greater cause in South Africa than "nigger-hunting," as an acquaintance of his suggests

(Gissing obviously doesn't agree with the acquaintance, and probably not with Rolfe's brand of imperialism either):

> There's more than that to do in South Africa [Rolfe says]. Who believes for a moment that England will remain satisfied with bits here and there? We have to swallow the whole, of course. We shall go on fighting and annexing until – until the decline and fall of the British Empire. That hasn't begun yet. Some of us are so over-civilized that it makes a reaction of wholesome barbarism in the rest. We shall fight like blazes in the twentieth century. (1977, p. 16)[2]

The Whirlpool appeared two years before the start of the Anglo-Boer War, and less than two decades before World War I. By this time, many British writers had produced novels that focused on the colonies and that typically supported the British Empire. These include a host of writers of boys' adventure novels, from Captain Frederick Marryat with his midshipmen novels in the 1830s through Robert Ballantyne's *The Coral Island* (1858) and Robert Louis Stevenson's *Treasure Island* (1883) to G. A. Henty's war novels in the 1890s. Many of these narratives, like H. Rider Haggard's *King Solomon's Mines* (1885), *She* (1887), and *Allan Quatermain* (1887), take their cues from explorers' journals such as David Livingstone's *Missionary Travels* (1857) and Henry Morton Stanley's *How I Found Livingstone* (1872).[3] As a means to thinking about some of the discourses these texts share, students might be asked to spend an hour or two examining passages from Livingstone's or Stanley's book, and relating it to one of Haggard's adventure tales.

Apart from adventure in exploration, in war, and on imperial frontiers, however, most Romantic and Victorian novels offer domestic themes and scenes, although these often, as in William Makepeace Thackeray's *Vanity Fair* (1848), Elizabeth Gaskell's *Mary Barton* (1848), or Charles Dickens's *Great Expectations* (1861), lead characters overseas to the colonies. In *Great Expectations*, the convict Abel Magwitch is transported to Australia, becomes wealthy as a sheep farmer, and returns to England illegally to see the "gentleman" he has made out of Pip. After Magwitch's death at the end of the novel, both Pip and Herbert Pocket are headed to Egypt as employees of Clarriker and Company. And from Sir Walter Scott's *Guy Mannering* (1815) and *The Surgeon's Daughter* (1827) through Flora Annie Steel's *On the Face of the Waters* (1896) and Rudyard Kipling's *Kim* (1901), India was a setting and topic in many British novels. Especially significant were Philip Meadows Taylor's bestselling *Confessions of a Thug* (1839), the most influential novel about India prior to *Kim,* and the many novels about the Indian "Mutiny" or Rebellion of 1857–58.[4] Thuggee was a cult whose believers practiced highway robbery and homicide, and Taylor, as a soldier and police officer in the service of the Nizam of Hyderabad, was instrumental in helping to eliminate it. For the British public, *Confessions* and the raft of "Mutiny" novels that soon followed helped to criminalize India while justifying British rule.[5] Slavery, too, was an important theme in British fiction from the Romantic through the Victorian periods. Parliament officially abolished slavery in all British territory in 1833, but because it persisted in the United States, in Africa, and in the Ottoman Empire, it also persisted in novels such as Charlotte Yonge's *The Daisy Chain* (1856). After 1833, the British navy patrolled the African coast and the Atlantic in search of slave ships, a matter of patriotic enthusiasm for the British. In Yonge's bestseller, Alan Ernescliffe is "a hero" who has "distinguished himself in encounters with slave ships, and in command of a prize that he had had to conduct to Sierra Leone, he had shown great coolness and seamanship . . ." (1876, pp. 9–10). (Sierra Leone had been established as a British colony for the relocation of former slaves.) The colonies and the Empire may have been secondary compared to domesticity in British fiction prior to the 1880s, but they are far more significant than criticism prior to 1978 allowed. And as we shall see, both India and slavery are not merely incidental but key aspects of Charlotte Brontë's great domestic novel, *Jane Eyre* (1847).

Claims by postcolonial critics that, as Firdous Azim puts it, "the novel is an imperialist project" may seem puzzling and certainly debatable to students of nineteenth-century fiction, especially since many novels have little or nothing to say about the colonies or the British Empire (1993, p. 37). Where is the Empire in, say, George Eliot's *Middlemarch* (1872) or Thomas Hardy's *Tess of the D'Urbervilles* (1891)? It is evident that the Empire plays a major role in some fiction, especially in the era of the "new imperialism" – roughly 1880 to World War I. Joseph Conrad's *Heart of Darkness* (1899) and *Kim* are major examples, the first very critical of imperialism, at least of the variety practised in King Leopold's Congo, and the second quite positive about British rule in India. *Heart of Darkness* and *Kim* both offer versions of the theme of "going native," one negative and the other positive. Reading these stories, students might wonder to what extent a Westerner living for long periods in any non-Western society could avoid "going native," or becoming a "mimic man" or woman in reverse?[6] At any rate, Kurtz is supposed to be an emissary of civilization, but has instead given in to his lowest impulses and become something worse than a "savage." In contrast, Kim is an Irish orphan who is more at home in India than the Indians. His delightful rambles through India, both as the *chela* or disciple of the Lama and as a juvenile espionage agent, help to foil a plot by French and Russian agents to weaken British rule on the northwestern frontier. Kim is "the Little Friend of all the World"; almost all the Indians he meets approve of whatever it is he is doing, and so does he! And so do the members of the British Secret Service, headed up by Col. Creighton. At the end of Kipling's tale, it seems a shame that Kim should have to grow older and become more English (not exactly Irish) in the process. If they read both *Heart of Darkness* and *Kim*, students might usefully analyse why going native is so negative in one instance and so positive in the other?

Azim's assertion that "the novel is an imperialist project" might prompt students to ask whether and how the British Empire empowered the novel and British novel readers? If slavery and the plantation economy of Antigua provided the wealth of the Bertram family in *Mansfield Park*, didn't it also provide the leisure and wealth for Jane Austen to write it and the literate British public to read it? Azim adds to her assertion by further asserting that that genre is "based on the forceful eradication and obliteration of the Other." This sounds as though she is accusing a literary genre of genocide, something like Mr Kurtz's "Exterminate all the brutes!" (Conrad, 2006, pp. 49–50). But while the actual "obliteration of the Other" involved the genocidal extinction of indigenous populations, Azim has in mind the annihilation of "the Other" in novels that depict the formation of "a sovereign subject." In domestic realism and particularly in the *Bildungsroman* such as Dickens's *David Copperfield* or George Eliot's *Mill on the Floss*, the goal is typically the protagonist's attainment of mature selfhood, signalled by the achievement of economic security and marriage. But there is no such ending for non-European "Others." When they appear in domestic novels, they are minor characters to be used, pitied, or laughed at, like the mulatta Miss Schwartz in *Vanity Fair* or like the "Native" in Dickens's *Dombey and Son* (1848), whom Major Bagstock has brought back from India as his servant. The poor "Native" has no role to play except to be insulted and beaten by the Major, and he never utters a word, which may indicate just how subordinate the Major – and perhaps Dickens also – believes India is or should be to Britain. Dickens obviously disapproves of the Major's abuse of the "Native," but he also treats that dehumanized character as a bit-part for slapstick humour.

More important than the "Native" is Jos Sedley, Amelia's brother, who is a fat, cowardly tax collector from the Indian backwater of Boggley-Wallah in *Vanity Fair*. Jos's role suggests that Thackeray viewed India as little more than an exotic and uncomfortable place from which the British could extract wealth. Like Rudyard Kipling later in the century, Thackeray was born in India, though he was sent to England at an early age and, unlike Kipling, never returned to the subcontinent. India is even more prominent in Thackeray's *The Newcomes* (1855), in which the failure of a shady Indian bank costs Colonel Newcome his fortune, just as a real bankruptcy of an Indian accounting house cost Thackeray the fortune he might have inherited. This experience seems to have led Thackeray to view all Indians and India itself as corrupt or criminal, though he also doesn't seem particularly interested in reforming it. Nevertheless, even in *The Newcomes* India seems more tangential than central to the main events, like Antigua in *Mansfield Park*. Since both Thackeray and Kipling were born in India, students could investigate how this affected their writing. They could do so by examining biographies of both authors, and by reading Kipling's brief account of his Indian childhood in his autobiography, *Something of Myself*.

British novels that feature the "colonies of white settlement" – Canada, Australia, South Africa, New Zealand – often also feature emigration. And many of the first novels written in those colonies – Catharine Parr Traill's *The Backwoods of Canada* (1836), for example, or Thomas Rowcroft's *Tales of the Colonies* (1843) – deal with the experiences of immigrants and settlers. The protagonist in Rowcroft's novel has to battle both bushrangers and Aborigines, but he manages to establish his farm and raise his family in Tasmania. Whether written by British or by colonial authors, as a theme emigration typically involves some amount of criticism of conditions the colonists leave behind. "England" may remain their beloved "home" which they remember nostalgically, but the colonists left it because, for one reason or another, life there was unsatisfactory. Whether personal problems like those that cause the Micawbers and the Peggottys to emigrate in Dickens's *David Copperfield*, or social problems like poverty and unemployment in Gaskell's *Mary Barton* or starvation in William Carleton's *The Emigrants of Ahadarra* (1848), the colonies beckon. Thus, emigration novels can be simultaneously works of social criticism even as they wax patriotic about the colonies and the British Empire. Any Dickens novel that features emigration could be used as a test case for how that theme operates both as social criticism and as an affirmation of life in the colonies or the Empire.

Reading empire in *Jane Eyre*

Even though Jane Eyre never leaves England, the colonies – specifically, Jamaica and India – are something more than mere background in Charlotte Brontë's novel. As a colony where slavery was practised before 1833, Jamaica hardly offered the attractions to potential settlers that made Canada or even Tasmania appealing. As in *Great Expectations* with Magwitch's return to England, *Jane Eyre* involves a version of reverse colonization: Mr Rochester and his "madwoman" wife are recent arrivals from Jamaica. On the other hand, St John Rivers, planning to become a missionary in India, proposes to Jane and hopes that she will accompany him there. She turns down this opportunity for a life of Christian action in the far reaches of the Empire in favour of life in "the healthy heart of England" (1996, p. 402). Jane also inherits a fortune from abroad, from an uncle who has been a wine merchant in Madeira. Of course, Madeira was not a British colony, but the idea of wealth coming from abroad is important in Brontë's story, just as it is in *Great Expectations*, *The Newcomes,* and *Mansfield Park*. Jane divides this fortune with her cousins, the Rivers siblings.

To explore further how *Jane Eyre* relates to the British Empire, students and teachers can ask several questions. Where did Rochester's fortune come from? What is his connection and also Bertha Mason's to slavery and the plantation economy of Jamaica both before and during the time when the main events of the novel occur?[7] What does Jane herself have to say about slavery and abolition? And is there any connection between abolitionism, imperialism, and the variety of feminism that Jane and Brontë express? Students might be asked to read a portion of Gayatri Spivak's essay on *Jane Eyre* to explore these questions. Also, what is the significance of St John Rivers's plan to go to India as a missionary? What does Jane think of that plan, and why does she reject his proposal of marriage? Does Brontë seem to approve or disapprove of missionary activity in India, which until 1813 was banned by the East India Company for fear it might arouse opposition by Hindus and Muslims? And does she approve or disapprove of the activities of the East India Company, or in other words of British expansion and exploitation in India? Finally, there are a couple of hints about "suttee" (*sāti*) or the ritual immolation of Hindu widows in *Jane Eyre*. How do these hints help to connect the issues of slavery and feminism, and what implications do they have for British imperialism in India?

Questions like these can help students begin thinking about the idea of empire as a context for nineteenth-century fiction via the text itself – before they have been asked to do any secondary reading at all. The Jane–Rochester–Bertha triangle can be used to demonstrate lots of things but is an especially rich seam when it comes to the issue of Victorian attitudes to race. When Jane becomes a governess at Thornfield Hall, its owner, Mr Rochester, has recently come back to England from Jamaica with his wife, Bertha Mason, whom he locks up as a madwoman. Rochester keeps his marriage and his prisoner a secret from Jane and his friends and neighbours. We never learn the nature of Bertha's madness, but it seems likely that it has something to do with her colonial origins – she like her mother is a "creole." That term can mean merely a person of European race who is born in a colony; but it can also mean someone who is of mixed racial "blood." Rochester's reference to Bertha's mother "the Creole" (p. 326) and Bertha's "purple face" (p. 328) suggest that her racial composition contains some African blood, even though her family, like Rochester's, have been plantation owners rather than slaves. After she first sees the phantom-like Bertha, Jane describes her "discoloured face – it was a savage face. I wish I could forget the roll of the red eyes and the fearful blackened inflation of the lineaments!" Rochester reacts to this description by saying that "ghosts are usually pale," but Jane insists Bertha's face "was purple: the lips were swelled and dark; the brow furrowed; the black eye-brows widely raised over the blood-shot eyes." It is a face that calls to mind, she adds, "the foul German spectre – the Vampyre" (p. 317), a Gothic and typically a racial alien, as in Bram Stoker's *Dracula*.[8]

As in the case of the passionate and frequently enraged Heathcliff in Emily Brontë's *Wuthering Heights* (1847), who may also be a racial hybrid – perhaps a gypsy, but perhaps also the offspring of a British sailor and an African slave[9] – Bertha's madness could be the product of miscegenation and the passionate sexuality many Europeans associated with the tropics. Students who read *Wuthering Heights* could be asked to try to figure out Heathcliff's racial origins. They could investigate gypsies in British society by dipping into Deborah Nord's recent study, *Gypsies and the British Imagination* (2006). Rochester's passionate nature, too, seems partially derived from his colonial, tropical background. In the nineteenth century, it was widely believed that living in the tropics caused Europeans to degenerate both psychologically and physically. It was even surmised by some medical authorities that whites living in Australia could over several generations be transformed into Aborigines (Anderson, 2002, p. 186).

At any rate, Rochester has returned to England from Jamaica freighted with sexual charisma and a past he wishes to escape – perhaps slavery as well as his insane wife (whom he brings with him, however). Both Bertha's madness and Rochester's excessive ardour and willfulness must be tamed or destroyed before Jane can settle down to a quiet domestic existence as Rochester's wife, her reward at the end of the novel. Despite Jane's refusal to marry St John Rivers and accompany him to India as a missionary's wife, her life in England as Rochester's wife has, Deirdre David argues, colonial implications: Jane undertakes the "reformation of the colonizer [that is, Rochester] rather than the colonized." Jane thus becomes "a symbolic governess of empire." David adds that Brontë's novel "is about a specific historical moment when women were called upon to be agents in the labor of both renovating and expanding Britannic rule" – women including Queen Victoria (1995, pp. 80–97).

Perhaps especially because Bertha Mason is a racial hybrid, does Rochester's locking her up suggest the way slaves, including his own, were treated in Jamaica? Does her breaking loose and torching Thornfield Hall, killing herself and blinding Rochester, suggest a slave rebellion? Slave rebellions occurred frequently, and a major one exploded in Jamaica in 1831.[10] Further, on what grounds has Rochester imprisoned Bertha in the first place? Was she really "mad" or insane before he incarcerated her, or perhaps just "mad" as in angry? Does Jane ever ask if Rochester's treatment of her was a cause – perhaps the main cause – of her madness? Bertha may have become a "maniac," a "savage" and a "hyena" (p. 328), and Rochester tells Jane he should have been aware of her tendencies toward degeneration before he married her. But why does Jane believe him? It may be difficult or impossible to answer this question, in part because of Jane's tendency to equate marriage with slavery in the first place: Bertha's imprisonment is perhaps only the extreme version of what all married women experience. The equation between marriage and slavery is clarified partly through Jane and Rochester's discussion of slavery in the Ottoman Empire, and partly through the novel's references to suttee.

On various occasions, Jane Eyre likens her own situation to being a slave. The abuse she receives from the Reed family puts her in "the mood of the revolted slave" (p. 22). Rochester later calls her working as a governess "slavery" (p. 303). When he also tells her he would not trade "this one little English girl for the grand Turk's whole seraglio" (p. 301), Jane responds: "If you have a fancy for anything in that line, away with you, sir, to the bazaars of Stamboul [Istanbul] without delay; and lay out in extensive slave-purchases some of that spare cash you seem at a loss to spend satisfactorily here" (p. 302).

Although the reference is to slavery in the Ottoman Empire rather than in Jamaica, that only generalizes the theme (together with its opposite, liberation) that runs through the novel: how can a young woman, in Jane Eyre's circumstances, gain freedom? What will Jane do, Rochester wonders, while he is buying female slaves in Istanbul to be his concubines? Jane retorts:

> I'll be preparing myself to go out as a missionary to preach liberty to them that are enslaved – your harem inmates amongst the rest. I'll get admitted there, and I'll stir up mutiny; and you, three-tailed bashaw as you are, sir, shall in a trice find yourself fettered amongst our hands: nor will I, for one, consent to cut your bonds till you have signed a charter, the most liberal that despot ever yet conferred. (p. 302)

So the "bashaw" who has imprisoned his wife is threatened by his future wife with imprisonment, as if he were himself a slave.

Gayatri Spivak, Deirdre David, Susan Meyer, and other critics have stressed the resemblance between "the self-immolation of Bertha Mason" and "widow-sacrifice" or suttee in India.[11] Shortly after the references to buying female slaves in Istanbul, Jane finds herself thinking that, even if she were to fall in love with Rochester and marry him, she would have "no intention of dying with him." Jane adds: "I had as good a right to die when my time came as he had: but I should bide that time, and not be hurried away in a suttee" (p. 306). Attempts by British officials in India to eradicate suttee were widely viewed, both by the British public and by Indian reformers such as Rommahun Roy, as a step toward liberating Hindu wives from bondage to their husbands and to a destructive tradition. The campaign against suttee comes up later in the novel, when Diana Rivers agrees with Jane's refusal to marry her brother and go with him to India. Diana tells Jane she is "much too pretty, as well as too good, to be grilled alive in Calcutta" (p. 462) – a phrase that may be a reference to the infamous Black Hole of Calcutta, or merely to the tropical climate, but that also evokes suttee.

Jane rejects St John Rivers for several reasons, not least because she realizes he does not love her, but is thinking of her only as a useful helper in his work as a missionary in India, and also because she now knows she loves Mr Rochester. But what does Jane – and Charlotte Brontë – think of Rivers' missionary ambitions in general? He may be "cold" and "austere," but he is also a "resolute, indefatigable pioneer," Jane writes at the end of the novel: "Firm, faithful, and devoted; full of energy, and zeal, and truth, he hews down like a giant the prejudices of creed and caste" that "encumber" India. Rivers "may be stern . . . but his is the sternness of the warrior Greatheart, who guards his pilgrim-convoy from the onslaught of Apollyon" in John Bunyan's *Pilgrims' Progress*. "His is the exaction of the apostle, who speaks but for Christ . . ." (p. 501). If imperial domination has meant slavery to Rochester in Jamaica, he has escaped from its "hell" to England, though bringing his wealth and his infernal, madwoman wife with him. For Rivers, in contrast, writes Suvendrini Perera, "empire is the active 'field' of English exercise and effort," a project both Jane Eyre and her author heartily endorse (1991, p. 83).

Just how, then, do slavery and imperialism in Jamaica and India relate to Jane Eyre's and Charlotte Brontë's emergent feminism? Jane sounds very much like Mary Wollstonecraft, author of *The Rights of Women* (1792), when she declares:

> It is in vain to say human beings ought to be satisfied with tranquillity: they must have action; and they will make it if they cannot find it. Millions are condemned to a stiller doom than mine, and millions are in silent revolt against their lot. Nobody knows how many rebellions besides political rebellions ferment in the masses of life which people earth. Women are supposed to be very calm generally: but women feel just as men feel; they need exercise for their faculties, and a field for their efforts as much as their brothers do; they suffer from too rigid a restraint, too absolute a stagnation, precisely as men would suffer; and it is narrow-minded in their more privileged fellow-creatures to say that they ought to confine themselves to making puddings and knitting stockings, to playing on the piano and embroidering bags. It is thoughtless to condemn them, or laugh at them, if they seek to do more or learn more than custom has pronounced necessary for their sex. (pp. 125–6)

At this point in the novel, Jane has not yet encountered Bertha Mason, or had her argument with Rochester over purchasing female slaves in Istanbul, or been tempted by St John Rivers to go with him to India. By the novel's end, she is happily married to Rochester. Has Jane simply given in to traditional patriarchal values? Can she be a liberated woman and still marry Rochester? Does she express any remorse over the death of Bertha Mason, or is the "madwoman's" "self-immolation" good riddance for both Jane and Rochester – a riddance, too, perhaps, of various burdens or blights from the colonies: slavery, racism, the oppression of one people by another . . . ? And do Jane and Brontë, the daughter of a parson, really expect missionaries like St John Rivers to succeed by ultimately converting all of India to Christianity? Finally, would the conversion of the subcontinent, in Brontë's mind, be in some sense its liberation – not from British imperialism, but from the "bondage" of "creed and caste"? Raising these questions about *Jane Eyre*, a teacher of nineteenth-century fiction might also want to look back to Wollstonecraft and forward to Virginia Woolf's *Three Guineas* (1938) with its feminist critique of imperialism and war.

In teaching about empire in nineteenth-century novels, having maps or a good atlas helps. A chronology or timetable, such as the one in my *Victorian Literature and Postcolonial Studies* is also useful. Knowing, even in very general terms, how the British Empire grew and developed from the 1600s into the twentieth century provides a context for reading such texts as *Jane Eyre, Great Expectations,* and *Heart of Darkness.* Knowing also how various modern sciences – geography, anthropology, biology – developed in tandem with the expansion of Britain's and the other European empires sheds light on many works of fiction. Summarizing Darwin's voyage on the *Beagle* can help students better understand the relations among imperial expansion, science, and literature. They may also find illuminating one or more of the many resources on-line and in books, such as Christopher Bayly's *Atlas of the British Empire.*

"The conquest of the earth," Marlow says in Conrad's *Heart of Darkness,* "which mostly means the taking it away from those who have a different complexion or slightly flatter noses than ourselves, is not a pretty thing when you look into it too much." At the end of a course of reading focused on imperialism and nineteenth-century fiction, do the students agree or disagree with Marlow's assessment?

Appendix: sample syllabus: Victorian literature: conceptions of history (postgraduate)

Main texts:
L743 Reader (available from Collegiate Copies)
William Buckler, ed., *The Major Victorian Poets* (Houghton-Mifflin)
Edward Hallett Carr, *What Is History?* (Vintage)
Thomas Carlyle, *Past and Present* (NYU Press)
Charles Darwin, *The Charles Darwin Reader* (Norton)
Karl Marx & Friedrich Engels, *The Marx-Engels Reader* (Norton)
William Morris, *News from Nowhere* (Penguin)
Walter Pater, *The Renaissance* (Oxford)
John Ruskin, *Unto This Last* (Penguin)
Sir Walter Scott, *Ivanhoe* (Penguin)
H. G. Wells, *Selected Short Stories* (Penguin).

Weekly schedule (based on two classes per week):
Week One: What *are* histories? For session two, read E. H. Carr, *What Is History?,* chapters I, IV, and V; Walter Benjamin, "Theses on the Philosophy of History," *L743 Reader.*

Week Two: For session one, read selections by Immanuel Kant and G. W. F. Hegel in *L743 Reader;* for session two, read selections by Thomas Babington

Macaulay in *L743 Reader*. Recommended: the other chapters of E. H. Carr, *What Is History?*

Week Three: For session one read first three or four chapters of *both* Sir Walter Scott, *Ivanhoe* and Thomas Carlyle, *Past and Present*. For second session, continue reading *Ivanhoe* and read Christopher Hill, "The Norman Yoke," in *L743 Reader*.

Week Four: For session one, read the essays by Peter Burke and Dominick LaCapra in *L743 Reader*. For session two, finish reading *Ivanhoe*. Recommended: Michel Foucault, "Nietzsche, Genealogy, History," in *L743 Reader*.

Week Five: For session one, finish reading *Past and Present*. For session two, read Karl Marx and Friedrich Engels, "The German Ideology," "The Communist Manifesto," etc., from *Marx-Engels Reader*.

Week Six: For session one, read selections by Auguste Comte and John Stuart Mill in *L743 Reader*. For session two, read John Ruskin, *Unto This Last*, "The Nature of Gothic," and "Traffic."

Week Seven: For session one, read selections from Charles Darwin, *Origin of Species* and *Descent of Man*. For session two, read selections by Herbert Spencer and Glyn Daniel in *L743 Reader*.

Week Eight: session one and session two: Poetry by Alfred Tennyson.

Week Nine: session one and Session two: Poetry by Matthew Arnold.

Week Ten: session one and session two: Walter Pater, *The Renaissance*. For session two, read Jean-François Lyotard, "Universal History . . .," in *L743 Reader*.

Week Eleven: Poetry by Robert Browning. The Pre-Raphaelites (handouts, slides).

Week Twelve: William Morris, *News from Nowhere*.

Week Thirteen: For session one, read Patrick Brantlinger, "Apocalypse 2001," in *L743 Reader;* H. G. Wells, *The Time Machine*.

Week Fourteen: Reports on final papers.

Week Fifteen: Reports on final papers.

Writing assignments and due dates:
Every student will write three "response papers," *no more than two pages, double-spaced*. These can be turned in any time during the semester, though everyone must turn in at least two before Week 9. Everyone will also write and turn in a proposal *or* outline for the final paper, *no later than Session one, Week 6.* If by Week four you haven't settled on a topic, please consult with me. Final papers should be 20–25 pages double-spaced, and should be turned in *no later than one week after the end of the course.*

Report:
Each student will give an oral report on her or his final paper, approximately 10 minutes in length, during the last two weeks of the semester. The tutor will assign times randomly; the papers don't have to be finished by the time of the reports. Also, each student will be required to lead one of the session two classes. This will involve writing and distributing a few discussion questions about the readings for that session, and then steering our conversation in any way that seems useful.

Notes

1. Since the appearance of *Orientalism* in 1978, many studies of nineteenth-century fiction and imperialism have adopted a "postcolonial" perspective. Besides the other works mentioned in this essay, see my *Victorian Literature and Postcolonial Studies* (Edinburgh: Edinburgh University Press, 2009). There are a number of good introductions to the history of the British Empire, particularly in the last two centuries. These include Bernard Porter, *The Lion's Share: A Short History of the British Empire*, 4th edn (Harlow, Essex, and New York: Pearson/Longman, 2004) and Denis Judd, *Empire: The British Imperial Experience from 1765 to the Present* (London: HarperCollins, 1996). Christopher Bayly, ed., *Atlas of the British Empire: The Rise and Fall of the Greatest Empire the World Has Ever Known* (New York: Facts on File, 1989) and Peter J. Marshall, ed., *Cambridge Illustrated History of the British Empire* (Cambridge: Cambridge University Press, 1996) are both useful, readable reference works.
2. George Gissing, *The Whirlpool* (Hassocks: Harvester Press, 1977), p. 16.
3. On boys' adventure fiction, see Kelly Boyd, *Manliness and the Boys' Story Paper in Britain: A Cultural History, 1855–1940* (New York: Palgrave Macmillan, 2003); Joseph Bristow, *Empire Boys: Adventures in a Man's World* (London: HarperCollins, 1991); and Jeffrey Richards, ed., *Imperialism and Juvenile Literature* (Manchester: Manchester University Press, 1889).
4. For *Confessions of a Thug*, see Javed Majeed, "Meadows Taylor's *Confessions of a Thug*: the Anglo-Indian novel as a genre in the making," *Writing India 1757–1990*, Bart Moore-Gilbert, ed. (Manchester: Manchester University Press, 1996), pp. 86–110. The best guide to novels about the Indian Rebellion is Gautam Chakravarty, *The Indian Mutiny and the British Imagination* (Cambridge: Cambridge University Press, 2005).
5. See Upamanyu Pablo Mukherjee, *Crime and Empire: The Colony in Nineteenth-Century Fictions of Crime* (Oxford: Oxford University Press, 2003).

6. For mimicry, see Homi K. Bhabha, "Of Mimicry and Man: The Ambivalence of Colonial Discourse," *The Location of Culture* (New York: Routledge, 1994), pp. 85–92. For going native, see Linda Colley, *Captives* (New York: Pantheon, 2002).

7. Adam Hochschild, *Bury the Chains: Prophets and Rebels in the Fight to Free an Empire's Slaves* (Boston: Houghton Mifflin, 2005) offers a recent, readable account of the antislavery movement. Students wishing to learn more about Jamaica and slavery in particular should consult Catherine Hall's *Civilising Subjects: Metropole and Colony in the English Imagination, 1830–1867* (Chicago: University of Chicago Press, 2002).

8. A good account of Bertha Mason and race in *Jane Eyre* is offered by Susan Meyer, *Imperialism at Home: Race and Victorian Women's Fiction* (Ithaca: Cornell University Press, 1996), pp. 69–81.

9. Heathcliff is sometimes called a "gypsy" in *Wuthering Heights*, but, partly because Mr Earnshaw found him on the streets in Liverpool, two different theories have been proposed concerning his race. Liverpool was Britain's main slave-trading port during the time the novel takes place, so in *Gothic Images of Race in Nineteenth-Century Britain* (Stanford: Stanford University Press, 1996), Howard Malchow suggests that Heathcliff may have been the mixed-race offspring of a British sailor and an enslaved African woman (pp. 39–40). But Emily Brontë was writing at the time of the Irish Famine of 1845–50, and Liverpool was a key destination for Irish immigrants escaping starvation, so in *Heathcliff and the Great Hunger: Studies in Irish Culture* (London: Verso, 1995), Terry Eagleton contends that "Heathcliff starts out as the image of the famished Irish immigrant, becomes a landless labourer set to work in the Heights, and ends up as a symbol of the constitutional nationalism of the Irish parliamentary party" (p. 19). In any event, Heathcliff is a dark, racial "other," and therefore an object of what Robert Young (among others) has called "colonial desire." See Young, *Colonial Desire: Hybridity in Theory, Culture and Race* (New York: Routledge, 1995).

10. Susan Meyer, op. cit., writes: "When Bertha escapes from her ten years" imprisonment periodically to stab and burn her oppressors alive, and, as Rochester says, to hang her 'black and scarlet visage over the nest of my dove' . . . , she is symbolically enacting precisely the sort of revolt feared by the British colonists in Jamaica" (pp. 70–1).

11. Gayatri Chakravorty Spivak, "Three women's texts and a critique of imperialism," *"Race," Writing, and Difference*, Henry Louis Gates, Jr., ed. (Chicago: The University of Chicago Press, 1986), p. 278. Deirdre David, op. cit., pp. 89–92. For the "debate" over suttee in general, see Lati Mana, *Contentious Traditions: The Debate on Sati in Colonial India* (Berkeley: University of California Press, 1998).

Works cited

Anderson, Warwick, *The Cultivation of Whiteness: Science, Health, and Racial Destiny in Australia* (Melbourne: Melbourne University Press, 2002).

Azim, Firdous, *The Colonial Rise of the Novel* (New York: Routledge, 1993).

Bayly, Christopher A., *Atlas of the British Empire: The Rise and Fall of the Greatest Empire the World Has Ever Known* (New York: Facts on File, 1989).

Brantlinger, Patrick, *Victorian Literature and Postcolonial Studies* (Edinburgh: Edinburgh University Press, 2009).

Brontë, Charlotte, *Jane Eyre*, 1847 (London: Penguin, 1996).

Conrad, Joseph, *Heart of Darkness*, 1899 (New York: W. W. Norton, 2006).

David, Deirdre, *Rule Britannia: Women, Empire, and Victorian Writing* (Ithaca: Cornell University Press, 1995).

Gissing, George, *The Whirlpool* (Hassocks: Harvester Press, 1977).

Nord, Deborah, *Gypsies and the British Imagination, 1807–1930* (New York: Columbia University Press, 2006).

Perera, Suvendrini, *Reaches of Empire: The English Novel from Edgeworth to Dickens* (New York: Columbia University Press, 1991).

Said, Edward, *Culture and Imperialism* (New York: Knopf, 1993).

Spivak, Gayatri Chakravorty, "Three women's texts and a critique of imperialism," *"Race," Writing, and Difference*, Henry Louis Gates, Jr. (ed.) (Chicago: The University of Chicago Press, 1986), pp. 262–80.

Yonge, Charlotte, *The Daisy Chain: or, Aspirations*, 1856 (London: Macmillan, 1876).

5
Interdisciplinarity and Cultural Contexts

Teresa Mangum

I

For those who teach nineteenth-century literature, both the past and future lives of novels matter deeply. Perhaps that is why so many of us teach novels that resonate with aesthetic, ethical, economic, social, and political issues we currently confront. Studying novels through the lens of legal, religious, or medical history invites students to consider how nineteenth-century literature engaged with its immediate world. At the same time, interdisciplinary approaches offer students a sense of their own history as they grasp both distinctions from and continuities with the past. In this essay, I begin by surveying conventional interdisciplinary approaches in the classroom, with an eye to their advantages and limitations. Then, I turn to two classroom activities that encourage students themselves to make choices and judgements about the benefits of studying nineteenth-century fiction in interdisciplinary contexts. While these activities would work with many texts, Bram Stoker's 1897 *Dracula* self-consciously references the contexts in which it was written, including the professions of law and medicine; disciplines of knowledge from theology to psychology; and technologies from the typewriter to the telegraph. *Dracula's* progeny – the innumerable plays, films, comic books, and postmodern re-workings in fiction – further contextualize print in the fields of sound and sight.

II

As scholars in other fields sometimes complain, literary critics too easily assume that their work subsumes other disciplines. Even when critics rely heavily on the practice of close reading alone, their attention to words and images locates traces of larger than literary contexts and disciplines. At a much deeper level, theoretical approaches from new historicism to cultural studies to discourse analysis to visual and material cultural studies have brought literary scholars into contact with history, the law, sociology, rhetoric, art history, and more. In fact, given that "English" departments often include linguistics, digital media, and film studies, defining a discipline is increasingly hard to do. Despite these mutations of "literary" studies, a 2007 special issue of the journal *Victorian Review: An Interdisciplinary Journal of Victorian Studies* (33.1) demonstrates how difficult and problematic it can be to move beyond one's own discipline. The issue includes twenty-one contributors, who reflect on definitions, practices, advantages, and liabilities of interdisciplinarity for the study of nineteenth-century literature. As many of them point out, genuine interdisciplinary scholarship requires being deeply educated in multiple disciplines, which few can claim. At best, scholars are likely to be "multi" disciplinary, planted in one field but fertilized by another. Something of this is evident in the contributions to well-known journals covering the period. Despite their titles, *Victorian Studies* and *Victorian Literature and Culture* tend to be dominated by studies of literature. Their ambitiously capacious titles represent a recognition that nineteenth-century novels (and genres) tend to be steeped in contemporary events and to draw on language and concepts from law, medicine, religion, and other arenas, the novels themselves call for contextualizing in those events and domains. Providing that context encourages "Victorianists" to describe their work as interdisciplinary. Those titles also represent a utopian longing to forge deep connections with the forms of knowledge, methodologies, and scholars across the disciplines. When scholars do work intensely across borders, their research so profoundly differs from their colleagues' that they often build new (inter) disciplines marked by separate departments, conferences, journals, and book series. Despite these realities, many literature scholars and teachers find their understanding of nineteenth-century novels so enriched by contact with other disciplines that the pleasure of searching for new practices outweighs the critiques that may follow.

Certainly, in an ideal world, teachers from two or more fields would co-teach genuinely interdisciplinary courses, but few institutions can afford that luxury. Instead, many of us alternate between short lectures – on religious dissenters, marriage laws, or workhouses – on one hand – and close reading of passages that invoke the "world" on the other: *Oliver Twist* (1837–38) and the Poor Laws or *Lady Audley's Secret* (1861–62) and "monomania." Frequently, a quick lecture is the most efficient way to link aesthetic and formal experiments with social or political issues. More ambitiously, we pair literary and visual materials or juxtapose primary texts by Charles Darwin or Herbert Spencer with novels by George Eliot and Thomas Hardy. This approach can be easy and appealing thanks to Broadview editions of novels with their provocative primary materials. Among the vast body of research on interdisciplinarity, a few sources offer efficient, concise, and pragmatic advice focused on classroom practices.[1] What we seldom clarify are our expectations. Students in a class with interdisciplinary ambitions must simultaneously read in radically different ways. First, most of us hold fast to our own disciplinary training as close readers. We expect students to discern the complex language play, formal characteristics, narrative structure, and genre markers that shape a novel and to describe these using the technical vocabularies of formalist criticism and even narratology. Second, we assume students can learn enough about an adjacent or alternative body of historical knowledge to risk interdisciplinary claims about the cultural significance of linguistic, formal, and structural features. For instance, we ask them to speculate about the sufferings of the labouring classes in Elizabeth Gaskell's *Mary Barton* (1848) or the stain of imperial guilt in Wilkie Collins's *The Moonstone* (1868). Or, third, we initiate students into current theories of social relations from anthropology or economics, hoping they can bring preoccupations at the forefront of other disciplines to bear on the literature of the past. An interdisciplinary approach to the novel also requires our students (and ourselves) to live in multiple temporalities – an imagined past, a self-conscious awareness of ourselves in our own historical moment reading the past, and a willingness to time travel in between, as we mark the incarnations of a text in the intervening historical and disciplinary presents. Who could possibly do so much and do it well?

But what would it mean to abandon fears of failing at interdisciplinarity – fears of not knowing all there is to know in multiple disciplines (impossible), of violating the expectations of our colleagues in other disciplines (inevitable), or of losing the autonomy that empowers English departments, if only as service units (improbable)? Taking my own dare, I want to argue, I hope not too irresponsibly, that undergraduate students can benefit from being plunged into the information networks that shape their world even when they briefly sample interdisciplinary reading practices. Where we do need to be vigilant is in teaching students to be self-conscious about the investments and character of disciplines. Without presuming to know other fields in depth, we can help students discriminate among the distinct views scholars in a given discipline share about what *matters*, from types of evidence to interpretive frameworks. Perhaps more daringly, I have also been asking how we might benefit by taking a lesson from experiential, immersive pedagogies that literature scholars often ignore because we define ourselves as a text-based discipline that dare not wander from the page. Rather than asking students to nibble at the crumbs of another discipline, I propose that we encourage them to get in the kitchen and cook. They may not become gourmets, but they can distinguish the complex flavours of different domains of knowledge. Those who develop a taste for "fusion" disciplines can learn to experiment with ingredients – research materials, cross-disciplinary interpretation, and arguments that acknowledge differences among kinds of information, ideas, evidence, and approach.

In my own case, I frequently teach in interdisciplinary arenas such as age studies, animal studies, and gender studies. Because these areas are in formation and flux, in class we are necessarily attentive to whether we are reading scholarship from sociology or psychology or biology. Taking a lesson from these courses, I now experiment with "provisional interdisciplinarity" in my Victorian literature courses. We consider the value and limits of bringing Elizabeth Gaskell's *Cranford* (1853) and Rudyard Kipling's *Kim* (1901) in conversation with psychological or historical studies of aging; we read Anna Sewell's *Black Beauty* (1878) and Kipling's *Jungle Book* (1894) as both Victorian novels and primary texts for animal studies. Students not only gather and absorb ideas, but also put their knowledge into play. But I am also increasingly interested in inventive assignments that actively engage students in disciplinary border-crossing. Pedagogical theorists variously call such "engaged" classroom approaches "experiential learning," "problem-solving," or "action research."

III

Engaged learning asks students to draw upon concepts, ideas, information, and, in a literature class, the text itself, to solve a problem or accomplish an agreed upon goal. This pedagogy therefore prompts attention to the interpretive communities in which we learn – from the classroom to the community of scholars who produce the informational and intellectual framework for a course. Engaged research is most familiar in applied studies where students are expected to translate what they learn into a product or services. Doing so requires not only synthesis and analysis but also attention to audience and context (for example an organizational management class might design a business plan for a local nonprofit organization).

It is possible to introduce this pedagogical approach to my students through the lens of what social anthropologist Jean Lave and Etienne Wenger, who worked in artificial intelligence, conceived of as "communities of practice." This community forms through the shared pursuit of knowledge and solutions. Working together, students can create a social identity as a class as they build a "shared repertoire" of vocabulary, procedures, values, or products (Wenger, 1999, pp. 73–84). Knowledge is conceived of as a complex and changing relation to ideas, skills, other people, the community of practice, and also to other, sometimes overlapping, communities, which in this case might include writers (and editors, publishers, readers, reviewers, etc.) of nineteenth-century novels; readers and scholars studying the novels now; and researchers in other disciplines, as well as the class. Assignments in a literature class might ask students to invent a topic or produce an interpretation of a text in an attempt to *create* a problem – or a thesis – for an audience of one. In projects "of practice" students encounter disciplinary concepts and experience the act of interpretation as solutions to situational problems – from how to construct a collaborative wiki project in and around a nineteenth-century novel to how to stage a live reading of a suffrage play.[2]

To suggest how interdisciplinary studies of literature might take advantage of engaged pedagogies, the remainder of this essay offers two recent approaches my classes have taken to *Dracula*. This "urban gothic," to use Kathleen Spencer's term (1992, pp. 197–225), begs for interdisciplinary experimentation. The novel also plunges readers into social and political issues haunting the 1890s: women's demands for access to power and men's fears of their sexual appetites, the Oscar Wilde trials which provided a crash course in gay culture; fears of moral and social decadence and degeneration; and anxieties over literal and moral contagion as well as diseases of the mind. The critical history of Bram Stoker's *Dracula* is also unusually diverse because the construction of the novel raises such provocative questions about form, structure, point of view, reliability of witnesses and documents, the nature of evidence, and the very act of interpretation.

My first example, a moot court project, turns to the overlapping practices of nineteenth-century literature and law. The second asks students to work with current visual culture as we explore the survival, reinterpretation, and critique of nineteenth-century literature and culture in the world of the graphic novel. Through cross-disciplinary analysis, students learn rudimentary vocabulary and analytic practices from the visual arts and yet another emerging sub-field, the sociology of art. The Norton Critical Edition provides students with easy access to excerpts from key scholarly articles for instructors who want to intertwine experiential learning and writing assignments in which students' continue to study uses of evidence but in secondary critical sources.[3] *Dracula* is also available online. The approaches illuminate disciplinary boundaries, without which "interdisciplinary" study has little meaning. In fact, ignoring those boundaries often leads to disappointment on the part of students and teacher alike, leading to that cruel moment in which the instructor has to explain how, when, where, and why a student's essay on the medical profession and its connections to *Middlemarch* (1872) has ceased to meet requirements for "literary analysis" and become a book report or a "history" paper that only superficially employs a novel for illustration.[4]

The first question, of course, is how to integrate another discipline into the literature classroom. Moisés Kaufman's play *Gross Indecency: The Three Trials of Oscar Wilde* (New York: Dramatists Play Service, 1999) offers an unexpected gateway to *Dracula*. This courtroom drama demonstrates how the 1890s legal system (and newspapers) could turn a man into monster by wilfully interpreting his words, practices, and associates against him. Drawing on multiple witnesses' accounts of the trial, the play thrusts students into the staged courtroom practices, the manipulation of language and evidence, and the kinds of "truth" the law can expose or suppress. Like *Dracula*, the play raises questions about form. Both texts weave various accounts and documents into a coherent whole without obscuring the interpretive challenges posed by questionable evidence, doubtful narrative authenticity, and conflicting beliefs. In addition, the play introduces students to the charges of criminal libel and gross indecency. Students can read the poignant anonymous account of Wilde's trials (and many others) at the online site "Studies in Scarlet: Marriage and Sexuality in the US & UK, 1815–1914," part of the Harvard University Library Virtual Collection.[5] The site includes reports from hundreds of trials, including a pamphlet titled *Oscar Wilde: three times tried* (Paris, privately printed, probably in 1905). By informally staging a few scenes as part of the discussion, students grasp the theatricality of the courtroom and the legal issues at the heart of the play.[6]

Turning to *Dracula*, we first discuss its imagined process of writing, compiling, editing, and reproducing documents, focusing on the secretarial Mina Harker. We address problems of belief, testimony, and evidence while noting the novel's clever refusal to reveal Dracula's point of view. We examine the competing discourses in the novel: science versus religion, medicine versus traditional remedies, and technology versus supernatural forces with attention to Van Helsing's (and Dracula's) mastery as inter-disciplinarians themselves. We speculate on the novel's fascination with different professions and domains of knowledge. We ask how the cultural work of the novel plays out in the anxieties a character or topic embodies, inspires, or deploys considering the social taboos literalized in the law. We examine the professions (and obsessions) of the characters and the discursive registers of their various narratives and documents, an interdisciplinary stew of medicine, science, business, and the law. We ask how and why these fail to account for or subdue the violations that constitute "Dracula."

We begin our study of legal issues with an online visit to "The Proceedings at the Old Bailey, London's Central Criminal Court, 1674–1913." Overseen by Tim Hitchcock and Robert Shoemaker, the website provides fully searchable accounts of over 100,000 criminal trials held at London's central criminal court. A wealth of information is available, including images of the court, a discussion of trial proceedings, descriptions and actual examples) of various charges, crimes, and consequences. The site provides more than enough information to sketch the broad outlines for a moot court assignment. We supplement the broad brush strokes of the Old Bailey site by studying a second website, which includes a useful glossary of legal categories and crimes, the "Early Modern Crime and the Law: Glossary." The online 1911 *Encyclopedia Britannica* also describes specific crimes. We have our moment of disciplinary humility, discussing what, with these resources, we have not and could not grasp without the help of a legal historian.

Class members form two groups, a prosecuting team and a defence team. They immediately come up against the inflexibility of class difference as they decide who will serve as the (collective) attorney and "his" impoverished clerks, collecting evidence and witnesses, and who will be the independently wealthy barrister(s), swanning about in the actual courtroom drama. We discuss the difference between literary conventions that shape plots and rules of evidence – including circumstantiality and reasonable doubt – that structure narrative in a courtroom. We also contemplate strategies realist novels use to create the illusion of coherence, continuity, narrative time, and cause and effect. In contrast, we ponder the likely suspicion of narrative in a court and the need for each legal team to pick apart the other's narrative constructions. Together the students then decide which characters they will charge and with what crime. A few students bring laptop computers to class so that the groups can begin their research. I bring a handful of books about nineteenth-century crime and studies of legal history that I have placed on reserve at the library. In addition to sources already noted, having a classic reference like J. H. Baker's *An Introduction to English Legal History* is useful. In addition to an overview of possible offences, the Old Bailey site includes clear, accessible accounts of trial procedures. Due to time constraints, we review and then leap past the initial steps. We assume a crime has been reported, a magistrate has arrested the accused, and the clerk of court has drawn up an indictment. If the charge were murder, the case would have gone straight to court, otherwise it would have been approved by a Grand Jury, and then the defendant would enter a plea. In class we begin the trial at this point.

First, though, we must decide together which character will be accused and with what crime. Though the novel trains readers' attention on Dracula's transgressions, groups may charge Dracula's antagonists (and the novel's protagonists) with libel (Wilde's first, mad stroke against his lover's father) or even murder. During this session, we discuss what other forms of disciplinary knowledge would be necessary if we were seriously making these cases, and students discuss the differences in conceptions of "facts," "truth," form, and sources across disciplinary "communities of practice." My most energetic students have thrown themselves into one more round of research, turning to histories of psychology to contextualize Renfield's monomania or to historical accounts of Transylvanian history to better understand 1890s British perceptions of what we now call Eastern Europe.

Each student treats the text of *Dracula* as potential evidence provided by witnesses. I encourage them to seek alternate interpretations of that evidence in articles by literary scholars (which the Norton Critical Edition can simplify). The groups meet out of class to build a "legal" argument from literary evidence, to determine which characters they will call as witnesses, and to assign those roles. The prosecuting and defence teams assign members of their group to play the witnesses. (The defence team accepts the witnesses – and classmates – chosen by the prosecution but can then appoint their own additional witnesses from their group.) Each team deploys close reading to determine their witnesses' "testimony" – which must be quotations from the novel – and to rebut the implied interpretation of hostile witnesses' "testimony." They may also use historical and legal materials, including the records collected on the Old Bailey site, to learn more about the "crime" under discussion as they consider how historical differences or legal precedent might influence their choice of quotations.

The trial opens with the lead lawyer for the prosecution's brief summary of charges, account of past offences, and list of witnesses to be called. Witnesses for the prosecution are examined by a prosecutorial team (and are free to consult with the larger team), then cross-examined by the defence. Next, the defence team members call their own witnesses to testify and be cross-examined by the prosecution. The fact that an accused person was not allowed to speak as a witness on her or his own behalf until 1898 often solves the problem of what to do with Dracula himself. On the other hand, defendants could address the jury before the verdict was decided if they chose to do so. We conclude by allowing each team to discuss what arguments they can draw from the narratives and counter narratives they have heard and to pull together brief concluding remarks for the jury (the students not assigned to roles in the trial). The jury has five minutes to make a judgement.

During the trial, we allow a great deal of leeway. The goal is to grasp differences among forms of knowledge and the shifting status of what we usually think of as literary concerns – character, motive, conflict, figures of speech, point of view, what characters can and cannot know, the difference between characters' speech and actions, the interpretive gestures registered by irony, mood, context, and so forth. In all honesty, the trials can be fairly hilarious and raucous affairs. Nevertheless, students become deeply engaged in the selection of details from the novel, in intense debates over the interpretation of evidence, and in side arguments about the disciplinary as well as "legal" status of testimony. *Dracula* even encourages the summoning of expert witnesses, highlighting our assumptions about disciplinary differences.

Crucially, we include with a meta-discussion of the differences between the legal community's understanding of documents and literary critics' views of texts. We discuss the status of evidence in different domains: literary criticism, legal interpretation, medicine, psychology, religion, and even gossip. We also consider how a community of practice authorizes and deploys forms of evidence. To bring these distinctions home, I ask students to write a one-page informal "reflection" on what they have learned about disciplines as particular communities of practice, including the disciplines of literary studies and Victorian studies. They produce a more conventional critical essay on *Dracula* using three or more of the texts they consulted to define and argue a case for a claim they want to make about the novel. Students' use of evidence from the primary text is consistently more insightful, rigorous, and shrewd than I see even in strong students' papers otherwise.

IV

To suggest the diverse possibilities of engaged interdisciplinary practice, the final section of this essay deals with a more controversial approach involving the graphic novel *The League of Extraordinary Gentlemen, Vol. I*, written by Allan Moore and illustrated by Kevin O'Neill (first published in 1999 by Wildstorm Comics).[7] As Grace Moore notes elsewhere in this volume, the 2008 launch of the online *Journal of Neo-Victorian Studies* suggest a growing interest in the alternative nineteenth-century worlds that make up the "steampunk" sub-genre of science fiction as well as other postmodern reworkings or interpretations of familiar texts. Several essays in the first issue of the journal introduce readers to terms and categories. In all honesty,Wikipedia also offers fine essays on the genre in general and *The League* in particular and includes links to other useful sites.

In this approach to *Dracula*, students have a chance to become the authorities since they are usually far more knowledgeable about popular culture than their tutor. Drawing upon present day theories of visual culture, we explore the survival, reinterpretation, and critique of nineteenth-century literature and culture in the world of the graphic novel. Students work together to build a rudimentary vocabulary and analytic reading practices from the visual arts even as they themselves attempt the practices under analysis. (Students in Art Education go further; creating their own graphic interpretations of literature.) A crash course in reading practices might begin with Scott McCloud's *Understanding Comics* (1994). The book is itself a comic book by a master at the genre which teaches readers the conventions reflexively; the comic panels both explain and visualize the form and strategies of the genre. Jessica Abel's online "What is a 'graphic novel'?" is a smart, miniature two-page version of this learn-as-you-read approach and is freely available for use in the classroom.

The League plays with a comix subgenre, the "superhero team comic" (readers may recall comic series like the "Justice League" that brought together well-known super heroes and imagined "what if.") Moore's "team" gathers characters of nineteenth-century fiction such as Allan Quartermain, Dr Jekyll/Mr Hyde, Dr Moriarity, Captain Nemo, and in Vol. I, the now divorced Mina Harker. Their job is to defend a crumbling British empire against subversives.

London is transformed into a steampunk landscape of ornate, dystopic machines and skyscrapers that loom over the collapsing streets and houses of Limehouse and the Docklands. Like other "nineteenth-century" graphic novels, the visual world of *The League* borrows and mutilates fashion, architecture, and material culture of the period. O'Neill's witty play with nineteenth-century visual styles urges discussion of popular Victorian visual culture: panels include Beardsley imitations and a cover of the quarterly that popularized the decadents, the 1890s' *The Yellow Book*. Many panels quote the iconography through which Victorian popular culture collapsed all Indians or Chinese into stereotypes; others capture period architectural detail. To a sometimes shocking degree, *The League* parodies Victorian pornography and pictures extreme versions of *fin de siècle* sexism, racism, and xenophobia. As one student put it, the text "surfaces" imperialist currents in novels from *Jane Eyre* (1847) to H. Rider Haggard's *King Solomon's Mines* (1885). To my admiration, however, students usually quickly leap past their fascination (and horror) to a sharp analysis of the gender politics in *Dracula* that are "surfaced" in Moore's Wilhelmina. The manipulations spark their interest in paintings and photographs of Victorian London and Londoners but also illuminate fictional techniques through which novels invent and manipulate rather than reproduce details from their moment. The series has inspired obsessive fan sites, which students find fascinating. Jess Nevins's online "Notes on League of Extraordinary Gentlemen #1" is an excellent guide and highlights Moore's homage to Victorian style.

It is possible, then, to use *The League* as a counter text to Dracula, asking students how visual images of landscapes, London, technology, and characters are at once inspired by, alternatives to, and utterly different from their own interpretations of the novel. Classes can grapple with the differences between the representational systems of language and visual popular culture, and it is also possible to incorporate discussion of Victorian illustration. The growing number of nineteenth-century online periodicals and museum sites increasingly allows students to conduct primary research in Victorian visual culture.

We can then learn a great deal about the meaning-making, cohering practices of fiction as we study the ways the varying panels and graphics create their illusions of moving through time and space as narrative. Discussion of *The League* also provides a wonderful opportunity to review what students have learned all semester about the distinctive features of nineteenth-century fiction and culture. Working in small groups, students generate capacious definitions of the term "Victorian" that both draw upon and resist the fictive visual world of *The League*. At no moment are they more aware of themselves as a community of practice – sharing a surprisingly deep and wide knowledge of the novel – than in our return to the past through the presentist back door of Neo-Victorianism.

Appendix: sample syllabus: Literature and culture of the 19th century: stages of life and forms of fiction

Aims and Objectives: Victorians were increasingly interested in changes over the life course. Long circulating stereotypes such as "young turks" and old misers or innocent girls and "old maids" were joined by new age-based images of tomboys, juvenile delinquents, the young and independent "New Woman" and the male *flaneur*, and the urban elderly poor. Psychology and sociology asked how gender, class, and economics affected each stage of life. Magazines advised how to eat, sleep, dress, and behave "for your age."

Schools, job opportunities, urban life, and mass-produced consumer goods created age identities. This module considers how literature of the period engages with some of these preoccupations with age. We shall consider how life stages influenced literary form, the way for example, "autobiographical fiction" and the *bildungsroman* (or novel of formation) mark the passage from childhood to youth; how young adulthood structures marriage plot novels and empire adventure narratives; and the old abuse the young in late-century gothic fiction.

Primary Texts:

Elizabeth Gaskell, *Cranford* (1853)
Charles Dickens, *Great Expectations* (1861)
George Eliot, *Silas Marner* (1861)
Bram Stoker, *Dracula* (1897)
Rudyard Kipling, *Kim* (1901)
Jack Zipes, ed. *Victorian Fairy Tales*
Alan Moore and Kevin O'Neill, *The League of Extraordinary Gentleman, Vol I* (2002)

Assessment

Paper 1: *Narrating the Emotions of Childhood: Great Expectations* builds a complex picture of the emotional life of an imaginative child, challenging sentimental views of childhood yet critiquing Calvinistic beliefs. Choose an emotion the novel explores as crucial to childhood – at least Pip's childhood. Consider, for example, happiness, wonder, anticipation, misery, anger, selfishness, fear, guilt, pride, jealousy, revenge, longing, envy, love, or loss. Explore the multiple meanings of the term in the *Oxford English Dictionary* online. Then, make a case for the predominant emotion shaping Pip's character in the language and form of the novel.

Paper 2: Ask three people (of different ages) what they look forward to and dread most about being 70. Do you see connections with the Victorians' views of aging? With those ideas in mind, decide which text you'd like to discuss. Take notes on passages that raise questions about late life in the most intriguing ways and read at least three recent articles you locate through MLAB that help you think about representations of life stages in your chosen novel. Once you decide on one specific feature of aging – whether a fear, anxiety, or hope an individual feels about growing old OR an attitude people in Victorian society generally may have held about the older people around them – return to your literary text. Consider how the language, imagery, characterization, setting, and form of the novel capture this facet of late life. Topic proposals and annotated bibliographies are due two weeks before the paper deadline so that two classmates and I can offer advice.

Commentaries: 10 of a possible 15 one-page responses to weekly questions.

Final Exam: The exam includes one essay question comparing representations of matters "Victorian" in *The League* with what they have learned about "Victorian" fiction – using novels from the course to support their claims.

Schedule

Week 1: Fantasies of Victorian Childhood: Memory Meets Culture
William Barnes, "Rustic Childhood" (1846)
Thomas Hood, "I Remember" (1846)
Robert Louis Stevenson, "The Land of Counterpane" (1885)
From *Victorian Fairy Tales*:
George Cruikshank, "Cinderella and the Glass Slipper" (1854)
Charles Dickens, "The Magic Fishbone" (1868)
Anne Isabella Ritchie, "Cinderella" (1866)
Mary De Morgan, "The Toy Princess" (1877)

Weeks 2–4: The Doubled Perspective of "Autobiographical" Novels
Charles Dickens, *Great Expectations*
Additional reading: Dickens's Autobiographical Fragment
Elizabeth Barrett-Browning, "The Cry of the Children" (1843)
James Fitzjames Stephen, "Gentlemen," *Cornhill Magazine*, 1862
Samuel Smiles, "Character" (1871)
Dickens, "A Visit to Newgate" (1839)
Report from the Select Committee on Transportation (1838)

Week 5: Victorian Late Life: The "Paired Plot" of Youth and Age
George Eliot, *Silas Marner*
Matthew Arnold, "Growing Old" (1867)
Eliza Keary, "Old Age" (1874)
Frederick Tennyson, "Old Age" (1913)
Alfred Lord Tennyson, "Ulysses" (1842)

Weeks 7–9: Alternative Plots for Late Life: Paper I due
Elizabeth Gaskell, *Cranford*
Alice Meynell, "A Letter from a Girl to Her Own Old Age" (1873)
Dollie Radford, "Soliloquy of a Maiden Aunt" (1891)
Thomas Hardy, "Long Plighted" (1901)

Weeks 10–11: The "Undead": Transgressing Boundaries of Youth/Age and Life/ Death
Bram Stoker, *Dracula*
Moot court: Review capital crimes and courtroom procedures on the Old Bailey website
Plan meeting out of class to research and organize your "case"

Weeks 12–14: Youth, Age, and Narratives of Empire: Paper 2 due
Rudyard Kipling, *Kim*
Discussion of film clips in class – evolving visual culture of empire (and India)

Week 15
Alan Moore and Kevin O'Neill, *The League of Extraordinary Gentlemen, Vol. I*
Work through Jessica Abel's online "What is a 'graphic novel'?"
Mark Llewellyn, "What Is Neo-Victorian Studies?" 1st issue, http://www.
neovictorianstudies.com/

Final Exam

Notes

1. A useful starting point is Julie Thompson Klein's "Resources for Interdisciplinary Studies," *Change* (March/April 2006), pp. 52–8.
2. See my essay describing a class production of a suffrage play in the cluster, "The New Woman's Work: Past, Present, and Future." *Nineteenth-Century Gender Studies*, 3.1 (Summer 2007). http://www.ncgsjournal.com/issue32/issue32.htm
3. Others of course also make creative use of moot court assignments though for different ends. For example, *Glen Downey* who teaches at the University of British Columbia asks students to try Becky Sharp for the murder of Jos Sedley, in response to the ambiguous ending of Thackeray's *Vanity Fair*. He details the assignment online at http://www.victorianweb.org/authors/wmt/downey11.html.
4. Of course, an energetic sub-discipline, most generally referred to as "law and literature" has produced its own journals, provocative scholarship, pedagogical studies, and online resources. While my students focus on legal history and primary legal documents online given time limitations, a more advanced class (as well as we instructors) would want to dig deep into the issues and debates shaping the subfield. Excellent introductions and major journals such as *Cardozo Studies in Law and Literature*, *The Legal Studies Forum*, and *The Yale Journal of Law and the Humanities* are readily available. James Boyd White's *The Legal Imagination* (1973) was one of the first major books to discuss the relation of literary and legal language and narrative. Kieran Dolin's *A Critical Introduction to Law and Literature* (2007) moves beyond a focus on language to the web of legal values and concepts that constitute our and the Victorians' culture. His *Fiction and the Law: Legal Discourse in Victorian and Modernist Literature* (1999) is especially valuable for Victorian studies as are Jan-Melissa Schramm's *Testimony and Advocacy in Victorian Law, Literature, and Theology* (2000) and Alexander Welsh's *Strong Representations: Narrative and Circumstantial Evidence in England* (1992). For actual classroom use, Simon Petch's chapter "Legal" in the Blackwell *Companion to Victorian Literature and Culture* (1999) provides a concise historical introduction to the law. His essay "Law, Literature, and Victorian Studies" in *Victorian Studies* (2007) is excellent. Dolin offers a concise summary of the subjects constituting the interdisciplinary field thus far. They include fictional representations of the law, crime, and criminals; studies of rhetoric, narrative, and figures of speech in literature and in legal documents; the impact of law on publishing; the circulation of legal ideas in literature and vice versa; ideology and the

law; theories of interpretation; theatricality and spectacle in the courtroom; the impact of technologies on writing and publishing; and "narrative jurisprudence" or storytelling (Dolin, *A Critical Introduction to Law and Literature*, 10-11).
5. Thanks to Lisa Hager for sharing information about the site on the Victoria listserv.
6. For an excellent analysis of the fascinating issues that arise in comparing versions of the trials and their representation in film and that would also arise in discussion of Kaufman's play, see Leslie J. Moran's "On Realism and the Law Film: The Case of Oscar Wilde" in *Law's Moving Image*.
7. My thanks to Elizabeth Chang at the University of Missouri for sharing her unpublished MLA talk on "The Future of Victorian Character(s)." Elizabeth's presentation inspired this experiment.

Works cited

Baker, J. H., *An Introduction to English Legal History*, 4th edn. (London: Butterworths, 2002).

Chapman, Alison, Susan Doyle, Mary Elizabeth Leighton, Judith Mitchell and Lisa Surridge (eds.), *Victorian Review: An Interdisciplinary Journal of Victorian Studies*, 33.1 (Spring 2007).

Dolin, Kiernan, *Fiction and the Law: Legal Discourse in Victorian and Modernist Literature*, (Cambridge: Cambridge University Press, 1999).

——. *A Critical Introduction to Law and Literature* (Cambridge: Cambridge University Press, 2007).

Kaufman, Moisés, *Gross Indecency: The Three Trials of Oscar Wilde* (New York: Dramatists Play Service, 1999).

Klein, Julie Thompson, "Resources for Interdisciplinary Studies," *Change* (March/April 2006), pp. 52–8.

Lave, Jean and Wenger, Etienne, *Situated Learning: Legitimate Peripheral Participation* (New York: Cambridge University Press, 1991).

Mangum, Teresa, "The New Woman's Work: Past, Present, and Future," *Nineteenth-Century Gender Studies*, 3.1 (Summer 2007), http://www.ncgsjournal.com/issue32/issue32.htm

McCloud, Scott, *Understanding Comics: The Invisible Art* (New York: Harper Paperbacks, 1994).

Moore, Allan and Kevin O'Neill, *The League of Extraordinary Gentlemen, Vol. I.* (Wildstorm Comics, 1999).

Moran, Leslie J., "On Realism and the Law Film: The Case of Oscar Wilde." In *Law's Moving Image*. Eds. Leslie J. Moran, Emma Sandon, Elena Louizidou (London: GlassHouse Press, 2004), pp. 77–94.

Petch, Simon, "Legal," in *A Companion to Victorian Literature and Culture*. Ed. Herbert Tucker. (Oxford: Blackwell, 1999), pp. 155–69.

——. "Law, Literature, and Victorian Studies," *Victorian Studies*, 35 (2007), pp. 361–84.

Schramm, Jan-Melissa, *Testimony and Advocacy in Victorian Law, Literature, and Theology* (Cambridge: Cambridge University Press, 2000).

Spencer, Kathleen L., "Purity and Danger: *Dracula*, the Urban Gothic, and the Late Victorian Degeneracy Crisis," *ELH*, 59.1 (1992), pp. 197–225.

Stoker, Bram, *Dracula*. Eds. Nina Auerbach and David J. Skal (New York: W. W. Norton, 1996).

Welsh, Alexander, *Strong Representations: Narrative and Circumstantial Evidence in England* (Baltimore: Johns Hopkins University Press, 1995).

Wenger, Etienne, *Communities of Practice: Learning, Meaning, and Identity* (New York: Cambridge University Press, 1999).

White, James Boyd, *The Legal Imagination* (1973) (Chicago: University of Chicago Press, 1985).

Online resources

1911 Encyclopedia Britannica for legal terms
http://www.1911encyclopedia.org/

Dracula Online
http://www.literature.org/authors/stoker-bram/dracula/

Dictionary of Victorian London: Professions and Trades: Legal Profession
http://www.victorianlondon.org/

Early Modern Crime and the Law: Glossary
http://www.earlymodernweb.org.uk

Jess Nivens and divers hands: Notes on *League of Extraordinary Gentlemen* #1
http://www.geocities.com/Athens/Olympus/7160/league1.html

Journal of Neo-Victorian Studies
http://www.neovictorianstudies.com

Law and Humanities Website (extensive bibliography)
http://faculty.law.lsu.edu/ccorcos/lawhum/lawhum.htm

The Legal History Project
http://www.legalhistory.com/index.html

The Proceedings at the Old Bailey, London's Central Criminal Court, 1674–1913
http://www.oldbaileyonline.org/

Studies in Scarlet: Marriage and Sexuality in the US & UK, 1815–1914
   (Harvard University Libraries)
http://nrs.harvard.edu/urn-3:hul.eresource:sscarlet

The Victorian Web
http://www.victorianweb.org/

"What is a 'graphic novel'?" (Jessica Abel)
http://www.artbomb.net/comics/introgndld.jsp

6
Women's Writing

Talia Schaffer

I Introduction

To grow up in the nineteenth century meant negotiating a culture that made gender the organizing principle of daily life, that divided work, education, clothes, colours, food, rooms, hobbies, even handwriting into male and female counterparts. Nineteenth-century women writers had a lifetime's worth of work in engaging with the identity so insistently ascribed to them. So to teach courses on nineteenth-century women writers is not just to have a useful excuse for an Austen–Brontë–Eliot course (pleasant though that is); it is to read womanhood as it is constructed, contested, challenged, and reaffirmed, over decades and decades. It is to allow students to view marriage, patriarchy, motherhood, domestic management, illness, social networks, economic dependence, and political invisibility as the defining features of life. It is to inhabit a female character whose subjectivity misaligns with her culture's dominant ideology, and to feel the mute desperation of having elements of one's fundamental identity be unnameable and invisible. It is to imagine the point of view of the nineteenth-century female reader who wants her novel to offer a scenario of exhilarating escapism encased in a strong structure of reassuring convention. It is to try to imagine the labour of the female writer who needs to represent a complex lived reality within a language, and a culture, that did not easily accommodate it. To be a woman in the nineteenth-century meant, as Virginia Woolf noted, to be poor (1929, p. 28). To be a working woman in the nineteenth century usually meant labouring in some form of domestic service (Steedman, 2007, p. 21). Finally, to be a nineteenth-century woman writer is also to be insistently heterosexualized, and yet to be able to sustain public affective relations, and private bodily intimacy, with same-sex companions. When students tend to naturalize modern ideas of identity, nothing is more salutary than introducing them to a culture where drastically different ideas of sexual identity, gender behaviour, class status and racial hierarchy dominated.

Separate spheres, however, may not seem quite as alien as we might suppose. The division between women's and men's roles still feels acceptable to many students. Presented with a list of items and told that Victorians divided them by gender, students have no trouble whatsoever assigning each to the proper gender category. Beef, brown, biology = men. Puddings, pastels, poetry = women. Of course, many students are ardently feminist and decry "women's oppression," but the point is that they all can intuitively understand how mid-nineteenth-century society was organized, whether they approve or not. So whilst it can be useful to present students with a few documents about separate spheres it is also the case that (fortunately or unfortunately) they grasp the rules without much additional input. More productive perhaps is to encourage the idea of dialogue: a few conservative readings – John Ruskin, an excerpt from Sarah Stickney Ellis's *Women of England* or perhaps Eliza Lynn Linton's "Girl of the Period" essays – can be balanced with a few protofeminist texts – Florence Nightingale's "Cassandra," Frances Power Cobbe's "Criminals, Idiots, Women, and Minors," or Mona Caird's "Does Marriage Hinder a Woman's Self-Development?"[1] It can also be useful to spend some class time on women's dress, explaining how much it weighed, how difficult it was to wear, and how much it restricted physical mobility. This discussion goes nicely with a lesson about what exactly was involved in washing clothes, or baking cake, two operations that modern students find almost inconceivably difficult once you start asking where they got the materials they needed for these common operations. Showing the first episode of C4/PBS's 2000 series, *The 1900 House,* can make this especially vivid for students, as it demonstrates the dismay of a modern family forced to cope with turn-of-the-century technologies.

A word about syllabus selection. If one of the aims of a module is to offer as much of a representative sampling of nineteenth-century thought and culture as is possible, then it is worth offering students the opportunity to read texts that appealed to different classes and served different markets and readerly needs. As John Sutherland has estimated, there were probably about 60,000 novels published in the period 1837–1901, of which we habitually read only the smallest selection (1996, pp. xi–xii). While canonical texts are, obviously, quite different from each other, they all share two salient points. First, the culture's judges of value (professors, teachers, critics, publishers, reviewers, filmmakers, bookstore owners) have declared them worthwhile and that judgement has held for long enough to generate a critical industry. Second, they have been read by many people and exerted influence over subsequent texts. What these two factors mean is that the canonical text is, in some sense, always already familiarized. If the student hasn't read it, s/he has read something like it. But noncanonical texts may be quite strange. While that strangeness may or may not be successful for modern readers, one important function they can perform is to unsettle our assumptions about normative texts.

Two examples here are Florence Warden's *The House on the Marsh* (1884) and Margaret Oliphant's *Janet* (1891). These texts are retellings of *Jane Eyre*, half a century later, and can seem seem very derivative. Yet Warden's volume makes the master's sexual harassment (to use a modern term) much more threatening than in *Jane Eyre*, since he is more violent than Rochester and the governess is less attracted to him. And Oliphant's version, which makes the wife into the jailer of a mad husband, foregrounds fascinating gender equivalences. For instance, whereas Bertha's "intemperate and unchaste" behaviour marks her as mad, in *Janet* it is the husband's financial malfeasance that marks his madness. Women cannot be immoral; men cannot be insolvent. Both texts therefore highlight aspects of the great novel of the mid-nineteenth-century that that original story occludes or mystifies.

One way of getting students to think about issues of canon formation is to ask them on the first day of a course what criteria *they* would use if they had to pick the class readings. The most representative? The most popular? The most entertaining? The most critically acclaimed? The most easily accessible or the one with the best critical edition? The teacher's own rationale for choosing the course texts might go as follows: work that has some claim to being major: it was a best-seller, or it was hugely controversial, or it was written in an ambitious way yet failed to get the recognition for which it was angling. In other words, there has to be a positive reason to select this volume and only this volume from the vast storehouse of the dim and doomed. Given a semester that has (in the US, anyway) 14 teaching weeks, fewer if one's school uses a trimester system, given that an average Victorian novel takes about two or three weeks to finish, and given students' aggressive queries about why they have to read this obscure old stuff anyway, there needs to be a very good reason to put it on the syllabus.

The remainder of this article discusses some techniques for teaching nineteenth-century women writers. It begins with the canonical figures, the ones with whom most teachers have all had more or less experience, and suggests a few issues and a few possible solutions. It then moves on to focus on noncanonical women writers to discuss both why one should make this sort of teaching part of one's pedagogy and what specific kinds of problems arise from doing so. The descriptions are drawn from experience, are to some degree anecdotal and are rooted in the particular structure of American undergraduate and postgraduate coursework, and, even more specifically, in the experience of teaching at a diverse urban commuter campus attracting a wide range of students. It is hoped that readers can either find material adaptable to their own teaching cultures, or else, if the experience proves irreducibly foreign, enjoy the pleasures of tourism in this alternative realm.

II   Canonical women writers

This section deals with two writers for whom the main problem is student overidentification. Most of the students who would take a course explicitly labelled as "women writers" are female, and young feminists at that, ardently seeking for foremothers. Gratifying as it is to find students adoring the course readings, one soon finds that uncritical admiration doesn't conduce much to class discussion. For Jane Austen and Charlotte Brontë, there is a case for the teacher's role being that of an agent of estrangement.

Students tend to adore Jane Austen, and the limpidity of her style can give students the impression that they already fully understand it. Moreover, the spate of Austen movies in the 1990s gave (and continues to give) students a strong sense of visual pleasure in the material paraphernalia of the period (so much so that they will insist, against all textual evidence, that Austen novels are full of ballroom-gown details). So to read for race, for class, for attitudes to slavery, for construction of provincial society, for women's self-determination, can be seen as unnatural mud-slinging against a perfectly polished and pretty text. Students also feel an overriding compulsion to prove that Austen was feminist. It is very hard for them to accept that an author so beloved might have been quite a conservative writer. Thus teaching Austen is difficult for three reasons: students resist close-reading, they assume they already know what it's all about, and they believe that what it's about is all good. *Emma, Persuasion,* and *Mansfield Park* often work best in class because of their heroines' more problematic qualities, which (to some extent) deter enthusiastic identification. So, one way of contesting this attitude is to try to estrange Austen. Contextual material helps here: historical information about the Regency period, perhaps from Paul Keen's anthology, *Revolutions in Romantic Literature* (2004). There is scope, too, for exposing students to material on the abolition and slavery debates, women's legal rights, the reception of the French Revolution in England, Romanticism and the post-Enlightenment moment, the neoclassical movement, landscape design, industrialization, and rural and urban living patterns, to override the pretty candlelit generalities with a specific and alternative historical space.

In teaching *Jane Eyre,* one can run up against a somewhat different form of overidentification. Students often want to celebrate, not analyse; they can be defensively and strongly wedded to a pop-feminist view that Jane is a feisty, admirable, strong woman fighting against their society's oppression, not to mention a cinematic view that Rochester and Jane are soulmates who were meant to be. (There is, of course, some truth in both views; the point is that students are often so passionately enamoured of these positions that they are unwilling to complicate them.) Again, estrangement may be a teacher's best friend. Stressing the evangelical aspects of the novel, in particular, helps defamiliarize it sufficiently that it can be analysed as a document of a different culture rather than a triumphant journey. Jane's endorsement of repression and "Christian virtues" for women, its use of racial and slave rhetoric (most famously in Bertha), and its unflinching depiction of sexual aggression and class entitlement in Rochester, darken the story sufficiently to deter all but the most ardent sisterhood-seekers.[2]

Teaching *Wuthering Heights* and George Eliot novels introduce the opposite problem; students do not overidentify, but they find these texts so bewilderingly dark or incomprehensibly dense that they have little way in. Often students give up halfway through. The alterity of the early and mid-Victorians is very much on display here, but not in a way that often attracts modern students. *Wuthering Heights*'s violent scenes and dark rage leave them no space for easy or admiring identifications. Accustomed to think of Victorian novels as charming exercises in courtly wooing, teacup-holding, and language-of-flowers bouquets at the ball, students are blindsided by the crudities of *Wuthering Heights*'s living conditions (which, of course, makes it all the more necessary to teach it). However, because they do not generally have affectionate fidelity to *Wuthering Heights*, it is quite easy to teach it critically once one gets past the bewildered resistance. *Wuthering Heights* can become legible in terms of other discourses students can easily access. Though it does not fit their BBC or Masterpiece Theatre notion of nineteenth-century novels, it does tap into their usually quite extensive awareness of pathological psychology. They enjoy reading Heathcliff in terms of the corrosive effects of internalized racism or class-based self-hatred, Catherine in terms of eating disorders, and their relationship in terms of co-dependency, erotic addiction, incest, etc. The point here is not that one necessarily wants to encourage these often-anachronistic diagnoses, but that it is possible to open up student enthusiasm by moving the framework to pop psychology. (Nothing seems to make Joseph legible, however.)

Teaching Eliot is more challenging. Few students have ever encountered Eliot outside of the classroom and some tend to regard her much as they do Thomas Hardy, Henry James, and Joseph Conrad: one of those academic authors whom cruel professors use to get students bogged down in boringly, densely descriptive novels with too many characters and not enough action. This attitude flourishes even with the rather sensational plot of *Adam Bede*. It is also difficult to do *The Mill on the Floss* in the same course as *Jane Eyre*, since the characters are so similar. One would think it would create good comparisons, but students tend to just get bored when forced to read over a thousand consecutive pages of feisty girls forced to smooth their hair and do plain sewing. If *Mill* is too *Jane Eyre*-ish, *Adam Bede* and *Middlemarch* and *Daniel Deronda* are all too long and dense. Likewise it is difficult to imagine undergraduates coping with *Felix Holt* or *Romola*, at least not without considerable help, as they are set in such profoundly alternative cultural frameworks. Yet to teach the shorter Eliot, like *The Lifted Veil* or *Scenes from Clerical Life* or *Silas Marner*, can feel like a sell-out;

without denying the obvious value of these texts, there is a strong case for arguing that if students encounter only one Eliot novel it ought to be one of the major texts.

One way of teaching Eliot, is to turn students into the kind of reader Eliot wanted to produce. Dividing a novel into many short reading assignments (perhaps reading it according to the original serial divisions as Linda Hughes and Michael Lund suggest in Chapter 10 of the present volume) accompanied by one-page papers forces them to concentrate on details. Asking them to research some small object mentioned in the text opens up Eliot's rich historical knowledge; asking them to explain an aphorism makes them appreciate the deep philosophical musings, and assigning them to defend an unsympathetic character makes them see her profound sympathetic humanism.

Finally, one author with whom students neither overidentify nor regard with blank incomprehension, Elizabeth Gaskell, presents a different sort of problem. It is tempting to teach *Cranford,* both because of its relevance to questions of female roles in the nineteenth century and because of its welcome brevity and humour. Yet for younger students in particular, *Cranford* often feels irrelevant. They are annoyed by its cloying charm and irritated by the lack of plot. They can understand that Gaskell was trying to write lives outside the marriage plot and trying to show the texture of daily life for subjects who don't normally get fictional representation. They can be taught to appreciate it. But they adamantly insist that they don't care. Here, the simplest way is perhaps the most productive: read it aloud. *Cranford* is exceptionally well adapted to reading aloud, since so much of the humour is in the women's dialogue, as in the story of the cat who swallowed the lace or the conversation in which Mary tries to date Peter's departure from Cranford. Students will often catch on to the comedy in class, having missed it on their own. It may also be best to teach it in courses with more mature returning students (or, of course, at MA or Ph.D. level), where students identify with older people, and one doesn't have to fight to make people understand that mothers and grandmothers can have stories too.

III   Beyond the canon

Teaching the more canonical nineteenth-century women writers to undergraduates can be problematic in that students often have already strongly-held beliefs about these novels that they are unwilling to relinquish. By contrast, students tend to know nothing about the noncanonical novels and therefore they can keep an open mind about them. Indeed, the very rationale for reading these novels is up for debate, and is not the least useful aspect of teaching them. One immediately engages with some of the most profound issues of teaching literature. Why this writer and not others? How can we determine the value of this text, if any?

Value: it is often MA-level students who are most anxious to hold the line about "great books." Undergraduates pretty much assume that whatever you give them merits attention by the mere fact that it's been assigned, and, moreover, they live in a world of popular culture and alternative media, blogs, zines, websites, and suchlike, so they are quite comfortable with the idea that texts travel fluidly and occupy different niches at different times. Moreover, many noncanonical texts were popular best-sellers, easy to read and bearing familiar genre hallmarks (the detective story, the horror story), so students tend to enjoy them. They can be endearingly grateful to have a fun reading assignment. Meanwhile, Ph.D. students have read the theory and criticism of the canon (or will read it if you assign it) and are quite able to argue the theoretical case for expanding or exploding the canon, and because they are committed to a field, they will be personally interested in exploring its lesser-known paths. But MA students tend to be the most conservative of students, at least at my instutition. New York State's teaching laws require all secondary-school teachers to get an MA within five years, which means that our MA classes are overwhelmingly populated by teachers. Teachers are overworked and not necessarily well-trained in theoretical niceties. They tend to enforce the idea of great books that transcend time. They have had to justify their English major and English teacher career path, so they have repeated the great books idea often enough to make it part of their personal identity. They are often from generations that are not comfortable with postmodern media constructs and moral relativism. And because they are not necessarily interested in pursuing the field professionally, they don't see much purpose to reading "weird" stuff.

One policy is to do what Gerald Graff has called "teach the conflicts" (1993, p. 12). The teacher foregrounds the question of the book's literary value asking what criteria make a book valuable and what the signs might be that a book has met those criteria. The goal is to make students aware of their own assumptions when they judge a text. Once they have articulated their biases, they can evaluate them. For instance, students will often judge a text adversely if it contains dialect, but when they realize that the only reason for disliking it is that "it's hard to read," they concede that this is not a useful measure of literary quality. They will assume that a humorous novel cannot be an important text, until challenged.

More profoundly, students often assume that realism is the criteria for all texts. Some consider "it's not realistic" to be a crushing, unanswerable critique. One response is to ask whether the author intended the text to be realistic, how they can tell, and if not, what else might she have wanted the text to do and why. For instance, the flamboyant thunderstorm at the beginning of Marie Corelli's *Ardath* (1889) is in no sense realistic. It begins: "Deep in the heart of the Caucasus mountains a wild storm was gathering. Drear shadows drooped and thickened above the Pass of Dariel, that terrific gorge which, like a mere thread, seems to hang between the toppling frost-bound heights above and the black abysmal depths below . . . " and goes on like this for two pages (1889, p. 7). Students tend to laugh derisively at it. But when one recognizes that realism was not necessarily Corelli's goal, it is possible to imagine the appeal of other ways of writing, especially when the importance of melodrama in nineteenth-century popular culture is taken into account. Students might also be asked to imagine the kind of exotic, dramatic visual thrill readers might have wanted from literature in an era when travel was difficult and film virtually nonexistent.

While cases like the Corelli lesson work to teach students something they probably need to know, it is also the case that working on noncanonical texts in the classroom can actually produce an interesting democratization of the classroom. Reading noncanonical women writers can empower the students profoundly. It can give them a readerly authority they have never had before and may never have again. An anecdote may be useful here. When I give students noncanonical novels, I say, "in the past 150 years, there are only twenty or thirty people, as far as I know, who have read this book. I am really curious to know what you think of it." This is intended to remind students that that their opinion is important and that it is actually possible for them to make a real, original contribution to scholarship. I once taught Mary Brunton's *Self-Control* (1811), a novel about a virtuous woman pursued by a relentless stalker named Colonel Hargrave. A student ventured the thought that Hargrave resembled Satan. I hadn't noticed that before and told him that it was a real contribution, that nobody else had ever said this and he had found something genuinely important. Ten years later, I still remember how he sat up straight and his face shone with pride. He wrote his final paper on this point; he came to own this idea, to feel passionate about it and to want to prove it. Interestingly, this opportunity for real originality is most exciting for undergraduates, for whom English classes are too often a slog through well-worn comparisons of much-studied texts. Tired of figuring out if they've said the "right" thing about *David Copperfield,* students find a frightening but exhilarating freedom in charting their own course. (On a different note, assignments on these topics are also useful because it is very hard for students to plagiarize an essay on, say, Ouida's novels.)

This readerly authority, however, also empowers students in a way with which instructors might not be comfortable. It gives their subjective assessments of worth the validity of major critical pronouncements. This is not particularly dangerous with undergraduates, for they tend to accept whatever texts you give them and are eager to use their newly minted critical skills on the texts. In my experience, undergraduates will rarely dismiss a book for being "bad." First, many undergraduates don't much care about quality; they care much more about whether they can get the reading done than whether the reading meets some kind of higher standard, and, as discussed above, they pretty much assume it must be okay if you're assigning it. Even if they don't like the text, they don't necessarily think they have the credentials to condemn the text. This may not apply to the students of every university of course, and it is quite probable that students at more "elite" institutions are much more self-assertive.

Another anecdote. It is with the relatively conservative student population of the MA that one runs into trouble here. Valorizing their reactions can hijack the class. In teaching *East Lynne* to MA students, for instance, I had one student who was so disgusted by what he regarded as the lousy writing style that he could not get past the first chapter, nor could he bring himself to treat the text seriously, instead sneering at what he considered particularly egregious examples of Woods's style. Meanwhile, another student in the same class told me she stayed up all night, couldn't put the book down, and felt Isabel was an extremely sympathetic character with whom she identified intensely. These two squared off against each other in a battle neither could win, because neither had any criteria on which to base their likes or dislikes. While students might be embarrassed to reveal that they disliked, say, Dickens or Milton, they have no such scruples when it comes to noncanonical fiction, and this means that classroom discussion can often devolve into self-proclamation. Moreover, because MA students tend to be confident adults with years of experience in real jobs, usually in teaching (at least in New York state), most are not troubled by shyness or self-doubt in announcing their own feelings.

At the Ph.D. level (which in the US involves students taking some taught classes), telling students they have the authority to judge the text can be daunting for them, since so much of graduate study is about developing expertise and these students are suddenly being thrust into a position in which they feel they have zero knowledge. It can also be uncomfortable for the instructor, who runs into trouble when students, particularly those in their first year, attempt to use criteria that they have not fully mastered. On the first day of a course on nineteenth-century noncanonical women writers, I handed out a sample page with title and author obscured, the opening, as it happened, of Dinah Mulock Craik's *John Halifax, Gentleman,* and asked students how they would evaluate it. I wanted to see what textual clues they'd identify as signs of value. On this first page the narrator and his father quite literally bump into a street boy. Their servant scolds him, but the father remarks, "'thee need not go into the wet, my lad. Keep close to the wall, and there will be shelter enough both for us and thee,' said my father, as he pulled my little hand-carriage into the alley, under cover, from the pelting rain" (1903, p. 7). This scene led one student to spin out an admirable theory about the usefulness of reading Scottish literature, while another surmised that the characters were of a high class level because they were riding in a carriage. Of course, the dialogue is not Scottish but Quaker, and a hand-carriage was a wheelbarrow-like contraption for the disabled. Now, these are not important mistakes. They are fairly recondite points which I wouldn't necessarily expect a student to know. Moreover, since they were classroom comments, I was able to correct them before they went any further. Incidentally, the two students who had the courage to advance these theories went on to become the most outstanding members of that seminar. But when a student builds an elaborate structure of critical reading on a mistake, and when that mistake occurs in a presentation or final paper, it can be a ticklish situation for the instructor to correct it gently without embarrassing the student. Students can, of course, also make mistakes on canonical fiction, but they have more protection when difficult terms are footnoted and critical articles explain knotty points. With noncanonical fiction, students are very much on their own, which is an invaluable learning and professionalizing experience, but can also mean that they fall flat – an experience many of them have not had for years. Building a career on knowing all about literature means that confronting an unknown piece of literature, with basic questions that may not be answerable has the potential to be highly disconcerting.

IV   Writing and assessment

Alongside the challenges of the classroom are those which emerge when students are set the task of writing essays and research papers. In a course on noncanonical women's writing, students often need to write on under-read texts. In one sense, this is the easiest way to do a research paper; there's very little out there and much of it can be discounted (it often takes the form of encyclopedia entries, websites, wikipedia entries, and fan sites). Students don't feel overwhelmed, as they do when trying to research George Eliot or Jane Austen. It is currently quite easy to read everything that has been published on, for example, Ouida, in a day. Yet that also creates several challenges. First, the material is often hard to find, since it is not always in nearby libraries or available on the full-text databases that students like. Second, the little that's out there is often just plot summary or dated biographical anecdotes; students work hard to find this material and then naturally try to use it, only to be told, to their dismay, that the stuff is not worth citing. Yet it can also be challenging for students to be so free. They find that nobody has ever mapped out which scenes are important, what images characterize this text, how one reads the characters, what other texts influenced it. Sometimes nobody even knows much about the writer's life, or how this particular text fits into her oeuvre. In short, the basic ideas that are comfortably and readily available for canonical authors all have to be painstakingly thrashed out by the student, with absolutely no guarantee that s/he's got it right, and research sources that often constitute interference instead of assistance.

Of course, this student discomfort can be profoundly educational. In terms of acquiring skills, it can be wonderful for them to realize that information isn't automatically provided, and to discover how to track it down. It forces students to learn something of primary and archival research as well as the more usual critical or theoretical research. And it requires students to critically interrogate their sources. Undergraduate and MA students are especially prone to believing that whatever they find is legitimate. But many of the sources on noncanonical women writers are dodgy enough to provoke even the most trusting reader's scepticism, and this is an ideal opportunity for the instructor.

In preparation for this kind of assignment, it is perhaps worth spending serious class time teaching students how to sift good research from bad. I give my students four websites on Victorian etiquette to evaluate. Victorian gardens, fashions, or tea would work equally well; one wants a subject that generates fan websites as well as some scholarly sites for comparison. We look for signs of reliability: university affiliation, grammatical and historical accuracy, recent updates, a list of (quality) sources, more attention to text than graphics, not trying to sell anything. For example, Googling "Victorian etiquette" brings up a history project written by a Michigan high-school student, using Miss Manners and her textbook as sources. Clearly users of this site have no idea how to ascertain validity. After parsing sample websites in class, students have to find a website on their topic and turn in an assessment of its merits. Similarly, we review four sample biographical treatments of the death of the same subject, and four sample pieces of criticism on the same text. These work best when one chooses a text suffused with controversial contemporary issues, like William Blake's "The Little Black Boy" or Oscar Wilde's work. Students are amazed that early criticism on Blake does not deal with race, nor do early articles on Wilde discusss homoerotic desire. I spend a considerable amount of class time eliciting the approaches that underlie each biography or criticism, the way the scholar uses sources, the signs of reliability, the imagined audience, and the fact that the same writing can provoke fascinatingly and radically different interpretations. I often juxtapose criticism on the same text written in different decades, thus teaching students about changes in critical styles as well.

What students come to recognize with all this, is that professional writing can vary drastically. This is part of the larger process of helping students teach themselves to be scholars. By forcing them out beyond their (and perhaps our) comfort zone, showing them how much is not known, and treating them as partners in the process of discovering it, the teacher has a chance to help empower them beyond whatever topic the individual course may have.

V   Conclusions

I began this chapter by discussing what it felt like to survive in an intensely, unremittingly gendered world, and to immerse students in that world. But

I'd like to end by pointing out that we too are preparing students for immersion in a world whose codes are stringent and whose terms may be alien.

I am talking, in part, about modern models of gender identity. I think that it is enormously beneficial to help students get outside the sexualized and commodified and media-inflected terms in which they are encouraged to view themselves. Female students, especially, constantly police their own bodies as consumable artifacts to be maintained and marketed as the measure of their own self-worth. For example, introducing them to a mid-nineteenth-century notion of gender doesn't mean they will (or should!) return to it, but it does demonstrate how recent and how contingent our ideas are. Nineteenth-century femininities were defined as a preeminently internal sets of qualities, moral and emotional orientations, whose presence could be indicated by external markers of dress and deportment. It is very far indeed from our modern fetishization of the external body. Moreover, because nineteenth-century femininity privileged self-suppression, piety, and quasi-maternal caretaking, it provides a usefully alien model for students for whom femininity is about self-expression and sexual self-assertion. Nineteenth-century femininity's very alterity demonstrates to students that their own gender ideas are not natural in any way, that it is possible to have wildly different ideas about gender performance.

However, we are also responsible for helping students enter another world: academic discipline. We are training our students to perform and ultimately own an academic voice, resonant with the confidence and authority and seasoned judgements they may not feel remotely ready to produce. We are training our students to locate research sources, to sift through them for the best ones, and to sort through those in turn to find the most useful quotations, which, we insist, they need to analyse in turn. We are training our students to synthesize multiple sources and generate a powerful argument which must be both plausible and original, which must take account of previous critics yet go beyond them. And I'd argue that the best training for citizenship in the academic nation (a nation to which most students are recent immigrants, and will be staying at least four years) is thorough acquaintance with both canonical and noncanonical sources. While canonical texts offer them the experience of sorting through the critical record and locating themselves vis-a-vis generations of experts, noncanonical texts offer them the experience of *becoming* those experts themselves. To learn the critical commentary on *Jane Eyre* is a valuable educational experience, but to generate that commentary oneself on *Miss Marjoribanks* is a different and equally important intellectual achievement. I teach both Brontë and Oliphant because I think they are superb and significant writers and I want my students to enjoy them. But I value the process of self-authorization my students go through even more. And so the final reason for teaching noncanonical texts is not just to "teach women writers" but also to teach women, and men, how to become writers themselves.

Appendix: sample syllabus: "Reading the underread: Victorian women's noncanonical novels

Rationale: John Sutherland has pointed out that "the tiny working areas of the 'canon,' the 'syllabus,' and the paperbacked 'classics' are poor reflections of what the Victiorian novel actually meant to Victorians." In spite of the fact that roughly 60,000 works of fiction were published between 1837 and 1901, "generations of students have left their academies thinking that this richest of literary fields comprises half-a-shelf's length of works by Dickens, two Brontës, George Eliot and Hardy." What happened to the rest, and what can we learn by re-examining a few of them?

This course interrogates the processes of canon formation and canon revision, inquires about the politics and genres traditionally excluded from the canon, investigates the potential problems of constructing a category called the "noncanonical," and monitors case studies of Victorian women's novels with interestingly vexed relations to canonicity. We will look at popular fiction, trying to figure out what accounted for the enormous appeal of this work, how it accommodated social ideologies, and how popularity might mitigate against a work's survival as the literary marketplace altered and academic needs developed in the early twentieth century.

Primary texts:

Mary Elizabeth Braddon, *Lady Audley's Secret* (Penguin)
Marie Corelli *Wormwood* (Broadview)
Lucas Malet, *The History of Sir Richard Calmady* (Birmingham)
Margaret Oliphant, *Hester* (Penguin)
Margaret Oliphant, *Miss Marjoribanks* (Penguin)
Ouida, *Moths* (Broadview)
Ellen Wood, *East Lynne* (Broadview)
Charlotte Yonge, *The Clever Woman of the Family* (Broadview)
Charlotte Yonge, *The Daisy Chain* (Beautiful Feet)

Recommended books:

Adam C. Roberts, *Victorian Culture and Society*
A. N. Wilson, *The Victorians*

Secondary Reading:

Everything marked * will be available in the reserve reading folder on the library web site.

Assignments

One presentation (about 20 min.)	30%	
One long paper (about 20 pp.)	50%	
Effort grade	20%	

Weekly Schedule

Week 1

Feminist and canon theory: introduction: handouts (including Poovey–
   Homans debate, sample noncanonical work)

*Canon theory: Sutherland, Thompson, Herrnstein-Smith; *Domestic-
   fiction theory: Armstrong, Freedgood, Langland

Week 2

Domestic fiction: Yonge, *Clever,* *Wheatley

Week 3

Domestic fiction (cont'd): Yonge, *Daisy Chain,* *Budge

Week 4

Oliphant, *Miss Marjoribanks,* *Langland, *Cohen
Oliphant, *Hester* *Poovey, Introduction in edition

Week 5

Sensation fiction: Braddon, *Lady Audley's Secret,* *Nemesvari
Wood, *East Lynne,* first half, *Rosenman

Week 6

Sensation fiction (cont'd): Wood to end, *Pykett

Week 7

Fin de siècle: Ouida, *Moths,* first half; introduction in volume
Ouida to end, *Schaffer
Research paper proposals due

Week 8

Corelli, *Wormwood,* *Federico
Malet, *Sir Richard,* first half, *Lorimer-Lundberg

Week 9

Malet to end
Schaffer, introduction in edition
Final discussion

   Research papers due, with self-addressed stamped envelopes

Presentations:

Everyone has to give one brief presentation. Aim to keep it no longer than 20
min., which means about 8 double-spaced typed pages. Please give me a copy

of the presentation afterwards, and bring extra copies for anyone else in the class who might want it. If two people are scheduled for presentations on the same day, you need to meet with each other to coordinate your talks.

In the presentation, you should analyse the critical article for that day. *Do not summarize it.* Instead, briefly explain what the critic is arguing, isolate areas where you think the critic is wrong, and suggest alternative ways of explicating the text. End by asking a question to get the discussion rolling.

Writing:

Since the presentation engages with a single article, it will be quite different from the long paper. I recommend treating them separately from the beginning and planning to do them on different topics. However, if you find you want to develop your presentation into a long paper, talk to me about how to change its scope.

My idea about the long paper in this course is that it would be fun to do a case study. Analyse why a canonical figure achieved and maintained his/her reputation, or explore the fortunes of a noncanonical figure to determine why s/he remained obscure. You don't *have* to do this; if you prefer, you may do a more traditional research paper on the concerns of this class. You might want to focus on a particular text we did in this course, explore a relevant theoretical/critical issue like feminist analysis or canonicity, or examine a relevant cultural field (i.e. the changing publishing industry in the period).

Notes

1. Many of these works appear in recent anthologies: Susan Hamilton (ed.), *Criminals, Idiots, Women and Minors: Victorian Writing by Women on Women* (Peterborough: Broadview, 1995); Claudia Nelson and Ann Sumner Holmes (eds.), *Maternal Instincts: Visions of Motherhood and Sexuality in Britain 1875–1925* (London: Macmillan, 1997).
2. In contrast teaching *Villette* is a fascinating experience of readerly disorientation and dismay, a whole different experience from *Jane Eyre,* and although I have not tried *Shirley* at the undergraduate level I imagine that it would not present the overidentification issue either.

Works cited

Brunton, Mary, *Self-Control* (London: Pandora Press, 1986. First pub. 1810/1811).

Corelli, Marie, *Ardath* (New York: H. M. Caldwell Co., n.d. but first edn. 1889).

Craik, Dinah Mulock, *John Halifax, Gentleman* (1856; New York and London: Harper Brothers, 1903).

Graff, Gerald, *Beyond the Culture Wars: How Teaching the Conflicts Can Revitalize American Education* (New York. W. W. Norton, 1993).

Hamilton, Susan, *Criminals, Idiots, Women, and Minors: Victorian Writing By Women on Women* (Ontario: Broadview Press, 2004).

Keen, Paul, *Revolutions in Romantic Literature: An Anthology of Print Culture, 1780–1832* (Ontario: Broadview Press, 2004).

Moers, Ellen, *Literary Women* (London: Women's Press, 1978).

Nelson, Carolyn Christensen, *The New Woman Reader* (Ontario: Broadview Press, 2000).

Oliphant, Margaret, *Janet* (London: Hurst, 1891).

Rumsey, Frances, *Ascent* (London: John Lane, 1923).

Steedman, Carolyn, *Master and Servant: Love and Labour in the English Industrial Age* (Cambridge: Cambridge University Press, 2007).

Sutherland, John, "Foreword: The Underread." In *The New Nineteenth Century: Feminist Readings of Underread Fiction.* Ed. Barbarah Leah Harman and Susan Meyer (New York: Garland Publishing, 1996), pp. xi–xxv.

Warden, Florence, *The House on the Marsh* (New York: D. Appleton and Company, 1884).

Woolf, Virginia, *A Room of One's Own* (New York: Harcourt Brace Jovanovich, Inc., 1929).

7
Teaching Genre: The Sensation Novel

Jennifer Phegley

Over the past decade, studies of sensation fiction have flourished, due in large part to the foundational work of Anne Cvetkovich, Pamela K. Gilbert, Winifred Hughes, Lyn Pykett, Elaine Showalter, and others who wrote about the genre in the 1980s and 90s. Since the turn of the twenty-first century, a wide variety of publications have been devoted to sensationalism making it a bourgeoning trend in current literary scholarship.[1] Andrew Maunder accounts for this increasing scholarly interest in a formerly marginalized genre by suggesting that "It is now acknowledged that if sensation fiction is cut out of the picture it is impossible to gain an accurate sense of nineteenth-century literary historiography . . . . Sensation fiction and the critical furore it provoked is now seen as a key event . . . enriching our understanding of Victorian fiction generally" (2004, p. xii). However, the reprinting of sensation novels themselves has not kept up with this surge in critical attention. As a result, classroom integration of sensation fiction has necessarily lagged behind academic research on the genre, just as its movement into the canon has progressed more slowly than critical interest. In this essay, I will investigate how sensation fiction is currently being used in college classrooms and to what extent it can be considered newly canonical. As I follow Maunder's lead in making a case for the importance of the genre, I hope to suggest some productive ways these novels can be incorporated into our current curricula despite the somewhat limited availability of texts.

In an effort to map the use of sensation fiction in college English courses, I investigated both publishing houses and course syllabuses to determine what texts are being assigned to students and how they are being deployed in the classroom. My survey of sensation novels currently advertised in the on-line catalogues of three major publishers of scholarly editions – Broadview, Oxford, and Penguin – indicates that the select sensation novels in print are predominantly written by the three founders of the genre in the 1860s: Wilkie Collins, Mary Elizabeth Braddon, and Ellen Price Wood. Wilkie Collins is the most widely published of the "big three" with thirteen of his thirty novels in print. *The Woman in White* and *The Moonstone* are each sold by all three presses.[2] Collins's domination of the publishing scene is not surprising given his close relationship to Charles Dickens, the status of *The Woman in White* as the "original" sensation novel, and a long history of critical praise for *The Moonstone*. As a result, Collins seems to have been deemed the most canonical sensationalist. Mary Elizabeth Braddon, on the other hand, may not have fully recovered from the brutal critical reception of her novels by her contemporaries. She comes in a distant second with only three of the more than eighty novels she wrote currently in print. *Lady Audley's Secret*, her first best-selling novel, is the only one featured by all three publishers. Ellen Price Wood has fared worse than the others. While Wood wrote more than thirty books and enjoyed a fairly favourable critical reputation in her day, *East Lynne* is her only available novel. It is published by just two of the three presses.[3] While several more specialized publishers, including The Sensation Press and Valancourt Press, have recently begun publishing a wider range of sensation novels, their books are much more expensive and difficult to obtain. Though their novels are not as widely available as might be desired by those who research and teach sensation fiction, Collins, Braddon, and Wood have clearly benefited from being considered the defining figures of the genre whose early works form what can be termed the canon of sensation fiction.[4]

This investigation of the sensation novels readily available for classroom use led me to wonder how the publishers' offerings square with recent classroom curricula? Given that teachers' choices are limited by what is easily accessible to their students, I assumed that the books included on class reading lists would closely resemble publishers' lists. To determine if this is the case, I examined fifty-three syllabuses posted on the "Teaching Resources" section of the Victoria Research Web, including twelve Victorian literature surveys, twenty-five special topics courses, and sixteen novel courses.[5] While my expectations were mostly confirmed, there were some anomalies. *The Woman in White* and *The Moonstone* are, as anticipated, the most frequently represented sensation novels, included in four courses each. Also unsurprising is the fact that Ellen Wood fares about as well in the classroom as she does with publishers: *East Lynne* is included in only two of the courses surveyed. However, given that Collins has the healthiest publishing list of the three authors, I was somewhat surprised to learn that Braddon's novels are featured even more frequently than his on course reading lists. *Lady Audley's Secret* made the cut in eight courses and *Aurora Floyd* in one.[6] Among instructors who posted their course outlines, then, the same writers whose books are most often published by the top three presses prevail, though their presence does not follow absolutely in lock step with the publishers' preferences. Despite the publishers' emphasis on Collins, it may well be that a nineteenth-century association of women readers and writers with sensationalism coincides with a scholarly interest in women writers, allowing Braddon to edge Collins out when faculty members choose books for their courses. According to Marjorie Mather at Broadview Press, *Lady Audley's Secret* is its best-selling sensation novel, outperforming its closest competitor, *The Moonstone*, by two to one. Indeed, *Lady Audley's Secret* is a consistent top seller among the entire Broadview Edition list.[7] Mather also attests to *East Lynne*'s "solid and steady" sales, which indicate that it is "finding a place in more courses than you might expect." Wood's novel is currently just behind *The Moonstone* in sales and sells twice as many copies as its closest rival, *Aurora Floyd*.

The question remains: do these publishing lists and nineteen instances of sensation novels in fourteen of fifty-three syllabuses confirm that the genre is becoming a standard part of the literary canon as Maunder suggests? I think so. Not only are at least some sensation novels competing with other Victorian novels, as Mather notes, but these novels are also emerging as key components of well-rounded course plans. I'll admit I expected more than 26 per cent of the courses I surveyed to include sensation novels if the genre is, indeed, on the path toward canonical status. However, the slow but steady movement of the sensation novel into the mainstream comes into clearer focus if we look more carefully at this (admittedly unscientific) sample of courses. Only two sensation novels (*East Lynne* and *Lady Audley's Secret*) are included in the twelve nineteenth-century survey courses, which means a total of 17 per cent of them feature sensation fiction. However, since survey courses necessarily include fewer novels due to the impetus for coverage that leads to a focus on poetry and non-fiction, that rather low figure is not as meaningful as it initially seems. If we exclude surveys altogether and turn instead to special topics courses, that figure rises slightly to 20 per cent. As these courses tend to tap into the latest trends in Victorian studies (in this sample the topics include gender, deviance, and empire), they are more likely venues for teaching sensation novels. Out of twenty-five special topics courses, five contain sensation fiction, with nine total instances of assigned sensation novels. One of these special topics courses actually focuses on "Victorian Sensations" and features four sensation novels. This indicates that the more advanced the course and the more focused the topic, the more likely it is to highlight sensational works.

But it is in courses on the novel where sensationalism really emerges as a driving force: 44 per cent of them incorporate sensation fiction. In these syllabuses, sensation novels are integrated into seven of the sixteen courses, with a total of eight assigned sensation novels. Almost half of all novel courses posted, then, foreground the genre as a way of explaining the development of the form. As many of the courses aim to define "the novel," they seek to encompass the full range of novelistic genres. This leads to the frequent pairing of sensational fiction with realistic fiction and, often, to the inclusion of contemporary critical conversations about these "opposing" genres. In her review-essay "Remapping and Reframing the Victorian Novel," Elizabeth Winston acknowledges that sensationalism is a major topic in recent examinations of the Victorian novel, marking a trend toward providing a counterpoint to the much more thoroughly discussed realist novel (2002). Likewise, Robert R. Thomas points out that "almost every Victorian novel has at its heart some crime that must be uncovered, some false identity that must be unmasked, some secret that must be revealed, or some clandestine plot that must be exposed" (2001, p. 169). The fact that sensational elements are more pervasive than previously acknowledged indicates that they deserve to be more widely examined in the classroom and explains why they are most frequently explored in courses that focus on the novel. While sensation novels do seem to be creeping into the classroom and thereby into the canon, the genre has still not received attention from publishers and teachers consonant with their central role in the development of the novel in the nineteenth century. In the remainder of this essay, I will advocate for the importance of a sustained focus on the genre of sensation fiction that I hope will encourage more teachers to incorporate the genre into their classes, whether or not they are focused on the novel as a form.

In order to do this, I will examine the evolution of my own novel course over several years, focusing on the benefits of teaching sensation fiction as an important genre in and of itself. While my teaching experiences have convinced me that comparing and contrasting realism and sensationalism by reading novels that exemplify both genres can be beneficial, I have not found that approach as productive as focusing solely on the sensation novel while exploring elements of both realism and sensationalism within it. Approaches that set sensational novels up against realistic novels can simply reinforce the divisions between high and low culture that are more blurred than we sometimes like to admit. As Maunder explains, sensation provides a challenge for students and teachers today as it did for original readers and critics "especially if we are used to thinking of [novels] in terms of the artificially opposed 'high' and 'low' divide which separates works of 'value' from 'trash'" (2005, p. 23). Teaching sensation novels solo curbs the simplifying impulse to label one genre artistic and one commercial, one good and one bad. When students (and faculty) are asked to move beyond this black and white construction of the Victorian novel, they are more intellectually challenged and more likely to see genre as something that is constructed by readers/critics for their own political, economic, or academic purposes. When we focus on sensationalism as a valuable genre, we are better positioned to interrogate the literary canon and the criteria critics (past and present) have used to justify it.

The course I will focus on is one I have taught three times over the past six years. Geared toward a mixed group of advanced undergraduate and graduate students, "The Novel, 1740–1900" is described in the university catalogue as "an intensive study of no more than three major novelists." The first few times I taught the class, I chose a range of writers I thought could be defined as "major" with the aim of exposing students to a mixture of realistic and sensational novels. I intended to define these genres through case studies but also to show how their genre classifications break down under close scrutiny. The first time around I chose Braddon's *Lady Audley's Secret*, Elizabeth Gaskell's *Wives and Daughters*, and Charles Dickens's *Bleak House* (classifying Braddon as the sensationalist, Gaskell as the realist, and Dickens as a cross between the two with elements of sentimentalism and detective fiction thrown in for good measure). The second time I taught the course, I once again used Braddon (incorporating *Aurora Floyd* as an alternative to *Lady Audley's Secret*) and Gaskell. I decided to replace the Dickens novel with Collins's *The Moonstone* in order to focus more fully on detective fiction as a third genre derived from elements of both realism and sensationalism.

In both iterations of the course, I began by defining the genres separately, but constructed assignments that encouraged blurring the boundaries between them. For example, I asked groups of students to analyse Dickens's characterization in *Bleak House*, deciding to what extent particular characters were realistic, exaggerated, or sentimental. We then compared his characters with Braddon's in *Lady Audley's Secret*. While students felt that Braddon was generally more sensational in her plot development, they found Dickens was more sensational and sentimental in his characterization. Braddon's long passages of detailed exposition on characters' external appearances and internal motivations seemed, to them, more "real" than Dickens's playful use of exaggeration and stereotypes, particularly in his character names and use of repeated catch-phrases as a shorthand form of characterization.

On another occasion, after students read several very positive reviews of *Wives and Daughters*, I asked them to consider whether or not they agreed with the *Manchester Guardian's* assessment that "as to 'sensation' there is not the faintest shadow of its existence" (1866, p. 485)? Having just completed Braddon's *Aurora Floyd*, which raised the hackles of many critics, we focused on how Gaskell carries out Molly's sensational disgrace without alarming her reviewers. Students were able to point out the ways in which Gaskell borrows sensational themes but tones them down, or "domesticates" them. For example, one student noted how subtly Osborne's secret is handled and revealed in comparison to Aurora Floyd's secret. Both are heirs who have clandestinely married working-class people and both hide the fact from their parents, yet their secrets have varying levels of importance in driving the plots of the two novels, with Aurora's as a primary strand and Osborne's as a sub-plot. By pursuing such lines of inquiry, students could productively explore how realism and sensationalism intersected and diverged in particular novels.

Despite the fact that these assignments initially worked to achieve my goal of blurring genre boundaries by closely examining texts, I always seemed to hit a stumbling block when discussing the novels in more general terms. I found that my suggestion that Gaskell and Braddon, for example, could be seen as "separate but equal" always met with scepticism and a desire on the part of many students to revert to preconceived notions about canonical vs. non-canonical works. Even students with little literary training are aware of the differences between high and low cultural works, which are often delineated in movie reviews and other forms they regularly encounter. Though students could identify ways in which Braddon was realistic and Gaskell was sensational, they did not willingly question their genre classifications or their status as authors. Likewise, students were reluctant to question the preeminence of Dickens, though they were also less engaged with his work than with Braddon's. Just as students can be aware of their enjoyment of romantic comedies or action films but continue to believe that independent films are of a higher quality, they often find Braddon more "modern" and "relevant," but maintain that Dickens is "better." I found these contradictions interesting though not unexpected. Students could easily see evidence of genre cross-fertilization on a micro level, but not on a macro level. I believe that this was the result of students reverting back to a "gut feeling" that one could never legitimately compare someone like Braddon to someone like Dickens. After all, students had known Dickens since they were children (typically from attending a performance of *A Christmas Carol*) and this Braddon person was a new (and apparently scandalous) entity. Why should they regard her in the same way they regarded Dickens? *How* could they?

When I was revising this course for the third time, I wanted to try to circumvent these prejudices by teaching three novelists with whom students would likely be unfamiliar. I also decided to foreground the class with critical discussions of genre and to focus on a single genre, the sensation novel. Rather than working with realism and sensationalism as oppositional forces from the start, I began with the idea of dissecting a series of supposedly low cultural novels to uncover the sensational and realistic (and sentimental and melodramatic) elements in each of them. Ultimately, I found this approach more satisfying and exciting for me and for my students as it allowed us to immerse ourselves in sensationalism and to see it on its own terms rather than in opposition to something "better."

During the sixteen-week semester we read three novels serialized within a few years of each other: Collins's *The Woman in White* (serialized from November 1859–August 1860 in *All the Year Round*), Wood's *East Lynne* (serialized from January 1860–February 1861 in *The New Monthly Magazine*), and Braddon's *Aurora Floyd* (serialized from January 1862–January 1863 in *Temple Bar*). I asked students to read the novels simultaneously in serial parts within their original periodical contexts, arranging our reading so that we focused on Collins every Monday and Wood every Wednesday for the first half of the semester and on Braddon every Monday and Wood every Wednesday for the second half of the term. Attempting to recreate the simultaneous serial reading experience better approximated the ways in which the original audience received the novels and would allow for more interconnections among the three works. We also focused on genre theory and periodical studies to loosen up students' preconceived notions of "good" vs. "bad" literature and help them understand the original publication contexts of the novels. I hoped that this course plan would provide a well-rounded picture of the Victorian literary marketplace even as we zeroed in on a single genre: the sensation novel.

On the first day of class, I asked the students to quickly write their own definitions of the terms "realistic" and "sensational," having several of them read their responses aloud before we considered the standard dictionary definitions that I distributed to the class. After comparing their own definitions with dictionary definitions, I divided them into groups to read small portions of the first section of Daniel Chandler's "An Introduction to Genre Theory" on "The Problem of Definition." This text is useful for a first-day assignment because it can be easily divided up and read in class and, if your classroom is networked, it can be accessed on-line by the students or projected on a screen in front of the class. Each group quickly read and discussed their assigned section of the essay and wrote a three-to-four-sentence summary of it on the board. Essentially, each group came away with some version of the idea that genres are inherently unstable, that "the classification and hierarchical taxonomy of genres is not a neutral and 'objective' procedure" (Chandler, 2005, p. 1). For many students who had considered genre – if they had considered it at all – as a monolithic construct, this activity justified how we might be able to identify elements of realism within sensationalism and vice versa. This reading framed the course with a scepticism for genre that encouraged students to question their assumptions and "gut feelings" about how literature should be valued.

For our second meeting, I assigned readings by Pamela K. Gilbert, Anne Cvetkovich, and Francis O'Gorman, which gave students the critical tools to theorize our definitions from the first day.[8] These readings helped us construct more sophisticated and detailed categorizations of the genres and further encouraged a healthy scepticism toward hierarchical taxonomies. Gilbert and Cvetkovich point out nineteenth-century reviewers' anxieties about sensationalism – particularly as they relate to gender, class, and the embodiment of feeling – that play into the genre's categorization as a low cultural form. In her essay, Gilbert uses sensationalism to point out how particular authors can be caught in a trap of genre labels: "once an author/ text is established within a certain generic domain, that is, coming from a certain 'location' within the marketplace . . . critics, publishers, authors, and readers will reinforce, through master-readings (reviews), packaging, textual references, and reading assumptions, a reading of that text which is congruent with its assigned generic pedigree" (1997, p. 59). Students found particularly helpful Gilbert's claim that "genre produces coherence within the multiplicity of the text, in some sense, it produces the text (the reading) itself"; they appreciated that she is not attempting to dismantle genre altogether, but to "render its operations suspect, and to redefine it as a dynamic process" (p. 60). Engaging with Cvetkovich helped students understand theories of affect and mass culture that she argues have influenced the reception of a genre defined "as inferior or second-rate fiction" by critics who simultaneously "constructed the category of high culture novels whose moral mission was to displace the popular forms that were entertaining and corrupting the mass reading public" (p. 17). Her juxtaposition of twentieth-century theories of mass culture (including Marx, Adorno and Horkheimer, Jameson, and Foucault) with psychoanalytic and feminist theory reveals the ways in which cultural and gender divisions are often anti-feminist and, indeed, elitist. O'Gorman's overview of the novel as a form likewise reveals the political motivations that underlie the construction of realism as synonymous with high culture (even if it has also been seen as naïve and unattainable) by providing brief summaries of and selections from critics such as George Levine, Catherine Belsey, D. A. Miller, and Nancy Armstrong. After reading these selections, students began to see how one critic might classify realism as progressive and another as conservative, just as sensationalism has been used for both progressive and conservative purposes. If both genres can be so easily co-opted by critics for various political ends, they become discourses that can and should be questioned and discussed together.

While these critical perspectives and the assigned articles on the periodical context of nineteenth-century fiction were important for students' understanding of how genres are constructed, maintained, and received by readers, the fiction itself was their primary guide to developing an understanding of the interpenetration of realism and sensationalism.[9] One might think that it would be difficult to develop definitions of realism while only reading sensational fiction. However, I maintain that we were able to develop more nuanced definitions based on our reading of a single genre. Most students were already familiar with at least some realist novels. If they had read Victorian fiction at all, it was typically one of the major realists, such as George Eliot or Thomas Hardy, which provided them with a basis for comparison. To further assist with their ability to identify and compare elements of various genres, though, I assigned a range of stories from *The Broadview Anthology of Victorian Short Stories*. Reading a series of stories and considering their narrative techniques, characterization, and plot development was an excellent way to quickly introduce students to elements of realism and sensationalism. Starting with these stories also had the benefit of allowing us to compare and contrast the writers we would focus on even before we had begun their longer works. My primary goal, however, was to showcase a range of genres including realistic, sensational, sentimental, and adventure fiction. In addition to stories from Braddon, Collins, and Wood, students read selections by Charles Dickens, Arthur Conan Doyle, Elizabeth Gaskell, Evelyn Sharp, and Anthony Trollope.[10] In class, I asked small groups of students to classify one story each by genre, providing evidence to support their conclusions. I also asked them to consider sub-genres such as domestic fiction, ghost stories, gothic tales, and detective fiction, noting where their assigned story might best fit into these narrower categories. As each group reported their responses, we determined how their classifications intersected with and diverged from those of other groups. By comparing these stories, students were confronted with the difficulties of classifying genres firsthand.

Following these varied introductory approaches to the course, we focused on closely examining the novels. First, I established an understanding of the complexities of the sensation novel itself by focusing on some of its gendered elements. Next, I troubled the genre's easy classification (and its often easy dismissal by critics). Early in the term, as we read Wood and Collins simultaneously, we explored the relationship between gender and genre classification. I hoped this would allow students to see possible gender differences within a genre typically labelled feminine and to reassess the value of feminine forms more generally. By urging the class to question the grounds for dismissing sensationalism, I hoped students might more greatly value, or at least understand, some of the genre's techniques and goals.

I brought in quotations from Jane Tompkins on the cultural work of sentimental forms and Ellen Bayuk Rosenman on gendered elements of suffering in Victorian melodrama. We looked at Tompkins's famous claim that "the popular domestic novel of the nineteenth century represents a monumental effort to reorganize culture from the woman's point of view" (1985, p. 124) and her explanation of the ways in which suffering, expressed through excessive tearfulness, is aimed at instituting social change through the only power available to women, their moral and religious superiority (pp. 126–7). Likewise, we used Rosenman's argument that "pain is gendered . . . in its meanings and aims" (2003, p. 22) as a basis for our comparison of Wood and Collins. Rosenman argues that "the glib association between femininity, weakness, and suffering makes masochism a particularly effective disguise for power: if women's pain appears to be natural, if it appears to conform to gender norms, it can smuggle its contraband desires unnoticed. Through melodramatic suffering, women assert themselves through the very emotions that seem to signify their lack of power" (p. 25). Using these interrelated critical perspectives as a framework, I asked students to compare Wood's articulation of these sentimental modes of powerful expression, which are most easily demonstrated through the penitent tears of Isabel Vane, with Collins's greater tendency to depict bodily excitement as a kind of empowerment that would likely be too scandalous for use by a woman writer (as it was so clearly in Braddon's much maligned works). I used the following prompt to guide a small group activity followed by a large class discussion:

Sentimentality and Sensationalism in Wood and Collins
Wood's novel frequently features crying and Collins's novel frequently features a variety of other sensations. The tears and sensations that each author incorporates are both bodily manifestations of emotions that allow their characters to express their otherwise unacceptable feelings and, potentially, to initiate change in their powerless situations.

Considering Tompkins's and Rosenman's claims, what specific function(s) do Wood's tears (see p. 95, 138, 148, 180, 189) and Collins's bodily sensations (see p. 51, 52–3, 61, 64, 67) have? Why do you think Wood uses tears and Collins uses other bodily sensations? What are the gendered implications of their modes of expression? In what ways are both kinds of emotional expression empowering?

The page numbers listed above point to a selection of Wood's repeated phrases that usually describe Isabel's tearful outbursts, including these: Isabel "flew into hysterics" (p. 95); "emotion overcame her and she burst into tears . . . sobs came forth hysterically" (p. 138); "Isabel . . . burst into a paroxysm of rebellious tears" (p. 148); and "Lady Isabel sat down and burst into tears and sobs" (189). In contrast, Collins's passages in Hartright's narrative focus on very different bodily sensations related to amorous feelings: upon meeting Laura Fairlie he wonders: "how can I separate her from my own sensations" (p. 51); comments on "the sensations that crowded on me, when my eyes first looked upon her – familiar sensations which we all know, which spring to life in most of our hearts" (pp. 52–3); laments that "The poor weak words which have failed to describe Miss Fairlie, have succeeded in betraying the sensations she awakened in me" (p. 64); and acknowledges "The sensations that I could trace to herself and to me, the unacknowledged sensations that we were feeling in common" (p. 67). The contrast between the feminine expression of suffering and the masculine expression of desire allows students to identify ways in which the two writers use related tactics to achieve different ends. For Wood, tears become a way to justify sensationalism as a purifying experience that allows women to occupy a position of moral authority, while for Collins, bodily sensations propel Hartight into the "heart" of an irresistible mystery that he is driven to solve in order to increase his power and status. While gender certainly is a factor in determining modes of expressive action for the characters, as one of my students pointed out, Hartight's frequent sensations actually feminize him. Since he is unable to resist feeling he is in a sense helpless just as Isabel is until she takes action to restore herself to her children. Hartright is only fortified into an acceptable masculine character by his self-imposed exile to America, where he becomes an appropriately stoic and adventurous hero;

this experience disciplines his heart so that he can return and save Laura from the villainous Sir Percival Glyde. Likewise, Isabel's tears are a sign of her transgressions, but also a sign of her repentance and eventual righteous empowerment. Through tears, she is able to rebuild herself into a respectable woman once more. While these uses of sentiment and sensation are clearly gendered, they accomplish similar ends within the two novels. This assignment allows students to explore some of the gendered complexities of sensation novels themselves, establishing the genre as culturally useful, following Tompkins' formulation. It also demonstrates that sensation fiction can hold up to close reading and analysis despite the fact that it has so often been written off as a shallow and empty form. Thus, students can appreciate the genre's expression of cultural anxieties as well as its artistic cleverness of design.

Nearer the end of the semester, when we focused on Braddon, I moved on to directly challenge the divisions between high and low culture, realism and sensationalism by considering *Aurora Floyd* as a realistic novel. To carry out this exercise of reformulating Braddon as a realist, we analysed the ways in which she directly contradicts her own classification as a sensationalist within the novel. Students read W. Fraser Rae's review labelling Braddon a writer who produces "pictures of daily life, wherein there are scenes so grossly untrue to nature, that we can hardly pardon the authoress if she drew them in ignorance" (1865, p. 591). I asked the class to juxtapose this claim with the efforts of Braddon's self-referential narrator, who attempts to convince readers that the novel is, in fact, realistic. Each group was charged with identifying specific passages that anticipate and refute charges of sensationalism.

One group cited a series of literary allusions to George Eliot, Shakespeare, and Tennyson, arguing that they are intended to imply that the narrator (as a signifier for Braddon) is a well-read and highly literary person. To support and expand on this claim, the students pointed to an interesting excerpt in which the narrator notes that Aurora's father found his daughter so fascinating that "the best book in Mr Mudie's collection" would pale in comparison to her: "Literary lions! Political Notabilities! Out upon them! When Sir Edward Bulwer Lytton and Mr Charles Dickens should call in Mr Makepeace Thackeray and Mr Wilkie Collins, to assist them in writing a work, in fifteen volumes or so, about Aurora" he would be interested in reading novels (Braddon, 1998, p. 278). Though this passage could be read as the narrator poking fun at Mr Floyd's excessive adoration of his daughter, students concluded that, combined with the extensive literary allusions, it marks Braddon as an intellectually capable author able to understand high culture and willing to reject it for a kind of literature that she found more exciting and more real. It also implies that Braddon has accomplished quite a feat by single-handedly penning the story of Aurora that Mr Floyd believes would require collaboration among some of the leading novelists of the day.

Another group focused on passages in which the narrator overtly denies that the story she is telling is sensational. For example, at the beginning of the novel, the narrator claims that:

> If this were a very romantic story, it would be perhaps only proper for Eliza Floyd to pine in her gilded bower, and misapply her energies in weeping for some abandoned lover, deserted in an evil hour of ambitious madness. But as my story is a true one – not only true in a general sense, but strictly true as to the leading facts which I am about to relate . . . I am bound also to be truthful here, and to set down as a fact that the love which Eliza Floyd bore for her husband was as pure and sincere an affection as ever man need hope to win from the generous heart of a good woman. (Braddon, 1998, p. 57)

Later, the narrator states that Aurora, "ought, no doubt, to have died of shame and sorrow after Talbot's cruel desertion" but "The lovers who die for love in our tragedies die in such a vast hurry, that there is generally some mistake or misapprehension about the business, and the tragedy must have been a comedy if the hero or heroine had only waited for a quarter of an hour. . . . people are, I hope and believe, a little wiser in real life . . . the worms very rarely get an honest meal off men and women who have died for love" (Braddon, 1998, p. 182). I asked the class whether or not they agreed that these kinds of passages, peppered throughout the novel, in fact move it away from pure sensationalism or if they are, as W. Fraser Rae argues, merely "hackneyed . . . blunders which a true artist would never commit" (1865, p. 585)? While students were about evenly divided on this question, they were all intrigued by the ways in which Braddon engages with the same questions of genre that we had been wrestling with all semester. Her purposeful attempt to shape her novel's reception in the face of hostile critics impressed students and made them think more critically about how and why the novel was designated "sensational." If nothing else, they could see Braddon as a very sophisticated manipulator of genre conventions and expectations.

A final group of students compared G. A. Sala's defence of Braddon and sensationalism in his *Belgravia* articles with the claims of Braddon's narrator. They argued that while Sala's support of the genre is founded on the assumption that sensation fiction is more "truthful" than realistic fiction because it depicts all aspects of life, Braddon actually uses her narrator to argue that "truth" is impossible to achieve in art. Sala famously claims that sensation novels depict the way "dwellers in the actual breathing world" behave (1867, p. 614). In contrast, Braddon's narrator questions the relationship between art and reality altogether by claiming that anything resembling real life would be a boring waste of time to read. This response framed a very provocative discussion about whether or not Braddon was aiming at realism or truth at all, whether or not she wanted to be a realistic writer or a writer who was actually far more sophisticated than the realists. Some students insisted that Braddon was truly ahead of her time in her questioning of the value of "Truth" and the possibility of reflecting reality in any meaningful way. This argument encouraged the class to at least consider whether or not sensationalism could be seen as superior to realism depending on what interpretive framework one chooses. As this group judged it, if one were to disregard the strict high/low cultural divide and accept Braddon's own complex redefinition of sensationalism, one might find oneself in a topsy-turvy world in which sensation rules! Ultimately, most students did not go this far in their analysis of Braddon. They did, however, seriously question genre classifications and the construction of the literary canon, which, of course, was the point of the entire class.

By the end of the semester, students were able to effectively discuss sensation fiction in a variety of ways that provide another perspective on what they learned in the course. I will quote extensively here from their final take-home exams, which included only one essay question asking them to define sensationalism, using specific examples and quotations from our course readings.[11] One student, Katie, follows Gilbert's lead in asking why sensation fiction seemed to emerge so dramatically in the 1860s. She cautions against overlooking the genre's many precursors, but does identify one important reason the genre received so much attention at mid-century: the growth of the popular periodical press. Katie argues that the press "provided reasons for more people to write popular fiction, and their writing was circulated to more readers." Furthermore, "critical writings about [these novels] also appeared" in magazines, giving sensation novels greater visibility "because critics . . . developed new ways of speaking about and classifying them." Katie also draws a connection between form and genre, noting that "The sensational features of the novels had to appear in a rhythm, usually leaving readers hanging at the end of each installment" with many of the themes and plots that engaged readers coming directly from the newspaper headlines. The press, she argues, is likewise featured in prominent ways by Braddon, Collins, and Wood as major plot points turn on discoveries printed in papers, including Anne's discovery of Laura's engagement to Percival in *The Woman in White*, the announcement of Isabel's death in *East Lynne*, and the revelation of James Conyers's demise in *Aurora Floyd*. Thus, Katie learned not only that the temporal boundary of the 1860s fails to contain sensation, but also that the genre routinely reached beyond its own page boundaries – within the periodicals in which it was published and from which it took many of its plots – to reach more readers and reviewers than earlier fictional forms.

Several other students focused on the idea that sensation fiction is actually very closely related to realist fiction (or at least to real life), that these boundaries, too, are permeable. Aaron claims that "Sensation novels recognize the tension between realism and romance and attempt to reconcile, then complicate, the two genres." He notes that "'Truth is stranger than fiction' is a cliché that resonates throughout sensationalism," citing Braddon as a concrete example of this marriage of "opposites" because she yokes realism in the form of "probable characters and settings" with the sensationalism of "an outrageous plot." Likewise, April explains that sensation novelists explored "realistic emotional responses to sensational scenarios" making "realistic behavior more entertaining than idealistic behavior" depicted in realist novels. Not only do these students question the terms by which sensationalism has typically been defined and explore its gendered elements, but they also link the genre intimately to real life, or at least to a sort of hyper-realism that destabilizes hegemonic genre categories.

Another student, Diane, conducts a meta-analysis of recent scholarship on the sensation novel, observing that it is "significant that the majority of literary scholars attempting to redefine sensationalism are women" considering that a genre "in which female writers were overrepresented was the one immediately dubbed 'low culture' by contemporary reviewers." She further elucidates the difficulties of defining the genre then and now, declaring that:

> [T]he distinction between the high-culture realist novel (George Eliot, Elizabeth Gaskell) and the low-culture sensation novel (Mary Elizabeth Braddon, Ellen Wood, Wilkie Collins) is socially constructed, and the lines between the two often blur past the point of usefulness. . . . Although Victorians often disagreed as to which genre certain novels belonged, few denied that there were certain signposts by which sensation novels could be recognized, elements that usually consigned them to be dismissed as low-culture reading material for women and servants. Among these were: plot-driven narrative, bigamy, murder mystery, sexual scandal, and, usually, location within contemporary, familiar settings. . . . These signposts, however, are inadequate to define the sensation novel because nearly all could be found in realist novels as well.

Katie similarly acknowledges the challenges faced by those who study sensation fiction with a series of questions that she claims have not been adequately addressed by current scholarship: "Are there traceable differences between Victorian sensation novels that were published serially and those that were published in book form first? What was the ratio of female to male authors of sensation fiction? What made certain subjects sensational and others not?" These questions and the other student comments I have quoted attest to the richness of sensation fiction that has too often been ignored. As Katie aptly concludes, sensation novels are so "wonderfully complex . . . I doubt that scholars will ever run out of questions to ask and angles to explore when studying this literature." As I continue to rethink and revise my approach to teaching the sensation novel, I will ask myself questions similar the ones Katie raises and try to come up with even better ways to address the diversity and complexity of sensationalism.

Appendix 1: sensation novels in print at Broadview Press, Oxford World's Classics, and Penguin (Fall 2007)

Braddon:

Aurora Floyd (Broadview 1998)
Lady Audley's Secret (Broadview 2003; Oxford 1998; Penguin 1998)
The Doctor's Wife (Oxford 1999)

Collins:

Armadale (Oxford 1999; Penguin 1995)
Basil (Oxford 2000)
Blind Love (Broadview 2003)
The Dead Secret (Oxford 1999)
The Evil Genius (Broadview 1994)
Heart and Science (Broadview 1996)
Hide and Seek (Oxford 1999)
The Law and the Lady (Oxford 1999; Penguin 1999)
No Name (Oxford 1998; Penguin 1995)
Man and Wife (Oxford 1999)
Miss or Mrs?, The Haunted Hotel, The Guilty River (Oxford 1999)
The Moonstone (Broadview 1999; Oxford 1999; Penguin 1999)
The Woman in White (Broadview 2006; Oxford 1998; Penguin 2003)

Wood:

East Lynne (Broadview 2000; Oxford 2005)

Appendix 2: percentage of courses from the Victoria Research Web featuring sensation novels

Victorian survey courses	Victorian special topics courses	Victorian novel courses
12 accessible syllabuses 2 courses; 2 sensation novels:	25 accessible syllabuses 5 courses; 9 sensation novels:	16 accessible syllabuses: 7 courses; 8 sensation novels:
• 1 *East Lynne* • 1 *Lady Audley's Secret*	• 3 *Lady Audley's Secret* • 2 *The Moonstone* • 2 *The Woman in White* • 1 *East Lynne* • 1 *Aurora Floyd*	• 2 *The Woman in White* • 2 *The Moonstone* • 4 *Lady Audley's Secret*
17%	20%	44%

Notes

1. Recent books that build on this earlier scholarship include Kimberly Harrison and Richard Fantina's *Victorian Sensations: Essays on a Scandalous Genre* (Ohio State UP, 2006); Andrew Mangham's *Wilkie Collins: Interdisciplinary Essays* (Cambridge Scholars Publishing, 2007); Andrew Maunder and Grace Moore's *Victorian Crime, Madness and Sensation* (Ashgate, 2004); Jennifer Phegley's *Educating the Proper Woman Reader: Victorian Family Literary Magazines and the Cultural Health of the Nation* (Ohio State UP, 2004); Natalie and Ronald Schroeder's *From Sensation to Society: Representations of Marriage in the Fiction of Mary Elizabeth Braddon, 1862–1866* (University of Delaware Press, 2006); Marlene Tromp's *The Private Rod: Marital Violence, Sensation, and the Law in Victorian Britain* (UP of Virginia, 2000); Tromp, Pamela Gilbert, and Aeron Haynie's *Beyond Sensation: Mary Elizabeth Braddon in Context* (SUNY Press, 2000); and Deborah Wynne's *The Sensation Novel And the Victorian Family Magazine* (Palgrave 2001).

2. Collins's *The Moonstone* is the most praised book of the genre, benefiting from T. S. Eliot's famous declaration that it is "The first . . . and the best of modern English detective novels" (qtd. in Farmer, 1999, p. 10). This endorsement sets the novel apart from its brethren in both form and quality.

3. For a complete list of the novels published by these presses, see Appendix 1.

4. I agree wholeheartedly with Maunder's contention that "the sensation novel cannot be contained tidily within a single decade" (2004, p. xiii); however, my focus here remains on the 1860s due to the fact that the novels from this period are most readily available for classroom use. Maunder's own concerns about the lack of readily available sensational literature are borne out by my survey of classroom editions. He notes that "Whilst the revivals of Collins and Braddon are well underway, the fact that very few sensation novels by their contemporaries are in print today has made it extremely difficult to assess the genre's true place in the history and development of the novel" (2004, p. xii). Indeed, the purpose of Maunder's admirable *Varieties of Women's Sensation Fiction*, from which I quote, is to broaden our understanding of the genre. Unfortunately, the books contained in the six-volume series are priced beyond the means of most individual purchasers.

5. This website can be found at http://victorianresearch.org/. The list of courses I examined excludes links that were broken and pages that were no longer accessible, which amounted to twenty-three total courses. I searched these pages on 7 August 2007.

6. For a complete overview of my findings, see Appendix 2.

7. Mather further explains: "I think that a small group of sensation novels is finding its way into the literary canon and onto syllabuses. It also seems that there is room there for one or two works by each author, and that their other works, however worthy, tend to fall by the wayside. We at Broadview see a similar phenomenon in other genres and eras, as well; when we publish more than one work by an author, particularly an author whose status in the canon is less secure, the majority of the sales tend to focus on one work while others are neglected. This is frustrating both for us and for scholars who are interested in making other works by authors like Braddon or Wood available. I'm not sure if the problem is that the group of scholars that are enthusiastic and knowledgeable about these authors' lesser-known works is quite small in the overall pool of English literature instructors, or that the courses in which these titles are used have limited enrolments – or, most likely, both" (Email Communication on 12/18/07).

8. I assigned Chapter Two of Gilbert's book, "Genre: The Social Construction of Sensation"; Chapters One, "Marketing Affect: The Nineteenth-Century Sensation Novel," and Two, "Theorizing Affect: Twentieth-Century Mass Culture Criticism," of Cvetkovich's book; and Chapter Four of Francis O'Gorman's book on "Realism."

9. The articles on periodical studies included: Laurel Brake's "Writing, Cultural Production, and the Periodical Press in the Nineteenth Century" in *Writing and Victorianism*, Ed. J. B. Bullen (London: Longman, 1997): 54–72; Linda Hughes and Michael Lund's "Textual/Sexual Pleasure and Serial Publication" in *Literature in the Marketplace: Nineteenth-Century British Publishing and Reading Practices*, Eds., John O. Jordan and Robert L. Patten (Cambridge: Cambridge UP, 1995): 143–164; and Lyn Pykett's "Reading the Periodical Press: Text and Context" *Victorian Periodicals Review* 22 (Fall 1989): 100–108.

10. I assigned Braddon's "Eveline's Visitant," Collins's "A Terribly Strange Bed," Dickens's "The Bloomsbury Christening," Gaskell's "The Great Cranford Panic," Conan Doyle's "A Scandal in Bohemia," Sharp's "In Dull Brown," and Trollope's "George Walker at Suez." Unfortunately, no stories by Wood are included in the Broadview anthology so I assigned an online version of "The Self-Convicted," which can be found at The Literary Heritage of the West Midlands website (www. literaryheritage.org.uk).

11. I am grateful to April Austin, Katie Manning, Diane Sager, and Aaron Slusher for being such interesting and engaged students and for graciously allowing me to quote from their work.

Works cited

Braddon, Mary Elizabeth, *Aurora Floyd,* Richard Nemesvari and Lisa Surridge (eds.). (Peterborough, Ontario: Broadview Press, 1998).

Chandler, Daniel (2005) "An Introduction to Genre Theory," http://www.aber.ac.uk/ media/Documents/intgenre/intgenre.html.

Collins, Wilkie, *The Woman in White*, Matthew Sweet (ed.) (New York: Penguin, 2003).

Cvetkovich, Ann, *Mixed Feelings: Feminism, Mass Culture, and Victorian Sensationalism*. (New Brunswick, NJ: Rutgers University Press, 1992).

Denisoff, Dennis (ed.), *The Broadview Anthology of Victorian Short Stories* (Peterborough, Ontario: Broadview Press, 2004).

Farmer, Steve (ed.), "Introduction," *The Moonstone* by Wilkie Collins (Peterborough, Ontario: Broadview Press, 1999), pp. 9–34.

Gilbert, Pamela K., *Disease, Desire, and the Body in Victorian Women's Popular Novels* (Cambridge: Cambridge University Press, 1997).

Manchester Guardian (1 May 1866: 7) Review of *Wives and Daughters* by Elizabeth Gaskell, Reprinted in *Elizabeth Gaskell: The Critical Heritage*, Angus Easson (ed.), (New York: Routledge, 1991), pp. 483–6.

Maunder, Andrew, "General Introduction," *Varieties of Women's Sensation Fiction: 1855–1890*, Volume 1: *Sensationalism and the Sensation Debate* (London: Pickering and Chatto, 2004), p. vii–xxxii.

——. "Mapping the Victorian Sensation Novel," *Literature Compass*, 2.1 (2005), pp. 1–33.

O'Gorman, Francis, *The Victorian Novel: A Guide to Criticism* (Oxford: Blackwell Publishing, 2002).

[Rae, W. Fraser] (1865) "Sensation Novelists: Miss Braddon," Reprinted in *Aurora Floyd*, pp. 583–92.

Rosenman, Ellen Bayuk, "'Mimic Sorrows': Masochism and the Gendering of Pain in Victorian Melodrama," *Studies in the Novel*, 35.1 (2003), pp. 22–43.

Sala, George Augustus (1867) "The Cant of Modern Criticism," Reprinted in *Aurora Floyd*, pp. 607–19.

Thomas, Robert R., "Detection and the Victorian Novel," *Cambridge Companion to the Victorian Novel*, Dierdre David (ed.), (Cambridge: Cambridge University Press, 2001), pp. 169–91.

Tompkins, Jane, *Sensational Designs: The Cultural Work of American Fiction, 1790–1860* (Oxford: Oxford University Press, 1985).

Winston, Elizabeth "Remapping and Reframing the Victorian Novel," *Nineteenth-Century Studies*, 16 (2002), pp. 103–13.

Wood, Price Ellen, *East Lynne*, Andrew Maunder (ed.), (Peterborough, Ontario: Broadview Press, 2000).

8
The Short Story: Ghosts and Spectres

Ruth Robbins

I   Introduction

> It is not worth telling this story of mine – at least, not worth writing.
> Told . . . to a circle of intelligent eager faces, lighted up by a good after-
> dinner fire of a winter's evening, with a cold wind rising and wailing
> outside, and all snug and cosy within, it has gone off . . . indifferent well.
> But it is a venture to do as you would have me. Pen, ink and paper are
> cold vehicles for the marvellous, and a "reader" decidedly a more critical
> animal than a "listener."
>
> (Le Fanu in Cox and Gilbert, 1991, p. 19)

So begins J. Sheridan Le Fanu's ghost story "An Account of Some Strange
Disturbances in Aungier Street" (1853). Its opening is in some ways genre-
defining in that it provides us with a typical situation for the ghost story's
dissemination: it is a tale told on a winter's night (preferably at Christmas),
when the weather is suitably stormy and the room pleasantly cosy in both
senses of the word (both warm and safe), in stark contrast to the dangers
without, and the horrors about to be told. This set-up introduces a truly
creepy tale in which a hanging judge infests the rooms of two young students: infests is the right word, since he sometimes appears in the guise of a
giant rat, and one of the creepiest things about the story is the "slap, slap"
of his naked feet on the stairs outside the narrator's bedroom which nearly
drives one of the students to suicide. Here is another subject for early debate:
what frightens us, and how and why are we afraid of particular things? Are
there patterns in our fear? It is a chilling subject for conversation, but it is
also, paradoxically, a pretty good icebreaker.

Perhaps most important for my purposes here, Le Fanu's narrator makes a
telling point about the valuation of the ghost story: it is not an aesthetically
respectable form, and therefore it is not worth writing down. The narrator of
this story announces a certain scepticism about the (literary) value of what
he is about to do. Telling a story orally, he suggests, is very different from

writing it, as it were, in cold blood, and readers are more critical than listeners. That is a moot point, of course, but one which first-year students might usefully begin to debate at the outset of their higher education studies. And if it is not "literary" enough to write down, perhaps it is also not worth writing about. The narrator speaks as if in fore-knowledge of the fact that, with a few well-known exceptions, criticism has not taken kindly to the Victorian ghost story: in fact, criticism has hardly noticed it at all.[1] As Harold Orel has noted, the short-story form in general was often distrusted even by its writers in the Victorian period, for whom "novels were the central commodity, and short stories a by-product, filler-material" (1986, p. 2). Additionally the Victorians in the UK, unlike Edgar Allan Poe in America, did not theorize the short story, and so did not lend it the kind of critical respectability that Poe attempted to forge for this new form of fiction. Poe, the major theorist of the form in the United States, indeed, was not widely read and known in Britain, and as Orel points out, the British version of the short story developed more or less independently of the American writer's strictures on the philosophy of composition (1986, p. ix), one key difference being that the British short story in the nineteenth century tends to be rather longer than Poe preferred. This was in part explicable by market considerations, a response to the preference for British periodicals to serialize even relatively short fiction over an extended period. For all the basic difficulties of dealing with the form, however, there are good reasons for starting entry-level students with a good old-fashioned set of scary stories.

One reason for thinking about the ghost story as a suitable subject for the instruction of the young is that it is particularly rich in terms of offering contexts through which readers can begin to complicate their responses to reading. Commenting on the ways in which Henry James's tale of psychological haunting, *The Turn of the Screw* (1898) might be read, for instance, Bruce Robbins suggests that there are a number of different contexts for James's novella. There are contexts to do with the author's life in both American and Britain; contexts of the histories of female employment and emancipation and reactions to these issues during the nineteenth century; there are histories of childhood and education to consider; and there are histories of sexuality. Almost as an afterthought, Robbins comments: "The ghost story genre [also] has its own (literary) history. And then there is the social history of the literary marketplace where ghost stories 'sell' better than more 'serious' fiction" (1995, pp. 283–4).

That afterthought is part of what this chapter is about. Without some sense of the literary history of the ghost story, and, indeed, the marketplace in which the Victorian ghost story flourished, reading *The Turn of the Screw* with anything like adequate attention is actually rather difficult. The shape of James's narrative draws strongly on that history, even as it modifies it and changes its direction. The framing of the story as a tale told, if not by an idiot, at least by one whose credibility is severely undermined, the context of the telling in a country house at Christmas to a selected audience of ghost-story connoisseurs (reprised as a setting from multiple stories of the period, including Le Fanu's tale with which I began), and the governess' story itself, with the dislocation experienced by "a fluttered anxious girl out of a Hampshire vicarage" (James, 1999, p. 4) coming to a new life filled with the possibility of romance (though that romantic vision of the future is drastically destroyed in the story's telling), is a story which belongs chronologically, generically, and structurally, if not in terms of literary technique, to the Victorians. It is with *The Turn of the Screw* that my own teaching of the Victorian ghost story ends. But in order to get to that point in the module there is much to say about the tradition within which and against which James was writing.

There is no doubt about the critical respectability of James's ghost story,[2] which has garnered a very wide range of critical attention in the last hundred years or so, though ironically, one of the major critical strands in reading this particular ghost story is, of course, to deny the reality of the ghosts and to see the narrative as primarily concerned with the psychological abnormality of the woman to whom they either do or do not appear. The critical interest in *The Turn of the Screw* is a function of a longstanding preference amongst commentators on short fiction for seeing the short story as a quintessentially modern form, and perhaps necessarily therefore also as a modern*ist* one. Any survey of the genre quickly demonstrates that the main concentration of effort in discussions of short fiction is on the post-1900 period and there is a privileging of particular forms and particular modes of experimentation. As Clare Hanson suggests, although the traditional weird tale continued to appear right through the modernist revolution, a major distinction can be made between works "in which the major emphasis is on plot and those in which plot is subordinate to psychology and mood": her own preference – and that of most other critics – is for the latter, for what Hanson herself calls "plotless fictions" (Hanson 1985, pp. 5–6). *The Turn of the Screw* ticks critical boxes because in its elliptical narrative, which leaves readers uncertain about the nature of the plot, it appears to belong more to the modern(ist) tradition than to the Victorian one. Its intellectual and aesthetic challenges are thus often deemed more appropriate to serious study, to the extent that even the champions of the Victorian short and ghost story forms often appeal to a proto-modernist nihilism as part of their "excuse" for writing about such perilous stuff (see for instance, Sullivan, 1978, pp. 2–3). Paradoxically, of course, if mood, psychology and atmosphere are the dominant notes of modernist short fiction, they are also the *sine qua non* of the good ghostly tale.

That said, it is not my intention here to make great claims about the literary merits of the ghost story when compared to the works of high modernism: it is a comparison of apples and pears, and there are, after all, other reasons than a subjective standard of literary quality for choosing particular texts to teach. In my case, teaching the Victorian ghost story is in part a pragmatic response to the difficulties students have in discussing genre as an organizing concept for their knowledge of literature when the works they discuss are very lengthy. Genre can only be understood comparatively – by reading widely within its confines to uncover what the generic features of a particular mode of writing might be. In semesterized systems where time is short and art, particularly Victorian art, is long and sometimes also has its *longueurs*, early-stage under-graduates are inhibited from focused critical commentary, or are forced into unsupported generalization, because they simply cannot read widely enough in the time permitted. Pragmatism aside, however, there are also principles at stake here in terms of pedagogy. Firstly, there is no reason why students should not enjoy what they read. The Victorian ghost story was popular in its own period for a range of reasons, and it retains that popularity with contemporary readers, and not only as cynics might believe because it is a short form that is attractive to readers with attenuated attention spans.

Additionally, however, although Michael Cox and R. A. Gilbert, editors of *The Oxford Book of Victorian Ghost Stories* (1991), the anthology from which much of the material discussed here is drawn, comment that they have made their selection on the grounds that "the story must exhibit clear literary quality" (1991, p. x), in fact, many of the stories have plots and devices which creak and clank nearly as much as the chains of Wilde's Canterville Ghost. Inexperienced readers can take confidence from the fact that they can see the joins, and can work out how the writers have designs upon them in ways that they find much harder to do when they are confronted with more seamlessly and artfully constructed fictions. In terms of enabling discussions of contexts of production and reception, of placing a fiction in its time and backgrounds, the Victorian ghost story is very much *of its time*. It opens up discussions of key concepts such as class, gender, sexuality (ethnicity can be there, though it is more often absent) in their nineteenth-century guises. With short fiction, especially the creaky sort, close reading is possible and pleasurable because the students can see how it works – or, even more pleasurably perhaps – when it does *not* work. Ideas about narrative points of view and narrative credibility are especially significant in stories in which the main event is by its nature open to doubt: contrasts between the credible (often male, often middle-class and professional) and credulous (almost always female, often labouring class, often virtually "peasant") witnesses of ghostly goings-on open up wider discussions of the making of reliable narrators in any kind of fiction. Students can learn the conventions of reliability without breaking into a cold sweat – much harder for them to do in readings of the realist canon, where the art is employed precisely to conceal the conventions that elicit the reader's trust. Additionally, of course, the common plot element of dislocation – a family moving to a new "home," which they promptly find to be unhomely because it is haunted, permits discussions of the mechanisms for the provocation of fear, including, inevitably, Sigmund Freud's discussions of the Uncanny, thus introducing the possibilities of theoretical readings. And the material world in which the stories take place tells us a lot about the Victorians' investment in material things, suggesting that one of the spectres haunting Victorian England might well have been the (spiritual) possession that might come in the wake of the possession of objects. In short, the short ghost story allows for students to cut their critical teeth via textual analysis, understandings of context, and developing understandings of concept and discussion of generic features. It also broadens the field of literary discussion – even for very early-stage undergraduates – to include some of the range of theorized readings.

Lest there are continuing doubts, I would also want to suggest here that studying a popular fantasy form like the ghost story does not mean attempting readings emptied of a larger intellectual content. If many ghost stories are conservative in function, often serving as Rosemary Jackson observes "to reconfirm institutional order by supplying a vicarious fulfilment of desire and neutralizing an urge towards transgression" (1981, p. 72), others are philosophically radical and anything but "safe." Even the simplest ghost story offers an assault on the comforting structures of binary thought, since a ghost story functions primarily on the basis of the return not so much of the repressed (though that too) but of the dead, so that the key binary of living/dead is undermined. A number of ghost stories, notably works by J. Sheridan Le Fanu and Algernon Blackwood utterly challenge the possibility of a rational universe by presenting events that are not only inexplicable by natural science but which also evade the relatively simple moral schema of theological systems – Le Fanu and Blackwood's victims are in no sense "deserving" of their fates.[3] In Julia Briggs's words:

> The ghost story's "explanations" do not operate to rationalise or demystify the supernatural events, but rather to set them inside a kind of imaginative logic in which the normal laws of cause and effect are suspended . . . The ghost story reverts to a world in which imagination can produce physical effects. (2000, pp. 123–4)

The nihilism of this kind of narrative ought to satisfy the hankering after uncertainty of even the most dyed-in-the wool modernist in search of an epistemological crisis to shore up the sense that the modernist project is more serious than anything those aesthetically and philosophically naive Victorians could have produced. In other words, if the entry to ghost fiction appears simplistic it is not entirely without artistic, intellectual, or critical merit all the same.

II   The classroom

The following discussion is based on a module I currently deliver at Leeds Metropolitan, co-designed and taught with my colleague Dr Andrew Lawson. The module is a first semester, first-year course, and as such it is one of the first modules students encounter. Its aims are consequently introductory and part of its ethos is that one of the things that students need to learn very early is *how to learn*, particularly to learn more independently than perhaps they have done in their previous educational contexts. The module is called *Reading Short Narratives* and its focus is on nineteenth-century British and American ghost stories or tales of weird phenomena. One of its key purposes is to encourage students to discuss. In order to discuss, they need to read, and they need to prepare. The delivery of the module is meant to facilitate all these elements. The reading is not difficult – the stories are short and thrilling, and two or three can easily be read at sitting. Preparation is demanded beyond reading, though, and this is encouraged through one of the delivery mechanisms. Like many literature modules contact time is divided between lectures (which provide contexts and introductions to key concepts) and seminars (turned over usually to close readings of particular texts). Our experience has tended to show that lectures, despite well-founded doubts about their pedagogic usefulness, are popular and well attended, but that seminars provoke a variety of anxieties, especially when group sizes are large. In particular, we sought to design a module and delivery method which would help students to see the value of their own and their peer group's views of the texts before them. We were encouraged to do this because of a growing sense that students did not always value the seminar experience, preferring often to be told what to think rather than thinking for themselves. There has been in recent years, in our perception, a tendency to demand "spoon-feeding" and an ongoing resistance to engage with the idea that, until one has tried to articulate a view, whether in writing or orally, it is not clear that an individual actually knows what s/he thinks.

To that end, and to support the process of learning to learn using seminar methods, *Reading Short Narratives* makes extensive use of the University's Virtual Learning Environment (VLE). This is used for very standard elements – it is a repository for the module guide, the timetable, the assessment process, supporting documentation, staff availability information, bibliographies, links to selected websites and subscription databases, relevant images, explanations of key terms, lecture handouts and so on, for example, all of which are quite common uses of a VLE. Alongside all of these information elements, however, there is also a substantial section on seminar preparation, with guided reading and week-by-week exercises which are required work for the weekly seminar. To emphasize the importance we place on this preparatory work, the seminar preparation and participation form one of the elements of assessment for the module. Half the module's marks are devoted to a learning journal in which students are required to record: (a) their initial responses to the tasks in the weekly preparation exercises; (b) record modifications to those responses that arise from seminar discussions; and (c) to offer brief reflections on what and how they learned that week. The marking criteria for the learning journal include (a) completion (it is a requirement that all tasks be attempted with some degree of earnestness); (b) commitment (one-word answers and note form are not good enough); (c) evidence in the reflective elements of the student's understanding of and sense of responsibility for his/her own learning. The other half of the marks are given to a standard academic essay on some element of the ghost story, from tutor-generated questions.[4]

This supplement to standard forms of contact delivery is very useful and works very well on the whole. As a tool to enable seminar discussion it really does work. Students know in advance what they have been expected to do and they come prepared. As an assessment tool there are some areas of doubt. Most students do this exercise well; but there is clear internal evidence in many learning journals that they do not necessarily do it as they go along and some get into trouble because their time management did not stand up to the pressure of a weekly task. (Where students do not succeed in this element, it is almost always because of non-completion of elements, with a common pattern being real effort at the start but a subsequent waning of the work ethic.) Failure, of course, is not desirable. But in terms of the necessity here for continued commitment to a task over the first 6–8 weeks of this very early module, our view is that it does test an ongoing commitment and shows us where early intervention may be required, not least since the VLE enables us to track which students have accessed the materials, and which – more seriously – have not.

Those are the practical elements of the teaching and learning. What follows in the rest of this chapter is a discussion of key elements that the module offers its participants in terms of their intellectual engagement with the Victorian ghost story genre.

III   Considering genre

Satisfactory definitions of the ghost story as a genre are notoriously hard to come by and like all definitions of genre tend towards tautology – a ghost story is a story with a ghost in it. That said, however, the Victorian ghost story, according to Cox and Gilbert can be defined thus:

> [Victorian ghost stories] reveal to the reader a spectacle of the returning dead, or their agents, and their actions; there must be a dramatic interaction between the living and the dead, more often than not with the intention of frightening or unsettling the reader. (1991, p. x)

This brief and serviceable definition is part of their justification for the selection made in the anthology *The Oxford Book of Victorian Ghost Stories*. As such it is not quite a definition of genre per se, but of genre defined for a particular purpose – inclusion in the anthology.[5] It does, however, offer a place to start with for the student reader. Its focus is on content (the returning dead and the relationship between the living and the dead), and on the effects that the telling of the tale has on the reader, which raises questions of audience response. Although there is no precise fit between this definition and that offered by Poe in essays such as "The Philosophy of Composition" (1846) and elsewhere, Poe's ideas can be used to test the various case studies (Poe, 1979). The high aesthetic ideals enunciated by Poe are not always visible in the British ghost story, since almost all of the writers of these fictions were quite deliberately supplying a commercial market for fiction, a motive that probably affected Poe too, but which he excises from his account of what he was doing. At the same time, though, Poe's emphasis on tight plotting, the careful structuring of narrative leading to a shocking denouement and to the sustaining of reader excitement over a relatively short period of reading time can be found in most of the ghost narratives considered here, which is not a particular surprise since Poe made use of weird phenomena rather extensively in the fictions for which "The Philosophy of Composition" stands as justification.

Using the Cox and Gilbert anthology does enable the development of more nuanced definitions of genre and subgenre. For example the genre we might label the "haunted house story": a number of the stories in this anthology, notably Le Fanu's "An Account of Some Strange Disturbances in Aungier Street," with which I began, the anonymous "Story of Clifford House," Rhoda Broughton's "The Truth, the Whole Truth and Nothing but the Truth," B. M. Croker's "To Let" and "Thurnley Abbey" by Perceval Landon, published between 1853 and 1908, all begin with empty houses that are soon let or inhabited by owner-occupiers who have every reason, at the outset, to regard the house in question as a boon in their existence. In three of these stories a great deal of emphasis is placed on just how marvellous the houses are, and just how cheap their rents are. Detailed descriptions are offered of their furnishings and appointments; astonishment shading into suspicious scepticism is expressed about the rent: for instance, when the narrator's husband in "Clifford House" hears the rent, he opines that there's a "a screw loose somewhere" and starts to ask questions about the drains (Cox and Gilbert, pp. 219–20), so un-commercial are the terms offered; and Elizabeth de Wynt, one of the two correspondents in "The Truth, the Whole Truth and Nothing but the Truth" expects her friend Cecilia Montresor to be extremely dubious about the demand for a very low rent of three hundred pounds per annum: "you will immediately begin to hint that there must be some terrible unaccountable smell, or some odious, inexplicable noise haunting the reception rooms" (p. 75).[6]

For students reading three or four of these very short and very similarly-structured stories for a single week's discussion, a useful exercise for learning to think about genre is to compile a list of similarities between them. Superficially the stories are very different in tone – there are first-person narrators, in all of them, but some are male and some are female, some are jokey and some are deadly serious. Superficially, too they are also different in terms of setting. Two are London houses to be let for the fashionable social season; one is a student let (on which students often have rather trenchant comments) in Dublin; one is a country house; one is a bungalow to let in the foothills of the Himalayas to European ladies anxious to escape the heat of the hot dry summer season. And yet each house has been empty a long time. All are extremely cheap. All (except Le Fanu's house) are filled with every modern convenience and are beautifully furnished.

The hint that something is wrong with them tends to come first from what we might term the credulous witness with servant girls being particularly susceptible to ghostly goings-on, with all the assumptions that this raises about both class and gender in the period. The true nature of the horror arises when the credible witness (always middle class and usually male) starts to feel the effects of the haunting, with the further comments about gender and class that this might also imply. The students are highly likely to find that in fact they cannot always accurately recall what precisely happens in each story – the inter-changeability of the various plot elements points out to them the disadvantage of too close an adherence to generic rules since it renders the stories into formulaic and repetitive performances. That discussion allows them to talk about literary quality, and to make evaluative judgements reasonably securely: all are able to decide which is the most effective story and why (and they usually choose the Perceval Landon story, since this subverts the genre established in the others, and pulls a convincing surprise on the reader). As an early introduction in discussing texts, as an exercise that enables learning to talk in seminars, to co-operate in interpretation with their peers, it works extremely well. As an approach it is obviously limited, but it is only intended as a starting point for a single week's discussion. Other clusters of stories (those that focus on family dysfunction as a reason for subsequent haunting, as several in the anthology do, or those that focus on animated corpses or corpse-like objects like Algernon Blackwood's "The Kit-Bag" and Robert Louis Stevenson's "The Body-Snatchers") will produce lists that are both different and similar, opening discussions of some of the other subgenres within the genre.

IV   Contexts: producing fear

If it is people who are haunted, the locality of this unpleasant experience in ghost fiction is more often than not a house or its near relations (the inn, for example). In the words of Andrew Smith: "Typically in the ghost story the 'monster' lives with you, invading your domestic spaces, so that 'evil' acquires a proximity to the self" (2007, p. 87). From an early discussion of the sources of fear, there are easy routes into varieties of theorized readings, in particular, the Freudian concept of the Uncanny or *Unhemilich* (unhomely/uncanny), supplemented perhaps with a discussion of Julia

Kristeva's concept of abjection. But one can also very easily introduce a quasi-Marxist, materialist approach relating to the significance of objects in Victorian culture.

In Henry James's New England-set story, "The Romance of Certain Old Clothes" (1868), the clothes of the title take on a meaning that seems excessive to readers used to living in a world of plenty. But then, when clothing was expensive, handmade, difficult to obtain, important to keep well, in which clothes were a major marker of class status, which mattered enormously; in a world in which clothes were given as gifts to convey affection, were kept extremely carefully, mended, altered, and protected from moth, it was possible to be obsessed by clothes in a way that is no longer "real" to twenty-first-century readers who buy their clothes off the shelves in Primark. That context of relative scarcity, even for the wealthy, is part of the explanation for the force that the clothes exert on the minds of the protagonists.

Similarly, illustrations of what a Victorian interior might have been like to live in can be easily obtained as source materials for discussion. Matthew Arnold may have opined that the function of criticism is "to see the object as in itself it really is," but the remarkableness of that view is emphasized strongly by a focus on the material conditions in which the Victorians lived on the whole. In a world without electric light, where the sources of light at night were flickering, unreliable, and even dangerous (neither gas nor candle light was exactly safe), inanimate objects might appear to take on a life of their own. Modern-day children still know that there are monsters under the bed and in the wardrobe, those dark spaces where they cannot see clearly at all; for the original readers of the ghost stories, the shadows spread more widely through the houses they lived in. Thus, although the details of the objects in the houses and the creepiness they evoke may both seem remote from the present, if one can reconstruct the conditions of domesticity in the nineteenth century, one can also understand those fears more clearly. There are material reasons to do with the conduct of everyday life, which supplement the psychoanalytical focus on family/familiar relations rendered uncanny by shifts in focus, and which help to explain why the Victorians displaced their minor anxieties onto the vicarious pleasures and horrors of the ghost story.

From domestic considerations, to more public issues: these can also offer fertile ground for discussions of the Victorian ghost story. It is a truism that the Victorian period was both intensely religious and also saw religious faith under consistent assault from a variety of sources, including the Darwinian theory of evolution and the technical advances of the period. It is a paradox – though one with which we still live – that an age of scientific or technological progress may provoke a spiritual(ist) backlash. The popularity of the ghost story, a form originally oral and peasant, turned into an entertainment for the literate middle classes, enjoyed enormous popularity in the context of the craze for mediums in the 1850s and 1860s, in which very large parts of nineteenth-century society sought reassurance of the existence of an afterlife through spiritualist gatherings and through orgies of table tapping and turning. The vast majority of the mediums, as Peter Lamont and others have shown, were simple frauds, and relatively easily exposed as such. This did not stop them making a good living with their "shows."[7] There were also notorious cases of the new technology of photography being utilized for fraudulent purposes: the view that the camera never lies is demonstrably fallacious in any study of Victorian spirit photographs, but it is fascinating nonetheless that science was harnessed for the purpose "proving" the existence of ghosts. Much might also be made of the technology of telegraphy, with its ghostly tappings and rappings through copper wires as a possible supplement to explain the popularity of table-tapping events. As Marina Warner observes, the notorious early (and fraudulent) mediums, Kate and Margaretta Fox, who heard ghostly rappings in Rochester, New York in 1851, heard their spirit communicator precisely in the terms of the new communication medium, telegraphy, as if the spirit world spoke in Morse Code (2006, p. 222). A parodic ghost story such as Oscar Wilde's "The Canterville Ghost" (1891) derives most of its comic effects from the juxtaposition of technology (electric light) and modern consumer products (the Paragon stain remover which is used to attack the ghost's calling card, a pool of indelible blood, the proprietary brand of oil offered to stop his chains from squeaking) with a spirit world that does not understand these phenomena, an interesting reversal which renders the material world mysterious, at least to the ghost, and regards the spirit world as mundane. Contexts such as the Victorians' vaunted sense of their own modernity are perhaps at odds with the assumption that the ghost story is an oral or peasant form – Wilde's story makes the most of the era's incongruous fascination with this ancient form, not least through the reversal of hierarchies of value: peasant versus aristocratic, British versus American, spirit versus material, values versus prices.[8]

V   Making ghost stories modern(ist): seen and not heard, or: the strange case of *The Turn of the Screw*

> [I]n or about December 1910 human character changed. . . . In life, one can see the change, if I may use a homely illustration, in the character of one's cook. The Victorian cook lived like a leviathan in the lower depths, formidable, silent, obscure, inscrutable; the Georgian cook is a creature of sunshine and fresh air; in and out of the drawing-room, now to borrow the *Daily Herald*, now to ask advice about a hat. (Woolf, 1992, 70)

This startling moment of class arrogance, and blindness to diversity in her readership (how is your cook?) in the writings of Virginia Woolf nonetheless tells us something quite important about the relationships between masters and servants, at least the official relationships, in the Victorian age. Like children, one might say, servants were seen (though only dimly, and perhaps as monsters in Woolf's version) but not heard. This is an insight which the critic Bruce Robbins has made central to his various readings of *The Turn of the Screw*. In a partial reaction against the psychoanalytically inflected readings which were central to understanding the story for most of the twentieth century, and which certainly still have mileage for all kinds of readers, including early-stage undergraduates, Robbins sets out to argue for a materialist reality to James's ghosts. In a close reading of a passage where the unnamed governess apparently comes across her "vile" predecessor, Miss Jessel, for the second time, he makes an important suggestion. The passage reads thus:

> Seated at my own table in the clear noonday light I saw a person whom, without my previous experience, I should have taken at the first blush for some housemaid who might have stayed at home to look after the place, and who, availing herself of rare relief from observation and of the schoolroom table and my pens, ink, and paper, had applied herself to the considerable effort of a letter to her sweetheart. There was an effort in the way that, while her arms rested on the table, her hands, with evident weariness, supported her head; but at the moment I took this in I had already become aware that, in spite of my entrance, her attitude strangely persisted. (1995, p. 85)

The governess, of course goes on to identify the figure at her table as Miss Jessel's apparition. But what if, Robbins asks, this "ghost" really is a servant? After all, many of the signs – her physical weariness, her clear difficulty in writing (because she is only barely literate) – make such an interpretation of this figure reasonable. Indeed, it might even be regarded as a perverse interpretation to see the servant as a ghost, as the governess does. One of the reasons for her distorted vision is the distortions on which class relations depend. We are told at the outset of the novella, in Douglas's frame narrative that the household at Bly is made up of "Mrs Grose [the housekeeper] . . . and there were, further, a cook, a housemaid, a dairywoman, an old pony, an old groom, and an old gardener, all likewise thoroughly respectable" (26). As Robbins puts it:

> The point is, of course, made with the pony. Cooks, ponies and gardeners are equal, levelled out as items on a list of Bly's possessions; none of these servants counts more than an animal. Servants, like ghosts, are something less than human beings. (1995, p. 287)

When we examine the lives of Victorian servants, it becomes clear that Robbins is partly right. For instance, in many households, servants were not even named by the given names. As Liz Stanley's edition of the diaries of

Hannah Cullwick makes clear, servants might be addressed in a variety of ways, including by forename or by surname alone; and it was not unheard of for their individual identities to be subsumed into generic names for servants such as "Mary" (1984, p. 32), so that they're known for their function (Mary is a servant's name) not for their individuality. And this sense of liminality (or marginal status) is perennial in the writings about relations between masters and servants, including in the most famous Victorian governess novel of them all – *Jane Eyre*, where, like our governess, Jane is an upper servant in a world of rigid class hierarchy, placed between the two worlds of the masters (with whom she shares cultural capital) and the servants (with whom she shares worldly dependence). It is not too far-fetched to suggest that this liminality is related to ghostliness.

It is much easier for students to make sense of this story if they start with a knowledge of the Victorian ghost story genre, and its contexts, and if they have already spent time discussing the reliability of the credible and credulous witnesses to ghostly events, and if they have already spent time thinking about the functions of frame narratives in ghost stories, about the sources of fear, and about social and material contexts of production and reception. On the whole, credulous witnesses are those who, by reason of either gender or class (and often by reason of both), lack the cultural capital to be regarded as reliable or trustworthy when bearing witness to marvellous or supernatural events. The credulous witnesses include women in general, but particularly women whose class status is low or uncertain (housemaids go into hysterics with alarming regularity, governesses for different reasons are socially marginal); they include lower-class men; they include upper- and middle-class men whose manliness is in doubt in relation to outbursts of hysteria or extreme emotion; and credulous witnesses can very often include children. Both servants (very widely defined) and children (more narrowly defined, upper- and middle-class children)[9] are figures who are meant to be socially "protected" in the Victorian worldview, who are perceived as vulnerable – whose very protection in the social world bespeaks their vulnerability in it as well. That "protectiveness" is signalled in the French phrase, *pas devant*, short for *pas devant les enfants* – not in front of the children. It is about "not" speaking about scandal, sexuality, death, and any adult matter (politics, religion) in front of those considered vulnerable and/or socially inferior. And the habit of mind that leads to social silences, euphemism and elegant periphrases, where one never calls a spade a spade, is clearly a habit of mind that is related to *The Turn of the Screw*, where repeatedly, what is actually happening is not put clearly – the very language in which it is written is elliptical, distorted, digressive, and periphrastic rather than clear and straightforward. Much of the story takes place in the silences and gaps of the governess's descriptions: and a psychoanalytical critic could (many have) have a field day with the things she refuses to say clearly (many of which appear to be related to sexuality and death – the two great taboos).

If children and servants need protection, there is also a sense in which the wider community equally needs protection from them. The danger of children and servants is their relative anarchism, figured in the likelihood that they might say or do anything: might say or do something that will disrupt the social norms of propriety and careful speech and behaviour. *Pas devant* in part because one does not wish to give children or servants the ammunition to be rebellious. Each group, one by reason of class, the other by reason of immaturity, represents a chink in the social armour – this is how societies get haunted. The upper classes are torn between their need for servants and their desire to control them; love for their children, and necessity of controlling them. Servants and children are therefore uncanny figures in themselves, making houses into homes, and at the same time metonymically representing the disorder at the heart of that home.

Appendix: sample syllabus: The Victorian ghost story

Module Descriptor: This level one module is intended as an introduction to the study of narrative through the lens of literary studies. It focuses primarily on short narratives – largely short fiction and some short narrative poems – from nineteenth-century Britain and America. The short narrative has several advantages for an entry-level module. Because the primary texts are, by their nature, very brief, students are enabled to develop close-reading skills in prose and poetry in ways that are often not possible where the primary materials are longer. In addition, the brevity of the materials permits the study of genre and narrative techniques across a historical period. In this module students will be encouraged to develop their reading skills and critical vocabulary in relation to the conventions and techniques of narrative. The module lays important foundations for all subsequent literature modules that deal with fiction.

Additionally, this module is also the location for some of the Personal Development Planning material at Level 1, by making explicit, through both delivery and assessment, the founding skills for academic study in general, and for the discipline of English in particular. It thus provides the foundation for all subsequent literary study in the course of the degree

The module is arranged around one of the commonest uses of short narratives in prose and poetry in the nineteenth century – the ghost fiction, or tale of gothic or macabre circumstances – and its development during the century as a form that enabled the discussion of abnormal psychological states. In the course of the module students will discuss, through considerations of individual examples:

- The short narrative as a genre in history – from Edgar Allan Poe's *Tales of Mystery and Imagination* to Henry James's *The Turn of the Screw*;

- Narrative shapes and the language we use to describe them (kinds of narrator, kinds of [implied] audience, frame narratives, epistolary narratives, psychological narratives, mimesis, exegesis and diegesis, conventions signalling reliability and unreliability, etc.);
- Short narratives in their historical contexts of production and reception – the way they read and wrote "then," in the nineteenth century.

Learning Outcomes: By the end of the module, students should have acquired:

a) Knowledge and understanding of a wide range of short narratives in poetry and prose;
b) An understanding of the forms that short narratives can take, and an understanding of genre within a historical period;
c) Close reading skills and a critical vocabulary relating to the structures of narrative – both in prose and poetry;
d) Study skills in relation to finding basic learning resources, using computers, reflecting on their own learning styles and processes, and becoming more self-directed in their studies;
e) Appropriate knowledge of academic conventions and scholarly practice in relation to the presentation of written assignments;
f) The ability to synthesize the above skills in the production of an end-of-module essay.

Learning and Teaching Methods: The module is taught by a combination of methods. There will be a weekly lecture, which introduces a particular topic or concept, followed by a weekly seminar, in which students discuss a particular example of short narrative. As part of the preparation for both seminars and for the eventual assessment on this module, there will also be at least one hour per week of self-directed study, delivered via the VLE platform, aimed at emphasizing the levels and kinds of preparation required in an effective HE learner, and at encouraging independence in learning. The VLE materials, alongside the seminar activities, will form a learning diary which is one of the elements of assessment for this module, and which also forms part of the Personal Development curriculum in the English and History degree.

Assessment: There are 2 items of assessment for this module:

a) Learning journal made up of the preparatory work for seminars, and reflections on seminar performance to cover at least 6 weeks of classes. This assessment is weighted at 50% of the module's total allocation of marks (learning outcomes a, c, and d);

b) Formal academic essay of c. 1500 words. The essay will discuss in detail at least one aspect of the short narrative forms covered in the module content. The essay is weighted at 50% and covers learning outcomes a, b, c, e and f.

Schedule

Week 1

Lecture: Introduction to the Module and to the Virtual Learning Environment

Seminars: Case Study 1: "The Black Cat" (distributed to you during your induction session.)

This week's classes are aimed at getting you started and at introducing you to fellow students and staff.

The lecture will focus primarily on the module's workings – what is expected of you, how to access the Virtual Learning Environment for your seminar preparation work, and other issues. In particular, this is where you will get the basic advice on how to complete your first assignment – the learning journal, which makes up 50% of the marks for this module as a whole.

The seminars this week will require you to read *in advance* the short story by Edgar Allan Poe entitled "The Black Cat" which was distributed to you during Induction week.

Week 2

Lecture: Edgar Allan Poe: History, Genre, Text: Reading "The Tell-Tale Heart"

Seminar: Case Study 2: "The Tell-Tale Heart"

The lecture provides a brief history of the genesis of the short-story form by focusing on the work of one of its primary exponents – the American author, Edgar Allan Poe. It considers basic contexts in which Poe was writing to show the ways in which we must historicize a text (i.e. how we must see it in relation to its contexts).

For the seminar this week you must read "The Tell-Tale Heart." You will also find it useful to read Poe's definition of what he called the "tale" posted on Xstream this week. Read the story and prepare your responses to the questions at the end of the story – these need to go into your logbook. In the seminar we will also consider a Crime Pamphlet from Poe's own time which we know he read to consider the ways in which he adapts and alters the "true-crime" story for his fiction.

Week 3

Lecture: Nathaniel Hawthorne, "Young Goodman Brown": Ways of Reading: allegory and the Puritan Tradition.

Seminar: Case Study 3: Interpretations of "Young Goodman Brown."

This week the lecture focuses on Hawthorne's story, "Young Goodman Brown." It places the story in its historical contexts, and raises questions about how readers might appropriately set out to interpret its meanings. Amongst the contexts considered are: Hawthorne's biography and family history; the Puritan tradition of the American Founding Fathers; the Salem Witch Trials.

For the seminar this week you must read the Hawthorne story on the VLE and answer the questions published at the end of the story in your logbook. Bring your responses to the class, and don't forget to revisit them after the class – especially if anything that happens in your seminar modifies your original views.

Week 4

Lecture: Defining the short story – the questions of genre, narrator, point of view, structures and framing devices.

Seminar: Elizabeth Gaskell's "The Old Nurse's Story" and Henry James's "The Romance of Certain Old Clothes" – Old wives' tales? (Both stories are in the anthology.)

This week's lecture discusses the basic definitions of the short story genre – drawing in part on the materials from the writer Edgar Allan Poe, but also raising other kinds of question about the nature of short-story narratives. The aim of this lecture is to ensure that you have a vocabulary for describing the genre and its evolution.

It would also be helpful if you could read the selections from Poe's review of *Twice Told Tales* by Nathaniel Hawthorne, and the essay "The Philosophy of Composition" by Poe both available from the VLE.

Seminars this week will discuss two "feminine" stories – stories, that is, focused on feminine ghosts and feminine concerns. Before you come to the seminar you should:

a) ensure that you have read the two stories carefully
b) have written responses to the questions about these stories on the VLE for this week so that you are prepared for the seminar discussion.

Don't forget to bring your notes and your primary text (Cox and Gilbert) with you. And remember, after the seminar, to make notes on any issues that the class discussions raised, and any modifications to your original views.

Week 5

Lecture: The context of the ghost story: the popularity of the genre.

Seminar: Haunted Houses . . . Rhoda Broughton's "The Truth, the Whole Truth and Nothing but the Truth"; Anon "The Story of Clifford House"; B. M. Croker, "To Let"; Perceval Landon, "Thurnley Abbey."

The lecture this week discusses the contexts in which the nineteenth-century ghost stories and tales of weird phenomena that we are reading were first published – what we might call the *context of production*. It will consider issues such as the Victorian reading public, reading and publication practices, technological advances, shifts in patterns of belief in the period.

The seminar will consider a number of stories that are based on the idea of a haunted house. The stories to discuss cover quite a long period of history, but they do share some features; so we should be able to begin to produce a definition of the ghost story genre.

Week 6

Lecture: The Uncanny – Freud's concept for explaining fear.

Seminar: Disembodied bodies: Robert Louis Stevenson, "The Body Snatcher"; Bernard Capes, "The Eddy on the Floor," Algernon Blackwood, "The Kit Bag."

This week's lecture discusses one of Sigmund Freud's most important concepts – a concept that is particularly useful for the discussion of literary texts – the concept of the Uncanny. It sets out to offer a basic definition of Freud's views about the production and reproduction of fear in Western cultures.

Seminars will discuss three particularly gruesome stories in an attempt to uncover the source of their horror: if these stories make your flesh creep, why do they do so? And is Freud's concept a helpful one in explaining their effects?

Week 7

Lecture: Short Narratives in Poetic Form: the case of Robert Browning.

Seminar: Please read all three of the poems by Browning ("My Last Duchess," "The Laboratory" and "Porphyria's Lover"). The first two will be the focus of the lecture, and the last will make up the material for seminar discussion.

An interest in weird phenomena was not confined only to the writers of prose fiction in the nineteenth century. In this week's lecture discussion will focus on another mode for expressing the short narrative, the dramatic monologue poem. This kind of poem gives both readers and writers the opportunity to explore strained psychology in dramatic circumstances. The major poets of the period made use of this genre, but Robert Browning is the acknowledged master of the form.

The seminar is designed around a close-reading exercise of one of Browning's poems, and around the kinds of interpretative problems it produces. Answer the questions published on the VLE and bring your responses to the class.

Your logbook is due for submission this week.

Week 8

Lecture: Playing with Ghosts: Oscar Wilde and Parody.

Seminar: Oscar Wilde's "The Canterville Ghost." (If you enjoy this story, you might also like to look up other stories by Wilde: in this context "Lord Arthur Saville's Crime: A Study in Duty" is particularly interesting. But you might also want to examine Wilde's parodic and subversive use of the genre of the fairy story in *The Happy Prince and Other Stories*.)

This week the lecture focuses on what happens to a genre when its key features become very well known. Parody is a form of writing which to some extent mocks an original model. It may also be, though, that parody is a kind of homage to that model. The lecture raises questions about parody and suggests possible ways of reading the parodic text.

The seminar is based on closed reading of Wilde's story in order to try to elucidate the ways in which it makes use of an existing generic model for rather different purposes.

Week 9

Lecture: How to write an essay.

Seminar: Essay planning – a discussion.

In classes this week, we want to focus on the specific skill of essay writing. We're going to spend some time thinking about how essays should be planned – including what their purposes are, and what markers might be looking for. The lecture this week will be a presentation on key issues for essay writing; seminars will be centred on a debate around a particular essay example (not one you'll actually be doing, but a sample question to think about). There is no required reading for this week's sessions, but you should (of course) complete your VLE exercise for the week; and you should get on with reading Henry James's *The Turn of the Screw* which we will discuss next week.

Week 10

Lecture: *The Turn of the Screw:* Victorian Ghost Story?

Seminar: *The Turn of the Screw.*

The lecture for this week will introduce Henry James's famous novella, *The Turn of the Screw*. It will discuss issues such as the frame narrative structure of the story, its place in literary history, its borrowings from other novels and stories of the period, and will sketch out a psychoanalytical approach to the novel.

In seminars we will undertake close readings of the novella, taking the materials from the VLE exercises as our starting point.

Week 11
Lecture: *The Turn of the Screw 2:* The Modernist Story?
Seminar: *The Turn of the Screw* Continued.

A second lecture on *The Turn of the Screw* will focus on other possible readings of the novella. It will discuss the role of the children in the novel, and of the servants, to suggest the ways in which a combination of reading methods might be a particularly fruitful way of approaching this complex text.

The seminar this week will continue our discussions of the novella in relation to its critical history of reception, it will also act as a space in which to revise and rethink some of our thinking so far in final preparation for the essay.

Notes

1. There are some studies of the genre – including Jack Sullivan's *Elegant Nightmares* (1978) and Julia Briggs' *The Rise and Fall of the English Ghost Story* (1977). Briggs has also contributed a useful essay on the form to David Punter's *A Companion to the Gothic* (2000), and Punter himself discusses the form in Volume II of *The Literature of Terror* (1980; 2nd edn. 1996). There are also a number of collections which deal with particular authors: Algernon Blackwood, for instance, who was a major influence on the horror writer H. P. Lovecraft, has a small industry devoted to his works; similarly M. R. James, the Edwardian ghost-story writer is also a popular subject. But there are relatively few surveys of the field, and both Briggs and Sullivan's books have long been out of print and are basically unobtainable except by luck.

2. The critical interest in *The Turn of the Screw* shows no sign of abating. Amongst the useful source materials for students are the Norton Critical Edition of the novella, edited by Deborah Esch and Jonathan Warren (1999); Neil Cornwell and Maggie Malone's New Casebook on *The Turn of the Screw and What Maisie Knew* (1998); and Peter G. Beidler's New Bedford Books edition of the novella with selected commissioned essays, 1995).

3. As Jack Sullivan has suggested in relation to Le Fanu's famous tale "Green Tea," the victim, a harmless clergyman, is attacked by forces he cannot explain for reasons that are not vouchsafed to the reader either, until he is driven to suicide to escape the persecution he suffers. The reason for his haunting and horrible death (that he drinks green tea to excess) is an explanatory nonsense (1978, p. 47).

4. Some of the preparatory work in the VLE is designed to support the writing of such an essay, and one seminar and one lecture are devoted to the planning and writing-up process.

5. The use of anthologies has both advantages and pitfalls. Binding together the ephemeral products of Victorian magazines into a respectable, permanent and relatively solid structure such as an Oxford University Press paperback may give the impression that these have always enjoyed a solidity and respectability since their

original publication. This would, of course, be erroneous. Beyond that objection, there is also the problem of the peculiarities of editors' choices, which can be either unhelpfully conservative (do we need another copy of "The Yellow Wall-paper"?) or unhelpfully outré (when working with genre, one needs standard examples: just how weird should the weird tale be?). The first of these problems can be dealt with in classes by bringing or showing copies of nineteenth-century magazines and journals. Their fragility and disposability (at least at one end of the literary market-place) is at least a testament to the ways in which such works were not always given the imprimatur or colophon of official culture's approval. The second is harder to manage. Cox and Gilbert do have some advantages (coverage of period; wide range of authors and types of story, range of themes and narrative devices), but even so we supplement with other stories on occasion, drawn from internet sources such as The Victorian Web; the Gutenberg Galaxy; and sites dealing with particular authors. Links to appropriate material are on the VLE pages.

6. Those questions about the drains are actually quite a useful discussion point, by the bye. Since the Victorians lived for the most part in a period in which adequate sanitation was a very recent phenomenon, and in which water-borne epidemics had taken place in recent memory, this particular interest is a way in to a discussion of wider contexts for the ghost story. Since many ghosts make themselves known via olfactory assault, drains are perhaps a material context for the fictions.

7. The histories of various forms of weird phenomena make useful supplementary and contextual material for the Victorian ghost story. Peter Lamont's biography of nineteenth-century illusionist, Daniel Dunglas Home, *The First Psychic: The Peculiar Mystery of a Notorious Victorian Wizard* (2005), provides an extremely intriguing social history of the variety of weird phenomena which fascinated the Victorians. Home's link with literature is that he is the original of Browning's "Mr Sludge: the Medium." Similarly, Marina Warner's recent book *Phantasmagoria* has much to say about the ghostliness of everyday life and the fascination which accompanied such new technological forces as telegraphy and photography. There is also a wide literature on spirit photography (see works cited for details), and uncovering the details of the case of W. H. Mumler, prosecuted for fraudulent "spirit photography" in New York in 1869 (though subsequently acquitted) is a research task that students might well be set as part of an attempt to develop their research skills. All of these contexts can be brought to bear on the ghost story as partially explanatory background.

8. At more advanced levels of study, there is perhaps also something to be said for connecting the ghost-story phenomenon to advances in scholarship into ancient history (the writings of Vernon Lee and the slightly belated M. R. James, whose antiquarians are forever stumbling across haunted artefacts or possessed possessions, are useful examples here). And equally much can be said for placing the Freudian interests in animism (where inanimate objects are endowed with life), the Uncanny and psychological effects of terror into the contexts of emerging understandings of psychology before Freud, amongst his Victorian predecessors (see for instance, Bourne-Taylor and Shuttleworth 2000 for source materials). I don't do these things in the current module, but for anyone seeking to complicate the relatively simple issues being set out here, this could be useful material.

9. As Regenia Gagnier points out in *Subjectivities*, there is a real sense in which Victorian working-class children were never children at all, since their childhoods were truncated by the necessity of wage labour. Upper- and middle-class children on the other hand, had very artificially prolonged childhoods. See Gagnier 1991, pp. 150–1.

Works cited

Briggs, Julia, *Night Visitors: The Rise and Fall of the English Ghost Story* (London: Faber and Faber, 1977).

——. "The Ghost Story," in David Punter (ed.) *A Companion to the Gothic* (Oxford: Blackwell, 2000), pp. 122–31.

Cheroux, Clement, Pierre Apraxine, Andreas Fischer, Denis Canguilhem and Sophie Schmit, *The Perfect Medium: Photography and the Occult* (New Haven and London: Yale University Press, 2005).

Cornwell, Neil and Maggie Malone (eds.), *The Turn of the Screw and What Maisie Knew*, New Casebooks (Basingstoke: Palgrave Macmillan, 1998).

Cox, Michael and R. A. Gilbert (eds.), *The Oxford Book of Victorian Ghost Stories* (Oxford: Oxford University Press, 1991).

Freud, Sigmund, "The Uncanny" (1919), in *Penguin Freud Library, Volume 14: Art and Literature*, ed. Albert Dickson (Harmondsworth: Penguin, 1985), pp. 335–76.

Gagnier, Regenia, *Subjectivities: A History of Self-Representation in Britain, 1832–1920* (Oxford: Oxford University Press, 1991).

Hanson, Clare, *Short Stories and Short Fiction, 1880–1980* (London: Macmillan, 1985).

Hart-Davis, Adam, *What the Victorians Did for Us* (London: BBC Books, 2002).

Jackson, Rosemary, *Fantasy: The Literature of Subversion* (London: Methuen, 1981).

James, Henry, *The Turn of the Screw* (eds.) Deborah Esch and Jonathan Warren (New York: Norton, 1999).

Jolly, Martin, *Faces of the Living Dead: The Belief in Spirit Photography* (London: Mark Batty, 2006).

Lamont, Peter, *The First Psychic: The Peculiar Mystery of a Notorious Victorian Wizard* (London and New York: Little, Brown, 2005).

Orel, Harold, *The Victorian Short Story: Development and Triumph of a Literary Genre* (Cambridge: Cambridge University Press, 1986).

Poe, Edgar Allan, *Selected Writings of Edgar Allan Poe: Poems, Tales, Essays and Reviews* (Harmondsworth: Penguin, 1979).

Punter, David, *The Literature of Terror*, 2 volumes (London: Longman, 1980; 2nd edition 1996).

Renner, Stanley, "'Red hair, very red, close-curling': Sexual Hysteria, Physiognomical Bogeymen, and the 'Ghosts' in *The Turn of the Screw*," in Peter G. Beidler (ed.) *Henry James: The Turn of the Screw*, Case Studies in Contemporary Criticism (Boston and New York: Bedford Books, 1995), pp. 223–41

Robbins, Bruce,"'They don't count much, do they?': The Unfinished History of *The Turn of the Screw*" in Peter G. Beidler (ed.) *Henry James: The Turn of the Screw*, Case Studies in Contemporary Criticism (Boston and New York: Bedford Books, 1995), pp. 283–96.

Smith, Andrew, *Gothic Literature*, Edinburgh Critical Guides (Edinburgh: Edinburgh University Press, 2007).

Stanley, Liz (ed.), *The Diaries of Hannah Cullwick: Victorian Maidservant* (London: Virago, 1984).

Sullivan, Jack, *Elegant Nightmares: The English Ghost Story from Le Fanu to Blackwood* (Athens, OH: Ohio University Press, 1978).

Warner, Marina, *Phantasmagoria: Spirit Visions, Metaphors and Media* (Oxford and New York: Oxford University Press, 2006).

Woolf, Virginia, *A Woman's Essays*, ed. Rachel Bowlby (London: Penguin, 1992).

9

Fiction and the Visual Arts

Richard Pearson

I

Reading novels in the nineteenth century involved a process of engagement that is largely impossible to replicate today. The works of writers such as Charles Dickens and William Makepeace Thackeray appeared in forms that no longer exist as a commercial publishing mode. They were released in serial numbers, published month by month in their own part-issue wrappers containing illustrations and trade advertisements. Or they appeared as monthly or weekly serializations in magazines of the period, sometimes illustrated, and always surrounded by the articles and news items of other writers. After the serial run, their numbers were then usually gathered together and published as volumes. These were generally in three-volume format, designed specifically for the circulating libraries to be borrowed a volume at a time.

Today, students will invariably be sitting in the classroom with a text that bears little resemblance to the original. Not only do modern editions conceal the serial structure of the narrative, but they strip away the visual registers that provided the original context for the novel. In many ways, the modern visual register of these new editions symbolically imitates the transfer of a text from the popular marketplace into the canon of English Literature. In Penguin and Oxford World's Classics, we generally read Dickens under the wrappers of a fine art painting. Although some editions try to maintain a link between Dickens and the comic caricature, for example, and many now reprint the original illustrations to Dickens's text, the effect remains a distancing one. Current editions of Penguin's *Dombey and Son, Bleak House, Our Mutual Friend, Edwin Drood, Hard Times, The Old Curiosity Shop, Oliver Twist, Great Expectations, A Tale of Two Cities,* and even *Sketches by Boz,* all come wrapped in a Royal Academy painting, even if it is one of a street scene or scene of urban poverty.

Challenging this repackaging can be a rewarding experience for students, and can make them aware of the cultural transformations in which literary studies is itself engaged. Moving from the idea of the coherent, unified, and harmonious text of New Criticism to the complex play of signifiers and historicist contexts that is post-structuralism, can suggest to students the way extra-textual materials can deconstruct our ideas of a novel (O'Gorman, 2002, pp. 214–15). It is the purpose of this chapter to explore Dickens's relationship with both fine art and the field of popular illustration, and suggest ideas for investigating this visual material when studying his fiction – and nineteenth-century fiction more generally. As contributors to Carol T. Christ's and John O. Jordan's important collection *Victorian Literature and the Victorian Visual Imagination* (1995) make clear, this relationship is not a straightforward one in the nineteenth century; literature and art do not exist in isolation, but compete and similarly circulate in a relational marketplace that is at once different and symbiotic.[1] In today's internet culture, we see something of a return to the Victorian interdisciplinary exchange between image and text; in convergeance, we find a pervasive and insistent combination of media that moves us away from the mono-disciplines of the twentieth century. Making positive use of internet resources can help to establish those webs of association that demonstrate how seemingly disparate cultural productions are related, both in the professional and historical contingencies of a vibrant culture, and in the aesthetic relationships between cognate works in a complex network of industry, production, and commodification.

II

A lot has been written on Dickens and the visual, particularly in relation to his illustrators, Cruikshank and Phiz, but also on his relationship to visual caricature, and the additional meaning sometimes encoded in the illustrations. One of the more famous examples is the image of Edith Dombey descending a (also metaphorical) staircase, flanked at the bottom by statues of a voluptuous Venus and the sacrifice of Iphegenia in *Dombey and Son*.[2] Because of this familiarity, I will focus on two lesser known examples of Dickens's relationship with the visual arts: firstly, his dispute with the Pre-Raphaelites, and particularly John Everett Millais, in the 1850s, and, secondly, the complicated sequence of illustrators for *Great Expectations* (1860–1) and how visual interpretations of the ending of the novel can assist discussions of the novel in the classroom.

Dickens's writing existed in close proximity to the visual arts of the period. Not only did his first novelistic production, *The Pickwick Papers* (1836–7), emerge out of a series of comic prints by Robert Seymour, but throughout his life, Dickens's novels stimulated artists to paint his characters and scenes. As Andrew Sanders notes, Dickens was a close friend of the Irish artist, Daniel Maclise and the Royal Academician and theatre scenery painter, Clarkson Stanfield. He was also intimate with William Frith, Edwin Landseer, and

Augustus Egg (2003, p. 180). There are well-known oil portraits of Dickens by Maclise in 1839 and Frith in 1859. Indeed, the range of Hogarthian characterization and dramatic incident present in Frith's great contemporary paintings, *The Derby Day* (1858) and *The Railway Station* (1862), can be paralled to the vast and highly populated "canvases" of a Dickens novel. These latter works suggest a battle that was taking place in high art during the Victorian period; historical and classical paintings, landscapes and portraits that had long been the province of the Academy were giving way to street characters, urban vistas, and paintings reflecting the buildings and infrastructure of the new industrial age. The professionalization of the author and painter was taking place simultaneously. Like Dickens's novels, Frith's canvases cross the boundary between popular and high art, disturbing their distinctiveness and confronting traditional views.

Dickens's career was also bound up with the theatre, from his early plays in the 1830s like *The Village Coquettes*, *Is She His Wife?*, and *The Strange Gentleman*, to the mid-serial adaptations of his novels, his plays with Wilkie Collins and private theatricals at Tavistock House, and his arrangements to adapt novels like *A Tale of Two Cities* (Dubrez-Fawcett, 1952, pp. 13–14). Scenery painters, technical stage effects, and the costumery and physical theatre of the actors, all contributed to a visualization of Dickens's texts with which he interacted. Michael Slater has discussed Dickens's attendance at the theatre to watch dramatizations of, for example, *Nicholas Nickleby*, produced before he had written the ending to his novel (1982, p. 245). This was one of the effects of monthly serialization, but must have been both an odd experience for the writer and an influence, however subtle, on the way Dickens imagined the finished text.

Most of Dickens's novels were illustrated, and so it might seem slightly perverse to focus this chapter on one of the non-illustrated ones, *Great Expectations* (1860–1). However, this novel provides a good example of just how pervasive and insistent the visual could be in relation to Dickens's work, and how it was illustrated after all. It also provides students with an interesting connection to the world of the fine arts and helps us to reflect on Dickens's views on art and how we might consider his own aesthetic ideals in relation to his understanding of modern art.

Before getting to *Great Expectations*, we need to situate Dickens's work in relation to illustration and the art world. *Great Expectations* (December 1860–August 1861) followed *A Tale of Two Cities* (April–November 1859) in Dickens's own (unillustrated) magazine, *All the Year Round*. In order to maintain the popularity of the visual representations of his works, and probably to capitalize on the extended readership of a double market, Dickens's publishers, Chapman and Hall, brought out *A Tale of Two Cities* in a monthly collation of the weekly parts, and bound these with a set of two illustrations by Dickens's regular illustrator, Hablot Knight Browne ("Phiz").[3] At the same time, the novel was serialized in America, slightly behind the English edition, in *Harper's Magazine,* from May–December 1859. *Harper's* was illustrated and John McLenan rapidly drew an accompanying set of plates. Dickens was unhappy with the Phiz drawings and their professional relationship ended after running for almost all of Dickens's career, from *The Pickwick Papers.*[4] Phiz's last set of illustrations were something of a hybrid. They reflect the comic grotesques and caricatures he was well-known for and that had visualized Dickens's works for over two decades. Good representations of these are, for example, "A visit to the Brickmaker's" or "The Smallweed Family" from *Bleak House,*[5] or "The Marshalsea becomes an orphan" and "The family dignity is affronted" from *Little Dorrit.*[6] Students can be asked to consider how, and to what extent, the later illustrations seem to capture something of the new seriousness and darker mood of Dickens's work, and it was this side that Dickens seemed to want to stress more.

Dickens was moving on and beginning to distance himself from the visual iconography of the 1840s and early 1850s. Something of this is due to the breakdown of Dickens's family life (he left his wife for Ellen Ternan in 1858), and an attempt on his part to formulate a new public image. But part is also due to the changing tastes of the day. Illustrations in the 1860s were more "realistic," less "grotesque," more restrained in subject if perhaps more flowing in style. Marcus Stone, the son of Dickens's friend, the watercolourist Frank Stone, was chosen as illustrator for *Our Mutual Friend.* His work gives a good flavour of the new style in images such as "Pa's Lodger and Pa's Daughter" or "Mr. Wegg prepares a grindstone for Mr. Boffin's Nose,"[7] the latter being about as near to caricature as Stone gets (which isn't very far) but one can guess at what Phiz might have made of the subject. *Great Expectations,* then, falls on the threshold of a change in Dickens's approach to his work. The illustrations offer a new style for a new era in Dickens's life and career; the 1860s left the 1850s behind. Or did they?

In 1859, Dickens was drawn back to the early days of the 1850s and a heated debate over aesthetic principles that occupied him at that time. The occasion was his being approached by John Everett Millais to allow Dickens's favourite daughter, Katie, to sit for a painting, *The Black Brunswicker* (1860). Katie was getting to know the Pre-Raphaelite Brotherhood as she prepared to marry Wilkie Collins's artist brother, Charles Collins, a one-time associate of the PRB – a match that Dickens privately thought a mistake (she was 20, he was 32). When they married in 1860, William Holman Hunt, who had returned from the Middle East, was a guest. The significance of this event demonstrates how much Dickens's life overlapped with the development of the visual arts. At the same time as he was reconsidering the illustration of his works (and, indeed, the staging of his works, having worked closely but unhappily with Tom Taylor on the staging of an adaptation of *A Tale of Two Cities* in January 1860), he was being drawn to reconsider his views of an artistic movement he had notoriously attacked a decade earlier. And that movement itself was on the cusp of a significant change: *The Black*

Brunswicker marked the transition for Millais from the precision, detail, and confrontation of Pre-Raphaelite painting to a freer, more broadly realistic, and more domestic style. In the 1860s, Millais was to turn to illustration (of Trollope's novels, in particular), and become a member of the Royal Academy in 1863. Millais also illustrated for Thackeray's *Cornhill Magazine* and for the popular magazine, *Once a Week*, a rival to Dickens's *All the Year Round*. Collins, meanwhile, followed his brother Wilkie into the pages of *All the Year Round* with a series called "Our Eye-Witness," published as a volume in 1860.

A decade earlier, things had been very different. The Pre-Raphaelite Brotherhood ("PRB") had been founded in 1848 by a group of young paint-ers eager to reassess artistic ideals and challenge the conformity of the regular Royal Academy members, such as Maclise, Stanfield, and Eastlake. In 1849, Millais, Hunt, and James Collinson exhibited at the Royal Academy Exhibition, Millais's offering being *Isabella*.[8] Frank Stone wrote a review that criticized the new school of art in the *Athenaeum*, and received a scathing attack on his own work in return by Dante Gabriel Rossetti in *The Critic* in 1850. Stone launched a new and more withering denunciation of Pre-Raphaelite ideas, and his friend Dickens waded into the fray with an equally mocking article in *Household Words*, "Old Lamps for New Ones," on 15 June 1850.[9] The subject of Dickens's attack was Millais's materialistic and meticulously detailed *Christ in the House of his Parents*, showing the boy Christ cutting his hand in his father's carpentry workshop in a prophetic analogy to the crucifixion. Dickens called the painting "mean, odious, repulsive, and revolting" and described the figure of Christ as "a hideous, wry-necked, blubbering, red-headed boy, in a bed-gown." Mary he saw as "a kneeling woman, so horrible in her ugliness," whilst "nobody is paying any attention to a snuffy old woman who seems to have mistaken the shop for the tobacconist's next door, and to be hopelessly waiting at the counter to be served with half an ounce of her favourite mixture." Of Joseph and the carpenters, he said, "[t]heir very toes have walked out of St. Giles's" (qtd. in Slater, 1996, p. 245).

It is worth getting students to tease out some of the differences between the aesthetic ideas of Dickens's criticism and the new ideas of the PRB. At the heart of his comments lies his view that Art should inspire the human spirit. The new movement was rejecting everything from Raphael onwards, "all religious aspirations, all elevating thoughts; all tender, awful, sorrow-ful, ennobling, sacred, graceful, or beautiful associations" (p. 244). Students should be able to see that Dickens's aesthetic is infused with the sprit of progress and anything seeming to turn the clock back is to be resisted, what he calls "the great retrogressive principle." Medievalism intends for "the abolition of all but manuscript books," and Pugin, he says, will supply the world with these "in characters that nobody on earth shall be able to read" (pp. 246–7). Stylistically, he is also offended by the "subversion of all known rules and principles of perspective" in Pre-Raphaelite art, along with the "mere handicraft" implicit in a detailed dedication to realism without higher purpose. The PRB, he mocks, "[realize] Hogarth's idea of a man on a mountain several miles off, lighting his pipe at the upper window of a house in the foreground" and "every brick in the house will be a portrait; . . . the man's boots will be copied with the utmost fidelity from a pair of Bluchers sent up out of Northamptonshire for the purpose; and . . . the texture of his hands (including four chilblains is, a whitlow, and ten dirty nails) will be a triumph of the Painter's art" (p. 247). It is significant to note that when commencing *Great Expectations* with this article fresh again in his mind from the approach by Millais, Dickens engages with the question of class snobbery (hinted at in his own responses) and includes imagery and thematic ideas around bricks, "coarse hands and thick boots."

Aesthetically, and despite our frequent use of Dickens's descriptions as examples of the realities of Victorian society, he was against realism for its own sake. As Harry Stone remarks of *Great Expectations*, "it is a narrative that partakes of fairy-tale transformatic, a narrative that fuses autobiographical, sociological, psychological, and mythological elements into a deeply resonant unity, a unity that is at once esoteric and realistic" (1979, p. 337). A consideration of the principles comically expressed in "Old Lamps for New Ones" demonstrates how literature and painting responded to each other. Dickens as a journalist writes on the controversial subjects of his day, as much cultural issues as social ones. But a comparison of *Christ in the House of his Parents* with *Great Expectations*, or with Dickens's approach to realism more generally, is not just about Dickens's response to the Pre-Raphaelites. It invites students to think also about the cultural challenge those artists represented and their attack on the complacency of Progress they saw in Victorian society. It took Dickens until *A Tale of Two Cities* and *Great Expectations* to begin to reject the idea that self-help and a good heart were enough to build Copperfieldian happiness. As will be seen, he did so in a period where he re-fashioned his own self-image and found himself connecting with a Millais also embarked on a re-moulding of *his* artistic identity.

III

At the beginning of 1860, Millais applied to Dickens to allow Katie to sit for him, and this was agreed provided she was chaperoned by "an old lady friend" (Brown et al., *Letters* IX, 1997, p. 240).[10] The sitting and painting took three months, from February to April, and the finished painting was shown at the Royal Academy in May 1860. The marriage to Collins took place in June.

The Black Brunswicker is a painting about love and sorrow, about choices and mistakes, and different kinds of duty (military/domestic).[11] It plays in the gaps between the characters' blissful ignorance of impending catastrophe, the wife/female lover's intuitive sense of the wrongness of parting, and the audience's knowledge of the fate of the Brunswickers. The black Brunswickers, known from their black uniforms and death's head badges, with their motto "Death or Glory," suffered heavy losses at the battle of Quatre Bras in 1815, the prelude to Waterloo (foretold in the picture of Napoleon on horseback on the wall). Students may not be experienced in "reading" paintings but asking them a fairly straightforward question: *what do you see?*" can be a useful starting point. Millais symbolizes the clash of values between the couple – the Brunswicker's determination and controlled decision, seen in the way he tries to open the door, and his partner's equally determined criticism, trying to hold the door shut by the handle, pressing his breast, and looking away. The contrast between the black of his uniform and the white of her silk dress displays the tension between right and wrong, hope and death, whilst the splash of the red sash tied around the sleeves of the girl's dress presages the spilled blood of the soldier and the torn heart of the girl left behind (see Figure 9.1).

Dickens commenced the run of his serial novel six months after the picture was shown. Given that his daughter was the subject, it seems reasonable to suppose that he went to see it. Whether the painting influenced the novel or not is worth conjecturing. As students will hopefully realize, there are interesting thematic and aesthetic parallels. *Great Expectations* is a novel about parting and loss. It begins with a scene depicting the isolated orphan boy looking at the graves that mark the loss of his own family: a family that he will never find again (many of Dickens's early characters – like Oliver Twist, for example – find at least surrogate families, but Pip's fate is a darker and more lonely one). The parting from Joe to go to London, the loss of Estella, and then of Biddy, the death of Magwitch his creator-parent, and even the collapse of his own identity ("I was a brick in the house wall, and yet entreating to be released from the place where the builders had set me") (2002, pp. 482–3), all explore the theme of parting and loss, and particularly the ending in which Dickens famously originally intended to separate Pip and Estella entirely, and then was persuaded by Edward Bulwer-Lytton to make it more ambivalent.[12]

The Black Brunswicker also suggests a link to the theme of "expectations." Millais's painting posits that the soldier departs with his own high expectations, of success on the battlefield, of future glories and promotions of rank. Like Pip's, his journey will be a perilous one, a gamble in some ways, and may end in glory or death, as Pip's might end as a "gentleman" or on the gallows he sees in the first chapter and is later shown in Newgate (p. 55; p. 196). Both Millais and Dickens are interested in the vagaries of fortune and chance, and both play upon the reader's/audience's uncertainties about the fate of the central figures. As Martin Meisel describes, Victorian painting was inherently "narrative" and demanded to be "read" for the potential stories it revealed.[13] From a still image, Victorian painters wove a timeline that extended into the past and the future of the current moment. In *The*

Figure 9.1:   John Everett Millais, The Black Brunswicker. Reproduction courtesy of
Lady Lever Art Gallery, Liverpool.

Black Brunswicker, we piece together the history of this couple: their neatness and closeness together, the playfulness of the little dog towards the soldier that indicates he is a frequent and popular visitor. Perhaps there is a hint that their relationship is a snatched one, undertaken behind doors and in corners. But their love appears a genuine and tender one. Behind the couple, Napoleon's rearing horse indicates the battle to be fought, whilst the covered item or baggage on the floor has the ominous appearance of a gravestone.[14] The door symbolizes those future potential endings and the conflicts of home versus social duty, or commitment to a relationship versus commitment to the self.

Great Expectations is also a work about defeat. As the Brunswickers stride out to defeat at Quatre Bras, so Pip travels to London on top of his coach, full of the hopes and dreams of an ambitious young man, only to see these dreams fade and dashed. Dickens's novel is in the form of a *bildungsroman*, a self-narrative of a developmental journey to maturity. It is well-known that Dickens re-read *David Copperfield* prior to writing it, another archetypal *bildungsroman*.[15] What is different about *Great Expectations* is its arrival, not at the coalescence of personality or identity, but at its fragmentation, the alienation implied in Lyn Pykett's description of "the unmaking and remaking of Pip's identity as he is taken out of the forge and 'forged' as modern urban subject" (2002, p. 167). Pip does not arrive at family and marriage, in the traditional manner of the domestic novel. Instead, the "family" excludes him, and consists of Joe, Biddy, and "little Pip" ("his little likeness" (p. 522), whilst the marriage is uncertain.

Although Forster considered Pip and Estella to marry, Dickens nowhere states this but uses the ambiguous final line "I saw the shadow of no parting from her" (p. 503). This itself was revised from the manuscript's "I saw the shadow of no parting from her but one" – i.e. death; and, in the first volume edition, became "I saw no shadow of another parting from her." Clearly wrestling with the syntax of his final line, Dickens nevertheless presents us with something that mirrors the emotions of Millais's painting. The ambiguity is present in the single person narrative: initially, Pip sees the "shadow" of their union, which implies either its lack of completeness or distinctness, or its lack of actuality. In the revised version, Pip *foresaw* no shadow, but that seems not to preclude the possibility of the shadow arriving, and thus the parting taking place. That lack of knowledge of the future is the crux of Millais's *The Black Brunswicker*. The characters in the painting, whilst holding to each other, are lost in their separate thoughts: he with his eyes down and almost closed, she with her face and look averted. The touch between them is important, but their averted gaze and their touch of the door reflect the gap that exists between them as individuals. The looking away is a form of alienation, an expression of subjectivity, that precludes the one-ness that the situation demands. Their push/pull of the door indicates the difference of opinion about the future, their focus on self-defining, as wife, as hero.

Pip, too, imagines the narrative of himself as hero, a future projection that also fails to materialize (p. 261). *Great Expectations* ends with just such an existential individualism, a lack of mutuality and unreachable intersubjectivity, that stresses the isolation of the individual. This resistence to closure can best be seen in the illustrations to the ending of the novel.

IV

Although not illustrated in *All the Year Round*, *Great Expectations* was given illustrations, without Dickens's input, in the American edition for *Harper's Weekly*, and in subsequent volumes, beginning with the Library Edition of Dickens's Works that he oversaw himself in 1862. The *Harper's* illustrator was John McLenan who had also illustrated *A Tale of Two Cities*. Marcus Stone drew the eight plates for the Library Edition of 1862, and F. A. Fraser the 28 illustrations for Chapman and Hall's posthumous Household Edition of 1875. The 27 plates by Harry Furniss for the Charles Dickens Library Edition of 1910 are also an interesting comparison.[16] All are available online as a teaching resource.[17]

Keeping with the topic of "endings," students might be asked to consider the four illustrations of the final meeting between Pip and Estella. These provide us with a variety of interpretations, or "readings," of the final scene of the novel. They form an intriguing quartet in which four different readings are presented (there is no evidence to indicate that they knew each other's work before embarking on the illustrations, but this is a possibility, particularly for the later artists).

McLenan's "I saw the shadow of no parting from her" (Figure 9.2) shows an upright and heroic-looking Pip gazing off into the distance, whilst the demure Estella gazes longingly on his face under the moonlight. They clasp each other and stand together in a conventional pose that suggests their future marriage and the strength derived from their mutual sufferings. The ruined and overgrown walls of Satis House are behind them (literally and metaphorically) and they, or at least Pip, look to the future. Marcus Stone's drawing (Figure 9.3) is completely different. "With Estella After All" hints at the ambiguity of the ending in the double meaning of "after all we have been through" and "surprisingly, when it didn't seem likely." But the image of the rough and aged Pip being touched tenderly by the brighter, moonlit Estella, suggests the angelic influence of her name and nature (the starry sky above), and *her* future role as *his* support. Her timidity towards him is also caught though, and she leans in to him with a tentativeness that emphasizes the damage done to Pip. Both of these drawings suggest a coming together, but the first places the strength in Pip and the second in Estella.

Fraser's "We sat down on a bench that was near" (Figure 9.4) represents a more separate and emotionally cooler view of Pip and Estella. Pip looks more anxiously towards Estella, whilst she looks down less hopefully into her lap

Figure 9.2:   John McLenan, "I saw the shadow of no parting from her."[18]

and avoids his eye. There is a slight leaning together between them, but it is only slight, and Pip's phallic-looking gesture with his cane does not look likely to succeed. They appear more like a couple about to part than one about to marry. The weeds around them signify the withered nature of their love (alongside a rather sorry-looking rose), whilst the slender bench suggests a fragility and awkwardness to their meeting. Estella's unhappiness is plain to see, and Pip sits uncomfortably like the young boy who was always shy of her.

Philip V. Allingham comments how Fraser's illustration "in itself does not afford closure, only the fragile possibility of closure."[19] In the final image, Furniss's 1910 "Estella and Pip" (Figure 9.5), the individuated isolation of the two figures is even more strongly marked.

Figure 9.3:   Marcus Stone, "With Estella after all."

Looking like a wedding procession, but set in a textually inaccurate grave-yard, the image portrays a bowed and haggard Pip alongside an indifferent, upright, and unmoved Estella. Pip looks broken and defeated by life; Estella appears to be the same proud beauty she had always been. The willow tree behind captures this same contrast of robust springtime and weeping sorrows. Neither Pip nor Estella make the slightest effort to look at each other, and the relationship looks forced and unwanted. Pip's brokenness is final; his personality looks as though it will be subsumed in the powerful aura of his wife. There is no shadow of a happy ending here.

Although in this instance I have been considering the ending of the novel, illustrations generally are a useful way to enter a text and usually help students to identify and explore key scenes, characters and conflicts. These four illustrations to *Great Expectations* offer a way to read the ambiguity of the ending of the novel through four clearly different interpretations. They also demonstrate

Figure 9.4: F. A. Fraser, "We sat down on a bench that was near."

the complex relationship between the visual arts and fiction. Unlike Millais's painting, they are directly derived from the source of the novel, even, as with Stone's, connected directly to the author. But they also offer us a view of how illustration can be an intervention in meaning, a critical representation of the novel that can mirror the author's nuances or challenge and contradict them. Do they, students might be asked, reflect historical time – will an image from 1862 perforce be different from one produced in 1910? This is difficult to determine, especially with a text so well-known as *Great Expectations*, and where any illustrator is likely to be influenced by previous interpretations.

V

How then might visual material be incorporated into the classroom? The task is not difficult. Students, with their pervasive use of computer technologies, inhabit a visual-textual world that shapes their imaginations. As film adaptations of texts have provided a televisual orientation for reading and interpreting well-known novels, so illustration and art can provide a graphics/text interplay. There are plenty of good examples of visual materials to use in studying nineteenth-century literature: the Brontës were consummate drawers, especially Emily; Thackeray sketched his own illustrations;

Figure 9.5:   Harry Furniss, "Estella and Pip."

the Moxon Tennyson provides Pre-Raphaelite and Royal Academy artists'
illustrations to various poems; Rossetti and Morris worked in paint/print
and literary media; Beardsley's drawings can be used alongside studies of
Wilde or the Decadent poets. Students respond well to this material, but
it is important to have access to computer and data-projector facilities in
a seminar when using them. Where there are different illustrations of the
same scene, the seminar can be broken up into smaller groups and each
group tasked with providing a discussion of one illustration. Each can then
be discussed and comparisons made. For the more creative-minded, students
can be asked to sketch out an illustration for a scene themselves, either as a
group or individually, and then discuss it with their peers to come up with
a singular interpretation of a particular scene of the text. This encourages
them to identify key elements and visual imagery, as well as to encapsulate

the relationships between characters, the personality of an individual character, or the style of description used by an author.

One productive method is to use a mid-semester assignment of a "portfolio," where students research a topic and set out four or five "documents" and provide a commentary. One of these documents can be a visual image. The portfolio helps to develop student research skills and if they draw on other art forms it makes them think about the relationships between different modes of artistic expression. In the study of some writers, the mode of publication makes the study of the visual a key component anyway (*Alice in Wonderland* has really to be seen with John Tenniel's drawings, for instance). Studying the illustrations or connected artworks can improve students' technical language. Again like student discussions of films, they tend to have a limited vocabulary when it comes to things like film theory or the explanation of semiotics. Providing a framework within which to discuss the visual improves the overall sophistication of essay arguments.

The relationship between fine art and fiction is more subtle and problematic than that of illustration (which is always intended to be connected to the text). Millais's *The Black Brunswicker* has a direct and close connnection to Dickens and his family at a time of particular sensitivity. But it is impossible to say what if any conscious or unconscious influence the painting might have had on the composition of *Great Expectations*. That both works were engaging with a growing cultural awareness of individualism, and grappling with the issues connected to gender difference, may be the main reason why they approach similar themes. In order further to explore this, taking students to a relevant art gallery can be a rewarding experience. Obviously, galleries with a strong nineteenth-century art collection are the most readily applicable, where students can gain a sense of this commonality or shared experience that artists in a cultural period may possess. Setting students the task of identifying common themes in three paintings, or looking at the relationship between story and image in works that depict literary scenes, Biblical or mythological stories, enlivens the kind of topics indicated in this chapter. But contemporary galleries are also useful for exploring the differences between literary forms: realism and modernism, for instance, or the postmodern resistance to narrative.

The interrelationship between the arts, the pervasiveness of visual imagery in the printed texts of the period, and the networks of writers and artists who naturally crossed what have become disciplinary boundaries, present us with significant cultural contexts against which to study nineteenth-century fictional narratives. One hundred and fifty years ago people did not see forms of art as exclusive or self-contained as perhaps we do today. The idea of a novelist also being a poet, or a sculptor also being a playwright, is anathema in our own specialized times. For the literate population of mid-Victorian Britain, however, literary and visual expression were interactive and symbiotic, and the multimedia of our near future provides us with a good opportunity to explore such interactivity with our students.

Notes

1. See also: Karl Josef Höltgen, Peter M. Daly and Wolfgang Lottes (eds.) *Word and Visual Imagination* (Erlangen: Universitätsbund Erlangen-Numberg 1988); J. Hillis Miller *Illustration* (London: Harvard University Press, 1992); Stuart Sillars, *Visualisation in Popular Fiction, 1860–1960* (London: Routledge, 1995); Stephen Behrendt "Sibling Rivalries: author and artist in the earlier illustrated book" *Word & Image* 13.1 (1997), pp. 23–42; Peter Sinnema, *The Dynamics of the Printed Page* (London: Ashgate, 1998).
2. For a useful overview see: Stein, Richard L. "Dickens and illustration", in *The Cambridge Companion to Charles Dickens*. Ed. John O. Jordan (Cambridge University Press, 2001), pp. 167–88.
3. For a recent biography, see Valerie B. Lester, *Phiz: The Man who drew Dickens* (London: Chatto and Windus, 2006).
4. For a summary and examples of Phiz illustrations, including those for *A Tale of Two Cities*, see David Perdue's *Charles Dickens pages* at http://charlesdickenspage.com/illustrations.html.
5. Ibid., http://charlesdickenspage.com/illustrations-bleak_house.html
6. *The Victorian Web*, http://www.victorianweb.org/art/illustration/phiz/ld.html
7. *The Dickens Project* (University of California), http://dickens.ucsc.edu/OMF/illustrations.html
8. For a discussion of the painting see Paul Barlow, *Time Present and Time Past: The Art of John Everett Millais* (Aldershot: Ashgate, 2005), pp. 9–14.
9. For an account of the controversy, see Leonee Ormond, "Dickens and Painting: Contemporary Art," *The Dickensian*, 80 (1984), pp. 2–25.
10. For an account of the wedding by Frederick Lehmann, see the same volume, *The Letters of Charles Dickens* (eds.) Margaret Brown, Kathleen Tillotson, Graham Storey), Vol. 9, 1859–1861 (Oxford: Clarendon, 1997), p. 72.
11. The painting is at the Lever Gallery in Liverpool, see http://www.liverpoolmuseums.org.uk/ladylever/collections/blackbrunswicker.asp
12. See Dickens's letters reprinted, ibid., 521–2 and *Great Expectations* (London: Penguin, 1996), p. 508. The ending is also reproduced on *The Victorian Web*, http://www.victorianweb.org/authors/dickens/ge/ending.html
13. Martin Meisel, *Realizations: Narrative, Pictorial, and Theatrical Arts in Nineteenth-Century England* (Princeton: Princeton University Press, 1983).
14. Paul Barlow suggests this looks like a child's cradle and denotes "the couple's thwarted family prospects", Barlow, op. cit., p. 92.
15. *Great Expectations*, op. cit., pp. 517–18.
16. For more information on this edition, see Gareth Cordery, "Harry Furniss and the 'Boom in Boz'" (2 parts), *Dickens Quarterly*, 21.2 and 21.3 (2004), pp. 90–102, 143–54.
17. The four sets of images can be found under the illustrator's name on the Dickens pages at *The Victorian Web*, http://www.victorianweb.org/authors/dickens/ge/artov.html

18. Figures 9.2–9.4 reproduced with kind permission of Philip Allingham.
19. http://www.victorianweb.org/art/illustration/fraser/28.html

Works cited

Barlow, Paul, *Time Present and Time Past: The Art of John Everett Millais* (Aldershot: Ashgate, 2005).

Brown, Margaret, Kathleen Tillotson and Graham Storey (eds.), *The Letters of Charles Dickens*.Vol. 9, 1859–1861 (Oxford: Clarendon, 1997).

Christ, Carol T. and John O. Jordan (eds.), *Victorian Literature and the Victorian Visual Imagination* (University of California Press, 1995).

Cordery, Gareth,"Harry Furniss and the 'Boom in Boz'" (2 parts), *Dickens Quarterly*, 21.2 and 21.3 (2004), pp. 90–102, 143–54.

——. *The life and adventures of Nicholas Nickleby*, reproduced in facsimile from the original monthly parts of 1838–9, with an essay by Michael Slater (London: Scolar Press, 1982).

Dickens, Charles, *Great Expectations* (Ontario: Broadview, 2002).

Dubrez-Fawcett, F., *Dickens the Dramatist* (London: Allen, 1952), pp. 13–14.

Flint, Kate, *The Victorians and the Visual Imagination* (Cambridge: Cambridge University Press, 2000).

Jordan, John O. (ed.), *The Cambridge Companion to Charles Dickens* (Cambridge University Press, 2001).

Lester, Valerie, *Phiz: The Man who drew Dickens* (London: Chatto and Windus, 2006).

Meisel, Martin, *Realizations: Narrative, Pictorial, and Theatrical Arts in Nineteenth-Century England* (Princeton: Princeton University Press, 1983).

O'Gorman, Francis *The Victorian Novel: A Guide to Criticism* (Oxford: Blackwell, 2002).

Ormond, Leonée, "Dickens and Painting: Contemporary Art," *The Dickensian*, 80 (1984), pp. 2–25.

Pykett, Lyn, *Charles Dickens* (London: Palgrave – now Palgrave Macmillan, 2002).

Sanders, Andrew *Charles Dickens* (Oxford: Oxford University Press, 2003).

Slater, Michael (ed.), *Dickens's Journalism, Vol 2: The Amusements of the People: Reports, Essays and Reviews, 1834–51* (London: Weidenfeld and Nicolson, 1996), p. 245.

Stein, Richard L. "Dickens and illustration," in *The Cambridge Companion to Charles Dickens*, ed. John O. Jordan (Cambridge: Cambridge University Press, 2001), pp. 167–88.

Stone, Harry, *Dickens and the Invisible World* (Bloomington: Indiana University Press, 1979).

10
Serial Reading

Linda K. Hughes and Michael Lund

I Introduction

The first mass-media era began after 1830, when steam-driven trains and industrial distribution systems carried print to readers across regions and classes throughout Britain. From mid-century onward print also became an increasingly visual medium due to new engraving and production techniques; as steam-driven technology was applied to printing presses, moreover, the volume of print increased even while prices dropped. In this environment monthly magazines, weekly newspapers, and freestanding serial parts, not just books, became a crucial delivery system for popular and high-culture literature from the 1830s to the century's end.[1] This media revolution, the changing price, format, and availability of materials, as well as alterations in the audiences who purchased or read them, played a key role in shaping Victorian fiction. Our essay begins with this crucial publishing history and its profound impact on the production and reception of Victorian fiction, including the sheer bulk and multiplot structure of serial fiction; the plot-driven suspense of weekly serials; the realist effect of monthly-serial characters whom readers accompanied in print and visual illustrations over the course of twelve to nineteen months; and the profound intertextuality of magazine and weekly serials that encased installments of serial fiction in a miscellany of texts. What happens next in professional considerations of magazine culture must involve pedagogy, and we will propose some specific strategies by which this publishing history can serve students in their critical reading and in their understanding of culture.

II Serialization, publishing history, and serial aesthetics

When the monthly numbers of *Pickwick Papers* (1836–7), originally focused around its illustration of sporting scenes, exploded in popularity due to Dickens's winning narrative, its shilling parts began to sell over 20,000 copies each month, and the final double number sold almost 40,000 copies

(Patten, 1991, pp. 45–6, 64–8). If not a mass-market phenomenon in itself (at mid-century cheap illustrated weekly papers could sell half a million copies per issue), *Pickwick* represented a dramatic increase in sales and middle-class readership for an illustrated novel esteemed by critics and embraced by popular audiences. And serialization was crucial to this success. As opposed to the conventional book market affordable only to the wealthy, middle-class readers could purchase shilling parts one at a time and still undercut the standard price of a triple-decker novel – 31 shillings, 6 pence – when they had bought all 20 monthly parts.

The heyday of the Victorian novel published in 20 illustrated monthly parts, as Graham Law notes, lasted only through the 1840s (2000, p. 18). And some key titles of the age, including everything by the Brontë sisters, owed nothing to serialization. Nonetheless, the impact of serial fiction by Dickens, of *Vanity Fair* (1847–8) and later novels by W. M. Thackeray, and of numerous other serials was so profound that it shaped aesthetic sensibilities and reading practices as well as means of production and distribution until late in the century. The novel's identity as an emphatically long story unfolding over time, which had already been established by Sir Walter Scott and his precursors, was given temporal palpability as well as material heft by serialization. That is, serial readers learned to live with a story for as much as eighteen months, folding the story into their temporal daily rhythms (and conversations with other serial readers), asking themselves and others "what happens next" in their own stories and in the stories they were reading.

This material condition of serialization had other aesthetic effects as well: characters, too, like their readers, had duration, enhancing the seeming congruence between literary realism and reality. Serial readers also learned to experience the pleasures, and sometimes the frustrations, of anticipation. As we suggest in *The Victorian Serial*, the extended time and enforced interruptions of serial fiction also chimed with key developments in Victorian science, economics, and ideology (1991, pp. 1–14). That geology and evolutionary theory emphasized gradual development over expanses of time, for example, or that capitalism and Protestantism lauded the delay of gratification further helped to naturalize a serial aesthetic despite its innovation.

If the duration of serialization also encouraged the multiplot novel – fiction with several plot lines among which the serial author could switch from part to part until all converged at the end – that duration was not uniform. As Mark Turner points out, "no single rhythm' operates in Victorian print culture, "and the periodical press in particular moves to a number of different beats' (2002, pp. 186–7). Where serial fiction was concerned, the most important periodical rhythms were weekly and monthly. The penny weeklies such as *London Journal* or *Reynolds' Miscellany*, aimed at the lower middle classes and workers, regularly published serial fiction in the 1840s and 1850s. Though these papers reached larger audiences than their middle-class rivals, however, their serials were dismissed by middle-class critics as merely sensational and plot-driven, and few of these works are still widely read today – though digitized full-text reproductions are making it feasible to study them in twenty-first century classrooms. In the 1850s the most prominent weekly venue for serial fiction was the two-penny *Household Words*, founded by Dickens in 1850, which hosted novels ranging from his *Hard Times* (1 April–12 August 1854) to Elizabeth Gaskell's *Cranford* (13 December 1851–21 May 1853) and *North and South* (2 September 1854–27 January 1855). As Lorna Huett notes, Dickens's stroke of genius was to combine middle-class fare in a cheap unillustrated magazine that could attract not just the middle class but also downmarket buyers – especially since Dickens used the same paper stock as "penny dreadfuls" (as they were often termed) so that the feel of his pages and closely printed columns would have been familiar to this audience (2005, pp. 77–9).

Dickens innovated periodical publication and serial fiction yet again when, after a dispute with proprietors Bradbury and Evans, he founded his own periodical, *All the Year Round* (Oppenlander, 1984, pp. 4–6). This gave far more prominence to serial novels than had *Household Words* and hosted the first important serial identified with sensation fiction, Wilkie Collins's *The Woman in White* (26 November 1859–25 August 1860). Sensation fiction combined domestic realism and middle-class settings with crime, elements of gothic fiction, melodrama, and newspaper reports – a kind of synthesis, so to speak, of the penny weeklies and Dickens's *Household Words*. As Deborah Wynne argues, Dickens's *All the Year Round* helped make stories about crime and sensational events respectable by presenting them in the context of a family magazine (2001, pp. 22–8). To hostile critics weekly publication itself was reprehensible, presenting only a short burst of story culminating in suspense and keeping readers' interest at a high pitch because they had to wait mere days rather than weeks for a new installment. In an unsigned 1862 essay entitled "Sensation Novels" in *Blackwood's Edinburgh Magazine*, Margaret Oliphant contended that "The violent stimulant of serial publication – of *weekly* publication, with its necessity for frequent and rapid recurrence of piquant situation and startling incident – is the thing of all others most likely to develop the germ, and bring it to fuller and darker bearing" (1862, p. 568). Victorians subscribers, that is, were not being asked to wait long enough to learn and appreciate deeply what happens next.

Oliphant, of course, fired her salvo from within the safe confines of a monthly periodical that also serialized fiction. Monthly magazine serials, however, could suggest continuity with the parts-novels of the 1830s and 1840s, and the greater length afforded to monthly rather than weekly installments offered space for character development and richly detailed descriptions of setting or manners – qualities generally identified by critics as hallmarks of more artistic (versus plot-driven) novels. The launch of the monthly *Macmillan's Magazine* in 1859 and lavishly illustrated *Cornhill Magazine* in 1860 further raised the prestige of monthly magazine serials, especially when *Cornhill* proprietor George Smith was willing to pay hand-some fees that attracted prestigious writers. By this means *Framley Parsonage* (January 1860–April 1861) by Anthony Trollope, *Romola* (July 1862–August 1863) by George Eliot, and *Wives and Daughters* (August 1864–January 1866) by Elizabeth Gaskell all made their first appearance in print.

Whether issued in weeklies or monthly magazines, however, all peri-odical-based serial novels shared serial rhythms. Authors could carefully synchronize the calendars of their fictional worlds with the magazine's publishing schedule, another means of intensifying the realist effect of serial reading. The opening episode of *Great Expectations* – Pip's confronta-tion with Magwitch on Christmas Eve, his smuggling of a Christmas pie to the convict, and the convict's recapture on Christmas Day – crossed four installments published from 1–22 December 1860 in *All the Year Round*, con-cluding on the brink of Christmas. In *Far from the Madding Crowd* (January–December 1874) the July oat-harvest on Bathsheba's land fell within the July issue of *Cornhill Magazine*, and the disastrous Christmas-eve party appeared in *Cornhill's* December number. Some things happened next to simultane-ously in Victorian fiction and in Victorian reality.

Both weekly and monthly magazine serials were also defined by their profound intertextuality. Even part novels placed serial fiction in dialogue with surrounding ads and visual illustration, but magazine and newspaper serials intensified textual dialogues because fiction appeared alongside news, travel writing, scientific articles, poems, and even rival fiction in a single issue. As Deborah Wynne indicates, Dickens made important use of articles and short fiction in *All the Year Round* to extend or complicate the cultural preoccupations – disease, crime, new concepts of evolution – raised by serial novels in his periodical (2001, pp. 88–91). And Carol A. Martin confirms the importance of juxtaposed short and long serial fiction in her study of George Eliot's debut, *Scenes of Clerical Life*, which consisted of three short stories serialized in *Blackwood's Edinburgh Magazine* in 1857. Louisa Melville Fraser's short story, "Hester Benfield," like the opening installment of "Mr Gilfil's Love-Story" in the March issue of *Blackwood's*, featured a love triangle. As Martin notes, "Review columns in Victorian newspapers and journals demonstrate that readers encountered one story in a kind of mental juxtaposition with another," a condition of which the "Maga" editor had taken advantage in selecting contents for the March 1857 issue (1994, pp. 53–5). All the above elements of Victorian serial fic-tion in turn have important implications (and manifold possibilities) for pedagogy.

What happens next in this essay is a review of the pragmatic, historical, and theoretical reasons to introduce students to fiction in the context of serialization and a survey of a range of possible pedagogical strategies before exploring in detail an entire class structured as a collaboratively-produced magazine under the guidance of an editor-instructor.

III Pedagogical approaches to serial fiction: an overview

Serialization and its enforced interruptions in the reading process are the defining features of serial fiction pedagogy: students, too, read a novel in parts rather than completing the entire text prior to a set of lectures or discussions. The most obvious benefit of this approach is that students can better manage reading assignments and absorb a novel's details than if they race through 500–900 pages in a weekend – or simply skip reading altogether and rely on summaries they can easily obtain online. As Michael Lund remarks in one of the earliest essays to address serial teaching:

> for many of today's undergraduates, less familiar with literature and less able to handle long novels than earlier generations of students were, reading one or two installments is simply easier. Discussing smaller sections of the text in several classes at least a week apart also ensures a fuller, closer knowledge of the total novel. And this approach encourages teachers to reexperience the novel along with their students and, generally, to foster more (and more open) discussion in the classroom. (1984, p. 116)[2]

Serial pedagogy also has direct implications for the process of teaching. Because it cannot rely on an ending to confer meaning on the whole text, serial teaching fosters discussion and collaboration with students. Serial teaching also offers important resources to instructors interested in cultural politics or narratology. In the absence of an authoritative ending, student responses acquire a legitimacy that cannot be gainsaid, particularly since serial teaching tends to encourage students to read more carefully rather than hurriedly. Hence the serial fiction classroom tends to decenter the authority of the instructor (especially if instructors dare, as we have on occasion, to teach for the first time a novel in parts they have not previously read, putting them in the same role as students). The extended reading time and evidence offered by student responses to individual parts also creates an opportunity for instructors to consider how narrative might be reconceived when its long middle occupies more classroom time and potentially does more to shape literary meaning than an end point. Not only can teaching in parts energize students as readers and discussants (as Andrea Kaston Tange reports [2006, pp. 334–6]), then, but it can also energize their teachers.

There are several ways that serial teaching can be introduced: reading one serial novel throughout a semester in courses on the Victorian novel, surveys of British literature, or genre courses on fiction; or reading multiple novels in installments throughout a semester. Since novels like *Jane Eyre*, *The History of Henry Esmond*, *Adam Bede*, *The Mill on the Floss*, *Mary Barton*, *Sylvia's Lovers*, *The Warden*, and *Barchester Towers* were published in volume form only, reading 2–3 parts of a serial novel every 7 or 10 days throughout the semester can offset a number of assigned "whole" novels.[3] Or parts of a serial novel can be interspersed among assigned nineteenth-century poems, short fiction, and periodical essays in any course dealing with the nineteenth century. Reading numerous serial novels in parts throughout the semester in a Victorian novel course, alternatively, enables students to experience with written texts what they do with television or blogs: taking in several unfolding stories at once.

As the analogy to electronic media indicates, teaching serially is closely related to historical, media, and theoretical studies. At the very least serial pedagogy acquaints students with a customary Victorian reading practice and reinforces what all theoretical and historical instruction aims to teach: that literature and textuality are profoundly mediated rather than spontaneous in creation and transparent in meaning. For those with original parts-novels (and special collections with librarians willing to let students see or touch them) or hard-bound copies of periodicals in their libraries, letting students turn the pages of an individual serial part filled with ads, multiple type fonts, and prominent illustrations or the pages of magazines that juxtaposed serial and short fiction, news, articles, and images can teach through touch, sight, and (given decaying paper and dust) smell the historicity of serial fiction and the role of material conditions in shaping the reading process and literary meaning.

Serial pedagogy also enriches approaches to the novel as a form of media history when fiction is taught as a constituent part of nineteenth-century periodicals, and/or as an introduction to cultural studies, since reading parts of canonical novels alongside more ephemeral essays, illustrations, ads, and other periodical contents exposes the degree to which "high culture" bears an intrinsic relation to popular or "low" culture. The sheer array of competing periodicals and serial novels appearing at once, moreover, can be usefully linked to theories of dialogism, national identity, class politics, textuality, and reception – or, more simply, to the analogous complexity of contemporary media markets in which serialization and story-telling are also familiar features.[4] Finally, the new era of digitized periodicals made possible by the open-access Nineteenth Century Serials Edition project and Google Books, or through the expensive subscription databases offered by ProQuest and Gale, will make it possible to teach serial fiction as part of mass media – since students will have access to hundreds of periodicals aimed at workers, artisans, and niche markets as well as the middle-class readership that has largely defined study of the Victorian novel heretofore – or as part of a rethinking of textuality in a print or digital environment.

To explore the question of how we might teach serial fiction in an era in which printed texts are so often superseded by their remediated digital forms or compete with the allure of contemporary electronic media, we offer a case study of an alternative pedagogy centered on a novel that itself tugs at the distinctions we tend to draw between older print forms and an electronic era defined by the rise of the internet and gaming. What happens next is the application of these general theoretical frameworks to a specific magazine novel.

IV   *The Hand of Ethelberta* and the classroom as magazine

At the height of nineteenth-century magazine culture, the 1870s, when literary monthlies like *Cornhill*, *Macmillans*, and *Blackwoods* retained their prestige and syndication had opened multiple opportunities to authors, Thomas Hardy was among those writers beginning to question the form in which his own work was appearing. Strict editorial control fostered a climate in which the authors who would shape Modernism increasingly sought out book publishers offering more opportunities to explore currently forbidden topics. In *The Hand of Ethelberta*, for instance, Hardy faced a cautious *Cornhill* editor, Leslie Stephen, who questioned his depiction of romantic themes. However, Hardy in that novel looked backwards more than forward for a more appropriate method of literary conversation. And his exploration of traditional literary modes suggests a pedagogical approach for our own time. (A syllabus for a course in "The Victorian Magazine Novel" featuring this work appears in the Appendix, though the pedagogical strategies discussed below derive from several courses.)

As shaping a course on the dynamic of periodical reading unsettles some conventional ideas of classroom structure, Hardy's novel also offers an unconventional model as fictional heroine. Robert Schweik recently reassessed *The Hand of Ethelberta*, acknowledging that it has suffered a "critical history studded with declarations that it was a failure" (2002, p. 239). Schweik argues that this novel's comic nature (it was subtitled "A Comedy in Chapters") includes a "cynical narrative stance . . . that sets [it] apart from his other novels" (p. 240). Its distinctive quality lies also in its perhaps cynical criticism of the periodical medium in which it was appearing. Schweik passes over Ethelberta's "plan to financially assist her family by story telling" and focuses more on her use of marriage to achieve material security (p. 250). Her intention of earning "fame by writing an epic" is, according to Schweik, "an altogether appropriate final comic note" in her story. However, this heroine's advocacy of a specific literary mode can be seen as an important reconsideration of magazine fiction for Hardy's time and a possible guide for pedagogy in our own.

When, as we propose, the teacher accepts his or her position as a continuing student of a novel being read in installments, rather than a nearly omniscient scholarly figure outside of the text, he or she acknowledges a physical, material presence in the world occupied by students. Analogously, when the heroine of *Ethelberta* mounts a forest tree stump before a group of listeners of different ages and in different postures in the September 1875 *Cornhill*, she represents an ancient storyteller materially present with her audience:

> "It occurred to me," she continued, blushing slightly, "that tales of the weird kind were made to be told, not written. The action of a teller is

wanted to give due effect to all stories of incident; and I hope that a time will come when, as of old, instead of an unsocial reading of fiction at home alone, people will meet together cordially, and sit at the feet of a professed romancer." (Chapter XV, September 1875, p. 279)[5]

Ethelberta's insistence on the physical presence of the teller/novelist cannot be realized in the contemporary classroom, of course; but the shape of the author whose work is serialized in a magazine can be more substantial than it is in a book. Editorial comment about the "latest number" and letters to the editor about the continuing story called up the author to Victorian periodical subscribers in spaces that did not exist in the volume edition; and such contextual matter can do the same for students who engage the novel in print or virtual form.

The class structured as a periodical, which acknowledges shared experiences of teacher and students, derives, then, at least in part from storytelling traditions like those employed by Ethelberta. Her intention to perform in front of a group gathered in a lecture hall underscores the communal nature of the oral tradition:

> She drew from her pocket a folded paper, shook it abroad, and disclosed a rough draft of an announcement to the effect that Mrs. Petherwin, Professed Story-teller, would devote an evening to that ancient form of the romancer's art, at a well-known fashionable hall in London. (Chapter XV, September 1875, p. 279)

Here print (the "folded paper") is secondary to oral presentation (her own voice). And the origin of such performances is credited to perhaps the most elemental context for storytelling, family gatherings. She explains to Christopher, "It was a private rehearsal before my brothers and sisters – not with any view of obtaining their criticism, but that I might become accustomed to my own voice in the presence of listeners" (Chapter XV, September 1875, p. 279).

The teacher's plan for a course in which he or she reads serially along with students has a greater chance of veering from a fixed trajectory than a class where works are read one at a time and fixed within an anticipated frame of interpretation. The improvisational mode of oral storytelling is also ironically embedded in the composition and publication history of *Ethelberta*. This particular novel proved an unexpected departure from Hardy's earlier mode, and F. P. Pinion writes that the *Cornhill* and Leslie Stephen were "disappointed" with the novel (1992, p. 136) in magazine form. Nonetheless, the prestige of the *Cornhill* had encouraged Hardy to take these readers seriously, adjusting his voice to keep subscribers engaged. While Tim Dolin reports that Hardy took little time revising the novel for later editions (1997, p. xx), he did make changes when Stephen "suggested minor improvements" as manuscript and proofs arrived (Millgate, 1982, p. 170). And, in response to an early question about the subtitle (subsequently omitted from the magazine version), Hardy took the time to explain: "I should certainly deplore being thought to have set up in the large joke line – the genteelest of genteel comedy being as far as ever I should think it safe to go at any time" (Millgate, 1982, p. 175). The effort to conform to editorial and subscriber expectations and to establish an intimate relationship can be related to the Victorian family practice of the father's reading aloud to mother and children. Teaching novels in parts in the contemporary classroom also tends to promote closeness among readers as discussion rather than lecture is the appropriate pedagogical method.

We can equate lectures with a literary mode Hardy's heroine finds restrictive. In one of the novel's key scenes Ethelberta explains to Kit, after he interrupts her storytelling on the forest tree stump, that the conversational tone of a storyteller might offer greater power and authority than more formal literary modes of publishing:

> "Now did you ever consider what a power De Foe's manner would have if exercised by word of mouth? Indeed, it is a style which suits itself infinitely better to telling than to writing, abounding as it does in colloquialisms that are somewhat out of place on paper in these days, but have a wonderful power in making a narrative seem real. And so, in short, I am going to talk De Foe on a subject of my own. – Well?" (Chapter XV, September 1875, p. 279)

The complete body of Hardy's work, of course, explores and makes use of print to establish its relationship with readers; but at this moment in this novel, Hardy is considering the unique potential of the oral tradition to move author and readers closer together.

We believe that students, teacher, and the weeks of the semester can come together in a similar fashion to create dynamic social activity beyond one person's delivery and a group's reception of a series of lectures. In a communal engagement of periodicals over many weeks, the teacher does not enjoy absolutely the privileged position of speaker; in listening to and responding to students, the teacher becomes an audience just as Ethelberta does when Stephen questions her about her story, as well as when she establishes a new home in London. Although to those outside the family Ethelberta is the mistress of this household, her siblings know she is their older sister once at their social level. As they live together and share household duties, she teaches them, drawing on her experience as a widow and daughter-in-law in a higher class. She enjoys a certain privilege and authority, then, but also interacts with her "students" as one of them.

To make the semester's experience a more analogous recreation of its nineteenth-century model, all participants should agree to base discussion on what can be concluded from a magazine or its contents at the moment when a new issue is published and when no more material will appear until a specific period of time has passed. When such conditions are accepted, students can even find their classroom observations taken up by the teacher and integrated with his or her own understanding. Charles Swann has argued for this kind of interaction between editor (as one reader) and author after attempting to track down Hardy's reference to Defoe's having "the most amazing talent on record for telling lies" (1995, p. 203). Seeking the "modern critic" who, according to Hardy, made this claim, Swann suggests that "the place of periodical publication provides a solution . . . For the *Cornhill* was, of course, edited by Leslie Stephen and he had published an essay on Defoe there in 1868 which was reprinted in *Hours in a Library*, 1st series, in 1874. There he describes Defoe as having 'the most amazing power ever known of giving verisimilitude to his fictions; or, in other words again, he had the most amazing talent on record for telling lies'" (p. 3). While Swann cannot provide conclusive evidence that Hardy was referring to Stephen in this instance, he asserts that "the closeness of the relationship between Hardy and Stephen was much more than that of author and editor" (1995, p. 203).[6] While possessing more authority than students, perhaps, Stephen in this case may have found his comments helping to shape the author's story.

Using magazines and reading serially can, then, alter a traditional classroom hierarchy, which is not unlike Victorian social strata. Similarly, Hardy's novel unsettles the class structure of his time. His heroine's peculiar social position in *The Hand of Ethelberta* – aristocrat by marriage, commoner by birth, middle class by profession – has no recognized place in conventional Victorian society. She must break further from conventional models to become a storyteller. Fortunately in this regard, she is, as "a widow . . . to some extent sheltered to live in a way which might be considered a trifle free if indulged in by other young women" (Chapter XIX, October 1875, p. 504). Further, her public identity makes her "a person freed of her hampering and inconvenient sex, and, by virtue of her popularity, unfettered from the conventionalities of manner prescribed by custom for household womankind" (Chapter XXXIII, January 1876, p. 16). George Wotton claims that "Ethelberta is as subjected in the sight of her suitors as any other of Hardy's women who are subjected in the sight of men to the images those men have of them" (1985, p. 124). In her stance as public storyteller, however, Ethelberta achieves an authority denied her when she is simply a man's love interest. Over time it becomes necessary that Ethelberta disguise herself, her family, and her residence in order to protect this special role: "I have thought over every possible way of combining the dignified social position I must maintain to make my story-telling attractive, with my absolute lack of money, . . . A vital condition is that I do not have a soul in the house (beyond the lodgers) who is not one of my own relations" (Chapter XVII,

October 1875, pp. 498–9). Michael Slater notes that in London Ethelberta is "seeking to cheat the city through art . . . to assert her individuality in an extreme way, i.e. as a unique kind of artist" (1994, p. 49). Similar to the evolving Victorian magazine – in which fiction, poetry, and essays – were contained, then, Ethelberta creates a special context of her own by which she can frame her storytelling. And structuring a class on the dynamics of periodical reading similarly alters the traditional classroom hierarchy.

The classroom model offered here, in which all are readers of an ongoing tale without knowing its conclusion, creates a pedagogical process more difficult to classify than traditional modes of teaching. The kind of story Ethelberta tells in Hardy's novel is also hard to fix within conventional literary types. Hardy explains that the unusual way in which she tells her story, not its content, accounts for her success:

> What Ethelberta relied upon soon became evident. It was not upon the intrinsic merits of her story as a piece of construction, but upon her method of telling it. Whatever defects the tale possessed – and they were not a few – it had, as delivered by her, the one preeminent merit of seeming like truth. A modern critic has well observed of De Foe that he had the most amazing talent on record for telling lies; and Ethelberta, in wishing her fiction to appear like a real narrative of personal adventure, did wisely to make De Foe her model. (Chapter XVIII, October 1875, p. 496)

Ethelberta's performance earns her "a notice in some of the weekly reviews" (Chapter XVIII, October 1875, p. 498), so that Hardy imitates contemporary print forms alongside Ethelberta's return to an oral medium and underscores their interaction. One reviewer fails to see that her mode is not so much innovative as a return to an earlier format: "we believe that this is the first instance on record of a Novel-teller . . ." (Chapter XVIII, October 1875, p. 498). Another reviewer acknowledges the physical presence of the storyteller as a key part of the literary experience: "There spreads upon her face when in repose an air of innocence which is charmingly belied by the subtlety we discover beneath it when she begins her tale; and this amusing discrepancy between her physical presentment and the inner woman is further illustrated by the misgiving which seizes us on her entrance, that so impressionable a lady will never bear up in the face of so trying an audience . . . " (Chapter XX, October 1875, p. 499).

Teaching works in installments results in the juxtaposition of the instructor's more informed explanation of background against student questions and observations that mirror Ethelberta's apparent innocence and her subtlety. While this can occur with complete works studied one at a time, the discussion method encouraged by reading serially tends more consistently to invite the mixing of voices in class. The unique qualities of fiction in magazines can be similarly contrasted with less indirect or figurative presentation of other material surrounding it in a particular issue. Political essays, records of scientific discovery, or reviews of art and music differ in style and goals from the novel genre. Even illustrations accompanying a serial work, often done without an author's direct supervision, can contrast with the text. Placement of the ongoing tale is a measure of the editor's sense of its value relative to other comments, further underscoring the distinction between substance and presentation identified by the reviewer of Ethelberta's performance.

The pedagogical goals of engaging periodicals as a temporal experience often turn into sharpening reading skills more than mastering definitive readings of canonical texts, as careful attention to technique in early install-ments encourages students to practice the same interpretative strategies in reading subsequent parts in the same work. The students' ability to connect different works being read simultaneously in the course of a term is also sharpened when they are engaged in alternating sections. Hardy's tale at one point includes two stories continuing simultaneously and requires *Cornhill*'s readers to explore their relationship. Ethelberta's tale of a woman disguised as a man and threatened by a blind antagonist (Chapter 15 September 1875, p. 275) is a digression from the main plot of her effort to establish her literary career. Today's students, accustomed to multi-tasking and rapid shifts of attention online and in response to visual media, adapt easily to the digressive nature of such less formal and fragmented narratives. While students are often surprised to be asked to read many works in a magazine or many magazines simultaneously, they are in fact better prepared for such an experience than many professors who compartmentalize their study. While older faculty can be distracted by students talking to each other as lecture or directed discussion continues, the younger generation often find such chatter consistent with the way they view media in a group, trading comments in several directions at the same time they follow a central plot-line on television or the Internet. Many students work at computers with multiple screens open simultaneously – e-mail, browsers, music – while focused concentration on a single object is the tradition most faculty refine from graduate school through scholarly publication.[7] Yet even older faculty move about a periodical's context comfortably in their non-academic lives, so perhaps they would benefit from adapting to new learning modes.

V   Some conclusions

Classes taught in the manner of magazine publication and reception offer opportunities for students to interrupt a teacher's planned instruction and inspire different directions for discussion in individual sessions and even throughout the remainder of a course. Michael Millgate reminds us of how texts were juxtaposed, crossed, and sometimes merged in the Victorian read-ing public's mind. The *Westminster Review* in July 1876 noted that "it was fortunate that *The Hand of Ethelberta* had been published first [before Eliot's

Daniel Deronda], or else ill-natured critics would have declared that his principal character was a copy" (1982, p. 168) of Gwendolyn Harleth. Millgate notes, however, that Eliot had "in the same novel borrowed from *Far from the Madding Crowd* the designation 'Wessex' for certain south-western portions of contemporary England" (1982, p. 168), and that the 15 July 1876 *Examiner* also "made frequent and familiar use of 'Wessex' as of a term already in general circulation" (1982, p. 168). Thus, specific words and concepts wandered from magazine to magazine in this period, creating a web of interrelated persons and events.

Student interest in movie series, weekly television shows, and electronic media (graphic novels, fan fiction, focused chat room discussion) provide them with material that is often outside a professor's experience and that they can bring into a course on an older print culture. When they report on similar plot structures, character development, or transitional techniques in popular media, their shared expertise can reverse the instructor/student roles. Once such serials as the six *Star Wars* movies or the weekly television show *Grey's Anatomy* are introduced into class discussion, the links to antecedents from the nineteenth century (William Morris's *The Pilgrims of Hope* or Trollope's Palliser novels) can become major topics in succeeding classes. This additional material develops the courses in ways the instructor could not have envisioned, just as an editor's reservations can reshape an author's narrative. Stephen's resistance to the subtitle, "A Comedy in Chapters," was accepted by Hardy at the outset of serialization; thus the novel that followed in the magazine accommodated the editor's view. And when, in May 1875, according to Pinion, Stephen objected to the word "amorous" linked to Ethelberta, and in August to a "very close embrace," Hardy seems to have adjusted (1992, p. 132). Pinion notes that the editor "complimented Hardy on managing 'the rose-leaf incident'" (1992, p. 132) appropriately.

Another feature of teaching classes with periodicals involves the blurring of boundaries between reality and fiction. In *The Hand of Ethelberta* Kit interrupts Ethelberta's story in the woods because he is "concern[ed]" at "such a history of yourself since I last saw you" (Chapter XV, September 1875, p. 277), assuming that the heroine of her narration is herself; but, as she explains, "The story I was telling is entirely a fiction . . ." (Chapter XV, September 1875, p. 277). This confusion about fiction and reality in her tale "of the weird kind" (Chapter XV, September 1875, p. 279) is also consistent with the mixing of factual material and imaginative literature included in most issues of Victorian literary magazines. The same *Cornhill* issue in which Hardy's *The Hand of Ethelberta* began, for instance, included articles on "British Birds and Bird Lovers" and "Horace's Two Philosophies" as well as on women and literary tradition ("Penelope, and Other Women of Homer," contributed by John Addington Symonds) and popular tales ("Venetian Popular Legends").

Contemporary students also move from their own reality into imagined worlds – both historical and literary – as they read periodicals. When the reading is done serially, imitating the schedule of nineteenth-century sub-scribers, the movement from factual to fictional can be an aid to under-standing periodical culture. That is, nineteenth-century readers of the works of novelists like Elizabeth Gaskell, poems like Tennyson's *Idylls of the King*, or magazine series like George Lewes's *Studies in Animal Life* (in the 1860 *Cornhill*) often felt that characters and situations in literature were part of their own daily lives. Just as a reader might be pleased to meet a friend or relative not seen for some weeks, so did that same magazine subscriber feel pleasure at rejoining David Copperfield on his way to Dover or Dorothea Brooke during her honeymoon in Florence. As the semester advances, then, students should share an analogous experience when they come together like a Victorian audience to see what has happened to David or Dorothea, what has occurred in the last month of Victorian history, or what new dis-coveries in natural science have been reported.

There may be another benefit to the repeated movement from the material world to an imagined one in periodical reading: the separation of art from experience tends to be less than when a work is read and analysed in a single span of time. In that traditional approach, the work assigned and studied is packaged into a fixed form, ready to be recalled and compared in other analy-ses; but when a work is read over several months, its shape becomes more fluid. Not only do additional installments reshape what has been read, but the class's individual and collective experience in the gaps between parts affects the developing idea of individual works and their collective meaning. The traditional packaging of literary meaning into fixed forms for examination is often frustrating for students, who feel they must present the instructor's vision, unchanged by their own reading. In this context a work can easily become an object rather than the memory of a pleasurable experience.

Hardy similarly complains in *The Hand of Ethelberta* that contemporary Victorian literature and social life represent a divorce of form and content: "Ethelberta never discovered from the Belmaines whether her proposal [to visit Milton's tomb] had been an infliction or a charm, so perfectly were they practiced in sustaining that complete divorce between thinking and saying which is the hall-mark of high civilization" (Chapter XXIX, December 1875, pp. 746–7). Hardy here insists on the cost of allowing the separation of underlying human feeling and thought: "The town gentleman" he observes, "was not half so far removed from Sol and Dan, and the hard-handed order in general, in his passions as in his philosophy. He still continued to be the male of his species . . ." (Chapter XXX, December 1875, pp. 753). Hardy's conviction that language and reality are drifting apart helps account for the striking images of juxtaposition in the novel: "Sitting in the room that commanded this prospect a white butterfly among the apple-trees might be mistaken for the sails of a yacht far away on the sea; and in the evening, when the light was dim, what seemed like a fly crawling upon the window-pane would turn out to be a boat in the bay" (Chapter XXXIII,

January 1876, pp. 13). When Lord Montclere encounters the genuine form of Ethelberta juxtaposed with images of women in his favourite periodicals, he finds that latter to be no longer of interest: "What an eye was hers! There is not a girl among them so beautiful as she . . . Tipman! Come and take it away. I don't think I will subscribe to these papers any longer – how long have I subscribed? Never mind – I take no interest in these things . . ." (Chapter XXXIV, January 1876, p. 25).

Many former graduate students intending to devote their careers to scholarly publication, having taken positions with heavy teaching loads at the undergraduate level, find their past interests distant from what they must do day-to-day in the classroom. Like Lord Montclere, some feel the structures of analysis they subscribed to in order to pass exams and write a dissertation fail to excite their students; and they seek ways to restore the joy of reading that brought them to the profession in the first place. Given what we have learned in the last three decades about serialization, publishing history, and serial aesthetics, and about incorporating new pedagogical models for the teaching of literature, culture, and history into the shape of the curriculum, the profession would do well to conceive the classroom as a magazine, a genre characterized by multiple voices and forms, varied subject matter and interests, periodic consumption and continuation. Like the oral tradition, the oldest structure for literary experience, reading magazines within a periodical structure encourages active participation by both students and teacher that has the potential to inspire the immediate excitement and pleasure of shared experience. Put another way, it may be a moment in pedagogical history for instructors, reading periodically with students, to put aside the advantage of knowing what happens next.

Appendix: sample syllabus: the Victorian magazine novel

Schedule

Week 1
Introduction
Old Curiosity Shop (*Master Humphrey's Clock*, 25 April 1840–6 February 1841) Chapters 1–5 (Parts 1–4)
"Janet's Repentence" (*Blackwood's* July–November 1857) Chapters 1–4 (Part 1); *The Secret Life of Mrs. Beeton* (video; 10 minutes in parts each Friday throughout the semester)

Week 2
Lecture: overview of Victorian publishing
The Old Curiosity Shop Chapters 6–16 (Parts 5–10)
"Janet's Repentence" Chapters 5–15 (Parts 2–3)

Week 3
Old Curiosity Shop Chapters 17–26 (Parts 11–15)
"Janet's Repentence" 16–21 (Part 4)
The Old Curiosity Shop Chapters 27–37 (Parts 16–21)

Week 4
Woman in White (*All the Year Round*, 26 November 1859–25
    August 1860) Chapters 1–10 (Parts 1–4)
The Old Curiosity Shop Chapters 38–47 (Parts 22–26)
"Janet's Repentence" 22–28 (Part 5)

Week 5
Woman in White 11–15 (Parts 5–7)
The Old Curiosity Shop Chapters 48–57 (Parts 27–31)
Woman in White The Story Continued By Vincent Gilmore–First Epoch
    closes (Parts 8–11)

Week 6
The Old Curiosity Shop Chapters 58–65 (Parts 32–35)
Exam
The Belton Estate (*Fortnightly Review*, 15 May 1865–1 January 1866)
    Chapters 1–2 (Part 1)

Week 7
The Old Curiosity Shop Chapters 66–The Last 65 (Parts 36–40)
Woman in White The Second Epoch–Chapter V (Parts 12–16)
The Belton Estate Chapters 3–6 (Parts 2–3)

Week 8
Woman in White Chapters V–The Narrative of Walter
    Hartright (Parts 17–26)
The Belton Estate Chapters 7–12 (Parts 4–6)
Woman in White The Narrative of Walter Hartright – Second Epoch closes
    (Parts 23–26)

Week 9
Paper# 1
The Belton Estate Chapters 13–18 (Parts 7–9)
Woman in White The Third Epoch Chapters 1–9 (Parts 27–33)

Week 10
The Belton Estate 19–24 (Parts 10–12)
The Hand of Ethelberta Chapters 10–15 (Parts 3–4)
Woman in White The Third Epoch Chapter 10–The

Story Continued by Walter Hartright Chapter 1
(Parts 34–36)

Week 11
Reading Day: the role of illustrations
The Belton Estate Chapters 25–28 (Parts 13–14)
Woman in White Chapter 2 – The End (Parts 37–40)

Week 12
Exam
The Belton Estate Chapters 29–32 (Parts 15–16)
The Hand of Ethelberta Chapters 16–26 (Parts 5–6)

Week 13
Kidnapped (*Young Folks* 1 May 1886–31 July 1886) Chapters 1–9
The Hand of Ethelberta Chapters 29–36 (but do not
    read last two paragraphs of Chapter 32 (Parts 7–8; do not read last
    two paragraphs of Chapter 32)
Kidnapped Chapters 10–19

Week 14
The Hand of Ethelberta Chapters 35–42 (Parts 9–10)
Kidnapped Chapters 20–24
Paper# 2
The Hand of Ethelberta Chapters 43–Sequel (Part 11)

Notes

1. The indispensable source for the "industrialization" of print production and dis-
   tribution is Richard Altick's *The English Common Reader: A Social History of the Mass
   Reading Public, 1800–1900* 2nd edn. (Columbus: Ohio State University Press, 1998).
   See also Patricia Anderson, *The Printed Image and the Transformation of Popular
   Culture 1790–1860* (Oxford: Oxford University Press, 1991).
2. For a recent articulation of the difference made by serial reading, see Michael Lund
   and Leigha McReynolds, "The Class as Periodical: A Contemporary 'Humanities
   Lab'", *Pedagogy* 9.2 (Fall 2008), 289–313. Lund and McReynolds use extensive data
   from student essays to document the experience of collective, serial reading and
   compare it to the more traditional classroom experience in which individual works
   are read and studied one at a time.
3. Most of these novels were issued as two-, three-, or four-volume works in "library
   editions." And circulating libraries like the giant Mudie's offered subscription plans
   that encouraged checking books out one or two volumes at a time. So even works
   not issued serially were still often read in installments, and an author who constructed a traditional "triple-decker" conceived of the whole as made up of distinct
   volume units.

At the same time, private lending libraries such as the Portico Library in Manchester (to which William Gaskell belonged) permitted borrowers to check out individual installments of serial novels or magazines and so created the conditions by which patrons could circumvent the rhythms of serialization. For as surviving borrowers' records at the Portico indicate, individual borrowers checked out as many as five parts at a time of *David Copperfield* in the spring of 1850, when the novel was still in the midst of its serial run.

4. The ten articles that guest editor Teresa Mangum gathers in the special issue of *Victorian Periodicals Review* devoted to pedagogy, as well as her own afterword, offer a range of specific teaching strategies and theoretical frameworks to teachers. See: *VPR*, 39.4 (Winter 2006), pp. 307–444. See also: Benedict Anderson, *Imagined Communities: Reflections on the Origin and Spread of Nationalism* (London: Verso, 2006); Dallas Liddle, "Bakhtinian 'Journalization' and the Mid-Victorian Literary Marketplace", *Literature Compass* 4/5 (2007), pp. 1460–74.

5. *The Hand of Ethelberta* provides further evidence that, as Ivan Kreilkamp indicates, vocal culture was a far more important presence in Victorian England than is often acknowledged in scholarship attuned to print culture. Victorian novelists, Kreilkamp argues, evoked the fiction of an ancient storyteller's immediate relation to his audience by resuscitating within their own novels the figure of a storyteller who ostensibly speaks directly to an individual reader. This strategy, Kreilkamp suggests, enabled Victorian novelists to assuage their guilt over their complicity in hegemonic print culture. If Dickens's early success depended on readers" independently performing his serial parts within family circles, Dickens took control of reading aloud back from unruly masses when he emerged as a public vocal storyteller late in his career, implying that only the novelist's authorized (and authorizing) performance of the novel was authentic (2005, pp. 3–7, pp. 90–121).

Ethelberta represents an interesting departure from this paradigm. Rather than published novels, she performs unwritten stories (reworking some of Defoe's fiction by means of a modern idiom and delivery style – not least in that the storyteller is an independent woman). And though she has had a prior publishing success, she shifts genres from *vers de société* (which she can no longer write when she loses the financial and social support of her mother-in-law) to telling tales before listeners. Rather than positing the storyteller within a nostalgic framework, moreover, Hardy situates Ethelberta's storytelling as a business strategy deliberately designed for profit.

6. N. N. Feltes reminds us, speaking of Hardy's 1891 serialization of *Tess of the D'Urbervilles*, that *The Graphic's* established magazine identity "forced and shaped the 'sheer drudgery' of Hardy's [manuscript] revisions, surround[ing] his text with illustrations, tidbits and advertisements so as to interpellate its 'class' reader" (1986, p. 75).

7. For an intriguing discussion of pedagogy in an era of "hyper attention" encouraged by multiple online media and information streams, see Katherine Hayles, "Hyper and Deep Attention: The Generational Divide in Cognitive Modes", *Profession 2007* (New York: Modern Language Association, 2007), pp. 187–99.

Works cited

Altick, Richard D., *The English Common Reader: A Social History of the Mass Reading Public, 1800–1900,* 2nd edn. (Columbus: Ohio State University Press, 1998).

Anderson, Benedict, *Imagined Communities: Reflections on the Origin and Spread of Nationalism,* 2nd edn. (London: Verso, 2006).

Anderson, Patricia, *The Printed Image and the Transformation of Popular Culture 1790–1860* (Oxford: Oxford University Press, 1991).

Dolin, Tim, "Introduction," *Thomas Hardy: The Hand of Ethelberta* (London: Penguin, 1997), pp. xix–xli.

Feltes, N. N., *Modes of Production of Victorian Novels* (Chicago: University of Chicago Press, 1986).

Hayles, N. Katherine, "Hyper and Deep Attention: The Generational Divide in Cognitive Modes," *Profession 2007* (New York: Modern Language Association, 2007), pp. 187–99.

Huett, Lorna, "'Among the Unknown Public': *Household Words, All the Year Round*, and the Mass-Market Weekly Periodical in the Mid-Nineteenth Century," *Victorian Periodicals Review*, 38.1 (Spring 2005), pp. 61–82.

Hughes, Linda K. and Michael Lund, *The Victorian Serial* (Charlottesville: University Press of Virginia, 1991).

Jordan, John O. and Robert L. Patten (eds.), *Literature in the Marketplace: Nineteenth-Century British Publishing and Reading Practices* (Cambridge: Cambridge University Press, 1995).

Kreilkamp, Ivan, *Voice and the Victorian Storyteller* (Cambridge: Cambridge University Press, 2005).

Law, Graham, *Serializing Fiction in the Victorian Press* (Basingstoke: Palgrave – now Palgrave Macmillan, 2000).

Liddle, Dallas, "Bakhtinian 'Journalization' and the Mid-Victorian Literary Marketplace," *Literature Compass*, 4.5 (2007), pp. 1460–74.

Lund, Michael, "Testing by Installments the 'Undisciplined Heart' of *David Copperfield*'s Reader," in *Approaches to Teaching Dickens' David Copperfield*. Ed. Richard J. Dunn (New York: Modern Language Association of America, 1984), pp. 114–21.

Lund, Michael and Leigha McReynolds, "The Class as Periodical: A Contemporary 'Humanities Lab'", *Pedagogy*, 9.2 (Fall 2008), pp. 289–313.

Mangum, Teresa (ed.), *Victorian Periodicals Review* Special Issue on Pedagogy, 39.4 (Winter 2006), pp. 307–444.

Martin, Carol A., *George Eliot's Serial Fiction* (Columbus: Ohio State University Press, 1994).

Millgate, Michael, *Thomas Hardy: A Biography* (New York, Random House, 1982).

[Oliphant, Margaret], "Sensation Novels", *Blackwood's Edinburgh Magazine* 91 (May 1862), pp. 564–84.

Oppenlander, E. A. (ed.), *Dickens's All the Year Round: Descriptive Index and Contributor List* (Troy, NY: Whitston Publishing Company, 1984).

Patten, Robert L., *Charles Dickens and His Publishers* (1978; rpt. Santa Cruz: Dickens Project, 1991).

Pinion, F. B., *Thomas Hardy: His Life and Friends* (New York: St. Martin's Press – now Palgrave Macmillan, 1992).

Schweik, Robert C., "Hardy's 'Plunge in a New and Untried Direction': Comic Detachment in *The Hand of Ethelberta*," *English Studies*, 83.3 (June 2002), pp. 239–52.

Slater, Michael, "Hardy and the City," *New Perspectives on Thomas Hardy*. Ed. Charles P. C. Pettit (New York: St. Martin's Press – now Palgrave Macmillan, 1994), pp. 41–57.

Swann, Charles, "Hardy, Defoe, and Leslie Stephen," *Notes and Queries*, 42.2 (June 1995), p. 203.

Tange, Andrea Kaston, "'Becoming a Victorian Reader': The Serial Reading Process in the Modern Classroom," *Victorian Periodicals Review*, Special Issue on Periodical Pedagogy, Ed. Teresa Mangum, 39.4 (Winter 2006), pp. 330–42.

Turner, Mark, "Periodical Time in the Nineteenth Century," *Media History,* 8.2 (2002), pp. 183–96.

Wotton, George, *Thomas Hardy: Towards a Materialist Criticism* (Totowa, NJ: Barnes & Noble, 1985).

Wynne, Deborah, *The Sensation Novel and the Victorian Family Magazine.* (Basingstoke: Palgrave – now Palgrave Macmillan, 2001).

11
Film Adaptation: The Case of *Wuthering Heights*

Terry R. Wright

To talk of "using" film adaptations of novels in order to teach literature will immediately raise the hackles of all film and television critics who quite justifiably choose to focus on these media for their own sake. One of the reasons that adaptation studies has enjoyed a fairly low status among film critics is, as John Ellis notes, its employment in literary departments to encourage "recalcitrant students . . . to read the original novel" (qtd. Cardwell, 2002, p. 37). Ira Konisberg's entry on adaptation in *The Complete Film Dictionary* actually defines it as a "subliterary discourse" designed to show that "great novels" are resistant to filming (qtd. Griffith, 1997, p. 6). While recognizing the centrality of adaptation studies to "any history of culture" interested in "the transmission of texts and meanings in and across cultures," Mirceia Aragay also deplores the way it is "often taught in literature departments as a way of sugaring the pill of (canonical) literature for an increasingly cinema-oriented student population" (2005, p. 30). Robert Ray is even more dismissive of the way in which the "same unproductive layman's question (How does the film compare with the book?)" is transparently designed to elicit "the same unproductive answer (The book is better)" (2000, p. 44). That, of course, is not the model of such comparative study of novels with their adaptations which I want to advocate.

It is nevertheless the case that students are often more competent at following film and television narratives than novels and that asking them to compare two different ways of telling stories and achieving meaning can help to defamiliarize what they otherwise take to be "natural," highlighting the conventions they unwittingly employ in everyday practice. There is some point in asking Seymour Chatman's question, "What Novels Can Do that Films Can't (and Vice Versa)," [1] even if it needs to be answered inductively, with full attention to the possibilities of both media. There is something to be gained too in considering adaptations as creative interpretations of novels, engaging imaginatively and historically with literature produced in different times and with considerably different ideological assumptions. To highlight the interpretive decisions involved in any adaptation, to foreground the historical assumptions that lie behind the attempt to "make sense" of a nineteenth-century novel (both passively to decode and actively to recreate it) is a pedagogical practice worth defending. This is not, of course, to deny that the films should also function (and be recognized) as autonomous works of art and should not invoke what Sarah Cardwell describes as the inevitable "mistaken conclusion that the excellence of the film depends on similarity to the novel" (2002, p. 9)

In what follows I will attempt a brief history of adaptation studies, highlighting both its problems and what I believe still to be of value within it, before looking at the three English-speaking film adaptations of Emily Brontë's *Wuthering Heights*: William Wyler's of 1939, Robert Fuest's of 1970 and Peter Kosminsky's of 1992. I will attempt to consider what can be gained by exploring the conventions through which firstly the novelist and then the three film-makers respectively tell their stories. This will involve not only questions of narrative and plot but also of characterization and meaning. For there is always an ideological point to the telling of stories: narratives not only reflect the historical periods in which they are set but convey meanings about them. The pedagogical point of the comparative exercise is to enable students to note how these meanings alter with the conventions employed and with the time of telling, to appreciate that (and how) re-telling a story in a different medium at a different period of history inevitably brings new meanings into play.

First, however, I want to preface my discussion of these particular examples with a brief outline of the history of the study of adaptation, now over half a century old, which may serve to distinguish the methods and practices which I believe to be of pedagogical and theoretical validity from those which need to be jettisoned (or at least modified). Histories too, however, have (more or less hidden) meanings. So when Sarah Cardwell divides her narrative of adaptation into three phases (the "medium-specific" approach of the 1950s giving way to the "comparative" approach of the 1970s before the "pluralist" approach of the 1990s, when cultural studies critics entered the arena) she is signalling the perceived inadequacy in her view of the first two approaches. Kamilla Elliott ingeniously fits elements of *Wuthering Heights* into her classification of this evolution of adaptation studies from the first "psychic" approaches (in which films were seen attempting like Heathcliff to connect impressionistically with the "spirit" of the text) to the medium-specific "ventriloquist" (film throwing its own voice independently into the corpse of the book) to the "genetic" (the book, like the first Cathy, evolving or mutating structurally into the film, Cathy II). Recent theoretical developments, she also notes, have brought an exotic pluralism of approaches: the "De(Re)composing" (in which the texts merge underground, as in Reader-Response Criticism), the "Incarnational" (in which the original word is phenomenologically made flesh) and the "Trumping" (in which the film treats the original novel as a signifier for its own performance as Heathcliff wins

Wuthering Heights from Hindley) (2003, pp. 136–83). Rather than expand upon this already overloaded but nevertheless not comprehensive list, I would like to note some of the continuities between all these approaches, in particular the attempt to identify the characteristic properties of both media (whatever vocabulary is employed to describe them), and the recognition of adaptation as involving an interpretation, or at least an intertextual relationship of some kind, with the original.

All surveys of adaptation studies begin with George Bluestone, the reprinting in 2003 of whose seminal study of *Novels into Film,* first published in 1957, testifies to its continuing use in courses on adaptation in higher education. Bluestone makes much of the differences between the two media, identifying novels as "conceptual and discursive," operating linguistically through time in the mind, and films as "perceptual and presentational," seen literally in space with the eye (2003; p. xiii; p. 1). These distinctions may be valid enough as opening hypotheses for inductive verification or disproof. It is when he advances from them to universal generalizations about what novels can do that films cannot, for instance convey "mental states" (p. 48) or sustained periods of time (p. 57), that Bluestone opens himself to criticism, the inevitable production of examples when these are achieved in film.

Bluestone has been held largely responsible for the "word/image wars," which have bedevilled adaptation studies ever since (Elliott, 2004, p. 2). James Griffith, in his survey of "Bluestone's heritage" in critics of the 1970s, finds similarly objectionable generalizations in critics insisting that the novel is "uniquely privileged to explore thoughts and feelings, . . . to show the complex interpenetration of past and present, and to handle large abstractions" (1997, p. 27), or that "Film can show us *only* objects, *only* things, only indeed, people as things" (p. 29). Against this, however, Elliott produces equally biased contributions from early film theorists claiming that film had replaced novels "relay fashion," as novels had replaced epic (Metz qtd. Elliott, 2004, p. 5) or objecting to dialogue in film as "a reinfestation of film by literature" (Mast qtd. Elliott, p. 12). She also cites Sarah Kozloff having to defend the use of voice-over against "the conventional notion that films caught [it] (like the measles?) from novels" (1988, p. 23). Generalizations about what film should not do (for example admit any connection with language or literature) are clearly as inappropriate as generalizations about what it cannot do. They may work as exam questions, inviting disagreement and detailed probing, but not as the starting point for the study of adaptation.

Structuralism, I want to suggest, brought an advance in the "comparative" approach to adaptation, not only in a more systematic spelling out of the conventions of novel and film respectively but in the analysis of elements they shared such as narrative. As influential in this respect as Bluestone had been for earlier generations was Brian McFarlane's *Novel to Film* of 1996, which employed Roland Barthes's distinction between functions and indices (the former relating to story, the advancement of the narrative in terms of its basic events, the latter to the discourse or mode of telling the story, bringing additional layers of meaning in terms of character, theme and ideology). The basic functions of a novel's story, McFarlane argued, could be transferred directly to film but the indices required translation into cinematic terms (1996, pp. 13–14). It is a simple enough distinction but one which has proved extremely fruitful in the analysis of particular adaptations.

McFarlane, like many other critics of earlier studies of adaptation, is extremely critical of their obsession with the question of "fidelity" either to the letter or to the spirit of the original. Again, it is not that it isn't appropriate and useful to consider whether or not (and how) an adaptation differs from the novel but this should not be a criterion for aesthetic evaluation but simply the starting point for more interesting questions about the significance and effect of such changes. In characteristic structuralist fashion, critics have suggested different taxonomies of adaptation. Geoffrey Wagner proposing transposition, commentary, and analogy, Dudley Andrew fidelity, intersection, and borrowing and John Desmond close, intermediate, and loose to cover the spectrum from adaptations which aim to change very little of the original to those which opt for considerable intertextual variation. All of them, however, recognize the validity of each kind of adaptation. What needs challenging, as Robert Stam argues, is any assumption that "a novel 'contains' an extractable 'essence,'" which it is the duty of an adaptation to "deliver." A literary text, it is now commonly recognized, "is not a closed, but an open structure, . . . to be reworked by a boundless context" (Stam, 2000, p. 57).

Because a novel is open to different readings at different times, it makes sense for Robert Stam in his most recent contribution to the study of *Literature and Film* to propose viewing a "film adaptation as a form of criticism or 'reading' of the novel," a performance of "someone else's interpretation of the novel," re-accentuated (in Bakhtinian terms) in a set of different grids and discourses (2005, p. 8, p. 15). Neil Sinyard had suggested earlier that "adapting a literary text for the screen is essentially an act of literary criticism" (1986, p. x). But it is, of course, more than that, bringing all the conventions of cinema to a performance which brings out new possibilities in the original text. Stam argues that unlike the "single-track medium" of the novel, confined as it is to words, a "multi-track medium like film" engages not only with words but with music, sound-effects, and images through which it "transforms, modifies, elaborates, or extends" the original novel (2005, pp. 4–5).

All this, of course, sounds fine in theory but needs to be exemplified in practice, so I propose to consider the three Anglophone films of *Wuthering Heights* as intertextual and performative readings of this kind, which students can benefit from analysing. I will look in turn at questions of narrative, plot, characterization, and ideology to see in detail what Wyler, Fuest, and Kominsky make of Emily Brontë's original novel, one of the most complex and indeterminate of Victorian novels. Contemporary reviewers found it "a strange sort of book – baffling all regular criticism" – as a reviewer for *Douglas Jerrold's Weekly Newspaper* put it in January 1840, both because of its multiple narrators and because of its extreme contents: "the reader is shocked, disgusted, almost sickened by details of cruelty, inhumanity, and the most diabolical hate and vengeance" while also (at the other extreme) encountering "powerful testimony to the supreme power of love." Its women characters were found equally baffling, "of a strange fiendish-angelic nature, tantalizing, and terrible" (qtd. Sale & Dunn, in Brontë 1989, p. 302), while its "hero," Heathcliff, appeared to the *Examiner* "an incarnation of evil qualities: implacable hate, ingratitude, cruelty, falsehood, selfishness, and revenge," to name but a few (qtd. Sale & Dunn, 1989, p. 303). Gradually through the nineteenth-century, attitudes towards Heathcliff mellowed as readers came to see him as "the prototypical hero of Gothic Romance" (Haire Sargeant, 1999, p. 167). If later generations of schoolgirls have supposedly swooned over his swarthy charms, more recent critics, in more detached vein, have come to admire the novel's layered narrative, its undermining of conventional notions of gender and propriety, its exploration of class conflict, of power, and of patriarchy.[2]

The narrative structure of the novel (and then of the three films) is the first element I would expect students to notice. The novel is extraordinarily complicated in this respect, with two frame-narrators, firstly Lockwood, whose arrival at Wuthering Heights sparks his interest in a story which Nelly then tells him. But since she is a homodiegetic narrator, a character in the story she tells, who cannot witness every event, she relies upon no less than five other narrators to relay to her some of the events in which they participated: first Heathcliff, who tells her about the visit to Thrushcross Grange at which Cathy is bitten and also (later) his visit to her grave, then a maid, who tells Nelly what a milkman passes on to her (that Heathcliff and Isabella have eloped), then Isabella, who recounts in a letter her bitter experience of marriage to Heathcliff, then Cathy II, who relates her imprisonment and marriage there, and finally Zillah, Nelly's replacement as maid at Wuthering Heights, who continues the narrative of events there, before Nelly and Lockwood finally wrap up the narrative. A result of this complex layering of narrative, it is worth noting, is that there is little continuity of outlook between them. Even Nelly herself cannot be regarded as reliable. She tells Lockwood that her "heart invariably cleaved to [Edgar] the master's, in preference to Catherine's side . . . for he was kind, and trustful, and honourable" (Brontë, 1965, p. 146). She is also given to expressing conventional Victorian values, for instance that "people who do their duty are always finally rewarded" (p. 289). The inadequacy of both Nelly and Lockwood to conceive of emotions as powerful as those of Cathy and Heathcliff is evident throughout the text, forcing readers to read between the lines of their narrative to construct their own understanding of the events.

The film adaptations deal very differently with this narrative structure. Wyler begins with a titlecard of thick white letters placing the action in "the barren Yorkshire moors in England, a hundred years ago" as a stranger knocks "at the door of Wuthering Heights," the letters dissolving for the action to unfold on screen, the words being replaced by a visual image of the house (Elliott, 2003, p. 164). The backlighting creates a strange, uncanny effect against which the house looms "large, dark, threatening" (Harrington, 1981, p. 73). Lockwood's entry to the forbidding house to be attacked by its huge dogs and spurned by its inhospitable guests is then seen from his perspective. We also see his dream of Cathy on the other side of the window crying to be let in (an event which he later recounts to Nelly *as a dream*, insisting that he himself has no belief in ghosts, thus provoking her own narrative: "Maybe if I told you her story you would"). There follows the first of several dissolves from Nelly as narrator to camera portrayal of the action. This is periodically punctuated, however, by Nelly's voiceover commentary, which to some extent, imposes her point of view on the action. She dwells, for example, on the way Cathy is "torn between her love for Heathcliff and her new life at the Grange." She certainly imposes a romantic significance on the ending. It is "not a ghost" that lures Heathcliff to his death, she insists to Lockwood, "but Cathy's love, stronger than time itself." He is "not dead but with her . . . They've only just begun to live." In many respects, it could be argued, the film's Nelly is a more authoritative narrator than the novel's. She may not be so ubiquitous, disappearing for long stretches of the action, but when she does speak there is no suggestion that her perspective is inadequate or unreliable.

Fuest reduces Nelly's voiceover to the beginning of the film, after an introductory view of Cathy's funeral, when she simply reports on Mr Earnshaw's return to Wuthering Heights. She does comment briefly on "the deep and close friendship" between Cathy and Heathcliff, both "rude as savages," but she soon disappears as narrator, playing a more significant part as a character. It is made clear, for example, that she harbours a romantic attachment to Hindley; she is the only one to lament his departure for college and betrays visible disappointment both when he returns with a wife and when he despatches her to Thrushcross Grange with the newly-married Cathy. At the Grange, she voices firm disapproval (as character rather than narrator) of Heathcliff returning to make love first to Cathy and then to Isabella. So, although Fuest dispenses early on with her services as narrator, he retains her role as conventional disapproving moralist if only to encourage viewers to disagree with her.

Kosminsky departs most radically from the narrative strategy of the novel, introducing Emily Brontë herself as narrator. It is she rather than Lockwood who is depicted walking towards the gothic mansion on the windswept moor and it is she who is given authority over the narrative as she announces somewhat portentously, "Something whispered to my mind and I began to write," producing "a world of my imagining." This, as Patsy Stoneman has argued, dramatizes the Romantic belief in the author as the origin and arbiter of meaning (2006, pp. 19–25), invoking the whole Brontë myth of the passionate isolated heroine of romance (Brusberg-Kiermeier, 2004, p. 152). She intervenes in voiceover at frequent intervals in the film, returning in person at the end to pronounce authoritatively, as two riders on horseback gallop into the distance, "Together they are afraid of nothing. They would brave Satan and all his legions." There is an interesting twist to this, since the riders are subsequently identified as Hareton and Cathy II, clinching the way in which the second half of the novel helps to restore the values of love so threatened by the first.

In terms of plot, the analysis of which has been opened up by McFarlane's structuralist approach (which students may initially resist but come to recognize its uses), all three adaptations stick fairly close to the original novel apart from the significant omission by Wyler and Fuest of the second half of the novel, the reconciliation eventually achieved between Cathy II and Hareton. Fuest even has Hareton die before Heathcliff returns. Actual changes to cardinal functions in the original novel (significant events which alter the development of the plot) are kept to a minimum. None of the adaptations has the young Heathcliff blackmail Hindley out of a horse – in the novel Mr Earnshaw buys each of them a colt but Heathcliff's goes lame, whereupon he threatens Hindley with exposing the thrashings he has meted out (p. 80). Wyler actually inverts the scene, making Hindley bully Heathcliff out of his horse, presumably to avoid his hero losing audience sympathy at so early a stage of the film. Bluestone complains that some 30 scenes in Wyler (out of a total of 50) are invented but they can all be seen to have their origins in some aspect of the text (2003, p. 94). The fanciful games, for example that Wyler presents the young Cathy and Heathcliff playing on Pennistone Crag (itself mentioned in the novel but not given nearly as much prominence) arise out of clear references in the novel, in which Heathcliff invites Cathy for "a scamper on the moors" (p. 64) and Nelly records that "it was one of their chief amusements to run away to the moors in the morning and remain there all day" (p. 87). Even the games they play there pick up a suggestion made by Nelly in the novel: "Who knows, but your father was Emperor of China, and your mother an Indian queen" (p. 98). Wyler can be seen in these episodes to dramatize and expand upon elements that can be found in the original film.

Fuest and Kosminsky invent similar scenes which dramatize what the young lovers actually *do* on the moors. Fuest has the two lovers swear eternal vows of allegiance over a stone which will appear in the final scene of the film while Kosminsky has Heathcliff pretend to magical powers, sending Cathy's spirit into the tree under which they habitually meet, which plays the same role as Pennistone Crag in Wyler. There are similar variations in what the Linton children are seen doing in Thrushcross Grange which so fascinates the onlooking Cathy prior to her being bitten: in the novel they quarrel over a dog, in Wyler they are literally having a ball, in Fuest they are playing a kind of indoor tennis while in Kosminsky they quarrel over Isabella's music. But there are no major narrative ramifications, either in terms of functions or indices, resulting from these slight differences. In Wyler, of course, Heathcliff actually revisits Thrushcross Grange during yet another ball at which he will exchange significant glances followed by a balcony confrontation with Cathy but again, there is no interpretative difference which results from this change to the setting for this. Kosminsky has a penchant for staging church ceremonies (three funerals, two weddings and a baptism) but this, it can be argued, is a cinematic way of narrating what is simply given as information in the novel.

The only major plot differences between the films and the original novel, in fact, apart from the omission of the second generation, occur in their endings. None of the films can resist the cinematic possibilities of representing spirits on screen. Wyler accordingly ends with the two ghostly lovers walking towards Pennistone Crag (a change from the original screenplay which had restricted itself to two birds hovering over the crag) (Brusberg-Kiermeier, 2004, p. 152). Fuest has the ghostly Cathy lure Heathcliff away from her funeral (with which the film both begins and ends), only for Hindley to shoot him, after which the two spirits are seen to run off hand in hand. Kosminsky has the most dramatic spirit-presence, a Cathy all in white who takes Heathcliff by the hand and leads him to their special tree under which they embrace.

It is easy, of course, to laugh at these attempts to represent the spiritual world which is so important a dimension of the novel. Fiction has the ability to remain ambiguous, to suggest the presence of the supernatural, leaving the reader with the option of ascribing it to the imaginations of the characters. Film must decide either to show the spirits themselves or not. In each case, as we have seen, the directors go for real ghosts, which makes for a striking scene at the beginning of Kosminsky's film, when the branches of the tree which have been knocking against the window of Lockwood's room turn into Cathy's hands before his (and our) very eyes. In Wyler's film, as we have seen, Lockwood does claim to have dreamt what he (and we) have seen, which does achieve some of the ambiguity of the novel. It could also be argued that all the screen ghosts are to be understood metaphorically, as a way of representing the eternal dimension of love which may have had a resonance within the society portrayed but is not meant to be taken literally by a more sophisticated modern audience. It would certainly be a poor adaptation of *Wuthering Heights* which ignored the supernatural altogether.

The most significant differences between the novel and the three films, however, can be found in the softened characterization of the central characters (students, in my experience, find characterization the easiest area to analyse, whether in fiction or in film). Wyler's producer, Samuel Goldwyn, put the matter bluntly, not seeing "why an audience would pull for a capricious irresponsible girl and a hate-filled man bent on revenging his miserable childhood" (Haire Sargeant, 1999, p. 229). By omitting much of the second half of the novel, Wyler and Fuest manage to avoid showing the harshest elements of the "revenge" plot but both central characters need considerable softening from their depiction in the novel if they are going to be seen as romantic lovers, which does appear to be their role in all three films.

Part of the point of the novel, of course, is to present readers with a dilemma about its hero, a contradiction raised by Lockwood at the beginning when he describes him as both "a dark-skinned gypsy" and "a gentleman" (p. 47) with "an almost diabolical sneer" (p. 55). Even Earnshaw acknowledges that his adopted child is "as dark almost as if it came from the devil" (p. 77), a judgement confirmed by Nelly, who also detects something "diabolical" in him (p. 106), exacerbated as it is by his treatment by Hindley. Catherine herself has no illusions about his nature, telling Isabella that he's no "rough diamond" but "a fierce, pitiless, wolfish man" (p. 141). She compares him with Satan, since he rejoices like him in "inflicting misery" (p. 151), a comparison repeated by Cathy II, who calls him "lonely, like the devil, and envious like him" (351). These, of course, are all judgements made by other characters in the novel which it is possible for readers to dispute. But it would be difficult for the most sympathetic reader not to acknowledge the abusive nature of his treatment of Isabella, their son Linton, Cathy II and Hareton. He also has a tendency not only to hang dogs but to behave like them: Nelly recounts how he "gnashed at me, and foamed like a mad dog" (p. 195), dashing his head against a tree and howling "like a savage beast" when he hears of Cathy's death (p. 204).

Cathy too is no angel, a fact confirmed by her dream of being "flung" from heaven onto the moors by the "angry angels" (p. 120). Nelly is prepared to assign some of her childhood mischief to "high . . . spirits" (p. 83) but grows increasingly suspicious of her "ambition" and "double character" in encouraging Edgar at the Grange while laughing at him at the Heights (p. 107). Cathy is also prone to violence, pinching Nelly, shaking Hareton, and boxing Edgar himself on the ear. That she is deeply disturbed after Heathcliff's disappearance is apparent in her "fits," "rages" and "depression of spirits" (pp. 128 and 131) even before she starts "dashing her head against the arm of the sofa, and grinding her teeth" (p. 156). The terms that Nelly uses are those of illness: she is "deranged" (p. 159), suffering from "madness" (160), a victim of "mental illness" (p. 190). Again, we may as readers reject Nelly's labels, rejoicing with critics such as Sandra Gilbert over her Blakean subversion of the conventional models of good and evil, angels and devils (1993, pp. 131–60). But the point is that she is not portrayed in the novel as a conventional romantic heroine.

The three film versions of *Wuthering Heights* present very different versions of both Heathcliff and Cathy. Wyler, casting the glamorous Laurence Olivier as Heathcliff, presents him as a long-suffering, deep-feeling, faithful lover. Much is made of his possible exotic oriental origins, only suggested by Nelly in the novel as a means of comforting and encouraging him. There is absolutely no indication of diabolism; it is clear that his worst suffering is a result of his rejection by Cathy. "If your heart were only stronger than your dull fear of the world," he tells her on his return, she would not throw love away "for a handful of worldliness." His suffering prompts Heathcliff into such Byronic questions as "Why did God give me life? What is it but hunger and pain?" and "What do they know of heaven and hell who know nothing of life?" Later, on Cathy's deathbed, while the others pray in conventional Christian fashion for her salvation, the only prayer he can make is that she will "haunt" him. This Heathcliff, into which Olivier throws all the passion and feeling he can command, is a fully-fledged Romantic rebel against conventional propriety.

This romanticization of Heathcliff, of course, demands a corresponding change in Cathy. She may not be the "vulgar tease" and "common snob, the bitch-heroine luring her helpless male to destruction" which Wagner unkindly called her (1975, p. 240), but after her initial protestations of undying love for Heathcliff she is soon drawn towards the life of the Grange: "That's what I want," she tells him, "dancing and singing in a pretty world." He in turn, after her return from the Grange "a lady," warns her that she is turning into a "vain, weak, greedy fool." That she is "torn" between the two lives (in the words of Nelly's voiceover) is apparent in the way she tears off her new dress and runs off to Pennistone Crag once more, begging Heathcliff's forgiveness and asking him to "fill my arms with heather." From this point of the film she oscillates wildly between the two worlds, the polite respectability which Edgar offers and the genuine passion which sporadically breaks through Merle Oberon's frozen and clearly troubled visage. Only on her deathbed, as she asks a bemused Edgar to fetch heather from "the castle on the moors" and proclaims, "I was a Queen once," does she recognize the mistake she has made. Her story thus becomes a tragedy of inauthenticity, only partially redeemed by her belated recognition of the importance of love.

Wyler's film, of course, was released in April 1939 (on the day Italy invaded Albania) which helps to explain its dark and foreboding atmosphere (Lawson-Peebles, 1996, p. 1). Fuest's film was the product of a very different time (1970), at the end of a decade noted for its release from restraint (especially in areas of sexual morality). This helps to account for its "swashbuckling hero" played by a very young Timothy Dalton, offering unfettered passion and "rough sex" (Haire Sargeant, 1999, p. 181). Having earlier knocked Cathy about in the stable before making love to her, he presses Isabella roughly against a tree before asking her, with seventies insouciance, if she "fancies a tumble." In spite of this, Cathy (Anna Calder-Marshall) hurries out from the Grange with flowers in her hair, like Lady Chatterley, to join her lover in the woods, to be hurled to the ground and roll with him in the grass. There are vestiges of the suffering Heathcliff in his complaint to her that "I went through hell" and in his dashing his head against a tree on hearing of her death (as in the novel). But viewers are clearly expected to admire the Bond-like energy and relish with which he defeats Edgar's men, vaults some railings, kisses his sister, and rides off into the distance. Even in death he is not wholly defeated, his spirit, as we have seen, running off hand in hand with that of his lover.

Ralph Fiennes's Heathcliff in Kosminsky's film of 1992 is the only performance seriously to develop the harsh, sadistic side of his character in the novel. It too has been seen as a Heathcliff for his own time: complex, aloof, depressed (Haire Sargeant, 1999, p. 190). The 1990s, Sara Martin observes, was a time when abuse became something to be publicly exposed. There is accordingly no attempt in this portrait to play down his cruel treatment of Isabella and the second generation at Wuthering Heights (2005, p. 57). This Heathcliff is made to punish Cathy for her delayed return from the Grange by starving some baby lapwings, on the perverse ground that she had prevented him from showing them to her. Cathy, as played by Juliet Binoche, responds to Heathcliff's savagery somewhat strangely, forever giggling and laughing, presumably as a result of the "high spirits" attributed to her by Nelly in the novel as well as to try to improve his moods. Kosminsky, who often reproduces dialogue from the novel verbatim, certainly captures both the "diabolical" aspects of Heathcliff's character and his later haunting by Cathy, when he stares so wildly into the air that Nelly offers to "fetch the parson" (presumably to conduct an exorcism). The Brontë voiceover, on the evidence of this characterization, is quite justified in speaking of his preparedness to "brave Satan and all his legions" and to continue to "walk the moors."

I have attempted to give at least some idea of the different interpretations of *Wuthering Heights* provided by these three films and to suggest how the different periods of their making may account for some of these variations. There is clearly much more that students might be expected to identify as ideological elements in all three films. There are issues of race and class, for example, as well as the questions of gender discussed above. Christopher Heywood, in his introduction to the Broadview edition of the novel, makes a convincing case for regarding Heathcliff as black (Brontë, 2002, pp. 56–70). My main objective, however, has been to illustrate the continuing value of a "comparative" approach to adaptation, particularly in the teaching of Victorian fiction. To note the differences of interpretation displayed by these films *is* to encourage students to return once again to the text, which should produce a deepened understanding of the conventions of written narrative as well as film. Students should also discover that there are significant elements of indeterminacy in the novel, which these filmic interpretations attempt to resolve. There will never, of course, be a definitive interpretation of the novel on screen just as there cannot be one "correct" reading of any novel. For students to discover this through careful analysis of the conventions of both media, I suggest, is a genuinely useful outcome of the study of adaptation.

Finally: In the module I currently teach on adapting Victorian novels to screen, a sample syllabus for which is given at the end of this essay, I ask students to consider similar questions of narrative technique, plot, characterization and ideology in *Middlemarch, Daisy Miller, Tess of the d'Urbervilles* and *A Room with a View*. This involves drawing attention to some of the same technical devices (how to translate free indirect discourse into cinematic terms), of plot (Polanski's omission of cardinal functions in Hardy's novel) and gender (the way Daisy Miller and Tess can be seen as victims of male desire). There are additional questions about heritage raised by the BBC adaptation of *Middlemarch* and by Merchant Ivory in general, which are less significant in the adaptations of *Wuthering Heights*. The point is that students learn to look with new eyes not only at the films but at their Victorian originals. They also discover the processes involved in interpreting and translating the novels to a different medium in a different age.

Appendix: sample syllabus: real to reel: Victorian novel to film

Aims and Outcomes: The point of this course is to consider how narrative functions in a range of Victorian (and Edwardian) fiction and how it is transferred from the page to the screen. Special attention is given to questions of realism, how the novel and its adaptation attempt to present the "reality" of the world depicted. Students will be expected to test various theories about narrative against their experience of reading and watching four novels and their adaptations.

Weekly schedule

Week 1
- Lecture: Narrative Theory: An Introduction
- Seminar: Seymour Chatman, "What Novels Can Do that Films Can't (and Vice Versa)," in *Film Theory and Criticism,* ed. Gerald Mast, Marshall Cohen and Leo Braudy, Fifth edition (Oxford: Oxford University Press), pp. 403–28.
- Brian McFarlane, *Novel to Film: An Introduction to the Theory of Adaptation,* (Oxford: Clarendon Press), pp. 3–30.

Week 2
- Lecture: Narrator and characters: *Middlemarch*
- Seminar: David Lodge, "*Middlemarch* and the Idea of the Classic Realist Text" in David Lodge, *After Bakhtin* (London: Routledge, 1990), pp. 45–56.

Week 3
- Lecture: Ideology: *Middlemarch*
- Seminar: Kathleen Blake, "Vocation, Love and the Woman Question," in Kathleen Blake, *Love and the Woman Question* (Brighton: Harvester Press, 1982), pp. 44–53.

Week 4
- Lecture: Adaptation: *Middlemarch*
- Seminar: Ian MacKillop and Alison Platt, "Beholding in a Magic Panorama: Television and the Illustration of *Middlemarch*" in Robert Giddings and Erica Sheen, eds, *The Classic Novel: From Page to Screen* (Manchester: Manchester University Press, 2000), pp. 71–92.

Week 5
- Lecture: James's *Daisy Miller*
- Seminar: Robert Weisbuch, "Winterbourne and the Doom of Manhood," in Vivian R. Pollak, ed., *New Essays on James's "Daisy Miller" and "The Turn of the Screw"* (Cambridge: Cambridge University Press, 1993), pp. 65–89.

Week 6
- Lecture: Bogdanovich's *Daisy Miller*
- Seminar: David Cross, "Framing the Sketch: Bogdanovich's *Daisy Miller*," in John R. Bradley, ed., *Henry James on Stage and Screen* (Basingstoke: Palgrave – now Palgrave Macmillan, 2000), pp. 127–42.

Week 7
- Lecture Hardy's *Tess of the d'Urbervilles*
- Seminar: Penny Boumelha, "*Tess of the d'Urbervilles*: Sexual Ideology and Narrative Form," in Penny Boumelha, *Thomas Hardy and Women* (Brighton: Harvester, 1982), pp. 117–34

Week 8
- Lecture: Polanski's *Tess*
- Seminar: Peter Widdowson, "A Tragedy of Modern Life? Polanski's *Tess*," in Peter Widdowson, ed., *Tess of the d'Urbervilles: Contemporary Critical Essays* (Basingstoke: Macmillan – now Palgrave Macmillan, 1993 pp. 95–108).

Week 9
- Lecture: Forster's *A Room with a View*
- Seminar: E. M. Forster's *Aspects of the Novel,* chapter 4 "People (continued)," Harmondsworth: Penguin, 1990, pp. 71–84 + Jeffrey Heath, "Kissing and

Telling: Turning Round in *A Room with a View*," in J. H. Stape, ed., *E. M. Forster: Critical Assessments* (Mountfield (East Sussex): Helm Information, 1997), III, pp. 187–221

Week 10
- Lecture: Ivory's *A Room with a View*
- Seminar: June Perry Levine, "Two Rooms with a View: An Inquiry into Film Adaptation" in J. H. Stape (as above) vol. IV pp. 202–21 + Peter J. Hutchings, "A Disconnected View: Forster, Modernity and Film," in the New Casebook *E. M. Forster*, ed. Jeremy Tambling (Basingstoke: Macmillan – now Palgrave Macmillan, 1995), pp. 213–28.

Notes

1. The title of Seymour Chatman's article, reproduced in Leo Braudy and Marshall Cohen (eds.), *Film Theory and Criticism*, 5th edn. (Oxford: Oxford University Press, 1999), pp. 435–51.
2. See the essays by N. M. Jacobs, "Gendered and Layered Narrative in *Wuthering Heights*," by Terry Eagleton, "Myths of Power in *Wuthering Heights*," and Patricia Parker, "The (Self-)Identity of the Literary Text: Property, Proper Place, and Proper Name in *Wuthering Heights*," reprinted in Patsy Stoneman (ed.), *Wuthering Heights: Contemporary Critical Essays* (Basingstoke: Macmillan – now Palgrave Macmillan, 1993).

Works cited

Aragay, Mirceia (ed.), *Books in Motion: Adaptation, Intertextuality, Authorship* (Amsterdam: Rodopi, 2005).
Bluestone, George, *Novels into Film* (Baltimore: Johns Hopkins University Press, 2003)
Braudy, Leo and Marshall Cohen (eds.), *Film Theory and Criticism*, 5th edn. (Oxford: Oxford University Press, 1999).
Brontë, Emily, *Wuthering Heights*, ed. David Daiches (Harmondsworth: Penguin, 1965).
——. *Wuthering Heights,* ed. William Sale, Jr., and Richard J. Dunn (New York: Norton, 1989).
——. *Wuthering Heights,* ed. Christpher Heywood (Peterborough, Ontario: Broadview, 2002).
Brusberg-Kiermeier, Stefani, "Stormy Novel, Thorny Adaptation: Recent Appropriations of *Wuthering Heights*," in Eckhart Voigts-Virchow (ed.), *Janespotting and Beyond: British Heritage Retrovisions Since the Mid-1990s* (Tübingen: Narr, 2004), pp. 149–57.
Cardwell, Sarah, *Adaptation Revisited: Television and the Classic Novel* (Manchester: Manchester University Press, 2002).
Desmond, John M., *Adaptation: Studying Film and Literature* (Boston: McGraw Hill, 2005).
Elliot, Kamilla, *Rethinking the Novel/Film Debate* (Cambridge: Cambridge University Press, 2003).
——. "Novels, Films, and the Word/Image Wars," in Robert Stam and Alessandro Raengo (eds.), *A Companion to Literature and Film* (Oxford: Blackwell, 2004), pp. 1–17.

Ellis, John, "The Literary Adaptation," *Screen,* 23 (1982), pp. 6–19.

Gilbert, Sandra, "Looking Oppositely: Emily Brontë's Bible of Hell," repr. in Pasty Stoneman (ed.), *Wuthering Heights: Contemporary Critical Essays* (Basingstoke: Macmillan, 1993), pp. 131–60.

Griffith, James, *Adaptations as Imitations: Films from Novels* (London: Associated University Press, 1997).

Haire-Sargeant, Lin, "Sympathy for the Devil: The Problem of Heathcliff in Film Versions of *Wuthering Heights,*" in Barbara Tepa Lupack (ed.), *Nineteenth-Century Women at the Movies: Adapting Classic Women's Fiction to Film* (Bowling Green: Bowling Green State University Popular Press, 1999), pp. 164–91.

Harrington, John, "Wyler as Auteur," in *The English Novel at the Movies,* ed. Michael Klein and Gillian Parker (New York: Ungar, 1981), pp. 67–82.

Klein, Michael and Gillian Parker (eds.), *The English Novel at the Movies* (New York: Ungar, 1981).

Konigsberg, Ira (ed.), *The Complete Film Dictionary* (New York: New American Library, 1987).

Kozloff, Sarah, *Invisible Storytellers: Voice-Over Narrative in American Fiction Film* (Berkeley: University of California Press, 1988).

Lawson-Peebles, Robert, "European Conflict and Hollywood's Reconstruction of English Fiction," *Yearbook of English Studies,* 26 (1996), pp. 1–13.

Lonoff, Sue and Terry Hasseler (eds.), *Approaches to Teaching Emily Brontë's "Wuthering Heights"* (New York: Modern Language Association, 2006).

Martin, Sara, "What Does Heathcliff Look Like? Performance in Peter Kosminsky's Version of Emily Brontë's *Wuthering Heights,*" in Mirceia Aragay (ed.), *Books in Motion: Adaptation, Intertextuality, Authorship* (Amsterdam: Rodopi, 2005), pp. 51–67.

McConnell, Frank, D., *Storytelling and Mythmaking: Images from Film and Literature* (New York: Oxford University Press, 1979).

McFarlane, Brian, *Novel to Film: An Introduction to the Theory of Film Adaptation* (Oxford: Clarendon Press, 1996).

Mast, Gerald, *A Short History of the Movies* (Indianapolis: Bobbs Merrill, 1981), p. 185, quoted in Elliott, 2004.

Metz, Christian, *The Imaginary Signifier: Psychoanalysis and the Cinema* (Bloomingon: Indiana University Press, 1977).

Murray, Edward, *The Cinematic Imagination: Writers and the Motion Pictures* (New York: Ungar, 1972).

Ray, Robert "The Field of 'Literature and Film,'" in James Naremore (ed.), *Film Adaptation* (London: Athlone Press, 2000), pp. 38–53.

Sinyard, Neil, *Filming Literature: The Art of Screen Adaptation* (London: Croom Helm, 1986).

Stam, Robert, "Beyond Fidelity: The Dialogics of Adaptation," in James Naremore (ed.), *Film Adaptation* (London: Athlone Press, 2000), pp. 54–76.

——. *Literature Through Film: Realism, Magic, and the Art of Adaptation* (Oxford: Blackwell, 2005).

——. and Alessandra Raengo (eds.), *Literature and Film* (Oxford: Oxford University Press, 2005).

Stoneman, Patsy (ed.), *Wuthering Heights: Contemporary Critical Essays* Basingstoke: Macmillan – now Palgrave Macmillan, 1993).

Voigts-Virchow, Eckhart (ed.), *Janespotting and Beyond: British Heritage Retrovisions since the Mid-1990s* (Tübingen: Narr, 2004), pp. 149–57.

Wagner, Geoffrey, *The Novel and the Cinema* (London: The Tantivy Press, 1975).

12
Rehabilitating the Nineteenth Century: The Revisionist Novel

Grace Moore

I

Reinventing the nineteenth century is certainly not a new phenomenon, although the last twenty years have seen a veritable explosion of novels that revise or memorialize the period. Raphael Samuel has attributed this revival of interest to conservative efforts to assert so-called "Victorian values," although, of course, many writers of so-called "neo-Victorian" fiction return to the nineteenth century as a way of combating conservatism, rather than celebrating it. Samuel helpfully terms this re-animation of the past "resurrectionism," a term that neatly taps into the Dickensian idea of "recalling to life" (1984, p. 40). It is also a term that has been adopted by postcolonial critics, including Kathleen Renk, to encapsulate the way in which the past can impinge upon the present (1999). This chapter will consider some of the challenges associated with teaching the neo-Victorian novel and the role that revisionist texts can play in introducing students to the literature of the nineteenth century and a range of theoretical perspectives.

II

As is often noted, the nineteenth-century novel has a bad reputation among students with increasing demands on their time. As they have to work longer and longer hours in order to support themselves through college, the sheer difficulty of getting through a 900-page novel each week can deter bright, motivated students from electing to study the Victorians. The additional problem that we face as teachers of the nineteenth-century novel is that many students subscribe to the Bloomsbury-inspired myth that the Victorian period was gloomy, miserable, and repressed. Simon Joyce puts his finger on this difficulty when he writes of the dangers of:

> [A] continuing insistence on seeing the Victorians in terms that were established by self-defined modernists in their first moment of recoil.

Doing so . . . commits us to a perpetuation of modernism's sense of itself as a negation of the past, an attitude that has already helped generate more than a century of denigration and revivalist reversals. (2007, p. 174).

Many of our students have succumbed to this version of the nineteenth century and part of our role as educators is unquestionably to help them to understand the breadth and diversity of the Victorians. In a bid to assist students in reconsidering their perceptions of the nineteenth century – not to mention the Modernists – it can be useful to begin Victorian survey classes with an extract from Virginia Woolf's *Orlando*:

All was darkness; all was doubt; all was confusion. The Eighteenth century was over; the Nineteenth century had begun . . . The great grey cloud which hung, not only over London, but over the whole of the British Isles on the first day of the nineteenth century stayed . . . long enough to have extraordinary consequences upon those who lived beneath its shadow. Rain fell frequently, but only in fitful gusts, which were no sooner over than they began again . . . The damp struck within. Men felt the chill in their hearts: the damp in their minds. In a desperate effort to snuggle their feelings into some sort of warmth one subterfuge was tried after another. Love, birth, and death were all swaddled in a variety of fine phrases. The sexes drew further and further apart. No open conversation was tolerated. Evasions and concealments were practiced on both sides. (Woolf, pp. 156–7).

A close reading of this parody can help students to understand how the reputation of the Victorians suffered in the early twentieth century and can then segue into a discussion of why Woolf and her colleagues might have to represent the Victorians as dingy and uptight. Woolf's love-hate relationship with the nineteenth century also makes her a logical starting point for a neo-Victorian course and, when paired with extracts from Lytton Strachey's *Eminent Victorians* (1918), her willful misrepresentation of the nineteenth century can help students to think about the myth-making that surrounds the Victorians and the different agendas of those involved in re-imagining them.

One of the difficulties in teaching an undergraduate course entirely devoted to the neo-Victorian novel is that it is not safe to assume that the majority of students will be familiar with the "parent text" that is being revised or pastiched, or that they will have the historical background knowledge to put the novel(s) into context.[1] While it is possible to teach a novel like Lloyd Jones's *Mr. Pip* (2006) or Peter Carey's *Jack Maggs* (1997) to students who are unfamiliar with Dickens's *Great Expectations*, it is a difficult task that closes off the possibility of an in-depth discussion about original sources, influences, in-jokes, and revisionism, unless the teacher is prepared to devote class time to extensive plot summaries. Hand-outs can of course assist, but they are certainly no substitute for reading the novel in its entirety. As a consequence, the most effective neo-Victorian courses seem to be those that pair texts from the nineteenth century with an updated version, thus allowing students to gain a full understanding of the dialogue between the reinvented novel and its source.

There are numerous possibilities for the critical direction a neo-Victorian course can take, given the diverse political and creative agendas of those involved in re-writing the Victorian novel. A survey course might incorporate a number of different approaches, taking in nostalgic historical fictions like John Fowles's *The French Lieutenant's Woman* (1969) A. S. Byatt's *Possession* (1990), feminist texts including Jean Rhys's *Wide Sargasso Sea* (1966) or Sarah Waters' meticulously-researched trilogy of lesbian historical fictions – *Tipping the Velvet* (1998), *Affinity* (1999), *Fingersmith* (2003) – postcolonial works like V. S. Naipaul's *Guerillas* (1975) or J. G. Farrell's *The Siege of Krishnapur* (1974). For some upper-level students it can also be of interest to examine the trajectory of revisionism, looking at late-Victorian iconoclasts like Oscar Wilde and Samuel Butler, who resisted "high" Victorianism from within, then moving through Bloomsbury to the Victorian revival of the 1950s, taking in texts like Elizabeth Coles Taylor's *A Game of Hide-and-Seek* (1951) or Marghanita Laski's *The Victorian Chaise-Longue* (1953), before looking at better-known contemporary novels like Gail Jones's *Sixty Lights* (2004) or Julian Barnes's account of Arthur Conan Doyle's defence of George Edalji, *Arthur and George* (2005).

From a teaching perspective, the post-World War II period offers a particularly valuable opportunity to consider the ebbs and flows in the reputation of the Victorians in Britain. Following the wide scale destruction of Victorian buildings and monuments during the Blitz, the 1950s saw a revival of interest in nineteenth-century heritage. As James Thompson has suggested, the BBC was at the forefront of this re-evaluation of the Victorian past, and students may find it interesting to think more broadly about the role of costume dramas, interior design, and heritage movements in conserving and celebrating the nineteenth century (2004, pp. 150–66). While students may not have encountered either Victorian or neo-Victorian novels before, they are likely to have been exposed to a range of Victoriana, whether through purchasing replica Victorian trinkets or decorations (or visiting heritage theme parks like "Dickens World" in Kent, where visitors can enjoy activities from a "Great Expectations Boat Ride" to a stint in the 1890s classroom). These re-workings of Victorianism can provide a point of access, both in terms of studying the nineteenth-century novel and in considering why there is such extraordinary nostalgia for the Victorian period. Students can be encouraged to think about the presence of the Victorian in their daily lives – whether it be in the form of art, architecture, literature, or more popular culture – and this type of general discussion may gradually be steered towards a consideration of Victorian influence and the Victorian afterlife.

An interdisciplinary course focusing on the recycling of Victorian culture across a range of media can ease the burden on students who simply do not have the time to commit to a large amount of reading. Graphic novels like Alan Moore's and Kevin O'Neill's *The League of Extraordinary Gentlemen* (1999) and *From Hell (1991)* or Tom Phillips's "treated" Victorian novel, *A Humument* (1980) offer visual versions of Victorianism that can be assimilated rapidly, but nevertheless offer enormous potential for discussion. Film offers similar opportunities, whether it is through analysing a well-executed costume drama or, indeed, debating why it is that "period" dramas also need to be revised and updated to remain "current," even as they memorialize the past. Andrew Davies, for instance, recently (2008) remade *Little Dorrit* as a sequence of thirty-minute episodes to reflect an "authentic" Dickensian reading experience of weekly instalments, displacing Christine Edzard's somewhat hefty two-part film version of 1987. Davies's update perhaps reflects a growing public awareness of the Victorian reading experience. Given that both versions appeared at times of global economic uncertainty, they may also point to a need for a twenty-first century interpretation of a novel depicting widespread financial collapse. Discussions can also centre around questions like the appeal of the Victorian to a film-maker like Jane Campion, whose *The Piano* (1993) has been discussed extensively as an exemplar of neo-Victorian cinema. Writing on Campion, Cora Kaplan has noted that the immediacy and affect of film can assist us in understanding revisionism, its relation to history and our ongoing desire to consume updated versions of Victorian stories:

> The cinema frames much more graphically . . . questions about our need – and our ability – to know and possess the past. Film's enhanced capacity to arouse us highlights the accompanying affective and ethical implications of such desires and identifications. It also raises the important but often ignored issue of what or where the "historical" is in Victoriana. (2007, p. 126)

While I would argue that one can be just as moved by Charles Palliser's portrait of Victorian orphanhood in *The Quincunx* (1989) as by Campion's mute Ada and her loveless marriage of convenience, the sheer popularity of films like *The Piano* should alert us to a broader public need to "know and possess" the Victorians, even while that Victorianism is being creatively reconfigured.

Integrating film into both nineteenth-century and neo-Victorian classes can undoubtedly bring the period to life for students lacking a firm contextual grounding, and it can generate interest in returning to written texts. When teaching the Jack the Ripper murders on a Victorian Crime course that is otherwise concerned with fiction, I always try to screen the 2001

Hughes Brothers' movie, *From Hell*. After the initial excitement at watching Johnny Depp has subsided, the students are very responsive to the idea of thinking about fictionalizing actual historical events (the film is based on Moore's graphic novel, which in turn owes a debt to Stephen Knight's *Jack the Ripper: The Final Solution*). In addition to considering the Whitechapel murders in context, the students often discuss Victorian sources, thinking about how Gustave Doré's engravings from *London: A Pilgrimage* (1870) have influenced the set design and considering the role of postmodernism in this drama of opium dreams, conspiracies, and revised endings. In many ways *From Hell* is a densely literary text and can be taught alongside extracts from Wilkie Collins's *The Moonstone* or late-Victorian slumming expeditions to show students how it connects to its nineteenth-century context. Other areas for study on a course that visualizes the Victorians might include the rise of the Merchant-Ivory costume drama as a way of considering the heritage industry, or an analysis of the process of what Jay Clayton has termed "hacking" the Victorians via the Japanese animated film *Steamboy* (2004).

Clayton cleverly adapts the language of information technology to think about the ruptures that occur in many neo-Victorian fictions, particularly those by authors writing with a postmodern agenda:

> To hack the nineteenth century in a literary work means altering the temporal order of events, deliberately creating anachronisms in a representational world . . . . To be interesting, anachronism must first establish a creative relationship with the received wisdom about a period. Variations, however ingenious, must have a logic or plausibility that stems from accepted features of the past. Second, anachronism should suggest intriguing perspectives on the contemporary world. Whether as cautionary fable, satire, or allegory, the anachronisms of alternative history implicitly comment on present conditions. (2003, p. 195)

As Clayton suggests here, the preconceptions that we, and our students, bring to the nineteenth century have a vital role in engaging with the chronological playfulness that is a hallmark of steampunk and speculative fiction. His comments also suggest that the conversation that we enter into with history when we read a neo-Victorian novel is a two-way process. At a time when Victorian studies is experiencing something of a crisis of identity, the idea that anachronism can help us to revive student interest in our field *and* put misapprehensions of Victorian culture to work in the classroom is a compelling one that needs further debate.[2] Certainly, students need to be distrustful of the idea that there is a single "authentic" Victorianism waiting for them to discover, but they also need to understand that the authors they are considering are not simply being irresponsible with history, but are instead creating multiple, competing versions of the past that often form dialogues with one another.

Steampunk is a genre that exemplifies the kinds of anachronisms Clayton has in mind and simply revels in its own artifice. It is highly popular with students – many of whom read it for pleasure – and it offers an accessible introduction to postmodern aspects of neo-Victorianism, particularly if students are aware of the works of late nineteenth-century science fiction writers like H. G. Wells. Written texts that work well in the classroom include Paul di Filippo's *Steampunk Trilogy* and Kage Baker's "Speed, Speed the Cable." Still within the realms of speculative fiction, although not technically steampunk, is Neal Stephenson's *The Diamond Age* (1996). Although many students find this novel confusing in the first instance, they inevitably have strong reactions to Stephenson's writing, with some finding his bricoleur's approach to history exhilarating, while others regard it as exasperating. Stephenson's character Hackworth, an inventor, sheds light on the neo-Victorian venture as a whole, when he explains to his employer, Lord Finkle-Mcgraw:

> My life was not without periods of excessive, unreasoning discipline, usually imposed capriciously by those responsible for laxity in the first place. That combined with my historical studies led me, as many others, to the conclusion that there was little in the previous century worthy of emulation, and that we must look to the nineteenth century instead for stable models. (1996, p. 24)

For Hackworth, a return to Victorian values signals a retreat from the more recent past and a nostalgic yearning for an era when rules and regulations seemed to be more rigidly applied. Of course, Hackworth's version of Victorianism is heavily romanticized and reveals more about his need for a sense of an elsewhere, than anything about the first Victorians. As a corrective to Hackworth's longing, Stephenson also provides us with a Bloomsbury-inflected view of Victorianism, when he describes his central character Nell's studies:

> They studied the most ghastly parts of Dickens, which Miss Bowlware carefully explained was *called* Victorian literature because it was *written* during the reign of Victoria I, but was actually *about* pre-Victorian times, and that the mores of the original Victorians – the ones who built the old British Empire – were actually a reaction against the sort of bad behavior engaged in by their parents and grandparents and so convincingly detailed by Dickens, their most popular novelist.
>   The girls actually got to sit at their desks and play a few ractives showing what it was like to live during this time: generally not very nice, even if you selected the option that turned off all the diseases. At this point, Mrs Disher stepped in to say, if you thought *that* was scary, look at how poor people lived in the late twentieth century. Indeed, after ractives told

them about the life of an inner-city Washington, D.C. child during the 1990s, most students had to agree that they'd take a workhouse in pre-Victorian England over *that* any day. (Stephenson, p. 313)

This passage alerts us to Stephenson's somewhat cavalier approach to historical facts, in that unpleasant aspects of Victorian culture and society become pre-Victorian because the neo-Victorians do not wish to be reminded of similar problems within their own hierarchical society. The juxtaposition of the Victorian with futuristic devices like the "ractive" nicely skews the reader's sense of history and defamiliarizes the nineteenth century. Nell, for instance, resists her namesake, Little Nell's destiny and, although she is similarly passive, she is on the whole a much more rounded and engaging character than Dickens's somewhat insipid original. Stephenson succeeds in de-centering our understanding of the chronology and context of *The Diamond Age* by redrawing maps and national boundaries, juxtaposing advanced nanotechnology and matter compilers with top hats and velocipedes, and then complicating matters still further, by adding contemporary corporations like McDonald's or Kentucky Fried Chicken into the mix. However, Stephenson's collapsing together of times and cultural artefacts helps students to identify Victoriana and to consider the presence of the Victorian in the present.

Neo-Victorianism can aid students in understanding and appreciating the nineteenth-century novel. Adding a revisionist text like David Lodge's *Nice Work* (1988) to a syllabus that otherwise examines Victorian works can help students to realize why they might want to study these "loose baggy monsters" of the past. With its academic protagonist and factory setting, *Nice Work* is what Robin Gilmour has termed a "research novel" in that it highlights the prominence of Victorian literature and culture in modern academic life (2000, p. 190).[3] Drawing most heavily upon Gaskell's *North and South*, with references to *Sybil, Hard Times, Alton Locke* and, moving into the twentieth century, Forster's *Howards End*, Lodge demonstrates clear parallels between the industrial wasteland of 1980s Birmingham and Manchester of the 1850s. The novel points to common concerns, such as class tensions between the North and the South and the need for workplace reforms in the past and the present. Furthermore, the extracts from lectures on the nineteenth-century novel given by the central character, Robyn Penrose, are especially useful from a pedagogical perspective, as they help students to understand the links between the past and the present, as well as providing contextual information in an accessible form. A campus novel is almost always appealing to students, since it represents the world that they inhabit, and when teamed with "Condition of England" novels a text like *Nice Work* can provide relief, both in terms of its length and its comparative accessibility. As Sue Lonoff has noted in the light of a survey of early career academics, "one clear message (is) the need for giving students a sense of the issues that Victorian literature manifests and, indeed, develops" (2002, p. 172, my parentheses). Through its intertextuality and contemporaneity the revisionist text can inform our reading of the nineteenth-century novel, problematizing issues like race and class and highlighting concerns that remain topical in the here and now. It can also often assist with the introduction of theoretical approaches and, as a literary theorist himself, Lodge interweaves a number of theoretical approaches, including feminism, structuralism, and post-structuralism, into *Nice Work*, ensuring that the novel can work just as well on a course introducing theory as it does in a neo-Victorian context.

Nancy Armstrong's provocative assertion that "postmodernism is a consequence and acknowledgement of the Victorian definition of the nation" (in Kucich & Sadoff, (2000, p. 312), like Lodge's novel, offers a bridge not just between past and present, but also between forms of historical fiction. Her comment invites us to draw connections between postmodernism and postcolonialism and is useful in terms of thinking through the logic underpinning a survey course of neo-Victorian novels. Armstrong's assertion can provide an excellent starting point for students to begin to make connections across sub-genres of neo-Victorian texts and to help them to arrive at a holistic understanding of how different types of historical fictions have evolved alongside developments in literary theory and broader social change.

III

In *Postcolonial Con-Texts: Writing Back to the Canon* (2001), John Thieme argues that there is little to connect the diverse texts that "write back" to the nineteenth-century novel and he contends that the differences between cultures are simply too vast, making it impossible to construct a single, neat theory to bind them all together. Thieme argues that a novel like the Canadian Jane Urquart's *Changing Heaven* (1993), a novel loosely based on *Wuthering Heights* and featuring the ghost of Emily Brontë, can have little in common with revisions of the same novel penned by, for example, Guadaloupan writer Maryse Condé in *Windward Heights* (1999) or the English poet Anne Carson. Such heterogeneity can, though, be a source of extraordinary richness in the classroom if it is managed carefully and discussions are steered towards thinking about common themes and approaches, for instance the difference between revising the Victorian in a decolonized nation, versus revisions from former dominions or the imperial centre. Harold Bloom's *Agon* (1983), with its discussion of wilful misreadings and struggles between strong and weak poets can be a productive way of introducing students to the idea of clearing creative space to set the historical record straight, enabling the group to consider the aesthetics of reinvention alongside broader political concerns. While a novelist like Margaret Scott pays tribute to the Victorian past in *Family Album* (2000), revisionist novels like Carey's *Jack Maggs* are driven by anger and frustration at the constrictions imposed by Britain's colonial literary legacy and Bloom's work can help students to think about how feminist, Marxist, and postcolonial novelists engage with deliberately warping the "parent" text. Sometimes this re-shaping can take the form of deliberate misrepresentation, such as when Peter Carey shows Dickens's sister-in-law, Mary Hogarth dying of a botched abortion in *Jack Maggs* after she has fallen pregnant by Tobias Oates, the novel's Dickens figure.[4] At others, the "warping" of the Victorian can involve a reconfiguration or subversion of "Victorian values," such as in Michel Faber's *The Crimson Petal and the White* (2002), where Faber positions an unrepentant prostitute as his engaging and likeable heroine in a brilliant, but distinctly un-Victorian move.

A postcolonial course shaped around historical fictions can bring together theoretical work with a variety of re-workings from across the globe, allowing students to adopt a comparative approach and to consider a broad range of postcolonial concerns. Since there are common issues associated with decolonization and the novel – for instance mimicry, animosity towards the English literary canon, or the quest to find an "authentic" voice – as well as radically different ones, it is relatively easy for the instructor to find threads that will draw together a diverse selection of novelists from a number of different geographical contexts. Students will be able to think through postcolonialism's often awkward relationship with the Victorians and look back to British imperial pageantry. In a longer, sixteen week semester it would even be possible to incorporate material such as clips from Queen Victoria's Diamond Jubilee celebrations, critiques of jingoism appearing in sources like *Punch*, or even late Victorian adventure novels by the likes of Rider Haggard, so that students are aware of just why postcolonial responses to the Victorians can be so vehement.

Simon Gikandi in an essay on C. L. R. James has written of the "embarrassment of Victorianism" (2000, p. 157) and its legacy in the decolonized world, reflecting on the role of the "classic" Victorian novel in the colonial and postcolonial classroom and its importance in shaping identity in relation to the colonial centre. As Patrick Brantlinger notes elsewhere in the present volume, race and colonialism are concerns that loom large in our teaching of the nineteenth-century novel and postcolonial revisions of popular Victorian texts are extremely useful in helping students to probe silences, to understand the often unpalatable nature of Victorian attitudes to racial others, as well as the damage done to other cultures in the name of the English literary canon. Peter Carey's *Jack Maggs* advances the debate about postcolonial updates of the Victorian novel and because of Carey's status as a white expatriate Australian, the novel presents a range of important questions about the postcolonial voice and the representation (or lack there of) of indigenous Australians. Carey is, I would argue, too responsible a postcolonial writer to attempt to speak on behalf of another group, but his work has been controversial because of this omission and his somewhat cursory depictions of aboriginal peoples in *Oscar and Lucinda* (1988) and *The True History of the Kelly Gang* (2000).

The Victorians have been an important source for Peter Carey as a novelist and have, as his work has developed, become inextricably bound up with his attempt to find a voice as an Australian writer. Carey has, throughout his career, positioned himself as constricted most especially by Charles Dickens's work, but also, like so many postcolonial writers, by the form and conventions of the European, and particularly the English, novel. He has developed a deep-rooted and very public resentment for the ways in which English writers, particularly those of the nineteenth century held up as "classic authors," became complicit in the colonization process by speaking *for* Australia. While Carey's early engagement with the Victorians *Oscar and Lucinda* begins as a loving homage, it gradually degenerates into an onslaught, as Carey demonstrates the futility and dangers of transporting English cultural icons to the Australian Bush. While this novel engages with Edmund Gosse's *Father and Son* (1907), as well as making fleeting references to George Eliot and borrowing heavily from Dickens, it is in *Jack Maggs* that Carey begins to work through his conflicting feelings of hostility and affection for the nineteenth-century novel and this text is particularly useful in introducing the feelings of entrapment that the Victorians can evoke in modern-day postcolonial authors. For Carey, it is not only *Great Expectations* that has formed a type of creative prison, but rather a whole literary tradition. With its depiction of Dickens as an upstart philandering plagiarist, *Jack Maggs* is in many ways a transitional jail-breaking work in which Carey explicitly confronts and wrestles free from the literary past that has haunted his writing up until this point in his career. Significantly, he ends the novel with the burning and mutilation of manuscripts by his Dickens figure, Tobias Oates, and these acts of destruction seem to pave the way for his subsequent nineteenth-century "settler" novel, *True History of the Kelly Gang*. This text therefore works well not only on a postcolonial course, but also as an example of the type of Agonistic relationship posited by Bloom.

As ever more revisionist novels appear, it is clear that they have a vital role to play on university curricula. They can also, I would argue, play an important part in rehabilitating our students' attitudes towards both the nineteenth-century novel and courses structured around it. Just as Carey uses his fury towards the Victorians to fuel his creativity, so we can deploy the neo-Victorian novel to stimulate students' interest in the dauntingly lengthy works that we teach and to demonstrate the currency of Victorian concerns. Far from being dark and dreary as Woolf suggested, the Victorian novel remains a dynamic, developing, changing form and neo-Victorianism can help us and our students to understand it better.

Appendix: sample syllabus: the neo-Victorian novel

Aims and Objectives: This course aims to introduce students to the neo-Victorian novel by pairing classic nineteenth-century texts with more modern updates. Beginning with a discussion of Bloom's theories of wilful misreading and the struggles that writers go through to "make it new," we shall consider what it means to re-write or revise a Victorian text. We will examine examples of neo-Victorianism from across the globe, thinking about how the Victorians continue to "speak" to or "haunt" the contemporary reader and examining the role of the nineteenth-century novel in decolonized nations. We will consider why creative, original writers choose to revise or update Victorian works and we will approach these texts from a variety of critical perspectives, including Marxism (Lodge and Gaskell), post-colonialism (Dickens and Carey) and feminism (Brontë and Rhys, Carroll and Roiphe). We will also discuss the at times strained relationship between the "parent" text and its successors.

Schedule

Week 1
Introduction. Harold Bloom, "A Meditation upon Priority." *The Critical Tradition: Classic Texts and Contemporary Trends*. Ed. David H. Richter. Boston: Bedford, 1998. 1028–33.

Week 2
Charlotte Brontë, *Jane Eyre*.

Week 3
Jean Rhys, *Wide Sargasso Sea*.

Week 4
Emily Brontë, *Wuthering Heights*.

Week 5
Jane Urquhart, *Changing Heaven*.

Week 6
Elizabeth Gaskell, *North and South*.

Week 7
David Lodge, *Nice Work*.

Week 8
Charles Dickens, *Great Expectations*.

Week 9
Peter Carey, *Jack Maggs.*

Week 10
Lewis Carroll, *Alice in Wonderland.*

Week 11
Katie Roiphe, *Still She Haunts Me.*

Week 12
Arthur Conan Doyle, selected Sherlock Holmes short stories.

Week 13
Michael Dibdin, *The Last Sherlock Holmes Story.*

Week 14
Film: *The League of Extraordinary Gentlemen.*

Notes

1. In a recent chapter on the future of Victorian studies, Ruth Robbins laments: "Perhaps because the Victorian period is now more than a century away from us in time, and thus is no longer within living memory . . . there is a real necessity to provide very basic information about what was happening politically and culturally in nineteenth-century Britain" (2008, p. 207). The realist novel's dialogue with the Condition of England Question makes it impossible to teach the nineteenth-century novel without providing some kind of historical overview. When revisionist novels are added, it is also often necessary to introduce theoretical concepts such as postcolonial theory, feminism or postmodernism, as well as contextualizing the twentieth/twenty-first-century novel and its author. The time spent on providing this overview is time that has to be subtracted from the study of the texts themselves and as we often only have a semester in which to cover a substantial amount of material, there are real challenges involved in making sure that students have enough contextual and theoretical knowledge to be able to grapple with the major concerns of the texts.

2. As I have noted elsewhere (see Moore, "Twentieth-Century Re-Workings of the Victorian Novel" *Literature Compass* 5 (January 2008), pp. 134–44) the journal *Victorian Poetry* has recently devoted two volumes to future directions for the study of nineteenth-century poetry, incorporating two reflections on the role of Victorian poetry in the post-September 11 world. *Victorian Studies* has also dedicated a special issue to reviewing the state of the field and outlining how the study of Victorian literature and culture will change in the twenty-first century, including Kate Flint's radical jettisoning of the term "Victorian."

3. Gilmour's essay provides a list of six "uses" to which neo-Victorian fiction has been put, helpfully distinguishing between types of neo-Victorian novel, including

the pastiche and parody of a work like Palliser's *The Qunicunx* and the reworking or "updating" of a classic Victorian novel such as Emma Tennant's *Tess* (1993).
4. Oates's name reflects both Carey's treachery to his original, as well as the betrayal that he attributes to Dickens, embodying as it does the name of the traitor, Titus Oates, along with the word "bias."

Works cited

Bloom, Harold, *Agon: Towards a Theory of Revisionism* (Oxford: Oxford University Press, 1982).

Campion, Jane (dir.), *The Piano* (film), Miramax, 1993.

Carey, Peter, *Jack Maggs* (London: Faber & Faber, 1997).

Clayton, Jay, *Charles Dickens in Cyberspace: the Afterlife of the Nineteenth Century in Postmodern Culture* (New York: Oxford University Press, 2003).

Gikandi, Simon, "The Embarrassment of Victorianism: Colonial Subjects and English Identities," in *Victorian Afterlife,* eds. John Kucich and Dianne Sardoff (Minneapolis: University of Minnesota Press, 2000), pp. 157–85.

Gilmour, Robin, "Using the Victorians" in Alice Jenkins and Juliet John (eds.) *Rereading Victorian Fiction* (New York: St. Martin's Press – now Palgrave Macmillan, 2000).

Hughes, Albert and Allen Hughes (dirs.), *From Hell* (film), Twentieth-Century Fox, 2001.

Joyce, Simon, *The Victorians in the Rearview Mirror* (Athens: Ohio University Press, 2007).

Kaplan, Cora, *Victoriana: Histories, Fictions, Criticism* (Edinburgh: Edinburgh University Press, 2007).

Knight, Stephen, *Jack the Ripper: The Final Solution* (Chicago: Academy Chicago Publishers, 1986).

Kucich, John and Dianne F. Sadoff, *Victorian Afterlife: Postmodern Culture Rewrites the Nineteenth Century* (Minneapolis: University of Minnesota Press, 2000).

Lodge, David, *Nice Work* (London: Secker & Warburg, 1988).

Lonoff, Sue, "Disseminating Victorian Culture in the Postmillennial Classroom" in Christine L. Krueger (ed.), *The Function of Victorian Culture at the Present Time* (Athens: Ohio University Press, 2002).

Moore, Grace, "Twentieth-Century Re-Workings of the Victorian Novel," *Literature Compass*, 5.1 (January 2008), pp. 134–44.

Renk, Kathleen J., *Caribbean Shadows and Victorian Ghosts: Women's Writing and Decolonization* (Charlottesville: University Press of Virginia, 1999).

Robbins, Ruth, "Mapping the Future of Victorian Studies" in Alexandra Warwick and Martin Willis (eds.), *The Victorian Literature Handbook* (London: Continuum, 2008).

Samuel, Raphael, *Theatres of Memory* (New York: Verso, 1984).

Stephenson, Neal, *The Diamond Age* (London: Penguin, 1996).

Thompson, James, "The BBC and the Victorians," in M. Taylor and M. Wolff (eds.), *The Victorians Since 1901* (Manchester: Manchester University Press, 2004), pp. 150–66.

Taylor, Miles and Michael Wolff (eds.), *The Victorians Since 1901: Histories, Representations and Revisions* (Manchester: Manchester University Press, 2004).

Thieme, John, *Postcolonial Con-Texts: Writing Back to the Canon* (London: Continuum, 2001).

Woolf, Virgina, *Orlando* (1928) (Harmondsworth: Penguin, 2004).

13
Transatlanticism

Sofia Ahlberg

I Introduction

Until relatively recently, nineteenth-century English fiction has been taught from a nationalist perspective. Students encouraged to address the themes that preoccupied many nineteenth-century writers who wrote about the foreign – including religion, race, capitalism, and colonialism – have generally done so within a nationally framed literary history. The division of literary studies into British and American often goes unquestioned in English departments. This is not to say that contemporary cultural and literary critics have not investigated Atlantic history. Famously, in *The Black Atlantic: Modernity as Double Consciousness*, Paul Gilroy revisits Atlantic history through the image of the ship in motion. "Ships," he suggests, "focus attention on the middle passage, on the various projects for redemptive return to an African homeland, on the circulation of ideas and activities as well as the movement of key cultural and political artefacts" (1993, p. 4). That the fluidity and connectivity of the Atlantic Ocean enables Gilroy to embark on his pan-Africanist project is clear, but how might the same body of water prompt us to reconsider the ways English fiction of the nineteenth century is taught?

The Atlantic offers a vantage point that is not national, but polynational; not territorial, but relational. Though studies such as Gilroy's remind us of the breadth and magnitude of circum-Atlantic history, the following chapter proposes to focus specifically on the significance of Anglo-American relations for students of nineteenth-century fiction. Imaginary and real acts of reciprocity and exchange that occur over and beneath the Atlantic border invite students to consider nineteenth-century literary history without privileging the centre. While influence and reception studies have already taught students the value of such traffic, both emphasize origins and roots, a viewpoint that is proving pedagogically limiting for the twenty-first century. Specifically, a transatlantic model of studying literature emphasizes the non-linear, alternative, distorted, anticipated, and deferred trajectories between

British and American cultures that are often overlooked in conventional national literary histories. Often, these paths overlap those of other minority studies, such as women's studies.[1]

As a counterpart to a traditional national literary history and as an exploration of the impact of the transatlantic universe on the teaching of the nineteenth-century novel, this chapter offers specific strategies for reading the Atlantic's metaphorical and actual presence. Broadly stated, its aim is twofold: first, to make explicit the pedagogical value of looking at nineteenth-century imaginary encounters between America and England from both sides of the Atlantic in several texts including Nathaniel Hawthorne's *The Scarlet Letter* (1850) and Oscar Wilde's "The Canterville Ghost" (1891); and secondly to demonstrate how a focus on the Atlantic as the intermediary, even interstitial zone, encourages students to consider the art of the novel in the nineteenth century as not exclusively a national art. As noted by Wai Chee Dimock in her celebrated essay "Deep Time: American Literature and World History," it is invariably the case that "neither a single nation nor a single race can yield an adequate frame for literary history" (2001, p. 757). Thus transatlanticism stresses the ontology of literary studies, not just for example the Victorian novel's relationship to American romanticism, but also literature's place in relation to other disciplines and media. The Latin prefix "trans" valorizes the possibilities of crossing over – linguistically, culturally, experientially, as well as generically. Indeed, a transatlantic approach to nineteenth-century literature tends to be generically inclusive.[2] Transatlantic readings have the potential to invigorate and stimulate the circulation of ideas, to reconstruct the flow of the Atlantic Ocean beyond temporal and spatial boundaries as a model for teaching nineteenth-century fiction. Transatlantic literary studies encourages students of nineteenth-century English fiction to view writers from this period in terms of what Edward Said calls their "worldliness" (1993, p. 13). As William C. Spengemann points out, it is unhelpful to think of Emerson, for example, as primarily a representative of American literature when his acknowledged teachers are Coleridge and Carlyle, yet this is what the current periodization of nineteenth-century literature into American literature on the one hand and English, on the other, suggests (1982, p. 156). Transatlantic literary studies, by comparison, widens the context between a work of fiction and the historical world of its characters and writer. Though it is well known that the rise of the novel coincided with the emergence of the nation state, the transatlantic novel explores the limits of national identity in nineteenth-century fiction.

II Confronting the transatlantic

When Edgar Allan Poe's narrator in "MS. Found in a Bottle" (1831) says, referring to the ocean, that "we are whirling dizzily, in immense concentric

circles, round and round the borders of a gigantic amphitheatre, the sum-
mit of whose walls is lost in the darkness and the distance," this is more
than literary metaphor (2000, p. 24). It suggests depths of perception
unique to the ocean. Closely reading passages that dramatise the Atlantic
or the transatlantic in works by Poe and others opens up a series of questions regarding the path to knowledge; enquiries that allow for reciprocal
exchange between teachers and students, areas of disciplines and cultures.
Often, these questions are those, in the Socratic tradition, to which there are
no "right" answers. Ultimately, such practices remind us that the object of
study is permanently under construction, and the conclusions of a literary
investigation cannot be prejudiced. For example, the following passage from
Nathaniel Hawthorne's *The Marble Faun* in which the narrator addresses the
reader gives insight into the distinct and complicated nature of transatlantic
narration – a narration which includes narrative gaps, conjecture, depth,
and surface and which encourages students to find meaning by reading
across on a horizontal, relational level:

> In weaving these mystic utterances into a continuous scene, we under-
> take a task resembling, in its perplexity, that of gathering up and piecing
> together the fragments of a letter, which has been torn and scattered to
> the winds. Many words of deep significance – many entire sentences,
> and those possibly the most important ones – have flown too far, on the
> winged breeze, to be recovered. If we insert our own conjectural amend-
> ments, we perhaps give a purport utterly at variance with the true one.
> Yet, unless we attempt something in this way, there must remain an
> unsightly gap, and a lack of continuousness and dependence in our nar-
> rative; so that it would arrive at certain inevitable catastrophes without
> due warning of their imminence. (1993, p. 929)

The allusion to the "winged breeze" draws attention to the movement of
the Atlantic itself and to the idea that a body of knowledge cannot be fixed;
it is always in motion. Reading as a form of reconstruction relies on "con-
jectural amendments" as much as facts, filling in gaps rather than digging
vertically into singular, incomplete aspects of the narrative. Similar leaps of
the imagination are commonly found in detective fiction. The entangled,
transatlantic pattern of cause and effect in Arthur Conan Doyle's *A Study in
Scarlet* (1887) is a good example. Beginning with the discovery of a corpse
in England, it then jumps to a Mormon community in the US in order to
present the reader with the motive for the crime. Playful allusions to Poe's
detective C. Auguste Dupin suggest innovative ways for broadening the
context of Doyle's fiction within a transatlantic syllabus.

A precursor to globalism, the hemispheric context of the nineteenth-
century text provides fascinating pointers on how to read literature in the
wider context of religion, race, capitalism, and colonialism – then and now.

A transatlantic reading encourages students to bring their own experience as global citizens into the classroom. More specifically, students are invited to consider and draw parallels between the dark crimson presence of the Atlantic Ocean in the nineteenth century and the borderless twenty-first-century world of white noise. As that which links people, cultures, and nations, the Atlantic works as a stylistic device in nineteenth-century transatlantic fiction in the same way that the impenetrable, yet all-encompassing World Wide Web informs much fiction of this century. Often the shape, form, and mood of the transatlantic novel takes after the Atlantic whose network reaches far beyond the sea itself. When the first message was sent over the Atlantic cable in 1858, it was anticipated that "the whole earth will be belted with the electric current, palpitating with human thoughts and emotions" (Briggs, 1858, p. 12). The depth of those palpitations had already been articulated in *Moby-Dick*: "He [Ahab] piled upon the whale's white hump the sum of all the general rage and hate felt by his whole race from Adam down; and then, as if his chest had been a mortar, he burst his hot heart's shell upon it" (Melville, 1922, p. 222). The Atlantic is a repository for a wide-range of feelings and when attempting to interpret their meaning, its surface reflects on the subjective act of interpretation by returning a mirror image of oneself. In some cases, the idea of a vantage point or a centre disappears altogether. For example, some nineteenth-century painters such as Edward Moran were drawn to the Atlantic not in the hope of discovering something new, but to revisit ancient mysteries that were thought to be buried, and consequently preserved at the bottom of the sea. Inspired by the popular belief that the aquatic world mirrored what was above, Moran's "The Valley in the Sea" (1862) depicts the ocean floor as the prairie.

III Reading the past in the present

How then might transatlanticism work in the classroom? A useful starting point is to stress the extent to which the field privileges network, circulation, and flow in place of the centre and the static. Similar to other fields of literary studies that challenge the authority of the nation and the mono-cultural, including postcolonialism and cosmopolitanism, transatlantic literary studies attributes meaning to a subject in its relation to another. While attentive to textual allusions, the student of transatlanticism needs to be profoundly tuned to influence that goes beyond or lies beneath the surface of the text itself. In *Atlantic Double-Cross*, Robert Weisbuch discusses the ambiguity of "plural cultural times" with regards to some nineteenth-century American authors to whom the nation represented both a new start as well as "the final, fatal outpost of a decrepit Euro-American civilization" (1986, p. 122). Some of this ambiguity can be found in Henry James's fiction, particularly in *The Golden Bowl* whose characters cling to the values of ancient European culture with all their might. The idea of a vantage point was crucial to James who believed that if he stayed in America, he would become a provincial writer (Spender, 1974, p. 53). He chose to live in London, rather than Paris, as a way of putting himself at the centre of the English language (p. 68). America's inferiority to Europe, particularly England, was above all else lingual according to James. In London, he dreamed about the formation of an Anglo-Saxon world in which the differences between America and England were negligible. In a letter to his brother, William James, he writes:

> I have not the least hesitation in saying that I aspire to write in such a way that it would be impossible to an outsider to say whether I am at a given moment an American writing about England or an Englishman writing about America (dealing as I do with both countries), and so far from being ashamed of such an ambiguity I should be exceedingly proud of it, for it would be highly civilized. (Spender, 1974, p. 69)

Having students note the differences between American and English protagonists in James's fiction, and then try to account for them, is a good way for them both to understand James's unique transatlanticist point of view and also see how that uniqueness violates nineteenth-century expectations of fiction conceived purely within national binaries. Such an exercise also provides opportunities for arguments about taste and value. Weisbuch's "plural cultural times" suggests that when taught within the framework of a broader historical narrative, the transatlantic novel conjures up a tidal movement of tales all jostling for a hearing. Most importantly, such polyphonic narratives do not presuppose that the influence is always European. Thus, the inspiration of Nathaniel Hawthorne's *The Scarlet Letter* on George Eliot's *Adam Bede*, to mention one example of many, illustrates transatlantic flow from the New World to the Old. Anglo-US literary exchanges, including reciprocity and cross-continental influence, draw attention to the ways nineteenth-century fiction is both history and literature.

Transatlanticism thus identifies the interplay between the undercurrents of history and the interpretation that brings history to the surface into clusters of the collective imagination. In so far as it gives students insight into questions of experience, a transatlantic syllabus benefits enormously from the inclusion of archival texts such as letters and journals. Those who wrote most candidly about the US in the nineteenth century were generally those who travelled there. Emigration from Britain to the US was at its peak in the first half of the nineteenth century. Travelogues demonstrate the degree to which identity is enmeshed with writing, and many nineteenth-century authors who wrote about America, including Charles Dickens, Frances Trollope, Henry James, and Robert Louis Stevenson, were fierce critics of their subject while also finding themselves increasingly drawn to the freedom that transatlantic travel enabled. The questioning and construction of identity that the traveller figure occasions, broadens our understanding of the periphery, as Judith Butler notes: "What was once thought of as a border, that which delimits and bounds, is a highly populated site, if not the very definition of the nation, confounding identity in what may well become a very auspicious direction" (2004, p. 49).

Just how relevant a new understanding of the border is to the teaching of transatlantic nineteenth-century fiction became apparent during a recent staging of such "confounded identity" from a passage in R. L. Stevenson's *The Amateur Emigrant* and the comments it provoked from the graduate students participating in the seminar. During the journey to America on board the *Devonia* in 1879, Stevenson experienced what it was like to travel out of himself. The following section illustrates the gist of his transformation:

> I found that I had what they call fallen in life with absolute success and verisimilitude. I was taken for a steerage passenger; no one seemed surprised that I should be so; and there was nothing but the brass plate between decks to remind me that I had once been a gentleman. (n.d., p. 73)

Unable to take advantage of his new found freedom, however, Stevenson dramatically exposes the limits of his world view. Assisting a disadvantaged woman who has fallen ill on deck, Stevenson is misconstrued by the crowd as being her husband. On account of her neglected appearance, he suffers shame and humiliation of the assumed association (p. 75). Troubled by what they judged to be the severe constraints to Stevenson's narrative, students were keen to discuss in small groups among themselves just how much identity involves both the act of perceiving as well as being perceived, and the literary means by which a transatlantic narrator passes from one to the other in the transitional space of travel.

In the way it foregrounds the ocean as a border where markers of familiarity are temporarily suspended, transatlantic literary studies shares a common understanding with comparative literary studies and translation studies. Particularly relevant is the latter's concern with literature as enabling the proliferation of other texts, interpretations, and translations. The Atlantic enabled the transportation of ideas, people, and products that in turn informed and shaped the work of the imagination.[3] To students of transatlantic fiction, the style, mood, and rhythm of the transatlantic novel are of equal significance to metaphors, similes, and other means of establishing a comparative paradigm of literary interpretation. As a narrative device, the Atlantic contributes to the "feel" of the novel, a means of transporting the reader back into the past. As a repository for memories, tales of immense suffering, and untold recriminations, the Atlantic is, in Paul Gilroy's words, "one single, complex unit of analysis" that defines "the modern world" (1993, p. 15). A good example of this comes in Ian Baucom's *Specters of the Atlantic* (2005), a book that analyses the tragedy of "the Zong" in 1783, when more than a hundred African slaves were sacrificed and thrown overboard for insurance money. Baucom focuses on one event and enlarges it to make his readers appreciate its magnitude and impact on the present. Time does not pass, it accumulates, weighs upon the reader of *Specters of the Atlantic*, who begins to realize the connections between the slave trade and modernity as we know it. To Baucom and many other transatlanticists, nineteenth-century European imperialism still casts a shadow over the twenty-first century. As we shall see, in works such as *The Scarlet Letter* this notion of "accumulated time" underscores the textual layers students can expect to find in their reading of transatlantic nineteenth-century fiction.

IV   Reading and writing *The Scarlet Letter*

If historians of the Atlantic agree that the past informs the present, how nineteenth-century fiction is read today influences the way history is written. A useful starting point here comes in *Freedom's Empire: Race and the Rise of the Novel in Atlantic Modernity, 1640–1940*, in which Laura Doyle includes a transatlantic reading on Nathaniel Hawthorne's *The Scarlet Letter*. Doyle uncovers the violence of colonization that informs Hawthorne's authorship and portrait of Hester Prynne. She correctly points to the often overlooked fact regarding Hester's solitary transatlantic migration, emblematic of "the exilic effects of Atlantic modernity" (1992, p. 301), but what about – we might ask – her escape to England and subsequent return to Salem? Though not explained in detail, these transatlantic journeys carry a cargo of implications, ramifications, nuances, and connotations concerning Hester Prynne's role in the novel. To what can we attribute the change that occurs on those transatlantic journeys and how can it be addressed through writing assignments?

Shifting students' attention from the textually rich narrative on land to the barely alluded to travels by sea is one way of encouraging them to create their own stories, mapping the landscape of history with a personal "tract of written space" (p. 169), as Hawthorne himself writes in relation to Dimmesdale's intellectual enterprise. The questions which can be addressed regarding the travels across the Atlantic undertaken by Hester and her daughter stretch across a series of disciplines, including gender studies, issues of genre, text and context studies and biographical studies (the importance of the sea to Hawthorne's authorship is well documented). An important advantage of looking at a multitude of issues within the parameters of a single spatial metaphor is that it helps students to assimilate the plethora of scholarly methodologies currently circulating in English departments around the world. Rather than using lectures to deliver knowledge and make conclusions it should be possible to transform a syllabus into a series of questions that will allow students to transfer what they already know to new contexts, not only by building interdisciplinary bridges and group assignments but also by student interventions in the form of suggestions for on-line extra-curricular material and class room presentations.

One approach to *The Scarlet Letter* would be to ask students to consider the book's preoccupation with femininity, ocean travel and the quest narrative. Through boarding the ship to England, Hester hopes to escape the scarlet letter; what the "forest cannot hide," the ocean shall "swallow" (p. 158). However, she discovers "there was a more real life for Hester Prynne here, in New England, than in that unknown region where Pearl had found a home" (p. 196) and returns to Salem to submit to the letter once again. A signifier of the Atlantic Ocean itself, the scarlet letter endures, especially when in the hands of Pearl, the illegitimate child of Hester and Dimmesdale. Attracting the attention of sailors, the little girl metamorphoses into something from the sea, "as if a flake of the sea-foam had taken the shape of a little maid" (p. 183). When not the embodiment of the Atlantic, Pearl resembles a creature from "dear old England" (p. 155). Simultaneously from the aquatic and the Old World, Pearl embodies plural cultural times, the symbol of that which has been left behind. When she returns to England in the company of her mother, she too is abandoned from a narrative point of view, never heard of again, save fleeting evidence that she has become the "American broad" overseas. The recipient of Chillingworth's substantial will and the attention of a lover of continental aristocracy, Pearl enters a mythical realm as potent as the Atlantic.

Equally suggestive, Hester's journey across the Atlantic and subsequent return to Europe and back again represents an alternative quest narrative. Students might be asked to close-read Hester's transatlantic passages, thinking about ways in which they could be said to indicate a shift of power and knowledge in which masculine authority gives way to female wisdom. Firstly, by migrating to the New World, Hester escapes a loveless marriage. Though made to suffer the consequences of adultery, she rises above her fate by becoming a Sister of Mercy held in high regard by the townspeople to whom the letter "A" means something different again, "They said that it meant Able, so strong was Hester Prynne, with a woman's strength" (p. 121). Secondly, Hester's final migration to New England singles her out as the survivor, adept at inhabiting a New World unlike Dimmesdale, "so inadequate to sustain the hardships of a forest life" (p. 161). Guided by her own rules of conduct ("The world's law was no law for her mind" [p. 122]), Hester's search for self-knowledge is cyclical rather than linear, transatlantic rather than national.

One of the activities students can be asked to do, is to re-write the transatlantic passage in their own words. Such an assignment can take different shapes. One way is to ask students to reconstruct the transatlantic journey in the style of the author, from the point of view of another passenger observing Hester and Pearl. Another would be to write a more socio-historical account, concerning for instance the ordeal of crossing the Atlantic as an unaccompanied woman. Doris Weatherford's *Foreign and Female: Immigrant Women in America, 1840–1930.* (1986) is an excellent point of departure. When read in tandem, both Hawthorne's novel and Weatherford's book are opened for investigation and scrutiny while also allowing a mode of comparison between the fictional and the historical narrative. Another approach might be to ask students to consider Hawthorne's own ambivalent attitude towards England as documented in *The English Notebooks* and *Our Old Home* and how his position as an American Consul in Liverpool 1853–1857 might influence a reading of *The Scarlet Letter.* Assuming the position of a reviewer in the latter case would very likely assist the student in getting started. The benefits of such creative work are many, including (1) to allow students to form a relationship with the author and the text by filling in the "blanks" in the text, (2) to encourage the students to engage closely with the author's individual written style, (3) to encourage students to familiarise themselves with the historical and cultural world that he or she has created, while (4) exploring and defining their own methods of research.

If one aim of literary studies is to deepen students' scholarly involvement and critical engagement with primary and secondary literature, then students must be encouraged to believe that how they respond to a text matters. As James F. Slevin puts it, students must be taught to appreciate their own contributions to scholarly work in order to become lasting members of the intellectual community at large. "Students have little idea how to recognize and disentangle the contradictions embedded in a cultural text," Slevin notes, "much less recognize the value of a text (including their own) that explores these contradictions" (2007, p. 207). The connections between student writing, the object of literary interrogation (in this case *The Scarlet Letter*), and scholarly criticism must be made more transparent if interest in nineteenth-century fiction is to be sustained and broadened through this century and beyond. Slevin's observation that "Most students do not value their writing, their minds, or their ideas as we do, or they do not value them at all" (2007, p. 207) is a serious one.

By shifting the emphasis from the territorial to the relational, transatlantic literary studies hopes to bridge the gap not only between author and reader, but also the chasm that exists between reader and reader. At all times, the transatlantic classroom emphasises the ability to see though the eyes of others. Through interaction and group work, it aims to create a non-competitive environment in which teaching and learning are "inextricably and elaborately linked," the ideal outcome identified by Paul Ramsden in *Learning to Teach in Higher Education* (2003, p. 8). Transatlantic approaches to studying nineteenth-century fiction accomplish these goals in that they introduce reading material that relate to already familiar knowledge of the subject. We are all subjects of transnationalism, whether by birth, upbringing, or consumerism. By reading across (transatlantically) rather than simply reading in (nationalistically), exclusive narratives of the nation and self are opened up and the task of essay writing becomes a deep learning experience with a sense of involvement.

V Transatlanticism and the fourth dimension

By way of concluding this discussion, it is perhaps useful to note that thoughtful and lasting student participation can be achieved without the weight of history. Oscar Wilde's light-hearted ghost story *The Canterville Ghost* – written after Wilde's celebrated lecture tour around America – escapes "deep time" and "accumulated time" in preference of the light and phosphorous. The humorous encounter with the Canterville ghost offers students insight into the transatlantic world and the faulty communication between the English and the Americans. Trans-experience of the fourth dimension offers citizens from both shores the opportunity to tease out points of conflict and collision, but also compromise and conciliation. Elegantly and profoundly, Wilde draws attention to how ideas and values are constructed and deconstructed, and stereotypes of self and others created and circumvented, by contrasting American versus English confrontation with the supernatural.

A transatlantic discussion lingers on the outward appearance of Wilde's story because it is there that negative and positive stereotypes surface. Rather than dismiss these as unfactual and unimportant, a transatlantic approach to nineteenth-century fiction would argue that they provide readers with a key to interpreting Anglo-American contact as content. Questions important to the student of nineteenth-century fiction should include the development of transatlantic stereotypes and their function. The American Minister's idea of a modern country is "that if there were such a thing as a ghost in Europe, we'd have it at home in a very short time in one of our public museums, or on the road as a show" (2003, p. 206). Discussions might also lead to the topic of fear, a topic highly relevant today, and a comparative study of transatlantic notions of fear in the nineteenth century. Though three centuries old, the ghost is not impervious to American enterprise and pragmatic solutions such as Pinkerton's Champion Stain Remover and Paragon Detergent and Tammany Rising Sun Lubricator which conspire to undermine his fearful influence on the all too living.

Stephen Spender in *Love-Hate Relations: A Study of Anglo-American Sensibilities*, notes that the idea that problems can and will be solved and that there is a cure for every predicament is, generally speaking, an American belief: "Historically, perhaps the outstanding, most persistent feature of the American culture has been the negative seeking to become a positive" (1972, p. 84). Wilde's story pokes fun at this proclivity towards resolution, not least in the narrative's own ending that sees the Canterville ghost laid to rest by, of all people, the American adolescent Virginia. In her own way, Virginia attempts to set the world right as evident in her rather prim counsel to the ghost:

> "the best thing you can do is to emigrate and improve your mind. My father will be only too happy to give you a free passage, and though there is a heavy duty on spirits of every kind, there will be no difficulty about the Custom House, as the officers are all Democrats." (p. 224)

As Virginia soon learns, however, the best thing for the Canterville ghost is not to emigrate to the New World, but to the Next, where he will be pardoned for his wicked sins with the help of the young maiden's forgiveness and thus cease to haunt the living. In its portrayal of new fantasies of participation – transatlantic and unearthly – *The Canterville Ghost* suggests interesting strategies for reading the nineteenth-century novel in the twenty-first century. By laying bare the possibilities and limitations of participation, Wilde invites the contemporary reader to draw parallels between the transferral of knowledge and experience then and now. With its connections to the fourth dimension, the Atlantic is looking less scarlet and all the more pale. The transatlantic community found in *The Canterville Ghost*, with its unlikely pairing of young American maiden and antique English ghost, presents the reader with fantasies of unity that displace nation states in the same way that web-based communities do today.

An interesting point of comparison here is with the similar longing to transcend social and biological rifts conveyed by H. G. Wells's narrator in the short story "In the Abyss" (1896). Here the narrator discovers denizens of the deep by means of a sophisticated diving apparatus. Overall, the story expresses a longing for technology to connect people from radically opposed geographies and to create an alternative kinship based on the sharing of information. In contrast, Wilde's ghost story recognizes that knowledge is not transparent and some experiences cannot be shared with others or otherwise pooled into a mutually accessible body of knowledge. Some years after Virginia has put the ghost of Canterville to rest, her husband Cecil asks that she discloses her account of what occurred:

> "Virginia, a wife should have no secrets from her husband."
> "Dear Cecil! I have no secrets from you."
> "Yes, you have," he answered, smiling, "you have never told me what happened to you when you were locked up with the ghost."
> "I have never told any one, Cecil," said Virginia gravely.
> "I know that, but you might tell me."
> "Please don't ask me, Cecil, I cannot tell you. Poor Sir Simon! I owe him a great deal. Yes, don't laugh, Cecil, I really do. He made me see what Life is, and what Death signifies, and why Love is stronger than both."
> The Duke rose and kissed his wife lovingly.

"You can have your secrets as long as I have your heart," he murmured.
"You have always had that, Cecil." (p. 234)

This exchange can perhaps be read as a sobering reminder to scholars in
any literary field, including transatlanticism, that no matter how faithfully
we read, not all will be disclosed. That some of this mystery (life, death
and love, according to Virginia above) is retained is of utter importance
to students of the nineteenth-century novel. Too often students are made
to assume that they are excluded from insight into a particular novel or
field of literary inquiry on account of their being at the beginning of their
careers, when in actual fact, all scholars and readers of literature are at
various times equally bewitched, bothered, and bewildered by a text. It is
crucial that our teaching practices reflect this view, with more attention
being given to how students approach a certain issue. More often than we
would like to acknowledge, when confronted with a work of literature, we
are all of us at sea.

Appendix: sample syllabus: horizontal readings: the Atlantic in nineteenth-century English fiction

Aims and Objectives: This module will consider a series of strategies for reading nineteenth-century fiction in the wider context of the Atlantic. On the
reading list are nineteenth-century English and American prose and non-
fiction that highlight the impact of the Atlantic as a significant zone of
real and metaphorical contact in the nineteenth century and beyond. The
module will introduce the concept of the Atlantic as a unique geographical
marker that discloses a series of correspondences and convergences between
the Old and the New, the centre and the periphery. Our goal will be to
demonstrate how the Atlantic presence puts American and British texts
in dialogue with each other and how they connect to the broader body of
nineteenth-century writing, bypassing traditional national narratives from
this era. We will investigate how transatlantic travel writing reorients nineteenth-century English identity with regards to class, race and gender. We
will also see how transatlantic fiction debunks assumptions about the status
of nineteenth-century women and we will interrogate the presence of the
Atlantic as a platform for critiquing the slave trade. Finally, we will develop
greater understanding of recent theoretical and practical approaches for
reading horizontally through time and place.

Schedule

Week 1
Introducing the subject; Learning to read across

Week 2
Crossing the Atlantic Then and Now
R. L. Stevenson, *The Amateur Emigrant*
R. L. Stevenson, *The Silverado Squatters* (excerpts)
Henry James, *The Art of Fiction*

Weeks 3 & 4
Sons and Mothers
Frances Trollope, Domestic *Manners of the Americans*
Edmund White, *Fanny: A Fiction*

Week 5 & 6
The English in the American South
Fanny Kemble, *The American Journals*
Gary Younge, *No Place Like Home: A Black Briton's Journey through the American South*

Week 7
The Transatlantic Quest/"A" for Atlantic
Nathaniel Hawthorne, *The Scarlet Letter*
Herman Melville, "Hawthorne and His Mosses"

Week 8
Transatlantic Murder and Mystery
Bram Stoker, "The Squaw"
E. A. Poe, "How to write a *Blackwood* Article," "The Predicament," "The Pit and the Pendulum"

Week 9
The Fourth Dimension
Oscar Wilde, "The Canterville Ghost"

Week 10
Transatlantic Investigations
Arthur Conan Doyle, *A Study in Scarlet*

Week 11
Trans-Atlantic Networks
Charles Dickens, *American Notes*

Week 12
Concluding Remarks and New Questions

Notes

1. Margaret McFadden's *Golden Cables of Sympathy: The Transatlantic Sources of Nineteenth-Century Feminism* (Lexington: University Press of Kentucky, 1999) is an exciting example of such an intersection of disciplines.

2. A recent collection of essays, *The Traffic in Poems*: *Nineteenth-Century Poetry and Transatlantic Exchange* (New Brunswick: Rutgers University Press, 2008), edited by Meredith L. McGill, illustrates in a compelling way how nineteenth-century poems from both sides of the Atlantic converge and collude as if inhabiting a transatlantic universe of thought.

3. Sarah Meer's *Uncle Tom Mania: Slavery, Minstrelsy and Transatlantic Culture in the 1850s* (Athens: University of Georgia Press, 2005) provides a stimulating account of such transatlantic creative currency in the nineteenth century.

Works cited

Briggs, C. F., and A. Maverick, *The Story of the Telegraph, and a History of the Great Atlantic Cable* (New York: Rudd and Carleton, 1858).

Butler, J., *Precarious Life*: *The Powers of Mourning and Violence* (London and New York: Verso, 2004).

Dimock, Wai Chee, "Deep Time: American Literature and World History," *American Literary History*, 13.4 (2001), pp. 755–75.

Doyle, Laura, "'A' for Atlantic in Hawthorne's *The Scarlet Letter*," in *Freedom's Empire*: *Race and the Rise of the Novel in Atlantic Modernity, 1640–1940* (Durham and London: Duke University Press, 2008).

Gilroy, Paul, *The Black Atlantic*: *Modernity and Double Consciousness* (London and New York: Verso, 1993).

Hawthorne, Nathaniel, *Novels* (New York: Viking Press, 1993).

——. *The Scarlet Letter* (Hertfordshire: Wordsworth Editions Limited, 1992).

Melville, Herman, *Moby-Dick or The Whale* (London: Oxford University Press, 1922).

Poe, Edgar Allen, "MS. Found in a Bottle" in S. Levine and S. F. Levine (eds.), *Thirty-Two Stories* (Indianapolis and Cambridge: Hackett Publishing Company, 2000).

Ramsden, Paul, *Learning to Teach in Higher Education* (London and New York: Routledge Falmer, 2003).

Said, Edward, *Culture and Imperialism* (London: Chatto & Windus, 1993).

Slevin, J. F., "Academic Literacy and the Discipline of English," *Profession 2007* (The Modern Language Association of America, 2007).

Spender, Stephen, *Love-Hate Relations*: *A Study of Anglo-American Sensibilities* (London: Hamish Hamilton, 1972).

Spengemann, William C., "Three Blind Men and an Elephant: The Problem of Nineteenth-Century English," *New Literary History*, 14.1 (1982), pp. 155–73.

Stevenson, Robert Louis, *The Amateur Emigrant, The Old & New Pacific Capitals, The Silverado Squatters* (London and Glasgow: Collins' Clear-Type Press, n.d.).

Weatherford, Doris, *Foreign and Female*: *Immigrant Women in America, 1840–1930* (New York: Schocken, 1986).

Weisbuch, R., *Atlantic Double-Cross: American Literature and British Influence in the Age of Emerson* (Chicago and London: The University of Chicago Press, 1986).

Wilde, Oscar, "The Canterville Ghost" in Ian Small (ed.) *Oscar Wilde: Complete Short Fiction* (London: Penguin, 2003).

14
Primary Sources and the MA Student

Josie Billington

I Introduction

I have a clear memory of the point at which, as a student of nineteenth-century literature, I became committed to what I was doing. We had read and discussed, closely and carefully, John Stuart Mill's "The Enfranchisement of Women" (*Westminster Review*, 1851).[1] In the following seminar we read Charlotte Brontë's *Villette* (1853), together with a letter (to Elizabeth Gaskell) recording the author's equivocal response to Mill's thesis, thus:

> I believe J. S. Mill would make a hard, dry, dismal world of it; and yet he speaks admirable sense through a great portion of his article – especially when he says that if there be a natural unfitness in women for men's employment, there is no need to make laws on the subject . . . In short J. S. Mill's head is, I dare say, very good, but I feel disposed to scorn his heart. You are right when you say there is a large margin in human nature over which the logicians have no dominion: glad am I that it is so. (qtd. in Gaskell 1996, p. 390)

Having just experienced, from the inside, the rich and complex resistance in *Villette* even to *narrative* explanation of its protagonist Lucy Snowe, the relative reductionism of Mill's logic was hard to deny. On the other hand, how did my acquiescence to Charlotte Brontë's criticism square with my rapt acceptance of Mill's thesis only a few days before? Was it worthless after all? What was the relation between these two discourses? How could or should one adjudicate between them? Or was it useless even to look for an arbiter between two essentially incommensurate modes of thought and language? I had no answers. But I had some serious and important questions to which I wanted answers. And so I was hooked.

What I was experiencing, without realizing it, was the challenge of contextuality. As review columns in nineteenth-century newspapers and journals remind us, contemporary readers invariably encountered a particular novel or short story in a kind of mental juxtaposition with other texts and ideas which is on one level irrecoverable. This was a point made by E. S. Dallas in 1863 when he noted how "a reader will go on reading novels to all eternity, and sometimes will have several in hand at once – a serial of Mr Trollope's here, a serial of Mr Dickens's there, and the last three-volume tale into the bargain (qtd. in Skilton, 1972, p. 144). Taking its cue from Dallas, this chapter argues that part of the training for students involves opening up different textual areas, recognizing the value of finding connections between apparently unrelated things, or for finding discontinuity between superficially connected areas.[2] Studying nineteenth-century fiction involves recognising the "large margins" of human mentality with which literature, uniquely among linguistic expressions of human experience, expresses and engages. Some of the training involves research – getting one's hands dirty, as it were – another part of it involves the imagination, engaging emotionally or conceptually, a task situated on the borderline between imagination and experience, between the inchoate inner life of the reader and the objectified finished one of the published text.[2] Of all things, the large loose "bagginess" of the nineteenth-century novel does not, and does not want to, fit rigid formal boundaries.

The discussion which follows thus considers some of the ways in which students might be encouraged to think outside the covers of the packaged, paperbacked classic, with its "old master" painting on the front. As I will show, working at micro-level, with manuscript or draft versions of novels is one way of doing this – making students aware of what Peter Barry has termed a text's "multitextuality' (2003, p. 48). But I also want to think about ways in which writing from extra-literary disciplines can be introduced as *primary* material, not in the sense of superseding the importance of the literary text or literary thinking, but in the sense of demanding equivalent mental and creative attention. (Barry terms this "contextuality".) Although, as has been noted elsewhere in the present volume (see Chapter 5), interdisciplinary thinking, or what passes for it, often seems to have replaced more literary modes of thought, this chapter will also explore practical ways in which primary sources can be used not only to preserve and foster literary thinking while incorporating non-literary discourses, but also to help make literary thought itself work in a flexibly interdisciplinary way.[3]

II Working at micro-level

A longstanding notion of higher level student work – particularly postgraduate study – is that this should involve a kind of deft tripartite movement between close analytical reading, developing argument or framing ideas, and wider conceptualization of specifically literary matters of form. One way of encouraging this is to look at published versions of poetry and prose in relation to manuscript or draft versions. Not only is this a reminder to students that texts do not just spring fully formed from the pen of a writer but that every word is there deliberately, chosen for a reason and thus repays close reading. The most famous example of text being changed is Charles Dickens's last minute amendment to the ending of *Great Expectations* (1860–1), following the advice of his friend and fellow novelist, Edward Bulwer Lytton. Several modern editions of Dickens's novel reprint both endings. However, I want to focus on a much more specific example of textual amendment, taking Elizabeth Gaskell's *Wives and Daughters* (1866) as my case study. The most obvious copy text for *Wives and Daughters* is the serialized 1864–6 *Cornhill Magazine* edition as it is the last Gaskell oversaw before her death and it was her practice tacitly to accept editorial decisions even where she did not explicitly approve them. Specifically, there are numerous examples where punctuation has been corrected in accordance with editorial convention and house style producing minute changes of meaning when compared with the original manuscript which seem significant in this deeply subtle prose writer.

A useful example of this is the scene where the morally dubious Cynthia Kirkpatrick – her duplicity in secretly engaging herself to another man having come to light – breaks off her engagement with Roger Hamley. The manuscript version reads:

> For a moment Cynthia's wilful fancy stretched after the object passing out of her grasp, – Roger's love became, for the instant, a treasure. But again
> ∧   she knew that in its entirety of high undoubting esteem, as well as of passionate regard, it would no longer be hers; and for the flaw which she herself had made she cast it away and would have none of it. Yet often in after years, when it was too late, – she wondered, and strove to penetrate the inscrutable mystery of "what would have been".[4]

The published version amends the punctuation thus:

> – Roger's love became for the instant a treasure; but, again, she knew

In Gaskell's original, the fleeting possibility (its very transience held a microsecond longer by the commas surrounding "for an instant") that Cynthia could yet change her own story hovers at the full stop before "But." The substituted semi-colon, in leaving open the sentence, paradoxically shuts out or closes down the implicit higher possibility. A similarly significant loss of richness happens when Cynthia announces her rejection of Roger to her family. Where the *Cornhill* has "I like him, I respect him; but I will not marry him" the manuscript reads: "I like him. I respect him. But I will not marry him" (p. 780). A writer who is often very casual about punctuation (dashes, as in these few examples, often stand in for full stops) is emphatic in her use of stops here where they seem to stop-up in Cynthia her desperate need for esteem, and to signal that that need, profoundly uncured by the rejection of Roger, exists in the interstices of her every consummate social utterance.

Gaskell's prose revisions prove a useful pedagogical tool both in exemplifying the rich resonance of minute details and in helping to make visible implicit formal dynamics, levels, or movements within this apparently seamless informal prose. So in this example, where the narration records first Molly Gibson's reaction to her father's news that he is to be remarried, and then, in a new paragraph, the father's own feelings in relation to his daughter:

> It was as if the piece of solid ground on which she stood had broken from the shore, and she was drifting out to the infinite sea alone.
>
> half-
> Mr Gibson saw that her silence was unnatural, and ∧ guessed at the cause of it. But he knew that she must have time to reconcile herself to the idea, and still believed that it would be for her eventual happiness. (p. 171)

In terms of classroom activity, there are several questions to be asked here. Students might consider what they think prompted the instinctive revision (made at the time of writing almost certainly). Does it exist in relation to "alone" which, drifting on at the end of the previous paragraph like a line ending in poetry, leaves Molly stranded in her own paragraph? Mr Gibson's guessing of the meaning of her silence cancels or closes the gap which opens up between father and daughter at the paragraph division – too readily perhaps: hence the sudden adjustment. Perhaps the insertion of "half" is produced in attentive, *en passant* acknowledgement of what the paragraph division really signifies. Molly is and is *not* alone. While her father is there, still, in that nearby next paragraph, he nonetheless inhabits temporal continuities ("She must have *time . . . still* believed . . . *eventual* happiness") which her own paragraph of ontological threshold experience seems to have left behind for ever. Relevant here is Henry James's contemporary (favourable) comment on the novel's formal temporality – "the hours spent in its perusal seem like actual hours spent" (qtd. Easson, 1993, p. 463) – together with its translation into the theoretical terms of Gérard Genette's *Narrative Discourse* (1980, pp. 33–5). "Scenes" of this kind seem to realize an equivalence between the time of the thing told (story time) and the time of the telling (narrative time). The insertion of "half" helps draw attention to the fact that something different is happening here, in the shift from one paragraph to another. While the successive paragraphs appear to follow on in time, in fact, in the life they depict, they happen simultaneously (and in the same space for all the language of the breaking of land). Father and daughter are together and apart in time, sharing the moment but never wholly sharing how it feels. Narrative time extends beyond story time in this instance to disclose the density of linear time's levels and layers, yet the extension happens within the successive movement of sentences down the page so that time both does and does not stop. The addition of "half" is a gain in this prose, quietly adding to the complexity, not taking away.

Manuscript exercises, in at once making visible the powerful effect of micro-events of syntax and suggesting their relationship to wider meta-physical concerns, indicate that paying close attention to the construction of primary sources has potential to put students in touch with their own inner resources, thus encouraging originality of thought and endeavor.

III Contextuality

If studying textual variants allows students to reflect on the possibilities inherent in close-reading, working with other contemporary texts can help extend students' awareness of significant ideas and concerns of the period and, more specifically, to encourage the kind of interdisciplinary thinking which prepares for higher level project or dissertation work. Reading discourse contemporary to the period alongside nineteenth-century fiction can provide a language for teasing out, or explicating, the significance of literary phenomena. Understanding how contemporary ideas were presented are often more enriching to our understanding of the novel than more recent critical approaches can be.

One obvious way of encouraging a sense of contextuality is to "pair" fictional and non-fictional texts together, for example:

The Idea of the Social/Social Thinking: John Ruskin, "The Nature of Gothic"; Elizabeth Gaskell, *North and South.*

The Woman Question: J. S. Mill "The Subjection of Women"; Margaret Oliphant, *Hester.*

Religious Questions: (Selections from) Feuerbach and Newman; George Eliot, *Daniel Deronda.*

Science and the Secular: (Selections from) Darwin and Paley; Tennyson's *In Memoriam.*

While there are clear relationships between the fictional and non-fictional texts in each case, it is also worth stressing the relative arbitrariness of these pairings. What they *do* offer, albeit in very restricted form, is a kind of saturation in nineteenth-century thinking, not only as a useful scholarly grounding for pursuing work in the period, but in order to make old ideas live again as they lived for nineteenth-century writers. The aim is to put students in the thick of the almost Malthusian proliferation of Victorian ideas – to get them to experience something of the "honest doubt" which beset serious-minded Victorians, so that in their writing they too had, frighteningly, to think their way out of a problem. Here, conclusions seem less important than creative engagement.

The point of putting Gaskell and Ruskin together is to try to explore the category "social" in relation to texts that are often uncritically identified with a socio-political agenda, which are ideologically sympathetic, yet do not straightforwardly or comfortably affirm one another. In "The Stones of Venice," Ruskin anticipates Karl Marx when he says:

> We have much studied and much perfected of late, the great civilized invention of the division of labour; only we give it a false name. It is not, truly speaking, the labour that is divided; but the men – broken into small fragments and crumbs of life; so that all the little piece of intelligence that is left in a man is not enough to make a pin, or a nail, but exhausts itself in making the point of a pin or the head of a nail. (1995, pp. 194–5)

What separates the Ruskinian vision from a Marxist one is that even amidst the expropriation of human essence by capitalist exploitation, essential humanity can yet be preserved and reclaimed:

> You must either make a tool of the creature, or a man of him. You cannot make both. Men were not intended to work with the accuracy of tools, to be precise and perfect in all their actions. If you will have that precision out of them, you must unhumanise them . . . look for the *thoughtful* part of them, and get that out of them whatever we lose for it, whatever faults and errors we are obliged to take with it. (pp. 194–5)

Alongside this example of "social" thinking students might read an episode from *North and South* in which Mrs Hale responds to the severe hardship suffered by Boucher and his family as a result of the strike. Her first impulse is to fulfil her keen sympathy with the family's trouble in immediate practical reality: she is "restlessly irritable till she could do something," directing a basket to be sent "there and then" to the Bouchers.

> [She] never gave herself breathing-time till the basket was sent out of the house. Then she said:
> "After all, we may have been doing wrong. It was only the last time Mr Thornton was here that he said, those were no true friends who helped to prolong the struggle by assisting the turn-outs. And this Boucher man was a turn-out was he not?" (1982, p. 157)

The humanity which was so anxious to assume priority is stalled at second thought ("*Then* she said") in the translation from a human to a social level. While Boucher the man remains more real for Mrs Hale than Boucher the striker – "turn-out" is an extraneous category imposed upon the man in need – she fears, nonetheless, that what she instinctively feels to be secondary might, in a world bigger than her own, be primary after all. In helping to "prolong the strike" a simple act of human kindness has become part of an alienated narrative sequence which has as little relation to its original starting point as Ruskin's pin-heads have to the "single living spirit," the loss of which is the human price of mass-production. Indeed, by the end of the episode, the kindness itself has apparently turned into its opposite ("why, it was clear that the kindest thing was to refuse all help") and the very possibility of knowing what is the humanly right thing to do has become lost to social process. In this instance, the alienation Ruskin describes as the division of the human against itself has got right inside humanity's feeling *for* itself. The humanly "thoughtful part," which Ruskin sought to rescue from insitutionalization, and even the very thought of the human, has become politicized – as if this unextraordinary event of industrial-domestic realism were showing the very mechanism by which the human essence is stolen from itself. Here novelistic-realist discourse, apparently operating at a level beneath ideas, brilliantly interrogates and tests the viability of the more formal categories and general laws possible in non-fictional discourse. An idea tested within the strictures of temporal sequence is found wanting. Fiction's "social" truth appears the more complete and complex one.

This is also the point at which to go back to the primary evidence of Ruskin and note that even Ruskin's most categorical general laws are nothing if not chary of category. Ruskin's prose gives priority to "completeness" of idea over generalized abstraction or even crude "exactness" and that Gaskell's and Ruskin's prose procedures are analogous in this respect. As the character of Gothic architecture is first extensively and scrupulously compared by Ruskin to the entangled composition of a rough mineral, and the painstaking analogy unapologetically and summarily withdrawn as soon as it risks producing imprecision of idea, so Ruskin's definition of the "grey, shadowy, many-pinnacled image of the Gothic spirit within us" evolves by delicate accretion and accumulation (and where necessary subsequent subtraction), in a process not unlike the form of Gaskell's realism.

Students might also be asked to consider the process by which Higgins (the workman) and Thornton (the mill-owner) in *North and South* begin to communicate directly, as offering a narrative illustration of Ruskin's theory – a sort of parable. As Higgins, whose first instinct following his initial reception by Thornton is to walk away, is impelled by thought from a different level of self to try again – "then the recollection of Boucher came over him, and he faced round with the greatest concession he could persuade himself to make" – so Thornton, at second thought, thinks better of the man he has summarily dismissed. "The conviction that went in . . . as if by some spell, and touched the latent tenderness of his heart; the patience of the man, the simple generosity of the motive, made him forget entirely the mere reasonings of justice, and overleap them by a diviner instinct." The mere rational principle is forgotten "entirely" and is overtaken by a Christian principle, which, though it happens second in time, is actually a prior "latent" part of

Thornton's being, so integral in fact as to have become vulnerable to being forgotten in the pragmatics of business. The likelihood of making ill-formed hasty judgements in such a time-pressured environment – that Higgins must wait for the busy Thornton so long is a measure of this – makes the possibility of space for second thoughts all the more necessary. In a recent student assignment, the writer argued that *North and South* puts its faith in such chances, just as Ruskin trusted unpredictable creativity to save humanity from mechanism. Higgins and Thornton's non-institutionalized second thoughts, not trapped by prior principle or pre-conception, seemed to this student directly related to Ruskin's notion of a labourer's "thoughtful" potential insofar as this capacity, for Ruskin, was the "divine" aspect of his workman. Here, of course, the student is himself enacting that Ruskinian principle in finding an original connection of this kind. Ruskin remains one of the best nineteenth-century models for how we might produce real, as opposed to merely borrowed, secondary or alienated thinking in our students.[5]

IV   Primary research

In this final section I discuss ways in which students can be encouraged to work on primary materials independently in a way which develops research skills and helps hatch ideas and foster commitment and conviction in relation to a new research area. My starting point is a short 15-credit module, "Literature and Social Thought," taught as part of the University of Liverpool's MA in Victorian Studies. It is designed at once to extend students' awareness of significant ideas and concerns of the period and, more specifically, to encourage the kind of thinking which would prepare for dissertation work. The assessment component of the module requires students to bring together for the purposes of contextual and/or philosophical illumination and dialogue, an example of Victorian literature with two examples of non-literary discourse from the period, using the resources housed at William Gladstone's Library, St Deiniol's (now part of the University Centre for Victorian Studies). Students write a 1500-word commentary on Victorian documents drawn from three different sources. One of these is a literary document: ideally, the other two documents are drawn from the library holdings during a one-day visit.

This kind of module assessment is labour-intensive. A preparatory class prior to the visit, which requires students to bring in and talk briefly about their chosen literary extract and the area(s) or discourses with which they might hope to match it, can provide some initial direction for research, especially if students have not done this kind of work previously. In advance of the session, students might usefully be given information packs on the library as a place (its history, layout, regulations) and as a resource (comprehensive details of the library's holdings, including the rich store of nineteenth-century pamphlets and periodicals) and encouraged to visit the library's website and familiarize themselves with the library catalogue. On the day itself, students can be free to work as they please but staff can be on call to help practically and conceptually.

The rewards from this kind of exercise can be immense and tangible. While some of this material might well have been available elsewhere, the significance of using a single library is that primary research becomes a real, physical event, as students wander through the richly varied sections (political, theological, scientific and so on) of the library. A useful analogy for students is to think of Gladstone's library as representing a big Victorian mind because the project was really about opening up possibilities for connections across different areas and modes of thinking.

Two examples from a recent cohort of students give some sense of the unrestricted range and richness of the intellectual encounters or connections made possible by this model of primary research. One student considered Caroline Helstone's anguished self-interrogation at the prospect of being excluded from a woman's "ordinary destiny" of marriage and children in Charlotte Brontë's *Shirley* ("Half a century of existence may lie before me. How am I to occupy it? What am I to do to fill the interval of time which spreads between me and the grave? . . . Where is my place in the world?"(2007, p. 149) in relation to two commentaries on woman's "place" or role in the Victorian world published in the same year as the novel – an article stridently opposed to female intellect in *The Leader* (1850) and George Henry Lewes's fierce critique of *Shirley* (1849) in the *Edinburgh Review* (1850). Lewes's view that "the grand function of woman, it must always be recollected, is, and ever must be *Maternity*" sparked off an interest in the relationship between maternity and writing in Lewes's partner (a childless author of course) which became a dissertation on George Eliot, Motherhood and Maternalism. Further archival work in relation to this study uncovered W. R. Greg's article "Why are women redundant?" (*National Review*, 1862) with its misogynistic misconception of an increase in the population of "surplus" single women, and the student is now undertaking Ph.D. research on women writers (Harriet Martineau, Charlotte Brontë, Margaret Oliphant) whose varied "single" status (spinster, spinster turned wife, widow) complicates the culturally generic category proposed by Greg.

The other project looked at M. Paul's "reading," via physical scrutiny, of Lucy Snowe in *Villette* in relation to: on the one hand, Johann Lavater's *Essays on Physiognomy* (a late eighteenth-century work widely popularized in mid-nineteenth-century) in which, as a theologian attempting to harmonize religion and science, he theorized a divinely pre-determined correlation between appearance and behaviour whereby consistent, knowable patterns linked the physical, psychological, and spiritual; on the other, to Herbert Spencer's evolutionary perspective on physical attractiveness as limited to an instinctual, biological level. The project inspired a dissertation which considered how interest in physiognomy (formulated in sight) took precedence among Victorian novelists over interest in the related pseudo-science of phrenology (formulated in touch); and which contrasted the relatively skilled physiognomists among Charlotte Brontë's characters both with the highly subjective and distorting interpretations under the direction of personal desire to be found in Hardy's people, and with the deliberate concealments and social masks which, in the work of Henry James, threaten the very notion of a coherent identity accessible through the workings of the human features. But this student's curiosity about the possibility that Lavater's scientific genealogies could make theological doctrine (that of inherited sin, for instance) a matter of living daily reality in the Victorian world, led to an interest in the Tractarian pursuit of a revitalized Anglican Church through the practical application in modern lives of ancient biblical truths; and thence, specifically, to John Henry Newman's belief in the personal influence of godly individuals and teachers as a kind of spiritual inheritance or genealogy tracing back to the apostles and their power.

Comments from student evaluation forms suggest that one of the benefits of this kind of assignment is the unmediated quality of the encounter.

"Dealing with these ideas in this primary way allows a far more immediate and individual impression, leading to one's own distinct lines of thought which are not influenced by the selection or agenda which governs their representation in secondary sources."

"Primary sources allow *you* to do the analysis and give you freedom to form an original argument."

"Primary sources can open up ideas behind or implicit in a text – they help you see the extent of an idea's influence on an author and how that idea works itself out in the text."

"Working with primary sources lends itself to a kind of joy of discovery, unveiling views that are non-existent in today's culture."

"Working with Lavater's texts was different to reading about him through a critic's perspective on his views because, though his ideas would be laughed at today, I could not dismiss the tone of seriousness with which he conducted his argument. The sheer bulk of information (his work is in several volumes) and his many diagrams showed he undertook the project like a scientist. In *Villette* M. Paul's fervour for Lucy, which can be viewed as Romantic exaggeration, also took on a new seriousness and validity with Lavater's ideas to illuminate the text."

"What can seem dead and finished when you first encounter it in a secondary text can come suddenly to life and hit you with force when you feel close to the original thing."

The point here is that these responses suggest the degree to which working with primary sources can be the direct contrary of a dry, scholarly exercise on "dead" material: rather, it can be a way of bringing to life of canonical and non-canonical texts, new and orthodox questions, alike. Research exercises can give students a sense of a personal stake in the material and the critical-theoretical debate surrounding it. With this approach, even hitherto heavily-scrutinized issues (the woman question or faith and doubt, for example) have the potential to become fresh and alive to students in ways which motivate a deeper mining of significances than over-saturation in secondary texts perhaps encourage (where, by definition, a student's first thoughts about material are someone else's). This is perhaps one way of overcoming the alienation which Ruskin feared for us all, and especially for our educational culture.

Appendix: sample syllabus: literature and social thought

Aims and Objectives: This six-week module aims to enable you to analyse the relationship between Victorian literature and various forms of social thought of the period. It aims to go further than simply contextualizing literature by familiarizing you with interdisciplinary approaches to Victorian writing. On a practical level, the module seeks to develop research skills by introducing you to archival library work – you will complete a portfolio project at St Deiniol's (Gladstone's) library. On a theoretical level, it asks you to consider the nature and value of both literature and interdisciplinary thought. As with all modules, seminar topics vary from year-to-year according to staffing and student interests: in addition to those listed below, topics have included Romanticism and Utilitarianism, Chartism, The Great Exhibition, The Oxford Movement, and Empire.

Schedule and Reading List

Week 1
The Idea of the Social/Social Thinking
John Ruskin, "The Nature of Gothic"; Elizabeth Gaskell, *North and South* (Oxford)

Week 2
The Woman Question
J. S. Mill "The Subjection of Women" in *On Liberty and Other Essays* (Oxford); Mrs Oliphant, *Hester* (Oxford)

Week 3
Religious Questions
(Selections from) Feuerbach, Mallock; George Eliot, *Daniel Deronda* (Oxford)

Week 4
Science and the Secular
(Selections from) Darwin; Tennyson's *In Memoriam*

Weeks 5 and 6
Session 5 will be a preparatory class for the library/archive research which
will consititute Session 6, based at St Deiniol's.

Notes

1. John Stuart Mill, "The Enfranchisement of Women," *Westminster Review*, 55 (July 1851), pp. 289–311. The article was attributed to Mill but was later admitted to be the work of Harriet Taylor (Mill's collaborator – and wife from 1851).
2. For a fuller discussion of literature as "a form of utterance that lies suspended *between* written speech and written fixity – making silent and implicit calls to be felt, innerly performed, translated and understood, and not just passively received" see Philip Davis's "The Place of the Implicit in Literary Discovery" in Tanya Agathocleous and Ann C. Dean (eds), (2003) *Teaching Literature: A Companion* (Basingstoke: Palgrave Macmillan), pp. 149–62.
3. On interdisciplinary studies, Gillian Beer writes, "Forms of knowledge do not readily merge; they may lie askance or cross-grained. But that does not imply failure. Disanalogy can prove to be a powerful heuristic tool. Indeed it is important not too readily to pair particular disciplines since that ignores indirection, the shared and dispersed other forms of experience and knowledge active in the time" *Open Fields: Science in Cultural Encounter* (Oxford: Oxford University Press, 1996), p. 115.
4. Elizabeth Gaskell, *Wives and Daughters*, MSS 877, John Rylands University Library of Manchester, 781–2. (For Cornhill versions and complete listing of variants see: Josie Billington (ed.), *Wives and Daughters*, in *Works of Elizabeth Gaskell*, ed. Joanne Shattock (London: Pickering and Chatto, 2006), pp. 445–6.
5. As Dinah Birch notes "The Nature of Gothic" . . . has not lost its power as an account of what education might mean, and should mean, for our own century. . . . [Ruskin's] plea for the courage that allows the freedom of creative engagement, rather than the security of measured precision, should be central to our understanding of the processes of education." *Our Victorian Education* (Oxford: Blackwell, 2007), pp. 140–2.

Works cited

Agathocleous, Tanya and Ann C. Dean (eds.), *Teaching Literature: A Companion* (Basingstoke: Palgrave Macmillan, 2003), pp. 149–62.

Barry, Peter, *English in Practice: In Pursuit of English Studies* (London: Arnold, 2003).

Beer, Gillian, *Open Fields: Science in Cultural Encounter* (Oxford: Oxford University Press, 1996).

Birch, Dinah, *Our Victorian Education* (Oxford: Blackwell, 2007).

Davis, Philip, "The Place of the Implicit in Literary Discovery: Creating New Courses," in Tanya Agathocleous and Ann C. Dean, *Teaching literature: A Companion* (Basingstoke: Palgrave Macmillan. 2003).

Easson, Angus (ed.), *Elizabeth Gaskell: The Critical Heritage* (London: Routledge, 1991).

Gaskell, Elizabeth, *North and South* (1854–5), ed. Angus Easson (Oxford: Oxford University Press,1982).

——. *The Life of Charlotte Brontë* (1857), ed. Angus Easson (Oxford: Oxford University Press, 1996).

——. *Wives and Daughters*, MSS 877, John Rylands University Library of Manchester, 781–2.

——. *Wives and Daughters* (1864) in *The Works of Elizabeth Gaskell*, ed. Joanne Shattock (London: Pickering and Chatto 2006).

Genette, Gerard, *Narrative Discourse*, trans. Jane E. Lewin (Oxford: Blackwell, 1980).

Raines, Melissa, "George Eliot's Grammar of Being," *Essays in Criticism*, 58:1 (2007), pp. 43–63.

Rosengarten, Herbert and Margaret Smith (eds.), *Charlotte Brontë: Shirley* [1849] (Oxford: Oxford University Press [1979], 2007), p. 149.

Ruskin, John, *Selected Writings: John Ruskin*, ed. Philip Davis (London: Everyman, 1995).

Skilton, David, "The Trollope Reader," in Jeremy Hawthorn (ed.), *The Nineteenth-Century Novel* (London: Edward Arnold, 1986), pp. 142–56.

15
Technology and the World Wide Web

Priti Joshi

I Introduction

Can technology foster learning in the nineteenth-century studies classroom? For many, the answer is an unequivocal "No!" Already burdened by triple-decker novels, epic-length poems, and prose essays, not to mention literary criticism, participants might well find the introduction of technology in the classroom a trendy encumbrance that diverts attention away from the text itself, particularly at a time when some students struggle with the prose style and locutions of the Victorians. These concerns are pertinent and have long informed a lack of initiative in deploying technology in classes. But on the other side of resistance is the oft-cited reason for adopting technology: it is ubiquitous and a "language" numbers of our students, if not *actually* conversant in, *think* is their natural medium. In my own case, having been prodded by an institutional culture that urged faculty to incorporate technology in courses and my own frustration with much of what was on the Web – and that I knew students were consulting – I decided to stop circumventing the putative elephant in the room and actually dissect it.[1] This essay serves two purposes: to discuss ways in which we might integrate technology to promote learning about the nineteenth century and to assess the strengths and weaknesses of various available technologies.

A word on terminology: "technology" is used in what follows as a self-evident term whose meaning is straightforward. It is of course no such thing: a vague term that can mean anything from "all that is new" to "electronic communication, storage, and retrieval" to the Web to Podcasts to Wikis. As the contributors to "Searching Questions: Digital Research and Victorian Culture," part of recent special issue of the *Journal of Victorian Culture*, made clear, "technology" can encompass a vast range of approaches, tools, software, and hardware.[2] I use the term, nonetheless, without further precision because I begin with the assumption that readers will have varying degrees of comfort with and resistance to technology, and largely too because I want to acknowledge that what constitutes "technology" for one might well be neither technological nor innovative for another (for some of my colleagues – those who still ask the department secretary to type a hand-written manuscript – the laptop counts as "technology," while for others it has achieved the status of the indispensable object we seldom notice).

II   Communication

Technological developments of the past decade have transformed how (and how often) we communicate with students. E-mail and social networking sites such as Facebook have become such a standard part of many lives that there is now a tongue-in-cheek term – Internet Addictive Disorder – and a blog-inspired self-help movement called "secular Sabbath" for those who cannot stay away from connectivity.[3] Such communication tools carry with them the danger of being on-call or overly-accessible, but in teaching they can be used to ease clerical duties such as communicating last-minute instructions or announcements. Increasingly, the class e-mail distribution list is being superseded by the communication tools on Course Management Systems (CMS) such as Blackboard or Moodle. These systems do a lot more (see "Assignments" below), but the benefit of a CMS for communicating is that students register themselves and the instructor merely types in a few keystrokes to distribute a message to all or a portion of the class.

Increasingly instructors also use their professional websites to "communicate" with students, especially about recurrent questions. Priya Joshi created a link on her website called "On asking professors for letters of recommendation" when she first started teaching at Berkeley in 1996. Over the years, that page has been joined by others, including a page on the proper way to cite sources, and tips on applying to graduate school, all gathered under "Advice to Students."[4] Dino Felluga, now at Purdue University, created the *Introductory Guide to Critical Theory* in 1996.[5] The site introduces various "schools" of theory and theorists and Felluga says he created it "because I was so dissatisfied with what was available out there."[6] He uses it as a supplement in his literature classes and is evidently not alone: since July 2002, it has had almost 6 *million* hits. In a slightly different vein, I have a link on my website called "I'm Reading" that offers short synopses of books I recommend.[7] I created it because at the start of every break students ask me for suggestions of books to read and, to the extent that many of the books listed are either accounts of the nineteenth century or "neo-Victorian" fiction, this site can be viewed as an extension of what I do in the classroom.

Some instructors are beginning to utilize blogs as pedagogical-communication tools. Blogs are commentary sites, generally updated daily or at regular intervals. A blog is a one-to-many format which means that the creator initiates and generates discussion by writing brief essays that readers can post responses to. This response or comment feature makes blogs interactive in contrast to websites that are static, and many instructors use blogs to create a virtual discussion space. For others, however, the blog creator's absolute control over the topic and tone of discussion can prevent students from being active and responsible for generating content. Such instructors ask students to also develop individual blogs on which they regularly post essays. Used this way, student blogs serve as a virtual and green version of the paper journal.

III   Nineteenth-century materials on the Web

To say that information and traffic on the Web has exploded is to say the banal, but the seismic changes that growth has wrought in our approaches to knowledge, ideas, and learning have only just begun to be registered or assessed. In nineteenth-century studies, the sheer growth in the number of sites has given rise to indices to gather and organize them, most substantial of which are Alan Liu's *Voice of the Shuttle: Victorian* and Jack Lynch's *Literary Resources: Victorian British*.[8] The assistance is welcome as ill-researched, poorly informed, and downright inaccurate sites share bandwidth with genuinely thoughtful and scholarly sites. Six years ago Chris Willis published an essay reviewing the best nineteenth-century research sites.[9] Her article is still pertinent as many of the sites she discussed continue to exist even if some have not been updated or completed, a not uncommon phenomenon (once funds, the initial enthusiasm, or the reality of the sheer labour involved sinks in, many sites are abandoned). My purpose in this section is not to rehash or update her essay, but to organize the plethora of materials into categories in order to assess their pedagogical potential. (Note: I discuss here only open-access sites, not proprietary resources for purchase; that would require a different essay, not to mention a robust budget.)

George Landow's *The Victorian Web* was a pioneer and model for creating a scholarly presence on the Web. The site offers primarily brief essays, originally written by his students, on various topics from intellectual, social, economic, and political history to literature and the arts. Due to Landow's boundless energy and capacious vision, the site is constantly evolving – it now includes a section on "Visual Arts" and another on *Punch* cartoons that contain images and occasional commentary. Despite its inclusion of such images, however, the sites' origins as a repository of secondary essays on the period's history, movements, and trends remains and was recently shored up by the introduction of excerpts from scholarly monographs (collected under "Victorian Web Books"). Landow's site has spawned numerous similar sites that I classify as "text-based" because they offer primarily commentary – some scholarly, some not – on Victorian subjects. Lesley Hall's erudite *History of Sexuality* is a curious mix of essays directed to a general audience – "The Condom" and "The Clitoris: historical myths and facts" – and scholarly essays on the history of medicine and sexuality.[10] Such sites are often consulted by student researchers and they function as Web sources that have established high standards of accuracy and detail. Sadly, such a claim cannot be made for much of the Web.

Several text-based sites that collect nineteenth-century *primary* documents have also had a salutary impact on teaching. Project Gutenberg is perhaps best-known for making available electronic versions (html and more recently MP3) of over 25,000 texts. The editions are not scholarly and can sometimes be replete with errors introduced in transcribing, but the vast scale of the project, sustained commitment to it, ease in downloading, and access can be harnessed to pedagogical purposes. For instance, a student working on a paper on *Bleak House* recently used a basic Control+F search on Project Gutenberg to check if she had missed references to her topic. Utilized thus, the source is useful – and harmless.[11] A more scholarly site is the *Victorian Women Writers Project*, the work of Perry Willett at Indiana University, that includes the works of some forty lesser-known women writers such as Dinah Craik, Sarah Ellis, Mathilde Blind, E. Nesbit, and Lucas Malet. It is a boon to researchers unable to travel to distant libraries and also allows us to make these texts available to students without having to rely on photocopies of old editions or hope for modern reprints.

The true promise of the Web is its graphic interface which allows for the transmission of images (still and moving) and sounds. The sites mentioned above are remnants of our text-reliant literacy, but a slew of new ones have emerged that marry text and "images" – broadly defined, as we will see shortly – to convey information. The most sustained and admirable of these is Jerome McGann's *The Rossetti Archive* out of the University of Virginia in which every image related to Rossetti's life and work – paintings, book bindings, furniture, manuscripts of poems – is accompanied by erudite commentary and bibliography.[12] In essence, the site is an open source or freeware version of the scholarly monograph, differing from it in ways we could all enumerate but also pointing to a future in which learned materials are widely available to those without access to a scholarly library. Other image-based sites are Anthony Wohl's *Punch* cartoon page put together by his students at Vassar in 1997 (sadly, the size and quality of the images are consonant with the technology available at the time) and the John Leech archive collection of *Punch* images.[13] The latter is unscholarly and poorly catalogued, but for the patient user provides access to dozens of quirkily-selected *Punch* images.

Sites that make available nineteenth-century primary documents in their original form are growing in number and a welcome development for teaching with technology. One of the most exciting is the *Proceedings of the Old Bailey, 1674–1913*, a collaboration between the Open University, and the Universities of Hertfordshire and Sheffield, which offers a searchable database of London crimes.[14] Searches yield both plain (html) text as well as a *page image* of the case as recorded in Old Bailey proceedings, complete with witnesses' and police testimony and verdict. These records offer an indispensable glimpse into a world of poverty and punishment, pettiness and neighbourliness, of objects of desire and modes of living, and the pedagogical possibilities they offer are staggering.[15] For instance, in the course of reading *Oliver Twist* one can ask students to search "theft" between 1825 and 1840 and use the returns to consider the types and reasons for theft that *were* brought to trial against Dickens's handkerchief thefts, thus prompting a rich discussion that contextualizes Dickens's portrait of the "underclass." Another project that aims to make primary texts accessible is Lyndsey Magrone's *Rediscovering Dickens: Making Connections Between Household Words and Hard Times*.[16] The site contains facsimiles of the editions of *Household Words* in which *Hard Times* first appeared in order to reposition readers in the novel's moment. The teaching opportunities the project generates – some explored by Jennifer Phegley in an assignment included in the "about this project" link – are numerous, and for those, such as myself, who wish to introduce students to the "look" of nineteenth-century periodicals and invite them to navigate this text-heavy medium, the site has immense potential. Unfortunately, the images of *Household Words* pages on the site are JPGs and therefore slow to load. A further limitation is that, unlike the Old Bailey site, *Rediscovering Dickens* is not searchable or tagged. Thus, locating material on it is well nigh impossible unless one uses the clumsy Control+F feature on each of the accompanying html pages until one finds one's term (such searches are not feasible on scanned facsimile pages unless they have been "translated" or "cleaned up" by Optical Character Recognition – see below).

Two sites that digitalize periodicals in a more researcher-friendly manner are the *Internet Library of Early Journals* which makes available approximately 20 years of each of three eighteenth- and nineteenth-century journals and the *Nineteenth-Century Serials Edition* that digitalizes six nineteenth-century periodicals.[17] Both use Optical Character Recognition (OCR) that makes image scans of text-filled pages searchable, a boon to researchers. Both aim to make scarce resources durable and can do so because they are well-funded and jointly-undertaken projects. Given the expensive equipment required for high-quality images and the intense, site-specific labour required to protect delicate source material, such resources are crucial for the successful completion of similar projects. Without them, not surprisingly, many projects are abandoned midway.

Let me conclude this section by underscoring what must already be apparent: websites that offer primary source material of nineteenth-century documents and artifacts, including less-accessible texts whether in html or properly scanned and tagged facsimile form, prove to be most useful for research and teaching purposes. Periodicals have been particularly promising and the renewed attention to them and pedagogical use of them is heartening. But other media – non-canonical literary texts as well as historical records such as Old Bailey records, pamphlets, posters, advertisements – have also fared well and are being increasingly introduced to students alongside nineteenth-century fiction.

IV   In the classroom

How, if at all, can we soberly incorporate such riches? The uses we put these materials to are limited only by our imaginations – and the inevitable disasters that follow when one attempts to use technology in front of an audience! In what follows I discuss ways in which instructors have drawn upon technology in literature classrooms, but first a clarification: my focus is not on the virtual classroom (a growing phenomenon that recently received a boost of respectability with the unveiling of MIT's OpenCourseWare), but on the utilization of technology in the "traditional" physical classroom with its face-to-fact encounter between instructor and students.

The clearest evidence that online resources have "made it" in teaching the nineteenth century is the introduction of "Norton Topics Online" to accompany the venerable Norton Anthology of English Literature series.[18] The nineteenth-century online resource covers topics such as Industrialism, Women, Empire, and "the Painterly Image in Poetry" and provides excerpts from primary texts (Ruskin's *Of Queen's Gardens*, Barrett Browning's "Cry of the Children") and the occasional image or map. A more robust incorporation of resources is evident in Katherine Harris's "British Literature 1800 to the Present" course at San Jose State University.[19] Harris integrates a wide range of supporting materials to guide her students through the literature of the period. She draws on, for instance, a scanned image of the hold of a slave ship or the table of contents of *Lyrical Ballads*, Pears soap ads, links to the "Victorian Periodicals and the Empire" site, audios of authors reading their work, even a student-created video on the "real" ending of *Jane Eyre*. The variety of materials and formats – images, scans of primary texts in their contexts, audio files, videos, maps – that Harris draws on and the ways she tightly integrates these materials so as to provide students with an informed context from which to understand and assess the literary texts is impressive and the outcome of considerable research and labour. The range of artifacts she draws on to produce a "thick description" of the nineteenth century would be extremely challenging to collect and introduce to students were it not for the technology that makes such materials durable, fungible, and accessible.

Not everyone uses as many primary sources nor as consistently as Harris. A recent query on the VICTORIA listserv[20] about using YouTube as a "resource" in classes prompted a series of responses, most of which indicate that instructors "use Youtube [*sic*] for lighthearted introductions/conclusions to various units,"[21] most frequently, it seems, in discussions of either empire or poetry. Martin Danahay is partial to "The Teletubby Uprising of

1883," while several members mention the comedian Eddie Izzard's routine about flags and yet others the Monty Python skit about climbing both peaks of Mt Kilimanjaro.[22] Recently, a member wrote: "In exhaustion, I used Youtube [*sic*] to teach Browning last week," only to find students responding positively to the "cheesy-but-fun" versions of "Porphyria's Lover" and "My Last Duchess."[23] As this sliver of conversation indicates, instructors use the popular and populist YouTube primarily to lighten and liven things up in the classroom. Aside from entertainment, however, such materials could be used as a springboard into the text and to press students to think about language and interpretation. For instance, the campy dramatization of "Porphyria's Lover" on YouTube[24] can initiate a conversation about Browning's language and the clues he intersperses that lead to the video's reading (novice readers often read Browning's speakers as trustworthy characters who are to be taken at their word; hence, "No pain felt she" is read as a statement of fact), thereby developing the skills of close-reading that are the bedrock of our discipline.

For some instructors, a "contemporary take" on nineteenth-century issues proves useful as it allows students to empathize and make connections or simply demonstrates the relevance of nineteenth-century concerns. This impulse is itself the progeny of the literary and intellectual trend some have called "neo-Victorianism" and others "afterlife studies" (see Grace Moore's Chapter 12 in the present volume). Examples of the first abound in the mini-industry of contemporary novels set in the nineteenth century that revise well-known narratives or retell the period's history from a new angle. Afterlife studies focuses critical attention on neo-nineteenth century novels and also on the unexpected continuities and fissures between that century and our own.[25] That there are such continuities should alert us to a danger in using twentieth-century routines about, say, the folly of the British empire as these run the risk of generating in students an attitude of moral superiority that "we" are better than those "less developed" nineteenth-century types. Such a stance is not only lazy and shallow – it prevents us from entering the debates and concerns of the nineteenth century from within its own framework and arsenal of intellectual tools – but also blinds us from our own intellectual and epistemological limitations.

In an attempt to introduce students to the period as they grappled to make sense of their world and developed mechanisms to understand it, I devised a successful classroom activity using tools on the Web to enhance my teaching of *Oliver Twist* in a seminar entitled "Industry and Empire in Nineteenth-Century Britain." I will describe here four instances in which I taught the material, each time incorporating more advanced "technology." As we read *Oliver Twist*, I draw students' attention to the role of the city in the novel. As Oliver enters and leaves London, Dickens practically draws a road map for his readers ("The Artful Dodger turned left by Sadler's Inn, by the walls of Clerkenwell prison to Holborn"). In pre-Web days, we would examine Dickens's text beside the writings of social investigators which lacked his precise directions and I asked students to consider why Dickens provided such exhaustive detail. They typically proposed that he used it for "authenticity" and to enhance his credentials, but seldom considered that his documentary realism might not simply be narrating "truth" but also creating an image of the poor and their neighbourhoods.

Some years later at the Dickens Project at University of California, Santa Cruz, I laid hands on a poster-sized copy of Cruchley's 1838 map of London, and this segment of the course became concretized. I asked students to compare Dickens's textual descriptions with the map and to examine his representation of London. While students readily noted that his directions were absolutely accurate, they had trouble grasping the differences between textual and geographical ways of viewing and narrating the world. This was largely because the map, while of good quality, is small and cramped and it requires considerable effort to make out details.

A few years later still, Greenwood's 1827 map of London became available on the Web.[26] The map is easy to navigate because it is divided into sections that users can zoom into and view in considerable detail (the sections keep the size of images transmitted manageable). The ability to get at the details on the map transformed this segment of our discussion of *Oliver Twist*. In a "smart classroom" that permits computer projection onto a large screen, I bring up the relevant section of the map and using a laser pointer and laser mouse stand amongst the students and navigate the map, pointing out relevant features (e.g., workhouses about which Dickens is silent). In a final iteration I taught this segment in a "genius classroom" in which the projection screen was equipped with an "electronic pen" and each student had a laptop. I familiarized students with the map and its features using the mark-up technology which was more interactive than the pointer as it allowed me to invite students to the "board" to identify features they noticed. Next, I asked students to navigate the map on their own laptops, keeping in mind several large questions: What sorts of "stories" does the map tell that Dickens leaves out? What sorts of "stories" does Dickens tell that the map cannot?

This last was by far the most successful experience I had teaching this material. Students were mesmerized and kept "discovering" new things – that the worst slums had many cemeteries but only a few hospitals; differences in the size of the streets and the lack of open spaces between neighbourhoods; the placement of parks, the density of buildings, etc. They came away with a complex sense of the epistemological differences between narrative and geographical representations (that maps and fictional texts had distinct purposes and stories to tell; that no matter how "accurate," Dickens's view was partial – but so was the map's take on London). They also recognized the "framing" that Dickens's narrative was involved in as it isolated parts of the town and segments of the population. Finally, students came to complicate the relationship between "authenticity" and "realism" and to understand viscerally that "realism" is about more than accuracy or truth-telling, but equally about the ability to create "truths." While I could certainly have lectured on these matters, the use of technology made students active and engaged learners of the material. (Note: this activity took about 45 minutes – although the preparation for it, of course, took much longer.)

V Assignments

This penultimate section discusses assignments that utilize technology and might enhance learning. Some instructors ask students to develop websites, and there are at least two directions to take in this assignment: the simplest is to ask students to write an essay on a given topic and to link all the students' essays off a main course page. In this vein, George Landow asks students to "create an annotated version . . . of Carlyle's 'Hudson's Statue'" in which they select terms Carlyle uses from history or myth, research them, and explain Carlyle's use of the term as it appears in the essay.[27] Readers arrive at the "annotation" (student essay) by clicking on the highlighted link in the text of the essay on the course webpage.[28] Jonathan Smith at the University of Michigan-Dearborn has developed *Charlotte's Web* and *Pip's World* to accompany his classes' reading of *Jane Eyre* and *Great Expectations*.[29] Both sites include links to numerous topics (Gypsies, History of Jamaican Slavery, London Fairs) that open to short essays by students and both have been developed over a number of years and represent the cumulative handiwork of dozens of students.

Landow's and Smith's assignments are text-based and their primary reason for making theirs Web projects appears to be to make information widely available and to expand the audience for student writing. Others who have introduced Web-design assignments have asked students to use the full promise of the Web.[30] I developed an assignment in a seminar on the Brontë sisters. We first spent class time examining, assessing, and critiquing a number of exiting sites (some on the Brontës, some not); next, we developed criteria for what scholarly sites should aim for and include; we then spent two classes in the computer lab learning how to develop Web pages; and finally I asked each student to research a topic, write up his/ her research, and then develop a Web page appropriate to the topic and research. Students were required to include appropriate images and links so this was not merely a matter of uploading text to a site.

Sadly, in a lesson about the ephemerality of such technology, the site did not survive my institution's shift from one server to another. While some of the pages students developed were thoughtful, demonstrating excellent research skills and absorption of historical material *as well as* innovation in rendering this information accessible and digestible by drawing on rich background materials (*Punch* cartoons on slavery, for instance), the vast majority of the pages were bland and banal. I have not repeated the assignment in eight years, less because I do not think it can be improved upon, but rather because I concluded that in balance the time this project took away from the fiction itself was too great to make it a worthwhile experience. (I should note, however, that while students initially resisted the project, the great majority concluded that it was the most useful assignment of the semester.)

Although some caution is recommended in using web assignments, one clear benefit of them is that they expand the audience for student writing – and with it arrive the gains that come of creating a broader audience than just the instructor for student work. Aside from Web pages, Classroom Management Systems such as Blackboard or Moodle are a popular way to get students talking to and writing for one another. Many instructors require students to regularly post ideas on Discussion Boards. Such postings can function as a virtual journal or way to monitor students' reading. Recently, wanting to create an arena for broader discussion, I developed a postings assignment in a seminar on *Bleak House* and *Middlemarch*. I required each student to post four "generative questions" and four "responses" to somebody else's question during the course of the semester. I provided careful guidelines (the questions could not be plot inquiries or speculations; they could not be brief one-liners, but needed to provide background and rationale for why the question was relevant, etc.) and due dates for each posting and its response. The results were encouraging. Students developed a lively virtual community, continuing discussions that began in class but were truncated by time constraints. They wrote mini-essays in posing questions and more pages in response to one another (more than one student responded to multiple queries). They even voluntarily chose to use this forum for their final paper proposals so they could get feedback from more than just me. What made this venture truly successful is that the virtual space served to promote and enhance active, person-to-person conversations both in class and outside it. Being able (asked) to develop a thought or promulgate a theory in some detail on a public forum raised the stakes and also promoted students' confidence: they wanted to convince one another of their ideas, they were open to revising them, they genuinely collaborated to understand the novels and assist one another in developing robust readings of them.

Collaboration is the entire purpose of wikis. A wiki, as defined by the grandest of all wikis, Wikipedia, is "a collection of web pages designed to enable anyone who accesses it to contribute or modify content, using a simplified markup language. Wikis are often used to create collaborative websites and to power community websites."[31] A wiki allows multiple users to pitch in and formulate content, but also leaves a trace or history of revisions and even allows reversions to a previous iteration. Instructors are beginning to experiment using wikis in their courses: one assignment is to ask students to write a joint response to a question (perhaps pertinent in summarizing a complex reading); another is to ask students to jointly develop a final essay prompt; yet another is to use the wiki format to create an open source site of original documents.[32] Students could be assigned to locate primary documents in the library around specific topics; the goal would be to collaboratively build a trove of relevant documents. Such an assignment would not only develop students' researching skills, but also immerse them into period concerns and debates in fresh ways. In any context where collaboration is desirable, wikis can be used productively and have the virtue of allowing each person to reflect and compose deliberately rather than try to write "in committee" which proves difficult for many. Anecdotal evidence indicates that students appear to prefer working on wikis over pen-and-ink collaborations.

VI Final words

The introduction of technology – particularly Web tools and materials – can, if used deliberately and sparingly, enhance students' understanding of the nineteenth century and its literary texts. The Web is most effective as a teaching tool when it offers scarce or historical primary documents, material that those with a New Historicist or Cultural Studies bent are more likely to draw on in their teaching of literary texts. To put it another way: in a New Critical classroom, the Web is less likely to prove a useful tool (although instruments such as class-developed websites that annotate a text or blogs to generate conversation/reflection or wikis to produce collaborated text can be used productively in such classrooms). For teachers who wish to place literary texts in a larger discourse or conversation, who view literature as participating in creating the context and conversation, the wealth of primary materials available on the Web can prove a boon in teaching.

Crafting activities and assignments from that material or using the new technologies is no simple task, but no different from the "old days" when instructors generated carefully-designed assignments to the rare-book room of the library: both require thought, care, and a dry run. It is important before asking students to work with primary documents on the Web, to run through them thoroughly and make sure you're aware of constraints or surprises. It is worth developing mock webpages with links so you can help the student for whom none of it seems to work. For assignments, think about carefully articulating all the steps of the assignment, being precise and fulsome in directions. On completion, think about *using* the materials you assign: nothing frustrates students more than being assigned a load of "extra" material with no attention or accountability to it. This only creates the impression that "context" is secondary. And finally, be prepared for failures, for trials and frustrations, but also for unexpected pleasures as students take charge of their learning as they make connections and arguments and teach *you* about the nineteenth century.

Appendix: sample syllabus: industry and empire in nineteenth-century Britain

Industry and Empire were the two processes that "book-ended" the nineteenth century, engendering simultaneously profound optimism and intense anxiety. Central to debates about both industry and empire were questions of gender – about women and their "proper" place, as well as men and masculinity. We will use these three questions – about industry, gender, and empire – as the lenses through which we approach the century's literature. We will begin by examining various responses to industrialism, particularly the crisis of poverty, the rise of class antagonism, and the criminalization of the poor. By the 1850s, as women's aspiration for greater voice and rights grew, the debate about industrial costs and class differences was replaced by anxieties about gender and attempts to define the role and nature of women and men, domesticity, and women's place in the nation. By the 1880s, gender concerns in turn were supplanted by, first, celebration and then consternation about Empire, its effects on England and the English, its costs and dangers. We will examine how these three concerns were resolved and how they reappeared in different guises and disguises as the century progressed. Throughout, we will examine how the character of "English" identity was produced and reproduced, asserted and altered in its engagement with these questions.

The guiding assumption of this course is that nineteenth-century literature cannot be read in isolation from the social debates of the day. For a variety of reasons having to do with the ways in which Victorian intellectual life was organized, nineteenth-century "literature" and writers were continually in conversation with essayists, journalists, philosophers, sociologists, economists, politicians, etc. In order to reconstruct some of these conversations, we will read literary texts alongside non-literary ones and consider the former as intervening and participating in the social and political debates of the day.

Required texts

The following books are on order at the university bookstore. It is preferable if you purchase the editions ordered as it will be difficult for you to keep up with the close textual work our class will be engaged in if you have a different edition.

Charlotte Brontë, *Jane Eyre* (Oxford, 1847)
Wilkie Collins, *Moonstone* (Oxford, 1868)
Charles Dickens, *Oliver Twist* (Oxford, 1837)
Elizabeth Gaskell, *Mary Barton* (Oxford, 1848)
H. Rider Haggard, *She* (Oxford, 1887)
Course packet.

Assessment

- *One 12–15 page final paper*: For this paper, you will research a 19th-century social, economic or political debate (a list of topics will be provided) and offer an analysis of how two or more of the novels engage, extend, challenge or participate in this debate.
- *Two 7-page papers*: For each novel we read (except *She*), the tutor will assign paper topics. In the course of the semester, you must write a 7-page paper each on *two* novels; the choice is up to you. Keep in mind, however, that you must hand in your paper on a novel *when it is due*. In other words, if you miss the deadline for the *Oliver Twist* paper, you cannot go back and write on it, even if you really, really want to. A word to the wise: don't procrastinate and leave both papers for the end of the semester.
- *Participation*: This is a seminar class and will be conducted as such. What does this mean? It means that YOU and your input are central to the success or failure of this class. The tutor will act as a guide, framing and shaping our entry into these texts, but you must be prepared to engage the texts and your peers. In other words, you should plan to fully and actively participate in class discussions, offer interpretations of texts, listen to your peers, revise your readings, and pose questions that forward our knowledge. What is valued is *not merely the quantity, but rather the* QUALITY *of your contribution* to our conversation.
- *Oral presentation*: Each student will do a 10 minute formal presentation on the central findings and argument of their final paper. The tutor will offer guidelines on these presentations. The order in which you go will be selected by lottery.
- *Peer feedback*: Each student will also offer oral and written feedback to two peers on their final paper presentation.

Grade breakdown

Final Paper (12–15 pages)	35%
Two short papers (20% each)	40%
Class participation	15%
Presentation	5%
Peer Feedback	5%

Papers: Papers must be typed and handed in on time (at the beginning of class). Late papers will be marked down one grade (i.e. A to B+) for *each class period* they are late and no papers will be accepted one week after the due date. Essays and papers will be graded for their argument, supporting evidence, analysis, and style (consult the Grading Criteria and Academic Paper guidelines in the Course Packet).

Plagiarism: To plagiarize means to take someone else's words and/or ideas and put them into writing as if they were your own. In the educational community, this is considered a theft – of intellectual property – and is unacceptable. There are many forms of plagiarism, but even the most "innocent" carries penalties (which range from failing the paper or class to suspension or expulsion). If you keep the following in mind, you will steer clear of trouble: (1) always put quotation marks around any direct statement from an author and provide a full citation that includes the source and page number; (2) cite the author even if you paraphrase or summarize her/his ideas; (3) remember that the Web too is a "source" and ideas gathered from the Internet should be properly cited; and (4) never ask or contract someone else to write a paper for you. Properly citing your work (please consult *The Logger* and the "Citation Guidelines" in the CP) is not only intellectually honest and keeps you free of the university's judicial system, but also allows you to develop more robust arguments of your own that may build upon others' ideas but allow you to develop your own voice.

And Finally . . . : Please turn off those cell phones, pagers, beepers, and other noise makers.

Weekly syllabus

Week 1
• Introduction

Week 2
Writing the Poor

• Thomas Malthus, selections from *An Essay on the Principle of Population* (1798 & 1803) [CP, p. 1]
• selections from the New Poor Law of 1834 [CP, p. 19]
• "Workhouse Life" [CP, p. 28]

Question: How does Malthus view the poor? What can his schema tell us about whom he values? What solutions does he offer for the crisis? In what regards is the NPL shaped by Malthus' vision? In what regards does it reject his vision? What is Carlyle's response to the NPL?

Week 3
Who REALLY is Poor? (The Social-Problem Novel)

• Charles Dickens, *Oliver Twist* (1837; pp. 1–226)
• Henry Mayhew, "Of the Jew Old-Clothes Men" from *London Labour and the London Poor* (1861–2) [CP, p. 46]

Question: What is Dickens's response to the NPL? Does he distinguish between types of poor? How so? What happens to the tone when the action moves from country to city?

Week 4
- *Oliver Twist* (pp. 226–440)

Question: According to the rhetoric of the novel, how should the problem of the poor be handled? By whom? Does the action of the novel follow its rhetoric?

Week 5
Discovering Poverty: The Investigative Discourse of the 1840s

- Selections by Peter Gaskell, Richard Guest, R. H. Horne, & Richard Carlile [CP, p. 50–57]
- Friedrich Engels, "The Industrial Proletariat" & "The Great Towns" from *The Condition of the Working Class in England* (1845) [CP, p. 58]
- Thomas Carlyle, from *Past and Present* (1843) [CP, p. 81]
- Henry Mayhew, from *London Labour and the London Poor* [CP, p. 87]
- Testimony of Child Textile & Mineworkers (1833 & 1842) [CP, p. 97]

Question: How does Engels speak of the poor? What perspective does he introduce that has been missing in the discussion thus far? Do the voices of the poor themselves offer an alternative vision of poverty, its causes and costs?

- *Oliver Twist* Paper Due

Week 6
Domesticating the Politicized Working Class (The Industrial Novel)

- Elizabeth Gaskell, *Mary Barton* (1848; pp. 1–236)
- readings on Chartism [CP, p. 103]

Question: How does Gaskell represent the poor? What are the problems of industrialism for her? How does Gaskell represent Chartism? Does she view it as the appropriate response to the "Condition of England" question?

Week 7
- *Mary Barton* (pp. 237–464)

Question: What happens to the story of industrial troubles? What resolution(s) does Gaskell offer to the CoE question?

Week 8
Are Women like the Poor or like Slaves? Gender, Work & Empire

- Charlotte Brontë, *Jane Eyre* (1847; pp. 7–220; thru vol. 2, ch. 5)
- *Mary Barton* paper due

Week 9
- *Jane Eyre* (220–452; to end)
- Bernard Martin Senior, from *Jamaica, as it was...* (1835) (account of 1831 Jamaican Slave Rebellion or Baptist War) [CP, p. 110]

Week 10
Critiquing and Justifying Empire (Detective Fiction/Imperial Gothic)

- Edmund Burke, "Impeachment of Warren Hastings" (1788) [CP, p. 125]
- Emigration Report to Poor Law Commissioners (1840) [CP, p. 133]
- Thomas Carlyle, "The Nigger Question" (1849) [CP, p. 134]
- William Gladstone, "Our Colonies" (1855) [CP, p. 144]

Question: What for Burke are the responsibilities a colony entails? What for Carlyle are the rights a colony bestows? How is the quest for imperial expansion explained and justified by Gladstone?

- *Jane Eyre* Paper due

Week 11
- Wilkie Collins , *Moonstone* (1868; 1–237*)*

Question: What crises does the "Mutiny" raise? How does Collins respond to it?

Week 12
- *Moonstone* (237–466)

Question: How is the work of detection presented? What are its successes and limitations? What does Collins's position on empire appear to be? How are the novel's crises resolved? Are all the loose ends tied?

Week 13
Race, Imperial Ambition, and Gender Trouble (Adventure Fiction)

- Henry Morton Stanley, from *Through the Dark Continent* (1878) [CP, p. 195]
- H. Rider Haggard, *She* (1887; pp. 1–157)
- *Moonstone* Paper due

Week 14
- *She* (158–317)

Week 15
- Oral presentations on papers

Week 16
Final paper due

Notes

1. A number of Victorianist pioneers have demonstrated that the Web and a scholarly approach to the period are not antithetical: George Landow's *The Victorian Web* (http://www.victorianweb.org/) started in 1987 as a class project at Brown University and Mitsuharu Matsuoka's *The Dickens Page* (http://www.lang.nagoya-u.ac.jp/~matsuoka/Dickens.html) and *The Gaskell Web* (http://www.lang.nagoya-u.ac.jp/~matsuoka/Gaskell.html) were launched in 1995.
2. See Helen Rogers et. al., "Searching Questions: Digital Research and Victorian Culture," *Journal of Victorian Culture*, 13.1 (Spring 2008), pp. 56–107.
3. See Mark Bittman, "I Need a Virtual Break. No, Really," *New York Times*, 2 March 2008. April 25, 2008. http://www.nytimes.com/2008/03/02/fashion/02sabbath.html?scp=3&sq=e-mail%20+%20bittman&st=cse
4. See http://astro.temple.edu/~pjoshi/advice.html
5. See http://www.cla.purdue.edu/academic/engl/theory/index.html
6. Personal e-mail communication with author, 27 March, 2008.
7. See http://www2.ups.edu/faculty/pjoshi/. The page is not a blog in which I write regularly.
8. See http://vos.ucsb.edu/browse.asp?id=2751 and http://andromeda.rutgers.edu/~jlynch/Lit/victoria.html. Neither appears to be actively maintained and both contain "dead" links that bring up the frustrating "404: Error" message.
9. Chris Willis, "'Out flew the web and floated wide': An overview of uses of the internet for Victorian research." *Journal of Victorian Culture* 7(2), 2002; 297–310. See also Patrick Leary, "Victorian Studies in the Digital Age." *The Victorians since 1901: Histories, Representations and Revisions*, eds. Miles Taylor and Michael Woolf (New York: Manchester University Press, 2004); 201–14.
10. http://homepages.primex.co.uk/~lesleyah/webdoc3.htm
11. Some scholars prefer to access primary sources from the more ambitious Google Books. This project can be a mixed blessing as available full-text versions are mainly those out of copyright. A recent search of *Jane Eyre*, for instance, brought up the 1908 Everyman edition, but the recent Penguin and St. Martin's editions were not available.
12. See http://www.rossettiarchive.org/. McGann is also the moving force behind NINES that makes digital scholarship available online, http://www.nines.org/
13. http://projects.vassar.edu/punch/ and http://www.john-leech-archive.org.uk/archive.htm
14. htttp://metropolisontrial.files.wordpress.com/2008/04/programmemetropolisontrial1.pdf
15. The July 2008 conference celebrating the completion of the project includes a panel on "Teaching from the Old Bailey Online." http://metropolisontrial.files.wordpress.com/2008/04/programmemetropolisontrial1.pdf

16. http://household.umkc.edu/
17. http://www.bodley.ox.ac.uk/ilej/ and http://ahds.ac.uk/ictguides/projects/ project.jsp?projectId=727
18. http://www.wwnorton.com/college/english/nael/welcome.htm
19. See http://www.sjsu.edu/faculty/harris/BritLitSurvey/Engl56B_Frame.htm for the Web version and http://newhorizons.eliterature.org/syl/harris.pdf for a pdf version.
20. This listserv, the brainchild of Patrick Leary, was begun single-handedly in 1993. It is one of the few listservs that fulfills the promise of a virtual community: the conversations on VICTORIA are always erudite, on topic (thanks to Leary's gentle monitoring), and cover research and pedagogy. The growing list of acknowledgments to VICTORIA members in monographs is only the most visible evidence of the robust role it has played in the intellectual lives of many.
21. Martin Danahay, "Youtube as a resource in Victorian Lit classes," 31 March 2008, VICTORIA 19th-Century British Culture & Society. http://listserv.indiana.edu/ archives/victoria.html [access to the archives requires a login].
22. Danahay; Kina Cavicchioli, "Re: comedy routines about the British Empire," 7 Apr 2007; and Alan Rauch, "Clips of Conquest," 6 Apr 2007, VICTORIA 19th-Century British Culture & Society.
23. Martha Stoddard-Holmes, "Youtube and teaching Victorian poetry," 26 Mar 2008, VICTORIA 19th-Century British Culture & Society.
24. http://www.youtube.com/watch?v=H0suKVEI9Wk
25. For the first, see *Cora Kaplan, Victoriana: Histories, Fictions, Criticism* (New York: Columbia University Pres, 2007); for the second, see Jay Clayton *Charles Dickens in Cyberspace: The Afterlife of the Nineteenth Century in Postmodern Culture* (Oxford University Press, 2003).
26. See http://users.bathspa.ac.uk/greenwood/home.html. Since I last taught this course, Cruchley's 1827 map has become available online in an excellent zoomable format: http://archivemaps.com/mapco/cruchley/cruchley.htm. For more historical maps of London, see http://archivemaps.com/mapco/london. htm and http://www.victorianlondon.org/frame-maps.htm
27. George Landow, *Hypertext 3.0: Critical Theory and New Media in an Era of Globalization* (Baltimore: The Johns Hopkins University Press, 2006); 104.
28. See http://www.victorianweb.org/authors/carlyle/hudson/hudson1.html
29. http://www.umd.umich.edu/casl/hum/eng/classes/434/charweb/index.html and http://www.umd.umich.edu/casl/hum/eng/classes/434/charweb/index.html
30. See http://www.sjsu.edu/faculty/harris/BritLitSurvey/Handouts/56B_Essay.pdf
31. See http://en.wikipedia.org/wiki/Wiki
32. Andrea Kaston Tange at Eastern Michigan University has created a wiki of primary documents that students continually add to, http://victoriancontexts. pbwiki.com/. For detailed directions to students, see Jennifer Phegley's linked "Transatlantic Authorship" syllabus.

Works cited

Bittman, Mark, "I Need a Virtual Break. No, Really," *New York Times*, 2 March 2008. April 25, 2008. http://www.nytimes.com/2008/03/02/fashion/02sabbath. html?scp=3&sq=e-mail%20+%20bittman&st=cse

Clayton, Jay, *Charles Dickens in Cyberspace: The Afterlife of the Nineteenth Century in Postmodern Culture* (Oxford University Press, 2003).

Kaplan, Cora, *Victoriana: Histories, Fictions, Criticism* (New York: Columbia University Press, 2007).

Landow, George, *Hypertext 3.0: Critical Theory and New Media in an Era of Globalization* (Baltimore: The Johns Hopkins University Press, 2006).

Leary, Parrick, "Victorian Studies in the Digital Age," *The Victorians since 1901: Histories, Representations and Revisions*, eds. Miles Taylor and Michael Woolf (New York: Manchester University Press, 2004), pp. 201–14.

Rogers, Helen et. al., "Searching Questions: Digital Research and Victorian Culture," *Journal of Victorian Culture*, 13.1 (Spring 2008), pp. 56–107.

Willis, Chris, "'Out flew the web and floated wide': An overview of uses of the internet for Victorian research," *Journal of Victorian Culture*, 7.2 (2002), pp. 297–310.

Further Reading

General books and articles on teaching literary studies

Agathocleous, Tanya and Ann C. Dean (eds.), *Teaching Literature: A Companion* (Basingstoke: Palgrave Macmillan, 2003).

Anderson, Judith H. and Christine R. Farris (eds.), *Integrating Literature and Writing Instruction* (New York: MLA, 2007).

Barricelli, Jean-Pierre, Joseph Gibaldi and Estella Lauter (eds.), *Teaching Literature and Other Arts* (New York, MLA, 1990).

Barry, Peter, *English in Practice: In Pursuit of English Studies* (London: Arnold, 2003).

Graff, Gerald, *Beyond the Culture Wars: How Teaching the Conflicts Can Revitalize American Education* (New York: W. W. Norton, 1993).

Hawkins, Ann R. (ed.), *Teaching Bibliography, Textual Criticism, and Book History* (London: Pickering and Chatto, 2006).

Slevin, James, "Academic Literacy and the Discipline of English," *Profession 2007* (The Modern Language Association of America).

——, and Art Young (eds.), *Critical Theory and the Teaching of Literature: Politics, Curriculum, Pedagogy* (Urbana: NCTE, 1996).

Books and articles on teaching nineteenth-century fiction

The Modern Language Association of America includes a large number of nineteenth-century writers and novels in its "Approaches to Teaching" series. The UK-based English Subject Centre Newsletter and website carry discussions of individual authors and texts (see: http://www.english.heacademy.ac.uk/). So, too, does the journal *Pedagogy: Critical Approaches to Teaching Literature, Language, Composition, and Culture*. In addition the following selections also contain useful discussions of teaching Victorian fiction:

Levine, George, "The Two Nations," *Pedagogy: Critical Approaches to Teaching Literature, Language, Composition, and Culture*, 1.1 (2001), pp. 7–19.

Lund, Michael and Leigha McReynolds, "The Class as Periodical: A Contemporary 'Humanities Lab,'" *Pedagogy*, 9.3 (Fall 2008).

Mangum, Teresa (ed.), *Victorian Periodicals Review* Special Issue on Pedagogy, 39.4 (Winter 2006), pp. 307–444.

Moskal, J. and S. R. Wooden (eds.), *Teaching British Women Writers 1750–1900* (New York: Peter Lang, 2003).

Student guides

Faced with the costs of buying primary texts, students may not have the resources to buy secondary material. However there are a large number of useful overviews directed towards student readers. The Cambridge University Press *Companion* series offers up to date essays on individual authors and their works, as does the British Council's longstanding "Writers and their Work" series and Oxford University Press's

"Authors in Context" series. The following books are directed specifically at undergraduate students.

Levine, George, *How to Read the Victorian* Novel (Oxford: Blackwell, 2007).
Moran, Maureen, *Victorian Literature and Culture* (New York: Continuum, 2006).
Purchase, Sean, *Key Concepts in Victorian Literature* (London: Palgrave Macmillan, 2006).
Roberts, Adam C., *Victorian Culture and Society* (London: Arnold, 2003).
Warwick, Alexandra and Martin Willis (eds.), *The Victorian Literature Handbook* (New York: Continuum, 2008).

Web sites

The Victoria Web:
The brain child of George Landow, this is a massive collection of biographical essays, contextual overviews, short essays, chronologies, and study questions written by teachers and students from around the world. Includes a section on sample syllabi and authors before 1837.
http://www.victorianweb.org/

The Dickens Project:
Includes links for teachers.
http://dickens.ucsc.edu/universe/universe.html

Professor Florence Boos's study questions:
An array of very worthwhile study questions relating to many nineteenth-century texts provided by Professor Florence Boos of the University of Iowa. The questions encourage close reading but also included are essays about the historical and social contexts of nineteenth-century fiction.
http://www.english.uiowa.edu/courses/boos/questions/index.htm

Victoria Research Web:
Resources maintained by Patrick Leary, administrator of the VICTORIA discussion list for Victorian Studies. Different sections offer links to archive catalogues, bibliographies, a listserv address, syllabi, specialist journals.
http://victorianresearch.org/

Project Gaslight:
A selection of obscure and hard-to-find texts (1800–1919) with an emphasis on crime fiction and the Gothic.
http://gaslight.mtroyal.ca/

Victorian Literary Studies Archive:
Maintained by Mitsu Matsuoka, a gateway to just about anything connected to nineteenth-century literature.
http://www.lang.nagoya-u.ac.jp/~matsuoka/Victorian.html

General

Alongside studies of individual authors and movements the following introductions usefully suggest the scope of nineteenth-century fiction and the different critical approaches that have emerged.

Brantlinger, Patrick, *The Reading Lesson: The Threat of Mass Literacy in Nineteenth-Century British Fiction* (Indiana: Indiana University Press, 1998).
A discussion of the contradictoriness of the nineteenth-century novel. Brantlinger writes in opposition to critics who see the novel as "*merely* an ideological or discursive tool for the forging and policing of bourgeois subjectivity." Eclectic in its scope, the book covers late-eighteenth-century Gothic fiction through the industrial novel, to the 1880s and the mass audiences at the time of Robert Louis Stevenson and George Gissing.

Brantlinger, Patrick, and William B. Thesing (eds.), *A Companion to the Victorian Novel* (Oxford: Blackwell 2002).
Twenty-six essays which aim to introduce readers to the historical and cultural contexts in which the novel was produced and consumed and aimed at supplementing a course on the period. There are accessible overviews of important historical contexts (class, gender, etc.) as well as the different genres and subgenres of the novel (realism, sensation, imperial romance). There is also discussion of recent theories about the Victorian novel and the genre's reception.

David, Deirdre (ed.), *The Cambridge Companion to the Victorian Novel* (Cambridge: Cambridge University Press, 2001).
Like Brantlinger and Thesing's *Companion*, this collection of essays, reviews, and key issues is intended as a supplementary guide, though it assumes prior knowledge. The introduction stresses the scope of the Victorian novel (which is "about so many things" and takes us "everywhere"). Chapters cover subjects such as readership, publishing, gender, sexuality, race, industrialism, and transatlantic studies, as well as the subgenres of detective fiction and sensation fiction.

Davis, Philip, *The Oxford English Literary History. Volume 8: 1830–1880: The Victorians* (Oxford: Oxford University Press, 2002).
A wide-ranging and detailed survey which argues for the seriousness of fiction produced in the period – its interest in the relationship between society and the individual, religion and faith and the possibility of democracy.

Feltes, N. N., *Modes of Production of Victorian Novels* (Chicago: University of Chicago Press, 1986).
A Marxist-influenced reading of nineteenth-century publishing practices and their impact on the Victorian novel. Five novels are covered: Dickens's *Pickwick Papers*, Thackeray's *Henry Esmond*, Eliot's *Middlemarch*, Hardy's *Tess of the d'Urbervilles*, and Forster's *Howards End*. Each represents a different publication format: part-issue, three-volume, bimonthly, magazine-serial, and single-volume.

Flint, Kate, *The Woman Reader 1837–1914* (Oxford: Clarendon Press 1993).
Flint provides an in-depth cultural study of Victorian and Edwardian attitudes toward women's reading practices. This study of the figure of the woman reader and her place is the point of contact for several important questions relating to Victorian literary culture: what should women read?; what shouldn't women read?; and why? Flint answers these questions by examining a wide variety of nineteenth and early twentieth-century texts, including medical books, psychological treatises, educational materials, diaries, periodicals, novels, and paintings.

Hughes, Linda K. and Michael Lund, *The Victorian Serial* (Charlottesville: University Press of Virginia, 1991).
A standard work for scholars of the period, which opens up new ways of reading and interpreting key Victorian texts. A central argument is that "[a] work's extended duration meant that serials could become entwined with readers' own sense of lived experience and passing time . . . ." For Hughes and Lund the serial novel's expansiveness was commensurate with the spirit of the age.

James, Louis, *The Victorian Novel* (Oxford: Blackwell, 2006).
A very accessible introduction to fiction of the period, with the student in mind. It contains time lines and contextual discussion as well as short biographies of forty Victorian authors and snapshots of thirty novels, as well as overviews of such topics as imperialism and industrialism.

Jordan, John O. and Robert L. Patten, (eds.), *Literature in the Marketplace: Nineteenth-Century British Publishing and Reading Practices* (Cambridge: Cambridge University Press, 1995).
A collection of essays focusing on issues in book history and the literary field. Essays consider different elements of the production, distribution, and reception of printed texts, and include accounts of serialization, anonymity, and the periodical press.

Miller, D. A., *The Novel and the Police* (Berkeley: University of California Press, 1988).
Taking Dickens, Trollope, and Collins as case studies, Miller argues for the novel as a form of social control, observing "a radical entanglement between the practice of the novel and the practice of the police" and seeing the "discipline inherent in the novel's technique of narration."

O'Gorman, Francis, *The Victorian Novel: A Guide to Criticism* (Oxford: Blackwell, 2002).
A survey of how the novel has been read over the past hundred years taking the works of Dickens, the Brontës, Eliot, Gaskell, Hardy, James, Thackeray and Trollope as exemplars. Nineteenth-century responses are followed by examples of more recent approaches including those which focus on ideas of genre, gender, politics, science, and the literary canon.

Robbins, Ruth, *Pater to Forster 1873–1924* (London: Palgrave – now Palgrave Macmillan, 2003).
A readable survey of the so-called "age of transition," spanning the end of the Victorian age and the rise of modernist aesthetics. Particularly good on the 1890s and in its coverage of decadence, New Woman writing, imperialism, and early modernism.

Shattock, Joanne (ed.), *Women and Literature in Britain 1800–1900* (Cambridge: Cambridge University Press, 2001).
An important collection bringing together leading scholars in the area of women's writing. The essays explore the roles played by women as novelists, poets, journalists, editors, translators, scholars, actresses, playwrights, autobiographers, and biographers.

Showalter, Elaine, *A Literature of their Own* (Princeton: Princeton University Press, 1977).
Highly influential since its first appearance in 1977, this feminist study of the long but neglected tradition of women writers in England remains essential reading.

Showalter breaks down the tradition into three stages – the Feminine (1840s–1880s); the Feminist (1880–1920); and the Female (1920–1970s).

Sutherland, John, *A Companion to Victorian Fiction* (London: Longman, (1989).
A justifiably celebrated reference work containing 900+ biographical entries on well-known and forgotten figures, synopses of 600 novels, plus material on leading publishing firms. An excellent starting point for research into the period.

Terry, R. C., *Victorian Popular Fiction 1860–1880* (London: Macmillan, 1983).
An account of the bookselling and reviewing practices in the middle-brow popular fiction market, followed by case studies of three authors: Margaret Oliphant, James Payn, and Rhoda Broughton. Good for a sense of the literary field and influence of the circulating libraries on production.

Thompson, Nicola, *Reviewing Sex: Gender and the Reception of Victorian Novels* (London: Macmillan, 1996).
Accessible investigation of the role played by gender in the reception of Victorian novels and the double standard which existed in the era which sometimes undervalued the work of women writers. While Thompson focuses on case studies of Charles Reade, Emily Brontë, Anthony Trollope, and Charlotte Yonge, the book provides a broader understanding of Victorian reviewing practices.

Tucker, Herbert, *A Companion to Victorian Literature and Culture* (Oxford: Blackwell, 1998).
Wide-ranging survey of the period broken down into five (eclectic) sections: "History in Focus," "Passages of Life," "Walks of Life," "Kinds of Writing," "Borders." Useful in the range of its coverage and pitched at the student who wants to explore more.

Wolfreys, Julian, *Dickens to Hardy 1837–1884: The Novel, the Past, and Cultural Memory in the Nineteenth Century* (Basingstoke: Palgrave Macmillan, 2007).
Readings of novels by Charles Dickens, Elizabeth Gaskell, Wilkie Collins, George Eliot, and Thomas Hardy with the emphasis on themes of identity, history, selfhood, and the modern.

Bibliography

Agathocleous, Tanya and Ann C. Dean (eds.), *Teaching Literature: A Companion* (Basingstoke: Palgrave Macmillan, 2003), pp. 149–62.

Altick, Richard D., *The English Common Reader: A Social History of the Mass Reading Public 1800–1900* (Chicago: University of Chicago Press, 1957).

Anderson, Benedict, *Imagined Communities: Reflections on the Origin and Spread of Nationalism* (London: Verso, 1983).

Anderson, Patricia, *The Printed Image and the Transformation of Popular Culture 1790–1860* (Oxford: Oxford University Press, 1991).

Anderson, Warwick, *The Cultivation of Whiteness: Science, Health, and Racial Destiny in Australia* (Melbourne: Melbourne University Press, 2002).

Anon, "Literature," *Tait's Edinburgh Magazine*, 19 (February 1852), pp. 118–289.

Aragay, Mireia (ed), *Books in Motion: Adaptation, Intertextuality, Authorship* (Amsterdam: Rodopi, 2005).

Arnold, Matthew (1869), *Culture and Anarchy*. Ed. J. Dover Wilson (Cambridge: Cambridge University Press, 1971).

Attridge, Derek, *The Singularity of Literature* (London: Routledge, 2004).

Azim, Firdous, *The Colonial Rise of the Novel* (New York: Routledge, 1993).

Baker, J. H., *An Introduction to English Legal History*, 4th edn. (London: Butterworths, 2002).

Barbaras, Renaud, *Desire and Distance: Introduction to a Phenomenology of Perception*. Trans. Paul B. Milan (Stanford: Stanford University Press, 2006).

Barlow, Paul, *Time Present and Time Past: The Art of John Everett Millais* (Aldershot: Ashgate, 2005).

Barry, Peter, *English in Practice: In Pursuit of English Studies* (London: Arnold, 2003).

Bayly, Christopher A., *Atlas of the British Empire* (London: Littlehampton, 1989).

Beer, Gillian, *Open Fields: Science in Cultural Encounter* (Oxford: Oxford University Press, 1996).

Beller, Anne-Marie, "Teaching Victorian Popular Fiction and the Problems of Literary Value," paper delivered at Victorian Literature: The Canon and Beyond Conference (University of Chester, 2006).

Birch, Dinah, *Our Victorian Education* (Oxford: Blackwell, 2007).

Bloom, Harold, *Agon: Towards a Theory of Revisionism* (Oxford: Oxford University Press, 1982).

Bluestone, George, *Novels into Film* (Baltimore: Johns Hopkins University Press, 2003).

Brake, Laurel, "Writing, cultural production, and the periodical press," in J. B. Bullen (ed.) *Writing and Victorianism* (London and New York: Longman Press, 1997), pp. 54–72.

Brantlinger, Patrick, *Victorian Literature and Postcolonial Studies* (Edinburgh: Edinburgh University Press, 2009).

Braudy, Leo and Marshall Cohen (eds.), *Film Theory and Criticism*, 5th edn. (Oxford: Oxford University Press, 1999).

Briggs, C. F., and A. Maverick, *The Story of the Telegraph, and a History of the Great Atlantic Cable* (New York: Rudd and Carleton, 1858).

Briggs, Julia, *Night Visitors: The Rise and Fall of the English Ghost Story* (London: Faber and Faber, 1977).

——, "The Ghost Story" in David Punter (ed.) *A Companion to the Gothic* (Oxford: Blackwell, 2000), pp. 122–31.

Brontë, Charlotte, *Jane Eyre*, 1847 (London: Penguin, 1996).

Brontë, Emily, *Wuthering Heights*, ed. David Daiches (Harmondsworth: Penguin, 1965).

——, *Wuthering Heights*, ed. William Sale, Jr., and Richard J. Dunn (New York: Norton, 1989).

——, *Wuthering Heights*, ed. Christpher Heywood (Peterborough, Ontario: Broadview, 2002).

Brown, Margaret, Kathleen Tillotson, and Graham Storey (eds), *The Letters of Charles Dickens*, Vol. 9, 1859–1861 (Oxford: Clarendon, 1997).

Brunton, Mary, *Self-Control* (London: Pandora Press, 1986). First pub. 1810/1811.

Burroughs, Catherine, "Teaching Women Playwrights from the British Romantic Period (1790–1840)," in J. Moskal and S. R. Wooden (eds.) *Teaching British Women Writers 1750–1900* (New York: Peter Lang, 2005), pp. 140–59.

Butler, J., *Precarious Life: The Powers of Mourning and Violence* (London and New York: Verso, 2004).

Campion, Jane (dir.), *The Piano* (film), Miramax, 1993.

Cardwell, Sarah, *Adaptation Revisited: Television and the Classic Novel* (Manchester: Manchester University Press, 2002).

Carey, Peter, *Jack Maggs* (London: Faber & Faber, 1997).

Chapman, Alison, Susan Doyle, Mary Elizabeth Leighton, Judith Mitchell, and Lisa Surridge (eds.), *Victorian Review: An Interdisciplinary Journal of Victorian Studies*, 33.1 (Spring 2007).

Cheroux, Clement, Pierre Apraxine, Andreas Fischer, Denis Canguilhem and Sophie Schmit, *The Perfect Medium: Photography and the Occult* (New Haven and London: Yale University Press, 2005).

Christ, Carol T., and John O. Jordan (eds.), *Victorian Literature and the Victorian Visual Imagination* (Berkeley and Los Angeles: University of California Press, 1995).

Clayton, Jay, *Charles Dickens and the Afterlife of the Nineteenth Century in Postmodern Culture* (Oxford: Oxford University Press, 2003).

Conrad, Joseph, *Heart of Darkness*, 1899 (New York: W. W. Norton, 2006).

Cordery, Gareth, "Harry Furniss and the 'Boom in Boz'" (2 parts), *Dickens Quarterly*, 21.2 and 21.3 (2004), pp. 90–102, 143–54.

Corelli, Marie, *Ardath* (New York: H. M. Caldwell Co., n.d. but first edn. 1889).

Cornwell, Neil and Maggie Malone (eds.), *The Turn of the Screw and What Maisie Knew*, New Casebooks (Basingstoke: Macmillan – Palgrave Macmillan, 1998).

Cox, Michael and R. A. Gilbert (eds.), *The Oxford Book of Victorian Ghost Stories* (Oxford: Oxford University Press, 1991).

Craik, Dinah Mulock, *John Halifax, Gentleman* (1856; New York and London: Harper Brothers, 1903).

David, Deirdre, *Rule Britannia: Women, Empire, and Victorian Writing* (Ithaca: Cornell University Press, 1995).

Davis, Philip, "The Place of the Implicit in Literary Discovery: Creating New Courses", in Tanya Agathocleous and Ann C. Dean, *Teaching Literature: A Companion* (Basingstoke: Palgrave Macmillan, 2003).

Davison, Margaret (ed.), *Bram Stoker's Dracula: Sucking Through the Century, 1897–1997* (Toronto: University of Toronto Press, 1997).

Dentith, Simon, "Reader, I Triumphed" Complicating the Appeal of *Jane Eyre, English Subject Centre Newsletter 9* (November 2005), pp. 19–25.

Derrida, Jacques, *The Derrida Reader: Writing Performances*. Ed. Julian Wolfreys (Edinburgh: Edinburgh University Press, 1998), pp. 264–93.

——, *The Gift of Death, Second Edition, and Literature in Secret*. Trans. David Wills (Chicago: University of Chicago Press, 2008).

Desmond, John M., *Adaptation: Studying Film and Literature* (Boston: McGraw Hill, 2005).

Dickens, Charles, *The Life and Adventures of Nicholas Nickleby*, reproduced in facsimile from the original monthly parts of 1838–9, with an essay by Michael Slater (London: Scolar Press, 1982).

——, *Sketches By Boz and Other Early Papers 1833–39*. Ed. Michael Slater (London: J. M. Dent, 1994).

——, *Selected Journalism 1850–1870*. Ed. and Int. David Pascoe (London: Penguin, 1997).

——, *Great Expectations* (Ontario: Broadview, 2002).

——, *Bleak House*. Ed. and Int. Nicola Bradbury. Preface Terry Eagleton. (London: Penguin, 2003).

Dimock, Wai Chee, "Deep Time: American Literature and World History," *American Literary History*, 13.4 (2001), pp. 755–75.

Dolin, Kieran, *Fiction and the Law: Legal Discourse in Victorian and Modernist Literature*, (Cambridge: Cambridge University Press, 1999).

——, *A Critical Introduction to Law and Literature* (Cambridge: Cambridge University Press, 2007).

Doyle, Laura, "'A' for Atlantic in Hawthorne's *The Scarlet Letter*," *Freedom's Empire*: *Race and the Rise of the Novel in Atlantic Modernity, 1640–1940* (Durham and London: Duke University Press, 2008), pp. 301–30.

Dubrez-Fawcett, F., *Dickens the Dramatist* (London: Allen, 1952).

Dunn, Richard J., (ed.), *Approaches to Teaching Dickens' David Copperfield* (New York: MLA, 1984).

Eagleton, Terry, *Criticism and Ideology: A Study in Marxist Literary Theory* (London: Verso, 1978).

Easson, Angus (ed.), *Elizabeth Gaskell: The Critical Heritage* (London: Routledge, 1991).

Easthope, Anthony, *Literary into Cultural Studies* (London: Routledge, 1991).

——, (2003) "But What is Cultural Studies," in *Studying British Cultures: An Introduction*, Ed. Susan Bassnett (London and New York: Routledge, 2003), pp. 3–19.

Elliot, Kamilla. *Rethinking the Novel/Film Debate* (Cambridge: Cambridge University Press, 2003).

——, "Novels, Films, and the Word/Image Wars," in Robert Stam and Alessandro Raengo (eds.), *A Companion to Literature and Film* (Oxford: Blackwell, 2004), pp. 1–17.

Ellis, John, "The Literary Adaptation," *Screen,* 23 (1982), pp. 6–19.

Feltes, N. N., *Modes of Production of Victorian Novels* (Chicago: University of Chicago Press, 1989).

Flint, Kate, *The Victorians and the Visual Imagination* (Cambridge: Cambridge University Press, 2000).

Freud, Sigmund, "The Uncanny" (1919), in *Penguin Freud Library, Volume 14: Art and Literature*, ed. Albert Dickson (Harmondsworth: Penguin, 1985), pp. 335–76.

Gagnier, Regenia, *Subjectivities: A History of Self-Representation in Britain, 1832–1920* (Oxford: Oxford University Press, 1991).

Gaskell, Elizabeth, *North and South* (1854–5) Ed. Angus Easson (Oxford: Oxford University Press, 1982).

——, *The Life of Charlotte Brontë* (1857). Ed. Angus Easson (Oxford: Oxford University Press, 1996).

——, *Cranford*. Ed. Elizabeth Porges Watson. Int. and notes Charlotte Mitchell (Oxford: Oxford University Press, 1998).

——, *Wives and Daughters* (1864) in *The Works of Elizabeth Gaskell*. Ed. Joanne Shattock (London: Pickering and Chatto, 2006).

——, *Wives and Daughters,* MSS 877, John Rylands University Library of Manchester, 781–2.

Genette, Gerard, *Narrative Discourse*. Trans. Jane E. Lewin (Oxford: Blackwell, 1980).

Gilbert, Pamela. K, *Disease, Desire and the Body in Victorian Women's Popular Novels* (Cambridge: Cambridge University Press, 1997).

——, *Mapping the Victorian Social Body* (New York: State University of New York Press, 2004).

Gilroy, Paul, *The Black Atlantic: Modernity and Double Consciousness* (London and New York: Verso, 1993).

Gissing, George, *The Whirlpool* (Hassocks: Harvester Press, 1977).

Graff, Gerald. *Beyond the Culture Wars: How Teaching the Conflicts Can Revitalize American Education* (New York: W. W. Norton, 1993).

Griffith, James, *Adaptations as Imitations: Films from Novels* (London: Associated University Press, 1997).

Guillory, John, *Cultural Capital: The Problem of Literary Canon Formation* (Chicago and London: The University of Chicago Press, 1993).

Hamilton, Susan (ed.), *Criminals, Idiots, Women, and Minors: Victorian Writing By Women on Women* (Ontario: Broadview Press, 2004).

Hammond, Mary, *Reading, Publishing and the Formation of Literary Taste* (Aldershot: Ashgate, 2006).

Hanson, Clare, *Short Stories and Short Fiction, 1880–1980* (London: Macmillan, 1985).

Hardy, Thomas, *The Hand of Ethelberta* (London: (London: Penguin, 1997).

——, *Far from the Madding Crowd*. Ed and Int. Rosemarie Morgan, with Shannon Russell (London: Penguin, 2000).

Hart-Davis, Adam, *What the Victorians Did for Us* (London: BBC Books, 2002).

Hawthorne, Nathaniel *Novels* (New York: Viking Press, 1938).

——, *The Scarlet Letter* (Ware: Wordsworth Editions Limited, 1992).

Hayles, N. Katherine, "Hyper and Deep Attention: The Generational Divide in Cognitive Models," *Profession*, 13 (2007), pp. 187–99.

Hegel, G. W. F., *Phenomenology of Spirit*. Trans. A. V. Miller. Foreword J. N. Findlay (Oxford: Oxford University Press, 1977).

Hernstein Smith, Barbara, *Contingencies of Value: Alternative Perspectives for Critical Theory* (Cambridge, MA: Harvard University Press, 1988).

Holberg, Jennifer L. and Marcy Taylor, "Editor's Introduction." *Pedagogy: Critical Approaches to Teaching Literature, Language, Composition, and Culture*, 1.1 (2001), pp. 1–5.

Hughes, Albert & Allen Hughes (dirs.), *From Hell* (film), Twentieth-Century Fox, 2001.

Hughes, Linda K., and Michael Lund, *The Victorian Serial* (Charlottesville: University Press of Virginia, 1991).

Hughes, Winifred, "The Sensation Novel," in P. Brantlinger and W. B. Thesing (eds.) *Companion to the Victorian Novel* (Malden, MA and Oxford: Blackwell Publishing, 2005), pp. 260–78.

Hutchinson, Linda, "Beginning to Theorize Postmodernism," *Textual Practice*, 1:1 (1987), pp. 10–31.

Jackson, Rosemary, *Fantasy: The Literature of Subversion* (London: Methuen, 1981).

James, Henry, *The Art of the Novel: Critical Prefaces* (London: Charles Scribner's, 1935).

——, *The Turn of the Screw* (eds.) Deborah Esch and Jonathan Warren (New York: Norton, 1999).

John, Juliet, and Alice Jenkins, *Rereading Victorian Fiction* (New York: St. Martin's Press – now Palgrave Macmillan, 2000).

Jolly, Martin, *Faces of the Living Dead: The Belief in Spirit Photography* (London: Mark Batty, 2006).

Jordan, John O., and Robert L. Patten (eds.), *Literature in the Marketplace* (Cambridge: Cambridge University Press, 1995).

Joyce, Simon, *The Victorians in the Rearview Mirror* (Athens: Ohio University Press, 2007).

Kaplan, Cora, *Victoriana: Histories, Fictions, Criticism* (Edinburgh: Edinburgh University Press, 2007).

Kaufman, Moisés, *Gross Indecency: The Three Trials of Oscar Wilde* (New York: Dramatists Play Service, 1999).

Keen, Paul. *Revolutions in Romantic Literature: An Anthology of Print Culture, 1780–1832* (Ontario: Broadview Press, 2004).

Klein, Julie Thompson, "Resources for Interdisciplinary Studies," *Change* (March/April 2006), pp. 52–8.

Klein, Michael and Gillian Parker (eds.), *The English Novel at the Movies* (New York: Ungar, 1981).

Knight, Stephen, *Jack the Ripper: The Final Solution* (Chicago: Academy Chicago Publisher, 1986).

Konigsberg, Ira (ed.), *The Complete Film Dictionary* (New York: New American Library, 1987).

Kozloff, Sarah, *Invisible Storytellers: Voice-Over Narrative in American Fiction Film* (Berkeley: University of California Press, 1988).

Kreilkamp, Ivan, *Voice and the Victorian Storyteller* (Cambridge: Cambridge University Press, 2005).

Kristeva, Julia, *Powers of Horror: An Essay on Abjection*. Trans. Leon S. Roudiez (New York: Columbia University Press, 1982).

Krueger, Christine L. (ed.), *The Function of Victorian Culture at the Present Time* (Athens: Ohio University Press, 2002).

Kucich, John and Dianne F. Sadoff, *Victorian Afterlife: Postmodern Culture Rewrites the Nineteenth Century* (Minneapolis: University of Minnesota Press, 2000).

Lacan, Jacques, "The Agency of the Letter in the Unconscious or Reason since Freud," *Écrits: A Selection*. Ed. and trans. Alan Bass (New York: W. W. Norton & Co., 1977), pp. 146–78.

Lamont, Peter, *The First Psychic: The Peculiar Mystery of a Notorious Victorian Wizard* (London and New York: Little, Brown, 2005).

Lave, Jean and Etienne, Wenger, *Situated Learning: Legitimate Peripheral Participation* (New York: Cambridge University Press, 1991).

Law, Graham, *Serializing Fiction in the Victorian Press* (Basingstoke: Palgrave – now Palgrave Macmillan, 2000).

Lawson-Peebles, Robert, "European Conflict and Hollywood's Reconstruction of English Fiction," *Yearbook of English Studies*, 26 (1996), pp. 1–13.

Leavis, F. R., *The Great Tradition: George Eliot, Henry James, Joseph Conrad* (Harmondsworth: Penguin, 1962).

Leitch, Vincent B., *American Literary Criticism from the Thirties to the Eighties* (New York: Columbia University Press, 1988).

Lester, Valerie, *Phiz: The Man who drew Dickens* (London: Chatto and Windus, 2006).

Levine, George, "The Two Nations." *Pedagogy: Critical Approaches to Teaching Literature, Language, Composition, and Culture*, 1.1 (2001), pp. 7–19.

——, "Foreword." Tanya Agathocleous and Ann C. Dean (eds.), *Teaching Literature: A Companion* (Palgrave Macmillan, 2003), pp. vii–xii.

Liddle, Dallas, "Bakhtinian 'Journalization' and the Mid-Victorian Literary Marketplace," *Literature Compass*, 4.5 (2007), pp. 1460–74.

Lodge, David, *Nice Work* (London: Secker & Warburg, 1988).

Lonoff, Sue and Terry Hasseler (eds.), *Approaches to Teaching Emily Brontë's "Wuthering Heights"* (New York: Modern Language Association, 2006).

Lootens, Tricia, *Lost Saints: Silence, Gender, and Victorian Literary Canonization* (Charlottesville, VA: University of Virginia Press, 1996).

Lukács, György, *The Theory Of The Novel: A Historico-Philosophical Essay on the Forms of Great Epic Literature* (London: MIT Press, 1971).

Lund, Michael, and Leigha McReynolds, "The Class as Periodical: A Contemporary 'Humanities Lab,'" *Pedagogy* 9.2 (Spring 2009), pp. 289–313.

Lupack, Barbara Tepa (ed.), *Nineteenth-Century Women at the Movies: Adapting Classic Women's Fiction to Film* (Bowling Green: Bowling Green State University Popular Press, 1999).

MacDonald, Peter D., *British Literary Culture and Publishing Practice 1880–1914* (Cambridge: Cambridge University Press, 1997).

Mangum, Teresa, "The New Woman's Work: Past, Present, and Future," *Nineteenth-Century Gender Studies*, 3.1 (Summer 2007).

——, (ed.), *Victorian Periodicals Review* Special Issue on Pedagogy, 39.4 (Winter 2006), pp. 307–444.

Martin, Carol A., *George Eliot's Serial Fiction* (Columbus: Ohio State University Press, 1994).

Mast, Gerald, *A Short History of the Movies* (Indianapolis: Bobbs Merrill, 1981).

Maunder, Andrew, "Mapping the Victorian Sensation Novel: Some Recent and Future Trends," *Literature Compass* (2005), pp. 1–32.

McCloud, Scott, *Understanding Comics: The Invisible Art* (New York: Harper Paperbacks, 1994).

McConnell, Frank, D., *Storytelling and Mythmaking: Images from Film and Literature* (New York: Oxford University Press, 1979).

McFarlane, Brian, *Novel to Film: An Introduction to the Theory of Film Adaptation* (Oxford: Clarendon Press, 1996).

McLaughlin, Kevin, "Losing One's Place: Displacement and Domesticity in Dickens's *Bleak House*," *MLN*, 108:5 (December 1993), pp. 875–90.

Meisel, Martin, *Realizations: Narrative, Pictorial, and Theatrical Arts in Nineteenth-Century England* (Princeton: Princeton University Press, 1983).

Melville, Herman *Moby-Dick or The Whale* (London: Oxford University Press, 1922).

Merleau-Ponty, Maurice, *The Prose of the World*. Ed. Claude Lefort. Trans. John O'Neil (Evanston: Northwestern University Press, 1973).

Metz, Christian, *The Imaginary Signifier: Psychoanalysis and the Cinema* (Bloomington: Indiana University Press, 1977).

Mighall, Robert, *A Geography of Victorian Gothic Fiction: Mapping History's Nightmares* (Oxford: Oxford University Press, 1999).

Miles, Robert, *Gothic Writing 1750–1820: A Genealogy* (London: Routledge, 1993).

Millgate, Michael, *Thomas Hardy: A Biography* (New York, Random House, 1982).

Moers, Ellen, *Literary Women* (London: Women's Press, 1978).

Moore, Allan and Kevin O'Neill, *The League of Extraordinary Gentlemen, Vol. I* (Wildstorm Comics, 1999).

Moore, Grace, "Twentieth-Century Re-Workings of the Victorian Novel," *Literature Compass*, 5:1 (January 2008), pp. 134–44.

Moran, Leslie J., "On Realism and the Law Film: The Case of Oscar Wilde," in *Law's Moving Image*. Eds. Leslie J. Moran, Emma Sandon, Elena Louizidou (London: GlassHouse Press, 2004), pp. 77–94.

Murray, Edward, *The Cinematic Imagination: Writers and the Motion Pictures* (New York: Ungar, 1972).

Natanson, Maurice, "Phenomenology, Anonymity, and Alienation," *New Literary History*, 10:3 (Spring, 1979), pp. 533–546.

Nelson, Carolyn Christensen. *The New Woman Reader* (Ontario: Broadview Press, 2000).

Nemesvari, Richard, "'Judged by a Purely Literary Standard': Sensation Fiction, Horizons of Expectation, and the Generic Construction of Victorian Realism," in K. Harrison and R. Fantina (eds.) *Victorian Sensations: Essays on a Scandalous Genre* (Columbus: The Ohio State University Press, 2006), pp. 15–28.

Nord, Deborah, *Gypsies and the British Imagination, 1807–1930* (New York: Columbia University Press, 2006).

O'Beebee, Thomas, *The Ideology of Genre: A Comparative Study of Generic Instability* (University Park, PA: The Pennsylvania State University Press, 1994).

O'Gorman, Francis, *The Victorian Novel: A Guide to Criticism* (Oxford: Blackwell, 2002).

Oliphant, Margaret, "The Byways of Literature: Reading for the Million," *Blackwood's Edinburgh Magazine*, 84 (1858), pp. 200–16.

——, "Novels", *Blackwood's Edinburgh Magazine*, 102 (1867), pp. 257–80.

——, *Janet* (London: Hurst, 1891).

Orel, Harold, *The Victorian Short Story: Development and Triumph of a Literary Genre* (Cambridge: Cambridge University Press, 1986).

Ormond, Leonée, "Dickens and Painting: Contemporary Art," *The Dickensian*, 80 (1984), pp. 2–25.

Patten, Robert L., *Charles Dickens and His Publishers* (Oxford: Oxford University Press, 1978).

Perera, Suvendrini, *Reaches of Empire: The English Novel from Edgeworth to Dickens* (New York: Columbia University Press, 1991).

Petch, Simon, "Law, Literature, and Victorian Studies," *Victorian Studies*, 35 (2007), pp. 361–84.

Pinion, F. B., *Thomas Hardy: His Life and Friends* (New York: St. Martin's Press – now Palgrave Macmillan, 1992).

Poe, Edgar Allen, *Selected Writings of Edgar Allen Poe: Poems, Tales, Essays and Reviews* (Harmondsworth: Penguin, 1979).

——, "MS. Found in a Bottle" in S. Levine and S. F. Levine (eds.) *Thirty-Two Stories* (Indianapolis and Cambridge: Hackett Publishing Company, 2000).

Poovey, Mary, *Uneven Developments: The Ideological Work of Gender in Mid-Victorian England* (Chicago: University of Chicago Press, 1988).

Punter, David, *The Literature of Terror*, 2 volumes (London: Longman, 1980; 2nd edition 1996).

Pykett, Lyn, *Charles Dickens* (London: Palgrave – now Palgrave Macmillan, 2002).

Raines, Melissa, "George Eliot's Grammar of Being," *Essays in Criticism*, 58:1 (2007), pp. 43–63.

Ramsden, Paul, *Learning to Teach in Higher Education* (London and New York: Routledge Falmer, 2003).

Ray, Robert "The Field of 'Literature and Film'", in James Naremore (ed.), *Film Adaptation* (London: Athlone Press, 2000), pp. 38–53.

Renk, Kathleen J., *Caribbean Shadows and Victorian Ghosts: Women's Writing and Decolonization* (Charlottesville: University Press of Virginia, 1999).

Renner, Stanley, "'Red hair, very red, close-curling': Sexual Hysteria, Physiognomical Bogeymen, and the 'Ghosts' in *The Turn of the Screw*," in Peter G. Beidler (ed.) *Henry James: The Turn of the Screw*, Case Studies in Contemporary Criticism (Boston and New York: Bedford Books, 1995), pp. 223–41.

Robbins, Bruce, "'They don't count much, do they?': The Unfinished History of *The Turn of the Screw*" in Peter G. Beidler (ed.) *Henry James: The Turn of the Screw*, Case Studies in Contemporary Criticism (Boston and New York: Bedford Books, 1995), pp. 283–96.

Rumsey, Frances. *Ascent* (London: John Lane, 1923).

Ruskin, John, *Selected Writings: John Ruskin*. Ed. Philip Davis (London: Everyman, 1995).

Said, Edward, *Culture and Imperialism* (New York: Knopf, 1993).

Sampson, George, *English for the English: A Chapter on National Education* (Cambridge: Cambridge University Press, 1921).

Samuel, Raphael, *Theatres of Memory* (New York: Verso, 1984).

Sanders, Andrew *Charles Dickens* (Oxford: Oxford University Press, 2003).

Sanders, Valerie, "Where Next in Victorian Literary Studies? – Historicism, Collaboration and Digital Editing," *Literature Compass*, 4 (2007), pp. 1292–302.

Schramm, Jan-Melissa, *Testimony and Advocacy in Victorian Law, Literature, and Theology* (Cambridge: Cambridge University Press, 2000).

Schweik, Robert C., "Hardy's 'Plunge in a New and Untried Direction': Comic Detachment in *The Hand of Ethelberta*," *English Studies* 83.3 (June 2002), pp. 239–52.

Showalter, Elaine, *Teaching Literature* (Oxford: Blackwell Publishing, 2003).

Simmons Jr., James. R, "Pedagogy and Oppositions: Teaching Non-Canonical British Women Writers at the Technical University," in J. Moskal and S. R. Wooden (eds.), *Teaching British Women Writers 1750–1900* (New York: Peter Lang, 2005), pp. 91–100.

Sinyard, Neil, *Filming Literature: The Art of Screen Adaptation* (London: Croom Helm, 1986).

Slater, Michael (ed.), "Hardy and the City," *New Perspectives on Thomas Hardy*. Ed. Charles P. C. Pettit (New York: St. Martin's Press – now Palgrave Macmillan, 1994), pp. 41–57.

——, *Dickens's Journalism, Vol 2: The Amusements of the People: Reports, Essays and Reviews, 1834–51* (London: Weidenfeld and Nicolson, 1996), p. 245.

Slevin, J. F., "Academic Literacy and the Discipline of English," *Profession 2007* (The Modern Language Association of America, 2007).

Smith, Andrew, *Gothic Literature*, Edinburgh Critical Guides (Edinburgh: Edinburgh University Press, 2007).

Spencer, Kathleen L., "Purity and Danger: *Dracula*, the Urban Gothic, and the Late Victorian Degeneracy Crisis," *ELH*, 59.1 (1992), pp. 197–225.

Spender, Stephen, *Love-Hate Relations: A Study of Anglo-American Sensibilities* (London: Hamish Hamilton, 1972).

Spengemann, William C., "Three Blind Men and an Elephant: The Problem of Nineteenth-Century English," *New Literary History*, 14.1 (1982), pp. 155–73.

Spivak, Gayatri Chakravorty, "Three women's texts and a critique of imperialism," *"Race," Writing, and Difference*, ed. Henry Louis Gates, Jr., (Chicago: The University of Chicago Press, 1986), pp. 262–80.

Stam, Robert, "Betond Fidelity: The Dialogics of Adaptation," in James Naremore (ed.), *Film Adaptation* (London: Athlone Press, 2000), pp. 54–76.

——, *Literature Through Film: Realism, Magic, and the Art of Adaptation* (Oxford: Blackwell, 2005).

——, and Alessandra Raengo (eds.), *Literature and Film* (Oxford: Oxford University Press, 2005).

Stanley, Liz (ed.), *The Diaries of Hannah Cullwick: Victorian Maidservant* (London: Virago, 1984).

Steedman, Carolyn, *Master and Servant: Love and Labour in the English Industrial Age* Cambridge: Cambridge University Press, 2007).

Stein, Richard L. "Dickens and illustration," in *The Cambridge Companion to Charles Dickens*, ed. John O. Jordan (Cambridge: Cambridge University Press, 2001), pp. 167–88.

Stephenson, Neal, *The Diamond Age* (London: Penguin, 1996).

Stevenson, Robert Louis, *The Amateur Emigrant, The Old & New Pacific Capitals, The Silverado Squatters* (London and Glasgow: Collins' Clear-Type Press, n.d.).

Stoker, Bram, *Dracula*. Eds. Nina Auerbach and David J. Skal (New York: W. W. Norton, 1996).

Stone, Harry, *Dickens and the Invisible World* (Bloomington: Indiana University Press, 1979).

Stoneman, Patsy (ed.), *Wuthering Heights: Contemporary Critical Essays* (Basingstoke: Macmillan – now Palgrave Macmillan, 1993).

Sullivan, Jack, *Elegant Nightmares: The English Ghost Story from Le Fanu to Blackwood* (Athens, OH: Ohio University Press, 1978).

Sutherland, John. "Foreword: The Underread," in *The New Nineteenth Century: Feminist Readings of Underread Fiction*. Ed. Barbarah Leah Harman, Susan Meyer (New York: Garland Publishing, 1996), pp. xi–xxv.

Swann, Charles, "Hardy, Defoe, and Leslie Stephen," *Notes and Queries*, 42.2 (June 1995), pp. 203–4.

Tange, Andrea Kaston, "Becoming a Victorian Reader: The Serial Reading Process in the Modern Classroom," special issue *Periodicals, Pedagogy, and Collaboration*, ed. Teresa Mangum, 39.4 (Winter 2006), pp. 330–42.

Taylor, Miles and Michael Wolff (eds.), *The Victorians Since 1901: Histories, Representations and Revisions* (Manchester: Manchester University Press, 2004).

Thieme, John, *Postcolonial Con-Texts: Writing Back to the Canon* (London: Continuum, 2001).

Trollope, Anthony, *Four Lectures*. Ed. Morris L. Parrish (London: Constable & Co., 1938).

Turner, Mark, "Periodical Time in the Nineteenth Century," *Media History*, 8.2 (2002), pp. 183–96.

Voigts-Virchow, Eckhart, (ed.), *Janespotting and Beyond: British Heritage Retrovisions since the Mid-1990s* (Tübingen: Narr, 2004), pp. 149–57.

Wagner, Geoffrey, *The Novel and the Cinema* (London: The Tantivy Press, 1975).

Waller, Philip, *Writers, Readers and Reputations: Literary Life in Britain 1870–1918* (Oxford: Oxford University Press, 2006).

Warden, Florence, *The House on the Marsh* (New York: D. Appleton and Company, 1884).

Warner, Marina, *Phantasmagoria: Spirit Visions, Metaphors and Media* (Oxford and New York: Oxford University Press, 2006).

Warwick, Alexander and Martin Willis (eds.) *Victorian Literature Handbook* (London: Continuum, 2008).

Weatherford, Doris, *Foreign and Female: Immigrant Women in America, 1840–1930* (New York: Schocken, 1986).

Weisbuch, R., *Atlantic Double-Cross: American Literature and British Influence in the Age of Emerson* (Chicago and London: The University of Chicago Press, 1986).

Wells, H. G., *The Country of the Blind* (London: Thomas Nelson and Sons, 1913).

Welsh, Alexander, *Strong Representations: Narrative and Circumstantial Evidence in England* (Baltimore: Johns Hopkins University Press, 1995).

Wenger, Etienne, *Communities of Practice: Learning, Meaning, and Identity* (New York: Cambridge University Press, 1999).

Whipple, Edwin. P., "Novels of the Season," *The North American Review,* 67 (1848), pp. 354–69.

White, James Boyd, *The Legal Imagination* (1973) (Chicago: University of Chicago Press, 1985).

Widdowson, Peter, *Re-reading English* (London: Methuen, 1982).

——, *Literature* (London and New York: Routledge, 1999).

Wilde, Oscar, "The Canterville Ghost" in Ian Small (ed.) *Oscar Wilde: Complete Short Fiction* (London: Penguin, 2003).

Williams, Carolyn, "Genre Matters: Response," *Victorian Studies,* 48:2 (2006), pp. 295–304.

Williams, Raymond, "When was Modernism?," in *The Politics of Modernism*, ed. Tony Pinkney (London: Verso, 1989), pp. 31–5.

Wiltshire, John, *Recreating Jane Austen* (Cambridge: Cambridge University Press, 2001).

Wolfreys, Julian, *Dickens to Hardy 1837–1884: The Novel, the Past, and Cultural Memory in the Nineteenth Century* (Basingstoke: Palgrave Macmillan, 2007).

Woolf, Virgina, *Orlando* (1928) (Harmondsworth: Penguin, 2004).

——, *A Room of One's Own* (New York: Harcourt Brace Jovanovich, Inc., 1929).

Wotton, George, *Thomas Hardy: Towards a Materialist Criticism* (Golden Bridge, Ireland: Gill and Macmillan, 1985).

Wynne, Deborah, *The Sensation Novel and the Victorian Family Magazine* (London: Macmillan, 2000).

Yonge, Charlotte, *The Daisy Chain: or, Aspirations,* 1856 (London: Macmillan, 1876).

Index